The
GREAT FAMINE
in Tralee and North Kerry

The
GREAT FAMINE
in Tralee and North Kerry

Bryan MacMahon

MERCIER PRESS

MERCIER PRESS
Cork
www.mercierpress.ie

© Bryan MacMahon, 2017
© Foreword: Ciarán Reilly

ISBN: 978 1 78117 829 4

Transferred to digital print on demand in 2025.

This book is sold subject to the condition that it shall not, by way of trade or otherwise, be lent, resold, hired out or otherwise circulated without the publisher's prior consent in any form of binding or cover other than that in which it is published and without a similar condition including this condition being imposed on the subsequent purchaser.

No part of this publication may be reproduced or transmitted in any form or by any means, electronic or mechanical, including photocopying, recording or any information or retrieval system, without the prior permission of the publisher in writing.

CONTENTS

Acknowledgements	7
Timeline	9
Abbreviations	12
Foreword	13
Introduction	17
1 'A dark and withered appearance': 1845	25
2 'Soft words no more': January–June 1846	30
3 'On the very verge of famine': July–December 1846	62
4 'A chill feeling of despair': January–June 1847	93
5 'What under Heaven are the people to do?': July–December 1847	152
6 'Graves call to you for vengeance': 1848	192
7 'The poor are sinking': 1849	219
8 'An unprecedented and unexpected influx of pauperism': 1850	252
9 'Take Fortune's tide – the world is wide': 1851	290
10 'Times are mending': 1852	314
Aftermath	324
Note on manuscript sources	335
Endnotes	340
Bibliography	373
Index	377

ACKNOWLEDGEMENTS

As well as general works on the Great Famine, I have consulted Relief Commission Papers in the National Archives of Ireland, Parliamentary Papers, Treasury Papers and local newspapers. The website www.irishnewsarchive.com has greatly facilitated my research in the newspapers of the period, as have microfilm copies of the newspapers in the National Library of Ireland and in Kerry County Library, Tralee. I have also consulted relevant local history publications, but I have not included folklore records. Board of guardian minute books for the Poor Law Unions of Tralee and Listowel are held in the archives of the Local Studies Department of Kerry County Library, and these have been a rich source of information. The minute books are incomplete, but some of the missing records of Tralee Union are available in the National Library of Ireland and in the Manuscripts and Archives Research Library of Trinity College, Dublin. Further details on manuscript sources consulted are included at the end of this book.

In recording the actual words of eyewitnesses, I have been influenced by the approach of Liam Swords in his book *In Their Own Words: The Famine in North Connacht 1845–49* and that of Noel Kissane in *The Irish Famine: A Documentary History*. I have adapted the timeline of Noel Kissane and have used the illustration 'Famine in Ireland' that I first found in his book. Underlying all my research is the encouragement I have taken from the observation of Ciarán Ó Murchadha that 'the immensity of what happened is perhaps best appreciated in the microcosmic detail of local experience'.[1]

I am grateful to all the following people for their assistance in my research: the ever-helpful staff of the National Library of Ireland, the National Archives and Trinity College Manuscripts Library; Michael Lynch, Kerry County Archivist, and the staff of Kerry County Archives; Fr John Joe Spring and Greg Harkin of All Hallows College; Noelle Dowling and Peter Sobolewski of the Dublin Diocesan Archives; Helen O'Carroll,

Director of Kerry County Museum; Maile Melrose and Amanda Barnes, great-granddaughters of H. N. Greenwell; Linde Lunney; Ursula Leslie; Pádraig Corkery; Trevor Giles; Paul Wright; Liam Doyle; Fr Tom Leane; Sr Columbanus Quirke; Micheál Ó hAllmhuráin; Felix Molski; Rob Gemmell; Aiden Feerick; Fr Declan O'Connor; and Rose Mary Logue.

A special word of thanks is due to John D. Pierse, who was completing his book *Teampall Bán: Aspects of the Famine in North Kerry 1845–1852* as I was beginning the research for this book, and who has generously shared his intimate knowledge of Listowel and its Famine history. The commemorative book *The Famine in Kerry*, edited by Michael Costello and published in 1997, has been a very useful resource, as has Shane Lehane's book *The Great Famine in Kerry*, which focuses on the Poor Law Unions of Dingle and Killarney.

I am very grateful once more to Julia Barrett for her invaluable research assistance. My sincere gratitude also goes to Dr Ciarán Reilly for his foreword. I have also benefitted greatly from the professional advice and guidance of Noel O'Regan and Wendy Logue in Mercier Press.

Finally, special thanks to my wife, Catherine, for her constant support and love.

TIMELINE

1845

August: Reports of blight. Partial crop failure.

November: Prime Minister Robert Peel orders purchase of Indian corn (named 'Peel's brimstone' because it was hard and unpalatable) in the USA for distribution to the needy.

November: Relief Commission established in response to the growing Irish crisis. It was governed by the relief commissioners.

1846

March: Public Works Act.

March: Sale of cheap Indian corn begins. In order not to interfere with market forces, this was not freely distributed but was sold, although sometimes at reduced prices.

June: Peel's government falls and Lord John Russell becomes prime minister.

August: General failure of potato crop.

August: Poor Employment Act – public works resumed.

November: Very severe winter begins. Fever, dysentery and starvation set in.

November/December: First deaths from starvation in Kerry.

1847

January: British Relief Association formed.

January: Government announces public works to be phased out and replaced by soup kitchens.

February: Temporary Relief Act or Soup Kitchen Act, allowing relief for three categories of people: the destitute and helpless; the destitute able-bodied who held no land; and the able-bodied with small land holdings.

This was intended as a transitional and temporary measure to deal with an immediate crisis.

March: 714,000 people employed on public works, such as the building of roads.

March: People begin to be laid off public works.

March: Soup kitchens begin to be set up to replace public works, but many are not established until summer.

May: Death of Daniel O'Connell.

May: Death of Earl of Bessborough, lord lieutenant.

May: Appointment of Earl of Clarendon as lord lieutenant.

July: 3,000,000 people in receipt of food aid through soup kitchens.

August: Poor Law Extension Act, making Irish property owners responsible for meeting the costs of relief through the poor rates levied by the Poor Law Unions. The intention was to force local landlords to take responsibility for local relief.

August: No blight, but potato crop is very small.

October: Soup kitchens closed. Poor Law Unions to provide relief.

1848

July: Young Ireland rebellion in Ballingarry, Co. Tipperary.

August: Encumbered Estates Act introduced.

August: General potato crop failure.

November: Cholera epidemic begins.

1849

March: Edward Twistleton, Chief Poor Law Commissioner, resigns in protest at government policy.

July: Rate-in-aid levy on all Poor Law Unions.

August: Visit of Queen Victoria.

August: Potato crop failure confined to west and south.

1850

May: Boundary changes transfer nine electoral divisions from Listowel Union to Tralee Union.

1851

March: Sixty-six people die in the workhouses of Listowel Union in one week.
May: A total of 5,627 in the workhouses of Listowel Union.
May: A total of 7,197 people in the workhouses of Tralee Union.

ABBREVIATIONS

CEx: *The Cork Examiner*
DED: District Electoral Division
JKAHS: *Journal of the Kerry Archaeological and Historical Society*
JP: Justice of the Peace
KCA: Kerry County Archives, Tralee
KEP: *The Kerry Evening Post*
KEx: *Kerry Examiner and Munster General Observer*
NAI: National Archives of Ireland
NLI: National Library of Ireland
PP: Parish Priest
RCC: Roman Catholic Curate
RN: Royal Navy
TCD: Trinity College, Dublin
TC: *The Tralee Chronicle and Killarney Echo*

A NOTE ON CURRENCY AND WEIGHTS

There were twelve pence (12d) in one shilling (1s) and twenty shillings in one pound (£1). Christine Kinealy in *Charity and the Great Hunger in Ireland: the Kindness of Strangers* (p. 14) cites an authoritative source for adopting an exchange rate of £1 in 1846 as equal to £100 in 2013.

Imperial measures of weight: 16 ounces is equal to 1 pound and 14 pounds equals 1 stone; 8 stone equals 1 hundredweight (cwt) and 20 hundredweight equals 1 ton.

1 pound equals 453 grams and 1 stone equals 6.35 kilograms.

FOREWORD

One million people died and one million people emigrated during the years of the Great Famine in Ireland, 1845 to 1851. These are the bare statistics in relation to Europe's worst social catastrophe. To put it more starkly, in that short period, one person died or emigrated every one-and-a-half seconds. The population of Ireland was decimated and, as I write, Ireland remains the only country in Europe that does not have at least the same population numbers as it did in 1841. However, for such a seismic event, the Famine was long avoided in Irish historical writing and, more importantly, in the social memory of local communities. In the decades that followed, a great silence prevailed. The sesquicentenary of the Great Famine in the mid-1990s changed that and there was an outpouring of both scholarly publication and local commemoration. The intervening twenty years or so have witnessed a continued interest in understanding the Famine, best exemplified in the hosting of the now annual National Famine Commemoration Day.

Few counties suffered as badly as Kerry during the Famine. Tralee, Listowel and north Kerry were devastated, and by the end of the Famine years the population of the county was reduced by over 20 per cent. In this book, Bryan MacMahon charts the various stages of how north Kerry was decimated, boring down in minute detail to even the most remote of places. The author has trawled through a multitude of sources, some more obscure than others, from the voluminous accounts provided by the Kerry newspapers to the journal of Lieutenant H. N. Greenwell located in the Kona Historical Society Archives in Hawaii. All these sources help bring to life the realities of this awful tragedy.

The key strength of this book is the fact that the reader is introduced to individual stories of hardship and hunger, relying on the voices of the people of Famine Kerry to tell their story. These voices remind us that these were real lives and real sufferings, something which can often be overlooked. Yet throughout we are conscious of the fact that some stories and depredations went unrecorded. We can only imagine the end for many men, women and children.

MacMahon's work poses and probes other questions about the Famine that deserve further analysis in the country as a whole. Perhaps key among these is the idea that people profited during these years of hunger, eviction and emigration. This 'greediness for gain' was exemplified in the actions of some merchants and shopkeepers who stood to gain from the severity of the times, when even the living were described as 'but crawling skeletons'. Such descriptions of the north Kerry famished are harrowing, none more so than the Tralee woman who 'begged while she carried her dead child strapped on her back, resisting all attempts to take the baby from her, saying that it was the only way she could get money to bury the child'. Elsewhere the dogs of north Kerry were said to have ravaged the graveyards, pulling limbs from the dead. Yet amidst these depredations, for many, life went on as normal. The celebrations at Ballyseedy Castle for the coming-of-age of Henry Blennerhassett in June 1847 were representative of this, when during an evening of celebration almost 120 gallons of whiskey were reportedly consumed.

No doubt such apathy or lack of concern for the poor was criticised and indeed some, such as Colonel John Day Stokes, believed that the Kerry gentry and those of means could not escape censure if they were unwilling to contribute to relief efforts. As MacMahon notes, the reaction of those of means displayed a mixture of 'paralysis, perplexity, perversity and philanthropy'. The experience of Colonel Stokes is just one of a number of the key personalities that this book considers. The efforts of the members of various relief committees and Poor Law Unions are examined alongside the indefatigable efforts of the north Kerry clergy who were also worthy of praise. Examining these, the author probes how the people of Kerry responded to the crisis and how the various levels of society treated the poor. However, even where there were conscientious efforts to provide for the poor, at times the spread of disease in the towns of Listowel, Tralee and elsewhere, where 'death is rife in every alley and lane', meant that there was simply no way of escaping the ravages of the Famine.

From the beginning this book sets out to answer the question – what happened in north Kerry during the Famine? In answering that question the book acknowledges the intentions and the good work of many conscientious people who laboured for the suffering and hungry people of Kerry during the Famine. It brings the reader closer to understanding the realities of life in north Kerry during the Great Famine. With an immense knowledge of his subject and landscape, Bryan MacMahon paints a horrifying picture of how thousands died, emigrated and were left traumatised by the event. No doubt the level of detail and analysis provided in *The Great Famine in Tralee and North Kerry* will offer a template for others to replicate across the country. Finally, the book sets out to remember all the 'traumatic events and distant lives' that the author stresses 'must never be forgotten'. The publication of *The Great Famine in Tralee and North Kerry* does just that, ensuring they will never be forgotten.

Dr Ciarán Reilly
Author of *Strokestown and the Great Irish Famine*

INTRODUCTION

Here and in the neighbouring parishes of Lixnaw and Irremore, fever and dysentery are making ghastly havoc. The people are dying and will die in hundreds. The government will make this doomed land one vast graveyard ...

'A voice from Listowel', *The Cork Examiner*, 7 February 1849

This book resulted from my desire to find out how Tralee and north Co. Kerry were affected by the Great Famine 170 years ago. I set out to answer the question: 'What happened in these areas during the Famine?' I have followed the sequence of events from the autumn of 1845 to the summer of 1852 in the area north of a line from Fenit to Tralee, Castleisland and Brosna, in order to convey some of the disastrous consequences of the potato blight, *Phytophthora infestans*, and also to record the various attempts to deal with the unprecedented catastrophe.

In trying to comprehend the ingrained beliefs and attitudes that prevailed in the 1840s, it is crucial to understand how poverty was seen, how the Irish people were seen by the British and how the business of government was conducted. This was an age when concepts such as human rights and democratic principles were alien, and property rights were paramount. Governments were slow to interfere with market forces, following the prevailing *laissez-faire* policies, and were keen to avoid creating dependence by giving food or monetary handouts, or raising unrealistic expectations of relief among the poor.

Poverty was equated with laziness, and the Irish were viewed in Britain as lazy, poor, lawless, feckless and dishonest. An editorial in *The Times* in 1848 declared: 'There are corners of Ireland which are the *ultima thule* [most distant region] of civilisation and where a Cimmerian gloom hangs over the human soul. The people there have always been listless, improvident and wretched, under whatever rulers.'[1] The words of a hymn composed in 1848 depicted a stratified society underpinned by divine sanction: 'The rich man in his castle/ The poor man at his gate/God made them high and lowly/And ordered their estate.'[2] It was a convenient belief for privileged elites of all kinds. Another convenient belief, which prevailed at the highest levels of government and administration and which influenced policy at all levels, was providentialism. This was the term used to describe the widespread belief that the Famine was sent by a vengeful God as a judgement or punishment on human beings.

The social structure in rural Ireland had landlords at its top, and they were part of a privileged elite with a security and status that they zealously guarded and promoted. Not all landlords were landowners; there was a complex structure of leasing land from other landowners and sub-letting. This was known as the middleman system, which could involve several tiers of letting. Along with the subdivision of land among all the sons of a family and the practice of giving long leases, the middleman system was one of the major defects of the landholding system in pre-Famine times. Middlemen would rent land from a landlord and then proceed to sub-divide the land and rent it to numbers of others, some of whom would then do likewise, a practice which encouraged squatting.[3]

Trinity College, Dublin was the owner of large tracts of land in north Kerry, but the management of the land was left to local landlords. Many landowners were absentees living in England or following careers elsewhere. Lord Listowel was an absentee, as was Sir Edward Denny, whose estate in and around Tralee extended over 21,000 acres, but their estates were under the management of conscientious resident agents, James Murray Home and William Denny respectively.

Large farmers were those who held fifteen acres or more. They kept animals and grew grain crops and so were shielded from the potato crop failure. Small farmers held five to fifteen acres, while cottiers had a small cottage and a holding of less than five acres, which provided enough potatoes for a family in normal years. At the bottom of the social scale were agricultural labourers, who rented land (conacre) to grow potatoes to feed their families; they lived in one-roomed cabins.

INTRODUCTION

In Tralee and Listowel there were professional and business classes, along with artisans, traders and shopkeepers. *Slater's Commercial Directory* of 1846 gives an overview of traders and professionals in these towns and many of the names and addresses of people who feature in this book can be seen there.[4] Women were confined to the domestic sphere and so did not usually feature prominently in public life; hence you will notice that few women appear in newspaper reports cited in this book.

There is a particular focus on the towns of Tralee and Listowel, as these were the centres of the Poor Law Unions at the time. These unions were established under the Poor Law Act of 1838, which divided the country into 130 unions and established workhouses; they were overseen by the Poor Law Commissioners.[5] They were administered by boards of guardians, which were responsible for raising funds for poor relief, through the collection of poor rates that were, in turn, based on property valuations. Workhouses were built in Tralee and Listowel in the early 1840s, and were under the jurisdiction of their respective Poor Law Unions. During the crisis of the Great Famine, these buildings did not have the capacity to accommodate the large numbers applying for admission and consequently auxiliary workhouses were established. These were typically unused stores, distilleries, breweries, farm buildings or warehouses that were usually rented by the unions. Although part of Tralee Poor Law Union until 1848, Dingle and west Kerry are not specifically included here except when the people from the area came to the workhouses in Tralee or where they are mentioned at board of guardians' meetings. The inmates of Tralee workhouse included many people from west Kerry until a workhouse was built in Dingle in 1849.

While much detailed information has been discovered about the effects of the Famine in north Kerry, there are still gaps in the surviving information, and the records leave many unanswered questions. Moreover, all of the sources consulted have their limitations and there is always a possibility of bias or exaggeration in reports. My survey of the newspapers is necessarily subjective and personal, and it is possible that I may have overlooked significant information. Some areas (for example, Knocknagoshel, Kilflynn and Asdee) seem not to feature prominently in the local newspapers.

Fortunately for researchers, three newspapers were published in Tralee in the mid-1800s and they are invaluable sources of eyewitness accounts of the Famine in the county. They were *The Kerry Evening Post*, *Kerry Examiner* and *The Tralee Chronicle*, all published in Tralee. *The Cork Examiner* also carried regular news reports from Kerry. The political persuasions of the three Tralee newspapers certainly coloured their presentation of events, and there were commercial rivalries and social tensions between them, although it should be noted that all four newspapers regularly reprinted news stories from each other.

The venerable *Kerry Evening Post* (hereafter *Post*) was first published in 1774. Owned by John and Jeffrey Eagar, it was the establishment newspaper, strongly Tory and Protestant. It therefore adopted a superior tone towards the nationalist or pro-Repeal papers, which supported the Repeal of the Act of Union of 1800 and Daniel O'Connell's Repeal Association. The Repeal of the Act of Union was the great nationalist cause of the period and the Repeal Association, under O'Connell's leadership, was a highly organised popular movement. The *Post* was steadfastly opposed to Repeal. *The Tralee Chronicle*, on the other hand, described itself as liberal and 'neutral in politics, enjoying the support of persons of all opinions, including landed proprietors, resident gentry and numerous visitors to this highly favoured locality'.[6] Its owner was James Raymond Eagar.

The third local paper, the *Kerry Examiner*, was strongly nationalist and Catholic, with this quotation from a French revolutionary hero, the Marquis de Lafayette, beneath its masthead: 'For a nation to be free it is sufficient that she wills it.' It described itself as liberal and as 'the special organ of the Roman Catholic clergy and people'.[7] It was owned and edited by Patrick O'Loughlin Byrne. *The Cork Examiner*, founded in 1841 by John Francis Maguire, was a strong supporter of Repeal and tenant rights, and was another source of reliable information.

There are of course problems with newspaper evidence. Anonymous articles and letters are not absolutely reliable, as some may have been written by the editors (often the owners of the papers) themselves to stir up controversy and generate sales. In fact, the editor of the *Kerry Examiner* accused other editors of writing such letters, 'a trick we have never stooped to'.[8] However, I believe that the news reports are generally reliable, and if one paper was in error, readers and other newspapers would quickly challenge it. The reporters were not observing events from a distance: they sat through discussions at board of guardians' meetings and wrote humane and graphic accounts of what they witnessed during visits to the workhouses and to the roadside hovels of the recently dispossessed.

Writing a narrative account based largely on newspaper reports has been akin to re-assembling an artefact from random fragmentary remains, and I am conscious of omissions and disjunctions. It was unusual for the lives of the ordinary poor to be documented in newspapers, which normally concentrated on international news, parliamentary affairs and, at local level, meetings of public bodies and the social lives of the wealthy and privileged. In a recent publication Michael Foley has pointed out that the Famine forced journalists 'to find new ways of reporting that would define how the press worked for the next fifty years'.[9] These new styles of reporting brought journalists closer to the people's experiences. The outrage displayed in their vivid and moving eyewitness accounts is an example of what Foley describes as the press contributing to developments as well as reporting on them.[10] Editors, reporters and correspondents performed an important service, speaking truth to power, challenging official policies and providing a voice for the powerless. The experience of journalists during the Famine led many of them into political careers later.[11]

The work of the parish clergy in providing material and spiritual comfort to the poor and in speaking out for them is a prominent theme of this book. Two men in particular stand out in this respect: Dr John McEnnery, parish priest (PP) of Tralee, and Fr Darby Mahony, parish priest of Listowel. (The former completed his PhD in the Sorbonne in Paris and is usually given the title 'Dr' in the sources.)

Local public figures displayed a range of responses to the events of 1845 to 1852, and the records show examples of paralysis, perplexity, perversity and philanthropy. Government officials were under obligation to implement decisions made in Dublin or London by superiors who could have had little appreciation of the extremely complex conditions experienced at local level. The accounts cited here are invaluable contemporary records of events and of reactions to them, and for that reason some are quoted at length. The emphasis throughout is on 'human interest' stories, the lived experiences of eyewitnesses to the events of 1845 to 1852.

Space does not permit a full treatment of the constantly evolving official strategies for dealing with the unprecedented crisis in Ireland in those years. For succinct overviews of government policies and the work of the various agencies involved in dealing with the Great Famine at national level, I recommend Ruán O'Donnell's *A Short History of Ireland's Famine* and Chapter 1 of Christine Kinealy's *Charity and the Great Hunger in Ireland: The Kindness of Strangers*, which deals with official responses to the Famine.

In deference to the journalists, clergy and public figures of the Famine period, and to today's readers, I have frequently chosen to rely on original words rather than provide a summary of what was written. The many individual voices included here are those of landlords and their agents, tenants, labourers, government inspectors, priests, parsons, philanthropists, relief officials, coroners, politicians, physicians, Poor Law guardians, overseas visitors, workhouse officials and inmates. These voices have been stilled for seventeen decades and their powerful testimonies have been largely hidden since then. It is time they were heard once more, in all their compassion and humanitarianism, their apathy and self-interest, their bewilderment and frustration, their outrage and fury, their sadness and despair. This book lifts the veil of history a little and looks at the vanished world that they inhabited and the desperate times through which they lived. That world was one in which the poor were always seen in the mass and were rarely identified as individuals; few of their voices have been recorded in the archives and what we have are the words of those who spoke on their behalf. In the words of

Hugh Dorian of Donegal, 'the poor were treated and despised as if they were beings of quite a different creation. The satiated never understand the emaciated.'[12] This last sentence was a rendering of the Irish proverb: *Ní thuigeann an sách an seang*.

I hope that this record of the actual words and responses of eyewitnesses will give readers a vivid and authentic sense of the unfolding crisis and of the developing responses of office holders and of the people of Tralee and north Kerry over the seven winters and six summers of desolation from 1845 to 1852, as well as a sense of how the small number of newspaper readers in particular experienced events week by week, month by month, year by year. Most of those readers were in comfortable drawing rooms and in offices, but some were in groups gathered around rural firesides, listening intently as the news reports were read aloud to them by an educated local person. The newspapers put a spotlight on the dark heart of the Famine in Kerry, as this book also attempts to do. The Irish people then endured the upheaval of a relentless onslaught of hunger, poverty, disease, death and emigration that in many respects finds echoes in the 'ghastly havoc' of migration crises today, which we, in our time, also experience through news reports.

The issue of where responsibility lay for the catastrophic events of 1845 to 1852 is too complex to be dealt with adequately here, but the conclusion of leading Famine historian Christine Kinealy is widely accepted: 'The response of the British government to the Famine was inadequate in terms of humanitarian criteria and, increasingly after 1847, systematically and deliberately so.'[13] The noted physician William Stokes (1804–1878), professor of medicine in Trinity College, wrote in a less direct and more indulgent tone:

> If many were lost, perhaps ignorantly, let us think on the number saved. We cannot suddenly be wise. Nations, as well as individuals, must purchase experience, even though the cost be ruinous. And whatever fault we may find with the modes adopted for relief to the sufferers in the famine of 1847, we must applaud the intention and be grateful for the efforts that were made.[14]

Among the lost were two brothers, Michael and James Mitchell, who died of starvation in Castlegregory in December 1846. They were sheltered in their last hours in the home of Cornelius Harnett and his wife, whose forename is not recorded. Michael was aged seven and James was aged three months. The post-mortem found that 'not the least trace of food was to be discovered in the stomach or bowels of either'.[15] They were among the first children in Kerry to die of starvation during the Famine. The unrelenting cycle of human tragedy and social havoc which began with the blight of 1845 was still evident in March 1851, when 129 people died in the Listowel workhouse over a two-week period. Eighty-nine of these were under the age of fifteen. It is often lamented that we do not know the names of those who died in the Famine years, but newspapers did report on individual deaths and the names of some people who died in the workhouses are recorded in the minute books of the Tralee and Listowel boards of guardians. When victims were identified, their names are included in this book.

This book is an attempt to honour those who died and to acknowledge the intentions and the good work of many conscientious people. If it brings readers closer to understanding how the catastrophic events of the Great Famine were experienced in Tralee and north Kerry, it will have achieved its purpose. The details are necessarily graphic because, in the words of Cormac Ó Gráda, gruesome reports are 'at the heart of the Famine story. They make it "a palpable thing".'[16]

These horrors occurred. These responses followed. These people were eyewitnesses.

Note:
The spelling of place names and townlands varies in the sources and some differ from today's spellings. Today's Kilmoyley, for example, was often spelled Kilmoily, and Ballyheigue could be Ballyheige. Some places had alternative names: Killury, for example, was the same as Causeway, and Rattoo was the same as Ballyduff. The spelling of personal names also varies in the sources; for example, sometimes McCarthy appears as McCartie, and Hurly as Hurley.

'A DARK AND WITHERED APPEARANCE'

1845

The Rev. Mr McCarthy, P.P. directed that a special committee ... should form a central meeting at Causeway once a fortnight to watch the progress of the disease.

Kerry Examiner, 14 November 1845

In August 1845 it was the price of potatoes rather than their quality that was of concern to the Kerry press, with reports that potatoes were selling at fourpence (4d) a stone in Listowel. This was considered expensive and the reason given was 'forestalling'.[1] The *Post* condemned this price-control practice, by which traders bought in bulk from farmers and then released the potatoes on the market in a controlled way in order to keep prices high. It stated that this was akin to usury, with the result that it was the poor who suffered most.

The concern with price, however, was followed by even more alarming concerns. Later in August of that year another newspaper carried a report from the *Sussex Advertiser* about the failure of the potato crop in that part of England. It remarked how a species of blight had suddenly attacked the crop, resulting in 'a dark and withered appearance', followed by 'a speedy decomposition of the vegetable matter ... causing an intolerable stench to arise'.[2] This heralded the arrival of the potato blight in England. On 7

October the *Kerry Examiner* (hereafter *Examiner*) reported that the disease had made an appearance in Cork. In mid-October, a report in the *Post* stated that 'Kerry, which was hitherto safe, is beginning to complain'.[3] The *Examiner* was concerned that prospects for the potato crop in Kerry were 'anything but encouraging', although the editor, Patrick O'Loughlin Byrne, was determined to be positive: 'But for our part, we have not yet seen one diseased potato; our market abounds with the finest potatoes … It may be that fear magnifies the danger, at least it is so to be hoped.'[4]

Constabulary reports show that there was no cause for general alarm in late October 1845. In Tralee, County Inspector Hawkshaw concluded that 'about one-fourth of the white potatoes or lumpers is in a diseased state and all sorts have been affected in a slight degree. The digging here is late and the state of the crop will not be ascertained till about 10th of November.'[5] From Listowel, Sub-Inspector Fletcher reported that digging and storing had already commenced and there was 'general complaint of rot but not to any great extent'. The farmers were afraid, however, that the crop might rot in the storage pit. Hawkshaw gave his view that, while statements were conflicting, 'the alarm at present is very considerable'. However, he went on to say that there was a vast quantity of sound potatoes in the country and that every year there was a crop failure to some degree.[6]

A correspondent to the *Examiner* gave advice on how to use diseased potatoes to make bread which was 'sweet, sound and wholesome', but others advised that neither man nor beast should consume the blighted crop.[7] This belief that some of the diseased potatoes could be salvaged and used to make starch was in general circulation for a short period, until it was found to be impractical. By November the editor of the *Examiner* was convinced that potato crop failure was the exception rather than the rule, that alarm was 'as groundless as it [was] mischievous' and that 'the alleged failure of the potato crop will be found to exist more in men's heated imaginations than in reality'.[8] He pointed out that the Maharees near Castlegregory had just produced the finest potatoes and that there were no complaints from the 'poor and wild district of Iveragh'.[9]

'A DARK AND WITHERED APPEARANCE'

There was, however, clear cause for alarm a short time later. After a meeting of parishioners held in Causeway, John Sheehy, a local Repeal warden (a representative and collector for the Repeal Association), wrote as follows to the *Examiner* about the experiences of farmers in Ballyheigue, Killury and Rattoo:

> I regret that the grievances set forth by many who had been present on the above occasion were most appalling. One man asserted that he saw a barrell [*sic*] of potatoes offered for one pound; others stated that they relinquished the digging of their potatoes altogether in consequence of finding them so unsound, while many more said that they had but a few weeks provisions and even those partially injured. I am happy to state that the Rev. Mr Plummer, a gentleman who is never wanting in the cause of humanity, presided at this meeting, offering his most strenuous support to meet the exgience [*sic*] of the time. Mr Maurice Cushion of Rattoo came forward also and offered to sacrifice the rents of his Con-acre land he had let, in consequence of the unsound state of the crop thereon. The Rev. Mr McCarthy P.P. directed that a special committee from each of the above parishes should form a central meeting at Causeway once a fortnight to watch the progress of the disease in the potato crop and to report thereon.[10]

The date of this meeting, 9 November, is significant, particularly as the first meeting of the Relief Commission, under the chairmanship of Edward Lucas, the under-secretary at Dublin Castle, did not take place in Dublin until 20 November. By then, the situation across the country was considered serious enough to warrant the setting up of this temporary commission to coordinate the work of local relief committees throughout the country and provide food distribution depots. However, the Relief Commission did not issue instructions to local relief committees until February 1846, in a deliberate policy of delaying any support in order to ensure that initiatives would be taken locally. Then the government could act in the guise of assisting local efforts.[11]

The Causeway proposal seems to have been among the earliest local responses to the looming crisis, although nobody then could have had any concept of the enormity of the catastrophe that lay ahead. Great credit is due to those involved in taking this prompt action, particularly Fr Eugene (or Owen) McCarthy, who was parish priest for Ballyheigue, Killury and Rattoo from 1822 to 1857; Rev. Plummer, who was rector of the Church of Ireland parish of Killury from 1833 to 1872; and the aforementioned John Sheehy.

The letter from John Sheehy contrasts with a report from a member of the coastguard in Ballyheigue, Henry Lawrence, RN (Royal Navy). He struck an optimistic note, expressing his confidence that reports of diseased potatoes were unfounded. His letter was written on 29 November 1845 to the Coastguard Office, Dublin, in response to a general query:

> I have much pleasure in stating for the information of the Inspector General that the crop of potatoes as previously dug and pitted in this district … is considerably beyond that of the last four or five years, consequently no apprehensions of scarcity are entertained in this locality. I have not heard of any injury happening to those dug early in the season.[12]

Reports in the Kerry-based newspapers were mixed. The editor of the *Examiner* remained sanguine. While he did express concern for the prospects of the poor in 1846, he saw 'no reason to apprehend an absolute famine'. He cited 'the most severely scourged' areas of the county as 'the districts of Kenmare, Ballyheigue and Ardfert, and the tract of country thence on by Rattoo to Ballylongford'.[13] Meanwhile the *Post* reported that accounts of the crop from around the county were 'chequered' but that 'from Castleisland and parts of Clanmaurice, accounts are very gloomy'.[14] A few weeks later it cited the area west of Dingle, as well as Castleisland, Ballylongford, Ballyheigue and parts of Kenmare, as the worst affected by crop failure.[15]

Nevertheless, by 26 November the *Post* was adamant that 'notwithstanding the croaking of the Repeal press, it is evident that disease in the potato is checked'. By 9 December the *Examiner* likewise believed that 'in this county at least, the alarm seems to have considerably subsided as to the failure of the potato crop'. Even so, it advised that 'immediate measures must be adopted for the relief of the real sufferers'. Noting that Killarney had taken prompt action, the paper posed a question about the 'sluggard' response in the county capital: 'What is Tralee doing?'[16]

John Hurly, who was chairman of Tralee board of guardians (the managerial board for the Tralee Poor Law Union) at the time, offered a clearer – albeit more negative – view of the situation. He reported to the government on 11 October 1845 that one-third of the potato crop thus far was totally lost and that no locality had been spared.[17] A great deal of the crop was still in the ground, but he was anxious about its quality. He was fearful for the future of the poor, anticipating price rises and the prospect of a much-reduced harvest the following year due to a lack of seed potatoes. He advised the government that every precaution should be taken. Having begun by stating that he was writing 'without any intention … of creating unnecessary alarm', Hurly's stance by the end of the report was that 'in the present case, alarm to a considerable extent is warranted'.[18] John Hurly's alarm would prove to be fully justified as events unfolded.

2

'SOFT WORDS NO MORE'

January–June 1846

We deem it due to ourselves as a board as well as to the electoral divisions which we represent to record upon our minutes the apprehension which we entertain in reference to this calamitous visitation of the Almighty.

Tralee board of guardians, *Kerry Evening Post*, 7 February 1846

Tralee

1846 began with a slowly growing sense of anxiety, but not yet alarm, at the unfolding events. John Lynch, a prominent solicitor and chairman of the Tralee Borough Commissioners (which managed the lighting, cleaning and maintenance of public spaces in the town), was also a member of the board of guardians. This was a difficult time for him as his son, also called John, had died suddenly in January, and his colleagues were sympathetic to this loss. Lynch's impatience with his fellow board members comes across clearly in press reports of their meetings around this time. He pressed them to seek practical remedies for the disease rather than waste precious time in inquiring about whether it existed at all. He said that the government would be discussing abstract questions of science 'until famine would come on accompanied by all its horrors, and when it did, they would have no place to obtain a supply of food for the people'.[1] In Lynch's opinion it was useless to speculate on the origins of the disease because he shared the providentialist view of many of his contemporaries regarding the outbreak and said that 'it could be traced at once to the will of God'.

Lynch had some clear proposals at this early stage, such as the idea that food should be allowed to come into every market free of duty. If there were to be duties, he argued, they should be on luxuries and applied only to those who could afford to pay them. He blamed 'the landlord legislature' for imposing the existing duties and reminded his colleagues that it was 'the bounden duty of the board to procure relief for the people by sustaining the legislature in their present efforts to repeal the Corn Laws'.[2] It is clear that Lynch had no great regard for landlords.

Replying to the queries of the Mansion House Committee, a famine relief organisation with headquarters in Dublin, the board stated in January that the disease was 'very much, though not entirely, checked'.[3] The following information was drawn up by the chairman, John Hurly, on the effects of the blight thus far: one-third of the crop of Tralee was lost, with some areas such as Taulaght and Fenit being comparatively free of the disease. One-quarter of the potatoes grown on workhouse land was lost. Cattle and pigs were reported as thriving on diseased potatoes. The disease had not yet affected applications for relief and no unsound potatoes had been fed to the workhouse inmates. There had been no attempts to make starch or meal from diseased potatoes. The expectation was that the only consequence of the crop failure would be higher prices for potatoes during the summer.[4]

However, in the issue of *The Tralee Chronicle* (hereafter *Chronicle*) which documented the guardians' reply to the Mansion House Committee, a report taken from the *Post* showed that there were concerns about the rising number of applicants to the workhouse. In mid-January, forty-five people sought admission, more than double the usual number. A week later, there were over sixty applicants. Many of these were families of rural labourers, driven to the workhouse because of the failure of their plots of score ground.[5] The report commented: 'This is one of the first symptoms of the failure of the food of the peasantry of which we have had cognisance and it is indeed alarming to see whole families this early in the year applying to get into the workhouse.' There was a clear admission in the *Post* that this scale of suffering was unexpected: 'This is a melancholy state of things for which we were quite unprepared.'[6]

Away from the homes of the peasantry, however, life went on as usual in Tralee. Captain Cruise and officers of Ballymullen Army Barracks, for example, entertained 'a very large party of the beauty and fashion of Kerry' at a garrison ball in late January 1846: 'The supper table was elegantly laid out and was covered with every delicacy of the season that money could procure.'[7] It was described by one who attended as 'one of the most elegant and agreeable parties ever seen in Tralee'. At the same time, at Brosna fair, 'cattle of every description, particularly milch cows and in-calf heifers carried high prices'.[8] In February the *Chronicle* was gratified to learn that 'the mills of our county are being well stocked with wheat'.[9]

The blight's stranglehold on the county, however, was undoubtedly growing. When the Tralee board of guardians held their weekly meeting on 2 February, many speakers expressed alarm at the rapid spread of the disease, the rising numbers in the workhouse and 'the expected famine' between April and August.[10] There was 'an unusually large number' of applicants to the workhouse and fifty-four were admitted on that day with only one rejected. Colonel John Day Stokes told his fellow board members at the meeting that while 'heretofore we have spoken of the potato disease as a thing likely to be attended with dreadful consequences, we may now speak of that state of things actually existing'. Famine, he said, 'was no longer problematical but certain'.[11]

Colonel Stokes was home on furlough in his native Tralee from military service in India. His authority and personal leadership qualities ensured that he was an influential member of the board of guardians for the duration of his leave. His advice to the government was that it should not only provide employment for the people but should also begin to provide food: 'Famine is certain if employment be not found for the people.' This followed John Lynch's warning of famine a month earlier, and was echoed by fellow board member Robert Hickson's warning that in west Kerry 'even within the next month, there is danger, I may say, of famine'.[12]

Stokes also had a blunt and uncomfortable message for the board members, one which he would continue to press while he remained in Tralee: 'If we do not come forward ourselves and willingly state our readiness to be taxed for the purpose, we shall deserve to have every censure heaped upon us.' He repeatedly urged that 'in a word, we ought to come forward and bear our share of the burden necessary to meet this state of things'.[13]

At the same acrimonious meeting, John Lynch repeated his view that they were far too late in taking action. He hectored the chairman, John Hurly:

> I tell you what you'll do sir, if you are now – even at the eleventh hour – really serious on this matter: call upon the government either to open the ports and let in foreign corn to the people or call upon them to shut the ports and prevent its exportation. Call upon them to do that and call upon them also to do this – to give employment to your unemployed and wretched population.[14]

Lynch went on to describe how farmers who would normally be providing potatoes to Tralee market were coming to the market to buy potatoes instead: 'Is not this an extraordinary anomaly? Is it not also an extraordinary anomaly that you only now admit the fact of failure, with certain want staring you in the face?' He reminded the chairman that he had spoken to the board much earlier about the scale of the crisis and was not heeded:

> You listened to me, sir, but my words fell on your ear as if I was speaking to the wall. Yet in the short period of three weeks, I find the very gentlemen who on that occasion met me in that spirit today admitting – what? Why, that there is indeed a prospect of famine. A most generous admission when it is too late to make it … I will expose the ulcer and it is this – the landed interests, the proprietors of land, did not like to approach this question so long as they could possibly keep it away from them.[15]

Lynch predicted famine not just in Ireland but also in England and Scotland, with consequences for other parts of Europe also. 'Where is this charity to come from to feed the millions who will be starving in a few months in England, Ireland and Scotland?' He accepted that the government could not solve everything, but the board should:

> ... ask them to do what they can do – to open the ports or shut the ports. Let them please themselves but they must do one or the other, or the people of these countries will be in that state that neither life nor property can be safe. Property most certainly will not be safe. A starving community cannot be kept in a state of discipline and self-control.[16]

He suggested that preventing the export of corn from Ireland would actually benefit the landlords and farmers, because prices would increase. 'You have the consumption at home for it. You have an immense population calling to you with both hands to give them something. If you let the corn go away, what will you have to give to them?'

Many Famine historians now identify the proposals by John Lynch as actions that ought to have taken place. He had other practical suggestions for employment projects too, particularly for work on the railway network, and on the roads and footpaths around Tralee that badly needed repairs. He also proposed a major project:

> ... to turn the course of the river which inundates Tralee, spreading disease through the wretched abodes of the inhabitants of our lanes and alleys. I say it would give employment to a great number of our people to make a short cut from near Ballybeggan in this direction, turning the body of water round by Ballymullen, outside Tralee altogether.[17]

Robert C. Hickson responded to what he called 'this angry invective' by saying that it was 'rather bad taste of Mr Lynch to introduce the torch of discord' into their proceedings. His comments show that there was still no sense of urgency among some board members:

> None of us is gifted with an unerring foresight. Some may have more of that gift than others. I did think, and still think, looking back on that period that there was great exaggeration then and that it was attended with some injurious consequences. I think it excited a panic among the people generally

– not that wholesome panic leading to the precaution of keeping the crop, but rather inducing fanciful ideas of coming relief. I am convinced that a great amount of potatoes – those partially diseased – were through the ignorance of the people given to pigs and cows.[18]

John Lynch was frequently at odds with the landlord members of the board of guardians, and an exchange on a later topic at the meeting had the landowning Thomas P. Trant tartly responding to him, 'We will beat you on that too, Mr Lynch.'

There was understandable concern from members of the board that the burden of relief was falling heavily on the town of Tralee. One board member, Peter Thompson, stated that out of 253 inmates in the workhouse, only 120 were from the town. The others came from various locations, including London, Liverpool, Cork, Newcastle, Cahersiveen and Castleisland. He added, to laughter, 'not forgetting Corkaguiny', and Thomas Trant responded in a mocking tone: 'You don't say so.'[19] By 28 February there would be 462 in the workhouse and very many would have been from the sorely stricken Corkaguiny barony.

Despite the differing views expressed at this meeting, a memorial was drawn up by the chairman of the board, John Hurly, and sent to the lord lieutenant. It referred to 'this calamitous visitation of the Almighty' and made the point that none of the actions that had been taken had stayed the disease. The memorial stated bluntly that 'potatoes will run short in April and peasants will have no food till 1st August. A moment's time should not therefore be lost in providing a food supply.' The memorial also dismissed the suggestion of making starch from diseased potatoes as 'nothing less than delusive' and advised that only corn meal would meet the needs of the people. It also appealed for prompt relief works to be undertaken, rejecting work on railways and drainage projects as not suitable because they could not begin immediately.[20]

The sense of crisis was mounting throughout the early months of 1846. Henry Stokes, county surveyor, wrote ominously and perceptively:

> I believe there can be little doubt now that our stock of food for the people will be very short next summer and many begin to have fears for 1847 on account of the bad seed; the spring here for the most part of this month is very mild and the potatoes shooting very early. I am sure all the late sowing will fail. I have got the magistrates to convene meetings in every barony but Clanmaurice to memorial for grant works to afford employment. I suppose the gross amount of the applications will be £50,000. If there is not at least a million put at the disposal of Government, there will be no perceptible good done in Ireland by their scheme for new public works.[21]

Public works had been used during previous times of food shortages as a means of providing relief to the poor. The work usually entailed building or improving roads, improving drainage and sometimes building walls and piers. In early 1846 government grants were given to the Irish Board of Works to administer public work schemes. In the case of road building, the government granted 50 per cent of the cost of road works and a local committee was expected to raise the other 50 per cent.

The bureaucratic delays and inefficiencies at national level, as well as incompetence and corruption at local level, made the whole system of public works very cumbersome and frustrating, as detailed by Christine Kinealy. A local committee had first to send a memorial requesting help to the lord lieutenant, which would then go to the relief commissioners for comment, and then to the Board of Works for scrutiny. Then it went to a local surveyor or engineer who would inspect the prospective project and report back to the board. If the work was approved, then the board would recommend it to the lord lieutenant and advise on the amount of money to be granted, for which he would then apply to the Treasury.[22] It is little wonder that there was great impatience with this slow procedure. Hopes of relief were raised among the people but often were not realised.

Fear of impending famine was widespread by March. This is particularly evident in a poem published by the *Examiner* with the lines: 'Striding nearer every day/Like a wolf in search of prey/Comes the Famine on its way.'[23] The

Chronicle urged that meetings should be held in every town in the county to ensure that there would not be any deaths from hunger: 'Let the gentry not only put down their names but their money. Let not the poorer classes of our towns be suffered to die from the want of a supply of suitable provision.'[24] An 'employment meeting' was held in Tralee, on the initiative of Rev. A. B. Rowan, the Church of Ireland rector of Kilgobbin, a well-regarded scholar and public figure. John Lynch spoke and told the assembly that credit for the initiative was not due to him but to Rev. Rowan. No Catholic clergyman is listed as being present on this occasion. One of the works suggested at the meeting was a road from Strand Street to the ship canal, through a part of the town notorious for poverty and deprivation known as the Quarry.[25]

John Lynch addressed another meeting in April, where he approved of the government's policy of not giving charity but rather keeping food prices down and giving employment in order that people could buy food: 'Nothing so debases the human character as to be obliged to ask for a general alms for a general people. It does not coerce them, as they ought to be coerced, to rely on their own resources.'[26]

There was dismay in Tralee at the end of May when major relief projects proposed for the town were rejected by the Board of Works. One scheme was the building of a road from Tralee to Abbeyfeale. Colonel John Day Stokes warned that the rejection would mean that 'numerous poor labourers will be without the means of earning a living during the summer months'.[27] Two other projects – the creation of a new marketplace and the diversion of the river to prevent flooding – were also rejected. John Lynch had been the main advocate for these projects and he asked: 'Is the government serious in its disposition to give employment to the people?' He warned that the authorities should be careful 'in a season of distress and trial such as this, before they provoke a patient, loyal and quiet people to the last extremity. They had better be cautious. Hunger will break through stone walls.'[28]

Lynch's warning was, like many of his contributions to public debate, prescient and accurate. In June Dr Blennerhassett, a prominent Tralee doctor, told the guardians that he had met a crowd of 200 labourers in the town carrying a black flag to signify their need of employment. Lynch's appeal for work for the people was echoed by Justin Supple, a fellow solicitor, who accused the government of 'playing fast and loose with the feelings of a hungry and unemployed people'.[29]

One desperate mother resorted to an extreme measure to provide care for her child, according to a news item under the heading 'A witty trick'. The story related how 'one of those female loungers who infest the shops of this town has got, by a disastrous expedient, employment for a while'. Another woman had come up to her and asked her to hold her baby while she ran after the parish priest, who had just passed by, to ask him for help. The 'lounger' was briefly charmed by the child but when she looked around, she discovered that the mother had disappeared.[30]

The project for a road from Tralee to Abbeyfeale was reinstated and work began at Ballybeggan during the early summer months, but the labourers on it were not paid regularly according to an article in *The Cork Examiner* headed 'Destitution in Tralee'.[31] Indian meal was given instead of wages, but at one point three days passed without even that being distributed. 'Hundreds are besetting and besieging everyone whom they calculate on being able to procure and provide them tickets for work – the tales of distress and destitution which we are forced to hear from some is harrowing.' Only three miles of road had been completed by July, and it ended in 'an inaccessible glen, where it would not be safe for a goat to venture'.[32]

In April 1846 William Denny, who acted as agent for his brother, Sir Edward Denny, the chief landowner of Tralee, wrote from Day Place, Tralee, requesting that Indian corn to the value of £500 be sent without delay, assuring the secretary of the Relief Commission in Dublin Castle that he would remit the money promptly. He wrote that 'the distress arising from the failure of the potato crop in this district and the extremely high price to which this article of food has consequently been raised calls for immediate and prompt relief'.[33]

In spite of all these concerns, it is surprising to read that social life went on as normal for many people in the first half of 1846. A steeplechase over eight stone walls took place near Tralee in April, followed by a ball in Benner's

Hotel where 'the anterooms were prepared with a supper of materials delicate and substantial, well-spread with well-arranged profusion'.[34] The ball went on from 11 p.m. to 6 a.m. and it 'was spoken of as one of the most delightful which had taken place for some time'.[35]

Tralee's new ship canal also opened to its first ship in early April 1846 and there was still a sense of optimism about improvements in the town:

> Tralee is now becoming what it ought to have been long since when we consider the flourishing state of trade and commerce for those years past. A new canal has been thrown open for the reception of our shipping; new corn stores are being built and three provisions stores are open and carrying on a flourishing trade. A gasometer will be erected before next winter; and we have this day to announce that unfailing accompaniment of commercial property, an auction mart, which has been established at No. 1, Denny St.[36]

Tralee Workhouse

Tralee workhouse first opened on 1 February 1844. It stood on ten acres of ground east of the town centre, near Rathass graveyard. The buildings cost £8,557 while the fittings cost £1,643. It had a capacity of 1,000.[37]

Before the onset of the Famine, it appears that the workhouse functioned efficiently and the fact that six months had passed without a visit from an assistant commissioner was interpreted as 'a striking compliment'.[38] Mr Hancock, Assistant Poor Law Commissioner, described Tralee workhouse as 'one of the best regulated and managed'.[39] During the summer of 1846 the visiting committee found that the house was remarkably clean and regular, and reflected considerable credit on the officers. It recommended that a good deal of the old clothing should be condemned and disposed of: the items were listed as 175 chemises, 175 shirts, 14 petticoats, 60 dark petticoats, 64 bed gowns, 44 women's caps, 91 aprons, 61 children's petticoats, 38 cotton neckerchiefs and 4 sheets.[40]

In early May 1846, when there were 533 people in the workhouse, twenty-two applicants had been admitted and twenty-four rejected, among whom were 'the wives and families of several men employed about the country who were endeavouring to get rid of their families during the present crisis'.[41] The board rejected all families unless the head of the family accompanied them. On 30 May 1846 there were 488 in the workhouse and the average cost per week of each pauper was 1s 6d.

There was dissension in the boardroom in June 1846 when John Hurly resigned as chairman after five years in the position. He stated that 'angry and protracted discussion' had prevented the harmonious conduct of business. The issue was an appeal to the Poor Law Commissioners to sanction the board's request that applicants should be medically examined before, rather than after, entering the boardroom; this was intended as a health precaution to protect the guardians from infection. The commissioners did not refuse the request but ordered that it be further discussed and Hurly resigned in protest at what he perceived as a snub to the board, tantamount to declaring its members incompetent. Justin Supple expressed 'utmost pain' at Hurly's resignation and the 'serious injury' that it would cause to the board. John Lynch then took over the role of chairman.[42]

In a discussion of the issue, Supple was opposed to the extra duty imposed on the medical officer of the workhouse, Dr Alton, in having to examine the applicants beforehand. Some guardians, such as Mr Denny, were afraid of contracting fever, but John Lynch said that he had no such fear. Dr Alton stated that he had no objection to examining applicants before they came into the boardroom, but he objected to being obliged to do so. He advised the members that all applicants with infectious diseases were sent to the fever hospital and did not come into the workhouse and therefore that there was no danger of them contracting fever.[43] Some other doctors must have anticipated the prospect of Dr Alton's resignation, because he felt the need to write to the press to inform anyone desiring to take his duties 'on his own Herculean shoulders' that there was no vacancy.[44]

At this time the board suffered another loss, when the highly regarded master of the workhouse, Mr Brereton, resigned in order to take up a position in the county infirmary.[45]

The necessity for burying inmates was first addressed by the guardians in 1845 when they were given permission to have burials in the grounds of the workhouse. The guardians decided that burials would not take place until the plot was walled in and nothing further appears to have been done until 1846.[46] In April 1846 it was decided that the north-east corner of the workhouse site was the most suitable place for a burial ground. Dr Blennerhassett said the plot would have to be consecrated before it could be used; otherwise the inmates would object to being buried there 'as they would to being buried within the walls of a gaol'.[47] Dr John McEnnery, parish priest of Tralee, then gave permission for burials in anticipation of a visit from the bishop in May to consecrate it officially.[48]

Listowel

Listowel's board of guardians discussed the impending crisis at a meeting in February 1846. Captain James Murray Home, the Scottish-born agent of absentee landlord Lord Listowel, argued that 'this visitation of Providence' should be met 'simply by making those having the means contribute out of their abundance for the alleviation of that evil'.[49] He echoed the sentiments of Colonel John Day Stokes in Tralee. Like most people, Home was familiar with the experience of partial potato crop failure and local food shortages, usually followed by a recovery in the subsequent year; in early 1846 it was believed that events would follow a similar pattern. Home went on with a proposal that landlords should share the short-term hardship for the sake of future benefits:

> If you get over the difficulty for the present year, everything is clear and simple for the future. Why should they not get over it? If it is necessary to limit our own expenditure and to live on potatoes and butter, it is better that we should do so and have our population ready to supply us with our usual incomes for the future.[50]

As the crisis deepened, an 'employment meeting' was held in Listowel on 2 April 1846, where Fr Jeremiah (Darby) Mahony, PP, told the assembly that he had seen 'one hundred families living on one meal for twenty-four hours, and that food too consisting of bad potatoes, and this diseased food, he feared, if sound provisions were not introduced into that locality, would generate sickness of every kind'.[51] He implored the gentlemen present not to depart without taking some steps for bringing food to the market. Lord Listowel immediately promised a loan of £200 for the purchase of food, through his agent Home; William Talbot Crosbie of Ardfert promised a loan of £100 and others followed suit.[52]

In Listowel, the central relief committee for the baronies of Clanmaurice and Iraghticonnor expressed concern at the delay in setting up public works, saying that their efforts to obtain relief had been 'unproductive of benefits'.[53] The committee cited memorials from Tarbert and from Ballyheigue as examples of initiatives that appeared to give people a false sense of imminent relief. Home was trying to establish a depot at Tarbert for the two baronies of Iraghticonnor and Clanmaurice, but he was finding it difficult to purchase meal at sufficiently low prices, despite being treasurer of the Listowel relief committee, which had subscriptions of £803. He ultimately did purchase forty tons of meal from Limerick and he also ordered a supply of Indian meal at his own expense.[54] The *Examiner* welcomed this prompt response and quoted from a Listowel correspondent who believed that Home's action was very beneficial to the town, 'as the machinery for acting practically under the Relief Commission now sitting in Dublin has, from conflicting opinions, become tedious in its working'.[55] Home's action could mean 'the preservation of the lives of thousands', declared the *Examiner*, which also denounced those who hoarded food as 'persons who speculate in human suffering and drive a trade in the sorrows of mankind'. These hoarders waited until market prices soared and then 'chuckled with a demonic grin at the success of their selfish cunning and their greedy calculations'.[56]

There was growing resentment too at absentee landlords who were not making a proper contribution to relief funds, not least from resident landlords who then had to shoulder more than their share of financial responsibility. One landlord, Mr Wilson Gun, said that the absentees should be sent a list of the destitute on their properties, and that the names of those absentees not contributing to relief should be published in the press: 'It was too bad that the resident gentry should be giving their time and their money for absentee proprietors who gave them nothing.'[57] There were frequent lists of contributors to relief funds in the press, with the *Chronicle* of 16 May listing subscribers to relief committees in Tralee, Listowel and Castleisland. 'Our local gentry and residential proprietary,' said the *Chronicle*, 'have come forward in a spirit of munificence to sustain our peaceable and well-deserving people in the hour of their visitation.'[58] In the same issue, the *Chronicle* highlighted how men of different political and religious persuasions had cooperated effectively, citing Mr Denny and John Lynch in Tralee: the former 'a high conservative', the latter 'a repealer of the first water'. The paper went on to excoriate absentees, 'four-fifths of whom have not even answered requests to them, and the majority who have done so have returned a cold refusal'. It reminded them of the long-established principle that 'property has its duties as well as its rights'.

One of those absentee landlords who responded to a request from Patrick Stokes, secretary of Listowel relief committee, was Peirce Mahony, who wrote from the Reform Club in London on 22 June 1846, declining to contribute to their funds. (Another address from which he wrote was the Colonnade Hotel, St James' Square, London.) He gave the reason that his agent, Mr Stack, had full instructions to deal with relief matters arising on his estate, as he had done for thirty years. Even if he had been disposed to contribute, Mahony went on indignantly, the threat in Stokes' letter that he would report Mahony to the lord lieutenant if he did not subscribe would have prevented him. Mahony stated that he had great respect for the lord lieutenant and his office, but that he had no right to interfere with how a landlord ran his estate. He advised that if Stokes did report him to the lord lieutenant, he should also inform him of how much he, Mahony, had already spent on his estate, amounting to almost £2,000 of his own funds. He concluded the letter with a rebuke that 'some ignorant busy persons have thought fit to send to the newspapers' about him.[59]

Mahony also gave details of his own elaborate scheme to provide relief works – the drainage of the rivers Feale, Gale, Cashion (Cashen), Brick and Crompane, encompassing about forty-seven miles in total length. He had submitted a proposal to the Board of Works which was deemed useful and viable as a long-term project, but of little advantage for the immediate crisis. He enlisted the support of all the landlords of the area affected, with the added attraction being the consequent increase in the value of their lands.[60] The government was willing to commit £22,000 to this project on condition that local landlords contributed £2,000. Ultimately, the large-scale project foundered when two major landowners, Lord Listowel and Sir John Benn-Walsh, refused to make the contributions levied on them – £700 and £370 respectively.[61]

In 1847 Scotsman Alexander Somerville visited Ireland as a reporter for the *Manchester Examiner*, and he wrote of his impressions of Peirce Mahony. The two men did not meet and Somerville began his assessment by reviewing Mahony's evidence to the Devon Commission, an inquiry into land tenure in Ireland that issued its report in 1845. He was sarcastic about the 'patriotic' Mahony's admission of his lack of awareness of drainage schemes in other parts of Ireland and dismissive of the mismanagement of government funding by landlords like him. Somerville considered that Irish landlords as a class were 'at the bottom of the scale of honest and honourable men'.[62] 'Ireland has vast capabilities for industrial wealth,' he wrote, 'but she has Peirce Mahonys who live on the industrial capabilities and eat them in the bud. Every germ of industry that shews [*sic*] itself in Ireland is eaten up by landlords and lawyers.' Somerville believed that agriculture in Kerry was 'almost entirely the prey of lawyers and law; what they leave, the potato disease has taken'. He concluded:

> And now famine is on all Kerry, not only for this year, but for years to come. Little progress, so little that it can hardly be named, is making towards seed sowing. Mr Mahony's estates are no exception. The work people have been [doing] all the spring on the public works, the best of the tenants saying they

cannot afford to employ them; and now those who are not on the public works are on the soup kitchens or on the public allowance of a pound and a half of bread per day; the land lying untilled and the landlord doing as much to it as the man of the moon.[63]

Castleisland and Brosna

The inland town of Castleisland was also suffering and a writer to the *Chronicle* complained that no public meetings had been held there and that there were 400 people whose only hope of subsistence was to procure employment but there was none to be had: 'what must be the suffering of these poor people?' he asked.[64]

The rector of Castleisland, Rev. F. R. Maunsell, was prominent on Castleisland's relief committee, acting as secretary and treasurer. On 27 April he requested fifty or sixty extra copies of an official sheet explaining the various ways of preparing Indian corn for eating, 'as there prevails among the poor of this locality much ignorance upon the subject and considerable prejudice against the meal which I hope will subside when they become better acquainted with it'.[65]

Maunsell was praised for his 'practical philanthropy' in selling meal in Brosna at the cost price of 1s 7d a stone. The parish priest of Brosna, Fr Naughten, wrote that the relief committee had lodged £350 in the bank and requested a corresponding grant in aid. He highlighted a problem about areas where there were no resident landlords or prominent figures: 'In our extensive and populous district there is not a single resident proprietor ... Our share of public works and consequently prospect of employment is extremely limited.'[66] Rev. Maunsell acknowledged receipt of £50 from Lady Headley and £20 from W. Meredith of Dicksgrove, who were local landowners. He sampled the bread made from Indian meal and apparently found it palatable and nutritious.[67]

In a letter addressed to the secretary of the relief commissioners, Rev. Edward Norman of the parsonage of Abbeyfeale described how Brosna dealt with the shortages in the summer of 1846:

Sir – In accordance with your letter of 13 May we formed a relief committee in this parish [Brosna] for the purpose of raising loans and subscriptions and since that time we have been purchasing and selling meal either at cost or reduced prices. As we had no public works of general utility to carry on or anything which would be worth doing with the small amount of funds at our command, we did not make any application to government for assistance but have been the means of bringing a good stock of provisions into the parish and keeping down the price of potatoes. We purchased our meal either at Castleisland, in whose district the parish is situated, or at Tralee, paying of course the full price for whatever we got. The Castleisland committee now refuse to sell us any more and the supply at Tralee is exhausted. Our small funds are nearly in a similar predicament, while the calls upon us have greatly increased and will continue to increase for about three weeks. May I therefore request you to be so kind as to lay this statement before the Relief Commissioners and to beg of them at this trying time to grant us two tons of Indian meal or the price of them and to permit us to purchase at cost price at the depots of Cork or Limerick or Castleisland. A prompt reply will much oblige.

Edward Norman, Rector of Brosna.
Secretary, Brosna relief committee.[68]

The reply was overwritten on the letter: 'State that the intervention of Government is merely auxiliary to local exertions and that if a second sub[scription] is raised, however small it may be, Government will immediately add a donation.'

In July there was a 'strike' of workers employed by the Castleisland relief committee. It was first stated that the reason was that wages were reduced from 9d to 7d per day, but a member of the committee disputed that and said the strike was over a demand for an increase in wages, which the committee refused, keeping to 9d a day. Reports of an attack on the meal stores in Castleisland were also denied.[69]

Ballylongford and Tarbert

On 26 March a group of hundreds of labourers marched to the house of the Ballylongford parish priest, Fr Daniel McCarthy, threatening to slaughter his cattle if they did not get work. He calmed them by assuring them that he would 'represent their awful situation to the authorities'.[70] The crowd then proceeded to the homes of Stephen Sandes at Carrigafoyle House and William Hickie, justice of the peace (JP), at Killelton House. On seeing what the *Post* described as 'a *posse comitatus*' approaching, the latter started to prepare for a siege, but no violence was offered and his assurances of representation on their behalf satisfied the labourers, who then dispersed quietly.[71]

Sub-Inspector R. B. Fletcher of Listowel played down the incident, stating that 'the people behaved very quietly and only said to Fr McCarthy that they would take some of his fat cows from him for food if they did not soon get relief'. He added that 'the town of Ballylongford is a very poor and impoverished place'. The spokesman for the crowd was named as Patrick McElligott and the people were described as 'complaining' rather than threatening.[72]

It is possible that the representations of Fr McCarthy, Stephen Sandes and William Hickie had an effect, as in early April two steamers with Indian meal came up the river to Tarbert, and they were 'cheered as lustily as half-starved lungs could effect it by the poor labourers from their gardens'.[73] This does not mean, of course, that all was suddenly well in the area. In the same edition of the *Chronicle* which reported the arrival of the steamers, it was also stated that some of the men on the public works in Tarbert were simply too weak to work and just lay down on the roadside.[74] Later in the month, a group of people in Tarbert tried to intercept a load of meal being transported to Ballybunion, but they were foiled when it was taken by sea instead, on the war steamer *Alban*.[75]

Stephen Sandes and another landlord, Stephen E. Collis of Ballydonoghue, were praised for their treatment of their tenants in Ballybunion. The leases of 230 families were due for renewal and they were fearful of rent increases.

However, to their great relief, the two landlords allowed the tenants to remain on the land on the same terms. This was a disappointment to others who had expected the lands to become available.[76] Later in the year Sandes wrote passionately about the hardships endured by the people of Ballylongford, stating: 'The wants of the people are beyond endurance and I must state that their forbearance under what I personally know them at this moment to be enduring is most praiseworthy.' He demanded that public works should commence immediately and that the price of meal should be reduced.[77]

Some attempts were certainly being made to combat the food shortages. Towards the end of April, for example, HMS *Stromboli* arrived in Tarbert with a hundred barrels of Indian meal. Two hundredweight was deposited on Tarbert Island and two hundredweight in the stores of the relief committee. The Indian meal was then sent by steamers to various places: the *Alban* went to Limerick, the *Myrmidon* to Clare and the *Vulcan* to Dingle. In total, 600 tons of meal were shipped to the Shannon area. The *Stromboli* also brought 300 tons of Indian corn into Tarbert in September.[78]

Issues remained with the distribution of the food. Thomas Sandes of Tarbert wrote to the relief commissioners in Dublin in April, complaining of delays in supplying corn, following requests to Captain Robert Mann of the coastguard and to the commissary general in Limerick:

> I feel constrained to avail myself of the opportunity to impress on the relief committee the very great danger of delay in the promised aid. The markets of the neighbourhood are scantily supplied with potatoes in a state of extreme decay for which prices far beyond the means of the labouring poor are demanded, and unless the holders of provisions, if any, are compelled to reduce the prices by the introduction of foreign food, the peace of this hitherto tranquil country may, and most probably will, be disturbed and the consequences necessarily most serious.[79]

Robert Mann had responsibility for Kilrush and Tarbert and he wrote that 'potatoes are coming to the market now as freely as is recollected and even more so'.⁸⁰ His explanation was that farmers were afraid to hold on to any potatoes in case they should rot. According to Mann, in some places the loss of the crop varied from a half to a third to a quarter, with some areas escaping altogether. He anticipated nothing more than a shortage of potatoes in the markets later on, in the hungry months of May to August. Mann blamed wet rot for the loss of many potatoes. He had visited Tarbert Coastguard Station where there was one officer and seven men. On the adjoining plot they had planted thirty acres of potatoes, and most of these, he claimed, had been lost due to wet rot caused by poor pitting.⁸¹

Regardless of the impending sense of doom, there were lavish celebrations in Tarbert to mark Robert Leslie's twenty-first birthday on 30 April, described then as 'attaining his majority' or coming of age, a significant rite of passage for the son destined to inherit the property. Leslie was the heir to Tarbert House and its estate. The celebrations involved a cavalcade, bonfires, banners, speeches, presentations and toasts. The reporter of the *Chronicle* described the occasion as 'one of the more touching and stirring scenes' he had ever witnessed. He saw the celebrations as a model of excellent relations between landlords and tenants:

> It was indeed a sight of which, as a Kerryman, we felt proud, characteristic as that whole demonstration was of that healthy kindly feeling which it is so delightful to see welling up from the hearts of an affectionate people to those amongst the proprietors of our green acres, who from father to son have lived amongst that people and reciprocated acts of goodwill towards that people. In sooth it was a scene from which our absentees might well be taught a lesson, a scene with regard to which the inhabitants of Tarbert, with whom especially originated this most creditable display of hereditary affection towards the lord of the soil, may well entertain feelings of self-congratulation.⁸²

Triumphal arches decorated the streets, and every house was decked out with green branches. The ships in the port hoisted their flags, and the fort, lighthouse and coastguard station flew banners in 'the meteor colours of England'.

Over the bridewell flew a white pennant, appropriately signifying the absence of crime in the area, according to the reporter. The parish priest, Fr McCarthy, and his curate, Fr McMahon, led a procession from Gallaher's Hotel to Tarbert House, the seat of 'the old and respected house of Leslie'. Robert Leslie was presented with an elegant velvet chair with a dais of rich crimson silk; the Leslie coat of arms was engraved on the chair, with a silver plaque marking the occasion. The chair cost twenty-five guineas and after it was presented to young Robert he was carried on it in procession through the town.[83]

Four large tables were set out on the lawn in front of the house for the banquet, each with a barrel of ale at the head and foot. The attendance included both the tenants and the gentry of the area, and the many fair young women were particularly mentioned. 'The happy faces of the dense mass of human beings composed of every class and creed, the Roman Catholic and the Protestant, the parson and the priest, each and all of these grouped into one picture, formed a spectacle not easily imagined and which it will still be more difficult to forget.' In all, 1,200 people dined at the feast. The parish priest, Fr Daniel McCarthy spoke of his warm personal regard for the Leslie family and praised young Robert's qualities, saying that he was 'confident that his tenantry – of whom there were none more deserving – would receive at his hands affectionate, straightforward and considerate treatment'. Rev. Richard Fitzgerald, the rector of Tarbert, was also present and the *Chronicle* reporter praised the spirit of goodwill that prevailed between the two clergymen.[84]

As night drew in, Tarbert was lit up and the report concluded with this description of the illuminations:

> These were on a brilliant scale, every house being lighted up while the residences of the gentry for a considerable distance around vied with them. In front of Gallahers blazed a monster bonfire and on the pillars of the large gateway leading into the yard, tar barrels of enormous size blazed out. Never did the waters of the Shannon reflect so many lights upon its bosom as it mirrored upon the night of 30 April 1846.

Rev. Fitzgerald was the only one of the banquet speakers to refer obliquely to the prevailing conditions for tenants: 'Kerry was an oasis in the desert, and in famine or destitution, in weal or wo [sic], the people of Tarbert had always conducted themselves like loyal and peaceable subjects and kind affectionate friends … He hoped that happiness would spread more and more amongst them, that the tenantry would be enabled to dwell in comfort and the labourer receive such ample wages as would enable him to live.'

Ironically, the report of the Tarbert festivities appeared alongside lists of donations to relief funds in Tralee and Listowel, showing how fragile and fleeting the celebratory mood really was.[85]

Ballyheigue Area

In January the editor of the *Examiner* wrote: 'We regret to say that the accounts which have reached us from Ballyheigue and other districts are anything but calculated to encourage the hopes we had entertained that the progress of the potato disease would be arrested in a very short time from its first manifestation.' Noting that a second variety of crop (the black minion) had by then been infected, the paper also condemned the practice of mixing sound and diseased potatoes for sale in the market.[86]

The *Examiner* continued with its criticism of the lack of action being taken in Tralee, saying that nothing was being done to relieve distress. It compared this delay with the prompt response adopted in the Causeway and Ballyheigue area, recommending it as a model for the kind of action which was required:

> Not so the good people of Causeway and Ballyheigue. The humble farmers of those districts not alone contributed to relieve the distress of the veriest [sic] poor amongst them, but on New Year's Day met after Mass and after passing some resolution in reference to the state of the potato crop, agreed to reduce, some one-third, some one-half, the amount of rent paid them by the poor conacre tenants who hold ground under them. What an admirable example have these worthy men set for the imitation of the high and wealthy, yet if

> the accounts we have received from that quarter be correct, it would appear that exactions of rents on the part of the land agents are directly in inverse proportion to the liberality of the humble farmers, who, though pressed down themselves, yet refuse not to share with their poorer neighbours the gifts for which they are indebted to Providence and their own industry. Where abatements had been made some years ago, the rents are this year raised to their former heights and exacted with a rigid hand. There is neither wisdom, policy nor prudence in such a course, to say nothing of its oppressiveness at a critical period like the present. We shall not further allude to this subject but reserve it to another day in the hope of a relaxation taking place in the interval.
>
> The farmers who have so nobly and with the true spirit of Christians come forward to the timely assistance of their fellow creatures in distress are deserving of the highest rewards. Among the many names before us are the Driscolls, the Leynes, the Connells, the Dillons, the Nolans, Fitzgeralds, Callaghans, Crowleys, Doolings, Joys, Leahys, etc. etc., all of which are worthy of honourable mention. We should not pass over another name, Mr Oliver Mason of Kilmore, who has reduced the rent of his conacre tenantry. We trust the landlords of Kerry will follow the example of the Ballyheigue farmers, and as for our friends the agents, we are most anxious for the opportunity of being enabled to record some instances of their philanthropy as benefactors of the human race.[87]

The *Examiner* concluded by suggesting that similar initiatives taken by the gentry of Killarney offered a precedent to counter the 'hesitating charity' of the gentry of Tralee: 'the sooner that hesitation takes wing and becomes active the better for all parties, for charity blesses those who give and those who receive'.[88] The *Post* echoed the same praise, stating that an example had been set in Ballyheigue which was 'worthy of imitation by greater and richer men'.[89]

Henry Lawrence, the Royal Navy officer based in Ballyheigue, reported to his superiors on 1 February 1846, explaining why his optimistic account of the potato crop to the Coastguard Office in November 1845 might not agree with other accounts:

> In representing the abundant quantity of potatoes in this district my statement may appear somewhat at variance with the opinion entertained by the Poor Law guardians of Tralee Union at their last meeting when it was agreed on that great apprehension of scarcity was to be dreaded, but I beg to observe that but a very small portion of this district is situated in that Union … I feel much pleasure in acquainting you that the disease has hitherto been very trifling and that there is a greater quantity of potatoes now in this district than has been remembered in any previous season or month.[90]

Lawrence had his own potato garden, which was unaffected by the blight, so perhaps this led him to believe that the disease was 'very trifling'.

On 15 January Joseph Dexter of the Ballybunion coastguard reported his surprise that potatoes were cheaper than they usually were at that time of year, 'which is really beyond my judgment to account for, if it is not that the people are glad to get rid of them where the wet rot has appeared in any of their store pits for fear they should also rot, which would be a dead loss to the owner'. The worst that Dexter anticipated was a shortage of potatoes later in the year.[91]

Evidence that the optimism of Lawrence was unfounded was provided at a large meeting in Ballyheigue just days after he had written his second letter. The outcome of the meeting was a heartfelt plea sent to the lord lieutenant. It was accompanied by a letter from Rev. James Chute, rector of Ballyheigue from 1821 until his death in 1848. Both of these documents give a very different picture from that of Lawrence. Chute wrote on 11 February 1846:

> Having been deputed at a very large and respectable meeting held at Ballyheigue on Monday last to forward the memorial to his Excellency the Lord Lieutenant then unanimously adopted, I have the honour to transmit it through you. I regret extremely that I am enabled from my intercourse with

the people as well as information which I have had on visiting each farm to bear testimony in this fullest sense to the disease of the potato advancing in this immediate locality to a frightful extent – the consequences of which are to be dreaded should not the case be met by immediate employment of the poor. Already have some robberies been committed in part of this district.[92]

Rev. Chute actually visited the farms of the area, where few of the occupants would have been his parishioners. It is significant that concern for the frightful consequences of the potato failure for the poor is followed by the observation that law and order had begun to break down; this was the great fear of the clergy, farmers and propertied classes.

The memorial accompanying the letter was couched in highly deferential terms:

> To his Excellency Baron Heytesbury, Lord Lieutenant General and General Governor of Ireland.
>
> May it please your Excellency.
>
> We, the magistrates, clergy, gentry, farmers and cess payers of Ballyheigue in the County of Kerry respectfully submit to your Excellency the necessity of adopting without loss of time, measures to provide for the employment of our poor people in the approaching months when we are threatened by a scarcity of provisions consequent upon the awful failure of the potato crop in this locality.
>
> That we are unwilling to suggest to your Excellency anything which could be deemed obtrusive, or bordering on what we wish to avoid in such a crisis, party or political measures, but would humbly recommend remunerative employment for the relief of the poor, by opening permanently useful roads through the district which will promote the industry and welfare of our people and give immediate relief.
>
> That in this district no such works have heretofore been carried on, though

in no part of the county could more permanent good be effected by them in the transit of sea manure, and a facility of procuring that most necessary article, fuel, so much wanted through this extensive district.

Memorialists therefore humbly solicit your Excellency to give such directions through the Board of Works as may promote these objects.

Which memorialists most respectfully submit.

The first three signatures to the memorial were Pierce Crosbie, Ballyheigue Castle, J. P. Chute, Rector, and Eugene McCarthy, PP, and there were eighty-three more signatures.[93]

The growing desperation of the people in need of food in this area can be seen in a tragic incident that took place in March. In coastal areas one of the places where sustenance could be found was the seashore, and people took risks in seeking out edible seaweeds. Two women lost their lives in Ballyheigue while gathering such food, as reported in the *Examiner*:

> Yesterday, as has been the custom in that neighbourhood, most particularly since food became so scarce there, some women went out amongst the cliffs to gather slouke [*sic*]. While so engaged, one slipped from a rock and in making some exertions to extricate herself, drew with her a second, both of whom, melancholy to relate, met with an untimely death.[94]

One of the unnamed women was the mother of a large family and the other was single.[95] A member of the coastguard named William Taylor went to the aid of the women and 'with the greatest intrepidity and indifference to personal danger' brought one woman out of the water but she died immediately. His example spurred onlookers, who had been standing by, to try to help the women. Taylor, aged twenty-five, had been a sailor for ten years and had previously saved a boy from drowning. The newspaper recommended that his superiors should reward him.[96]

A meeting in Listowel in early April established a relief committee, with a subcommittee for Dromkeen, Ballyheigue and Rattoo. This subcommittee included John Pierce, Thomas O'Connor, William Pope and Dominic Rice.[97] These names were subsequently added to the subcommittee: Thomas O'Connell, John Creagh, John Magee and Justin Rice.[98]

John Ball's Report on Ballyheigue, Causeway and Ardfert
John Ball was the Assistant Poor Law Commissioner and he was sent to north Kerry in April 1846 to report on conditions in the area.[99] Ball consulted first with Rev. Chute, 'a very active and benevolent clergyman', who told him that between half and three-quarters of the potato crop had been lost in the lowlands of Ballyheigue and that the loss was less severe in the higher ground, where the soil was lighter. Chute had undertaken a survey of the state of the parish and he gave details to Ball, who found that it understated the reality of food shortages. Ball visited houses in the village and found that, without exception, people had only diseased potatoes:

> In many cabins the people showed me some utterly corrupt, which the pigs now refuse to touch and declared that they had none others left. In one instance I found a family of nine dining upon limpets taken from the rocks near the village. The few sound potatoes which I saw, most of them bought by those who could afford it from the upland farmers, some supplied by Major Crosbie, were reserved by the owners for seed, but there must be a large number who are destitute of this resource, the only provision against future distress.

Chute proposed that Indian corn should be supplied for the people and that if employment were provided they could pay for it. He told Ball that the relief committee had proposed a new road from Ballyheigue to Lixnaw and had applied for £3,000 for it. This road through an inaccessible area would connect five parishes. If this amount was considered too large, Chute said that even if only six miles of road were built at £100 per mile, then the £600 provided in wages would give employment to 600 men for four weeks at ten pence a day. Ball approved of this and added that the drainage of the River

Brick would bring even greater benefits to the areas of Killury and Rattoo (Causeway and Ballyduff).

John Ball visited Captain Lawrence at the coastguard station located in Ballyheigue village and found that his potatoes, which had been grown in nearly pure sea-sand, were free of blight. The two men discussed the feasibility of building a boat harbour, but Lawrence said that the difficulties were 'insuperable' and that in any case, fish were to be found more on the southern side of Tralee Bay.

Ball then visited Fr Eugene McCarthy at Killury. He had prepared similar lists to Rev. Chute and they showed that 'out of a population of about 6,000 there are upwards of 2,000 actually in a state of want, having but insufficient or unwholesome food'. There were about 560 labourers with no employment. Ball found that the crop failure in Causeway was not as severe as in Ballyheigue.

He next visited Ardfert and met the landlord William Talbot Crosbie, whom he praised as 'a gentleman very active in carrying out improvements upon his estates, and who displays a proper solicitude for the condition of the poorer class within this district'. Crosbie was in favour of drainage work on the Brick as a means of providing employment.

Ball also visited some houses in the Commons area and found potatoes 'partially diseased' but in general less so than in Ballyheigue. Nevertheless, he judged that supplies were quite inadequate for the coming months. He found a few cases of fever and smallpox that were confined to seven or eight families.

Ball concluded his report by stating that the farmers of the area were 'for the most part in a very prosperous condition' and that they had a considerable store of provisions, including sound potatoes in some upland areas; they were, however, very concerned that the introduction of Indian corn would result in a fall in prices. But as their stores of potatoes would not be sufficient to meet the needs of the people, Ball saw no difficulty in introducing corn to Tralee, especially if the entire amount were to be sent at once rather than by a piecemeal distribution.

Despite the growing concern, there were celebrations in Ardfert Abbey, home of William Talbot Crosbie, for May Day, which also coincided with the birthday of one of his children. Villagers were entertained by a hobby horse and other amusements, and in the evening tenants danced around a maypole in the grounds of the great house: 'They were substantially regaled with porter, lemonade and bread in abundance.'[100]

State of the County

The lack of employment and the predicted famine was foremost in the columns of the *Examiner* in April: 'The cry of the approaching famine has been gradually swelling louder and louder on the ears of men. [The poor] calmly await with folded arms the approach of the gaunt monster HUNGER, whose capacious maw must be filled by human victims. What has been done as yet for the people of Kerry to save them from the havoc which HUNGER already threatens to make in their ranks?'[101]

At this point reports remained varied. The *Post*, for example, maintained the position that it was too early to be alarmist, believing that there was plenty of work available until the first week of June. It asserted that it was not being heartless or senseless in holding this view, as claimed by other newspapers that were 'croaking' about lack of employment.[102] By the end of May, however, the *Post* had come round to an appreciation of the crisis, condemning 'the apathy of our rulers in their indifference to the wants of the people of Tralee'.[103]

The Cork Examiner remained hopeful about the potato crop in May, singling out one area: 'We have heard encouraging accounts as to the supply of potatoes in the neighbourhood of Ballyheigue. This was one of the localities for which the worst fears were expressed at an early period of the season.' It noted that there were large quantities of potatoes in the Tralee market, equal to any previous year.[104]

The eminent historian of the Great Famine, Christine Kinealy, has written that 'the relief provided through the temporary relief commission in the summer and spring of 1846, was held to be successful, both by contemporaries and subsequently by many historians'.[105] In this regard, an editorial in the *Examiner* is of interest, as it gave an overview of the situation that was broadly optimistic and yet showed an acute awareness of the issue of employment. It is quoted in full here because it has a particular significance; twelve months later the picture would be entirely different:

> We are happy to perceive that the most active preliminary measures for the relief of the poor have been adopted in almost every district of the county. Meetings have been held, subscription lists opened, money subscribed and applications about to be made for more, so that provisions will, as far as circumstances permit, be kept down to a fair price and all deficiency be supplied by importation of foreign food. A vessel has just arrived in the Basin of the Canal with a cargo of Indian meal consigned to Mr Norris Russell of this town from whose stores it is to be sold, we understand, at 1s 8d per stone, which is considered rather high. However, we may now expect further arrivals of vessels chartered by the government, as at the meeting of the relief committee of this town on Wednesday a sum of over five hundred pounds was subscribed, *three hundred* of which was from Sir Edward Denny. The government no doubt will meet the subscribers half-way and send in a corresponding supply of meal. Committees have been formed in Listowel, Killorglin, Milltown, Brosna, and, we perceive, in Castleisland. The Killarney Committee, with their usual promptitude and energy, have imported from Cork *ten tons* of Indian meal which is being for the present sold out at three halfpence per pound. This seasonable supply has already produced its proper effects on the markets of the town. Now so far all is very good.
>
> But where, we ask, is the money to purchase a daily supply from each committee to feed the poor man's family? What will all avail without employment? In vain provisions may be made abundant and cheap if employment be wanting to enable the poor to purchase. Although a pound of meal cost but a penny, the penny must be earned and when earned, presented in payment for a pound of provision. We confess we are anything but pleased with the Government, notwithstanding all their professions of sympathy

and their display of 'good intentions' respecting the numerous public works for which applications *on their own solicitation* have been made. The Lord Lieutenant has been memorialed, the Board of Works has been memorialed, and yet not a spade, not a shovel, pick-axe or crow-bar has been put in requisition and the labouring class who were taught to expect immediate and profitable employment are beginning to despair. Supplies of provision and employment must go hand-in-hand to work out relief, for money becomes useless if there be no provisions to be purchased and the provisions almost equally useless if there be not money to purchase them.

The Government should be treated now to *remonstrances* and not to *memorials* – they have been pelted with grass to no purpose, a harder material might now be tried, when probably a few knocks might arouse them from their present apparently contemplative mood. If they have not given us stones for bread they have at least given us soft words – no more. But coercion, more than corn, seems to occupy their attention. Ireland still continues to be Sir Robert Peel's old 'difficulty' and we are much inclined to think that if he perseveres in his bad bill for Ireland, this 'difficulty' will be increased and ere long, by that very bill, be himself *coerced* – to resign – an event we should by no means desire in the present state of public affairs.[106]

Newspapers in June were optimistic about the harvest: 'The country looks beautiful. Every species of crop looks most promising. The weather is delightfully hot as summer weather should be and as things go on at present, we may, through the bounty of a merciful Providence, expect an abundant harvest.'[107] Three days later, there was continued optimism: 'Every day the country is improving in appearance, giving rich promise of an abundant harvest. As yet we think there is little likelihood of a failure in the potato crop similar to that of the crop of last year.'[108]

Such newspaper accounts were common in those warm early summer weeks, according to Ciarán Ó Murchadha, who describes them as 'poetic' and 'euphoric'. He attributes the optimism to 'a collective will that after all that had been endured up to now, the new potato harvest must not – could not – be anything but bountiful'.[109] There was a general sense of relief that nobody had died of hunger and that a crisis had been averted by responsible government policy. Christine Kinealy refers to 'a general mood of optimism and self-congratulation among the officers involved in providing relief'.[110]

The optimism would not last, however. On 11 August 1846 the *Examiner* published a poem entitled 'There must be something wrong':

> *When Earth produces free and fair*
> *The waving golden corn,*
> *When fragrant fruits perfume the air*
> *And fleecy flocks are shorn;*
> *Whilst thousands move with aching head*
> *And sing this ceaseless song:*
> *'We starve, we die, Oh give us bread'*
> *There must be something wrong …*
>
> *Then let the law give equal right*
> *To wealthy and to poor.*
> *Let freedom crush the arm of might,*
> *We ask for nothing more.*
> *Until this system is begun,*
> *The burden of our song*
> *Must be and can be only one:*
> *There must be something wrong.*

3

'ON THE VERY VERGE OF FAMINE'

July–December 1846

The people looked to me. I have nothing in my power; all I could do I did.

Fr Daniel McCarthy, PP of Tarbert and Ballylongford
The Tralee Chronicle, 5 December 1846

By July 1846 things had once again taken a turn for the worse. The *Examiner* recognised the 'increasing alarm' regarding the crop, although up until then the paper 'forebore to give alarm from our locality [but] now we anticipate a return of last year's calamity'.[1] There was specific mention of the neighbourhood of Ballyheigue, where 'the crop we have heard is much affected'. In August the paper declared: 'Where all was so lately verdant and promising, all is now black and withered. The potato crop in Kerry is ruined.'[2] The *Chronicle* echoed the same sentiment: 'The crop is totally ruined. It is lamentable but true.'[3]

Tralee

The funds of Tralee relief committee were almost exhausted by July 1846 and the administration of public works was chaotic. So many men turned up at public works it was impossible to manage them and the *Post* was outraged that in the confusion, some were able to shirk the work.[4] Moreover, the works were nowhere near completion and an investigation by the relief committee discovered that 'the really destitute' were not benefitting from the works: 'a large number of persons had been improperly admitted into employment … and very little value in the shape of labour was received from those in return for the large sums of money disbursed as hire'.[5] The prospects for the months ahead, until the potato harvest, were ominous. After considering their options and with enough to cover wages for just two further weeks, the committee decided to suspend the public works for three days in order to deal with the situation. The committee then decided that no man could work for more than three days a week and that payment would be by Indian meal rather than in money. A list of 517 men who were willing to work under these conditions was drawn up and they were issued with tickets which they were required to present to the stewards and paymasters of the public works.

However, a group of 200 to 300 – under six ringleaders – opposed these measures. They went to the site of relief work in Caherina (where a wall was being built) and threatened violence on the workers unless they left the works and joined the protest. The protestors assaulted and kicked the contractor and another official who tried to stop them. The efforts of magistrates George Day Stokes and William Denny and resident magistrate Mr Drummond to deter the protestors went unheeded, and the army was summoned. Soldiers under Captain Cruise lined up in Denny Street, from where they made ready to take control of the town. The police under George Stokes and Sub-Inspector Bolger also readied themselves for action.

When crowds assembled under a black flag near the Presbyterian church, Stokes intervened, striding into the crowd, seizing the flag and breaking its staff. Three men named Connor, Leahy and Healy were arrested, and the people, 'feeling the power of the law', dispersed. The *Post* wrote: 'Our streets might have been flowing with blood but for the prompt action of magistrates.'[6]

It was beyond doubt that the workers' frustration was beginning to boil over. A formal notice was presented to the master of the Tralee workhouse by a large deputation of labourers in late July. It read: 'Sir, Take notice that on the 30th day of July next, you will have to receive the number of 508 men in great distress; besides their families. Eight pence a day would not support these number of men and their families on the Board of Works line.'[7] The *Chronicle* simply commented that the notice spoke 'briefly yet eloquently of the distress of that class'.[8]

Some public works continued despite the difficulties. Work on the Ballybeggan road was approved and work on the Quarry road had also started. The latter project was commended by the *Post* as 'carrying civilisation, if we may so speak, into a locality which [is] the haunt and hot-bed of all the low profligacy of the town'.[9] Ten days after work began on the Ballybeggan road, however, labourers went on strike because wages were reduced from five shillings a week to four shillings.

In some respects, life went on as normal for some people: the races at Ballyeagh on the Cashen went off successfully, and 'every bed in that fashionable watering village of Ballybunion was engaged, 7s. 6d. being freely given'.[10] August also saw a regatta in The Spa, a string band playing at a ball in Listowel and a stag hunt in Killarney.[11] But the *Post* already anticipated the worst for the following year: 'We are afraid that the year 1846 will be mere child's play to the famine of 1847.'[12] The article also praised the actions of landlords who were described as 'discharging nobly the duties of their high position. To relieve the distress of their destitute fellow countrymen they are taxing their properties with a liberal – we might almost say a ruinous – hand.'

In September press reports stated that 'Tralee with a population of 18,000 souls is, at the present moment, suffering under extreme privation from scarcity of food in the markets and shops.'[13] The members of the relief committee decided to set an example, asking others to follow: each member promised a sum not less than £25 towards employment or food. They appealed for a food depot to be established in the town and informed the Lord of the Admiralty that 'we are already over-roaded and our district cannot supply more employment on public works'.[14] As alternatives to road building for the 'starving multitudes', embankments at various places such as Derrymore Point and Annagh Island, the Kerries to The Spa, and Barrow Harbour were proposed. The relief committee of Tralee also sent a 'piteous memorial' appealing for government action, stating that the area was starving and private enterprise had failed to provide food.[15]

The *Examiner* carried a strongly worded editorial on the subject of employment, stating that 'in the present crisis, employment – and thereby the means of procuring food – must be afforded to the people, or no human foresight or exertions can avail to save property, and we may add, in very many cases, to save life'.[16] It went on to warn of the violence which might follow if desperation set in among the poor:

> Blind and foolish indeed that man must be who would look for moderation from a starving crowd and whoever attends to the present state of the country must be most insensible if he perceive not that *immediate* and general employment must be given or very soon whole millions will be starving. Most portentous murmurs are being heard about the country. The mind cannot contemplate or imagine any state of society more dangerous or more awe-striking than that to which we have been reduced by the late visitation of Providence. In this state of things it rests with the government and with men of property, particularly the landlords of this country to save the people. They can do it. Will they do so?[17]

The *Examiner* warned that 'hunger will break through stone walls and may not be reasoned with', but it also acknowledged that the gentry of Kerry were 'alive to the necessity of providing employment for the people'.[18]

A new relief committee was formed in October as part of a restructuring of the relief system. The relief measures introduced during 1845–6 were all seen as temporary expedients for a temporary problem. When it became clear that the crop failure of 1846 was extensive and widespread, the government introduced revised relief procedures which Kinealy has summarised as follows: 'In a shift of emphasis, however, the public works were to be regarded as the main agency of relief'.[19] New instructions were issued regarding the formation of local relief committees, and each committee had to be approved by the lord lieutenant of the county. At national level, the number of local committees doubled as compared with 1845–6. These committees raised voluntary donations towards relief but instead of issuing tickets to those deemed eligible for work, they could only draw up lists of names and submit them to the Board of Works for a decision.[20]

In Tralee, the restructured committee consisted of only fifteen members instead of the forty members of the previous group. The chairman was John Lynch, solicitor, and the other members were four Protestant clergymen: Arthur and Henry Denny, A. B. Rowan and William Scott; four Catholic priests: John McEnnery, John Mawe, Patrick Foley and Thomas Enright; one Presbyterian minister, William Chestnut; two magistrates, William Denny and George Day Stokes; resident magistrate Mr Drummond; an officer of the constabulary, James Bolger; and the county surveyor and officer of the Board of Works, Henry Stokes.[21]

Regardless of these revisions to the relief system, the same problems persisted. The *Examiner* wrote that 'if employment was not given, food must be, and gratis, or again we repeat the consequences will be fearful'. It also posed some questions:

> What is the government doing? Where are their large importations? Where their depots? Where their liberal grants? Where are they themselves whilst a whole population is starving? They measure out not food but famine, an instance of which is to be found in the district of Dingle, where the government stores are closed amidst a people dying of hunger ... The poorhouses – that pulse by which to judge the increase of famine – are filled, but thousands, millions, think not of poorhouses but are struggling and dying in agony. The accounts of destitution are horrifying and maddening.[22]

The problems in Tralee were summarised as follows: the failure of the potato crop; prices of other foods rising so high as to be unattainable; the workhouse filling up and the number of applicants continuing to rise; funds of the union nearly exhausted with more liabilities being added daily, and the poor rates neither agreed nor collected.[23]

An 'extraordinary edition' of the *Chronicle* was published on 10 October. One of its features concerned a petition circulated by William Talbot Crosbie to be signed by the landlords and clergy of Kerry. This was an appeal for a national committee to be set up under the chairmanship of the Earl of Devon, 'to join in rescuing their country from its present evils and to promote its amelioration, so bringing good out of evil …'. The paper commended Crosbie's initiative, commenting that 'we feel much gratification in laying before our readers that [declaration] originated by William Talbot Crosbie'.[24]

A letter-writer outlined the rapidly deteriorating conditions in the town later in October: 'Crowds of starving fellow creatures are thronging our streets and besieging our doors and persons with the tale of their deplorable distress.'[25] The writer had a suggestion for readers fortunate to have regular meat dishes and a cook: that every family should tell the cook to preserve the liquor in which all joints of meat had been boiled, mix it with Indian meal and keep this in a large soup kettle which should be topped up regularly and provided to the destitute.

The number of guardians attending the weekly meetings of the board in Tralee was sometimes very low, with only six guardians at one meeting in early October and seven attending in late November. On one occasion (when 144 applicants were refused entry to the workhouse) the *Examiner* commented that 'the same few persons always constitute the board, labouring to discharge not only their own duties but those of others falsely calling themselves guardians'. The absentees were accused of 'negligence … and breach of trust towards the division for which they were elected'.[26] Among the most regular attendees were chairman John Lynch, Colonel John Day Stokes and John Hurly.[27]

Practical arrangements for public works appear to have been somewhat chaotic. Some of the pressing issues in Tralee were the non-payment of labourers in the town for nine or ten days in early November and the sudden dismissal of 400 labourers at works in Doon and Derrymore in December.[28]

No reason for the dismissals was cited in reports, but it is possible that funding for the works had run out. The *Post* reported that the people went 'en masse to the relief committee ... and represented their case, which appeared to be one of great hardship'. The committee merely told the people that they would 'communicate with the Board of Works on the subject' and the crowd dispersed.[29]

The following sums of money had been allocated by the Board of Works to public works in three baronies: Trughnanacmy – £16,000; Clanmaurice – £8,000; Corkaguiny – £11,300. The last named had applied for £40,000.[30] The sum allocated to Tralee town was £4,000 and this was derided in an editorial in the *Post* headed 'Public Works – Public Mockery'.[31] The public works in Tralee town area employed only 150 men when there were 2,000 in need of employment. The works undertaken were the arching of the river to Mulgrave Bridge, making new roads through the Quarry area in Tralee and at Glounaheenta between Tralee and Castleisland, and building a wall along the canal from Tralee to Blennerville. Moreover, arrangements for payment were not in place, leaving open the prospect of a repeat of an incident that happened at Skibbereen, where a man named Denis McKennedy died while on the public works because he had not received any wages to buy food.

The price of food also continued to be an issue. Richard Leahy, a Tralee merchant, returned from Liverpool where he had purchased 200 tons of wheat for milling. 'Is it not an anomaly,' asked the *Post*, 'that the gentleman finds it cheaper to import wheat from England than to purchase it in our own markets?'[32] Cargoes of food arrived into Tralee in late November. The *Eleutheria* was expected from New York with 500 tons of Indian corn and meal for the Tralee merchants Robert and William Hickson. The relief committee of Tralee had purchased ten tons to come from Liverpool. Other supplies came from Cork on board the following vessels: *St Patrick* and *Reliance* (530 sacks of Indian corn), *Nancy James* and *Ellen* (50 sacks) and *Isabella* (300 sacks). Wheat was selling at 1s 11d per stone, oats at 1s 2¼d per stone, and barley at 1s 3½d per stone. Noting that these prices were 10 per cent higher than the previous week, the *Post* added: 'We cannot too much condemn the cupidity of parties who at a season like the present for selfish and private purposes drive up the price of the poor man's food.'³³ A month earlier, a correspondent of the *Post* had also condemned 'the hungry vulture-like speculations of merchants without bowels, whose only look-out in the visitation of God on the land is to turn it to their own advantage, who are filling their stores to bursting and sparingly retailing it to the poor at exorbitant prices'.³⁴ Other concerns of the relief committee were that some of the Indian meal was going to the destitute of other districts outside Tralee and to better-off people in Tralee itself. The suggested solution was to set up special shops and institute a ticket system.³⁵

Among the individual responses to the crisis of the winter of 1846, the following were noted in the press: Rev. Rowland Bateman of Kilcara near Tralee employed forty labourers, and in Ardfert, David McEnnery, the brother of the Tralee parish priest, forgave tenants a year's rent. Dr Alton donated his quarter salary of £12 10s to relief funds in October.³⁶

Following the suggestion of the relief committee, a ladies relief committee was formed with the following members: Mrs Edward Day Stokes, Mrs William Denny, Mrs Nicholas Donovan, Mrs Anthony Denny, Mrs Bowles, Mrs John Day Stokes, Mrs John Eagar, Mrs Rutledge, Miss Foley, Mrs Murphy, Mrs George Hilliard, Mrs R. Fitzgerald, Mrs Neagle, Mrs Pembroke, Mrs John Busteed, Miss A. O'Leary, Miss Quill, the Misses Primrose, Miss Pembroke, Mrs Morris, Mrs J. Chambers and Miss Betty Chambers.³⁷ F. W. Jerningham, a military man, wrote to the English Catholic paper *The Tablet*, welcoming the initiative of the Tralee women, which he had heard of in a letter from one of them, 'a truly pious, virtuous and fair correspondent'.³⁸ She told him that they were feeding 800 to 1,000 a day. Jerningham had been quartered in Tralee before the Famine struck, and, remembering the miserable state of the people even then, he appealed for English charity and reminded readers that many Kerrymen had joined the 29th Regiment and served in India and at Waterloo: 'To them we owe a debt for the victories gained … and how can we repay it better than by coming forward at this moment and assisting them with the means at our command?'³⁹

Tralee town was divided into districts where the women would conduct a monthly collection towards a soup fund. A thousand persons received the grandly named *soup maigre* (i.e. thin soup) on 15 December. On Christmas Day the ladies relief committee distributed soup and bread to 556 persons, and meat and bread to 165 more. On St Stephen's Day 787 quarts of porridge were provided. Mrs Edward Day Stokes recorded that an extra boiler had been acquired and that they could now distribute 750 quarts of soup and porridge on alternate days.[40] Mrs John Day Stokes at Lassinagh in The Spa was distributing 120 quarts of soup to thirty-one distressed families of the area twice a week.[41] At Ballyseedy Mr Blennerhassett distributed soup three times a week to 120 paupers.[42] There was also a Blennerville ladies committee, which raised £14 12s 6d in January 1847.[43]

John Lynch continued his watchdog role with a strident address on the issues of bureaucratic waste and inefficiency. He drew attention 'in forcible language to the amount of salaries paid to check clerks, pay clerks, stewards, gangsmen, etc. on the public works and complained of the wasteful absorption of public funds intended for the relief of the destitute in that manner'.[44] Some examples of the abuses were specified in *The Cork Examiner* in December: non-payments for labourers on public works; non-adherence to the lists of those to be employed; non-completion of works such as the footpath to the workhouse; no fewer than twelve gangsmen being employed on a quarter-mile of road works near The Spa; farmers obtaining places on public works by bribing stewards; work specifications being altered by manipulation of Irish perches and English perches; and farmers whose fences had been damaged by roadworks offering to forego compensation if their horses were hired for the works.[45]

Tralee Workhouse
Applications to the workhouse increased dramatically in the autumn of 1846 and, with union funds depleted, the *Examiner* had a premonition of what lay ahead:

Without funds, the wretched inmates cannot be supported, and if not supported in the house, what is to become of them? And what, we may ask also, is to become of those who cannot gain admittance? If the applications continue so numerous as they have been, the house will be soon full, and it is really horrifying to think of turning a deaf ear to the prayers of starving creatures. Humanity is shocked and stunned by the appalling wretchedness which appears in the boardroom of a workhouse. The heart sickens to see a father or mother or both with a half dozen pallid children, Lazarus like, begging crumbs at the rich man's table. We are bound to admit however that humane feeling generally characterises the acts of the guardians of this Union. They have frequently strained the law to the utmost on the side of mercy.[46]

There were 670 inmates in the Tralee workhouse on 3 October and this rose to 780 a week later. Of 127 admitted on 10 October, eighty were children under fifteen. Several of these were admitted on their own, without parents, although this was contrary to regulations. The *Examiner* recommended mercy and compassion towards individual cases, as the board had shown a month earlier when accepting the two children of a widower.[47] Another applicant was a mother of five who asked that two of her children be admitted. Her eldest son was serving his time as a sawyer, but he said that if his mother went into the workhouse he would not complete his training but would enlist in the army. To reinforce her case, the woman stated that on the way into the room she had met the widower whose two children had just been admitted and she asked to be treated likewise.[48] Later, such special pleading fell on deaf ears. Even when Dr McEnnery appealed for three dying children named McKenna to be admitted, he was refused and told that the workhouse was full.[49] A Mrs Tangney with four children was admitted because her husband refused to support them; he was to be prosecuted for desertion. A boy whose stepfather refused to support him was admitted, but a group of illegitimate children had their admission cancelled when two of them were found to be suffering from smallpox.[50]

By 26 October numbers had risen dramatically to 1,060.[51] In early November 153 people were admitted, forty-five were rejected and there were 1,155 in the workhouse.[52] What the newspapers termed 'a riot' took place on 6 November when a group of about 100 able-bodied labourers stormed the workhouse, and 'having taken possession of the hall, insisted on getting their breakfast'. Soldiers from Ballymullen Barracks were summoned to restore order by ejecting the men and arresting the ringleaders.[53] On 10 November the board found it necessary to refuse admission to '200 destitute objects', all of whom were eligible for entry. The guardians believed that accommodation for 500 more was needed and proposed converting the dining area into dormitories and erecting temporary wooden sheds for dining. However, the Poor Law Commissioners gave approval for only 150 extra places and these were provided by adding sleeping galleries. The board also recommended that Dingle should be made a separate union with its own workhouse capable of accommodating 600. This did come about eventually, but not in time to help with the crisis of 1846–7.[54]

By the end of November numbers in the workhouse had risen far higher than its official capacity of 1,000. Eighty-six applicants were rejected and 102 were admitted on 24 November, bringing the total in the workhouse to 1,207. Dr Alton, medical officer of the workhouse, was asked by the board whether they should admit or reject applicants. He refused to be placed in the position of making that decision, saying that all he could advise was that the safe capacity of the house was 1,000, and that it was up to the board to make decisions about applicants.[55]

One solution to the accommodation problem was the conversion of schoolrooms to day-rooms, day-rooms to dining-rooms and dining-rooms to dormitories. This would impact on the room used for worship by the chaplain, Dr McEnnery, but he had no objection to the changes, saying that anywhere could be used for worship.[56]

Extra accommodation was provided in December 1846, and there was a plea for extra hospital accommodation also because there were 'single beds in which as many as five persons are crowded together', some of whom were suffering from contagious diseases.[57] In the face of a clamour for workhouse places by men who had been dismissed from public works, the board saw themselves as helpless: 'The workhouse cannot give them accommodation, however impressed the guardians are with the positive conviction that they only seek for it to save themselves from actual starvation.'[58] Later the guardians stated: 'The destitute poor of this locality are in an actual state of starvation (not to say destitution) and if some immediate assistance be not afforded, our labouring poor must perish for want of food and employment, for employment without food is valueless … Our people are perishing about us.'[59]

Most press reports from the proceedings of the board of guardians are formal, factual and objective, with only a rare comment or observation. However, towards the end of 1846, a reporter of *The Cork Examiner* gave a strong sense of immediacy and a rare insight into the workhouse. He referred particularly to the hardships of those who had come from the most distant part of the union, the areas west of Dingle. The board had applied for extra accommodation for 500 and had got sanction for only 250 spaces, the same number as had arrived seeking admission that same day:

> I have just returned from the workhouse leaving the chairman and a few guardians to deal with a mass of misery, which though it may be equalled in some places, cannot be exceeded anywhere. Only think of the workhouse hall being filled with disappointed supplicants who are literally – men, women and children – wedged together. Their number cannot be less than two hundred, and seven-eighths of these are from Dingle, forty miles distant from this. The number in the house this Monday was eleven hundred and twenty though it was designed for the reception of one thousand. Feeling the pressure from without, the guardians appealed to the commissioners for liberty to provide additional accommodation for 500. Their reply limited the number to be accommodated to 250. This exemplifies the value of theoretical superintendence. Accommodation is only to be obtained for just as many as were turned away from the door this day. Why, no less than a thousand should be provided for. This number must be accommodated in spite of cool economy.

All that could be rescued from a lingering death today were fifty. The report of the doctor on the state of the house recommended no more. This number was exhausted in sanctioning the provisional admissions alone. And the fortunate applicants were principally from Dingle. But independent of the two hundred whose claims could not at all be entered on, many from that locality were obliged to be rejected, and every rejection was announced with sorrow by the board and received with sobbing by the miserable applicants for workhouse protection. Many of those were children whom the law pronounces able-bodied paupers as being over fifteen, an age at which they are not presumed to be longer attached to the family. These little creatures were unable to undertake their forty-mile journey, and were it not for the humanity of the guardians in ordering them some bread before they were sent out, this night would be the last that some of them would ever see. As it is, how are they to manage when sent upon the wide world at four o'clock in the evening?

Yet what can the guardians do? The few present, the Chairman [John Lynch], Colonel Stokes, Dr Blennerhassett and Mr Gorham, in order to revise the house with a view of stowing some of these 'westerns', went through it, but after an examination, the gentlemen returned without being able to select one object undeserving of shelter. Every creature seemed an object worthy of being retained. I may remark that if the duty of guardians be 'to defend the poor and fatherless, to do justice to the afflicted and needy', a greater number than have lately attended should delight in participating in that laudable work. It should not be left on the shoulders of a few who are obliged to bear all the brunt of the harrowings which irremediable wretchedness must create – to hear children screaming with hunger, and see parents fainting with weakness and continue to witness these scenes until eight o'clock at night, is more than can be expected.

This is no time for shirking. It may to be sure be revolting to a susceptible mind to witness such scenes as the poorhouse presented today. I suppose that over thirty of these poor Dingle people who were admitted today could not come before the board for want of covering. The house could afford them none and they were obliged to take to the bed, which was their only alternative. Can misery exceed this? Can destitution be more sadly, more deplorably manifested? The house has not clothing, day clothing or night covering, for more than half the number. The condition of the house may then be well imagined. Poor human beings wallowing night and day in their habitual filth is a discouraging reflection to those at a distance, but to those who must witness it, who must in fact come in contact with such contagious impurities, is pollution itself.[60]

At Christmas there were 1,072 inmates in Tralee workhouse, along with forty-four in the fever hospital: '144 wretched applicants to the workhouse with every appearance of starvation about them were necessarily refused admission.'[61]

Listowel

Sub-Inspector Fletcher of Listowel Constabulary reported as follows on 5 September 1846 on the sorry state of the potato crop:

> I have to state that since my last report, the state of the potato crops is throughout my district now fearfully awful and the small portions of those that are brought into the markets are not eatable and numbers of the farmers are not digging them and others are offering fields of potatoes for nothing to the people for the sake of getting the potatoes out of the ground. I need only say this much, and I am creditably [sic] informed that there will not be a potato to be had for the people in November next. Only for the Indian corn and the employment given under the Board of Works, vast numbers of the labouring classes would be in a miserable and famishing state. Something should be immediately done for their relief.[62]

The relief committee for Listowel also anticipated that 'hunger, disease and famine will set in unless the people by employment are afforded means to purchase food'.[63] This was echoed by an anonymous letter-writer from the town:

> No man now living ever witnessed such a sight. The stalks are withered as if it were Christmas ... It is almost impossible to sit at table for the smell of rotting potatoes ... I never witnessed anything like it nor do I know what the poor will do. Last year the failure was grossly exaggerated but I defy them to exaggerate this year. I fear that sickness will come before starvation.[64]

The board of guardians acknowledged the total failure of the potato crop and anticipated that 'the people are likely to be in such a state of destitution as cannot be relieved by the retail trade'. It recommended that immediate employment be provided and that food should be sent to every village for sale. The board also stated that reports that the relief committee was to be dissolved 'produced much uneasiness and dismay in the public mind'.[65]

In late November, 'an alarming assemblage' of about 5,000 gathered in Listowel with the cry 'Bread or Blood' on their lips:

> The poor unhappy people presented all the appearance of want. Their bodies could scarcely be said to be clothed and their pallid visages showed what ravages gaunt famine had already made on their manly health and vigour. Heaven only knows where these things are to end, for it is to be feared that we have scarcely seen even the beginning of the misery that awaits our unhappy people.[66]

The fears of the *Chronicle* were well founded, as this hardship was only the beginning of five years of abject misery for the people. Fr Darby Mahony, the parish priest, went into the centre of the crowd and tried to pacify them. After some time remonstrating with the people, he collapsed in exhaustion. 'The sight before them of the parish priest and minister of Heaven in a faint as if his spirit had fled' had the effect of calming the people, and they dispersed quietly.[67] Fr Darby was held in high regard by the people, particularly for his refusal to give evidence against anyone over a notorious faction fight which took place at Ballyeagh in 1834 between the Cooleens and the Lawlors, in which at least twenty men were killed and many more were wounded; his reason was that giving evidence against individuals might 'injure or lessen his influence on his flock'.[68]

According to Fr Anthony Gaughan, the crowd that gathered in Listowel came mainly from the Beale-Kilconly area. He also records that as they dispersed, some of the people ate a wild plant near the workhouse and died as a result. This was probably *praiseach buí* or charlock, large quantities of which can be fatal.[69]

Castleisland and Brosna

A new relief committee was established in Brosna in September with landowner Charles G. Fairfield as chairman. He told the meeting that although there were numerous landowners in this area, 'a barren and mountainous tract of country', he was the only resident landlord within a radius of twenty miles of Brosna.[70] He said that he was 'in dread' that any measures the committee adopted 'would not be sufficient to support the people in the present crisis' but that 'the people should be fed at all events'. Fairfield was praised for the 'kind and friendly manner in which he came forward in the present necessity'. The parish priest of Brosna, Fr Richard Naughten, also spoke at the meeting and said that his parishioners were 'anxious and willing to lend their support' and that he had collected 'a reasonable sum' of money towards relief. He was also praised for his 'indefatigable exertions' on behalf of the poor.[71]

In Castleisland, by August the crop was totally destroyed and the *Post* was alarmed at the prospects for the area and the country:

> The potato fields in this locality are a scene of desolation. It wrings the heart of the farmer and the labourer with anguish and despair to behold the blighted aspect of that crop which a short time ago gladdened the hearts of all ... A nation's food is lost and the matter should not be treated with indifference.[72]

A notice was posted in Castleisland in October stating that there would be plunder unless public work was started; the men of the area could not 'bear the cries of children any longer'.[73] The town's relief committee published a formal appeal on 19 October, signed by chairman William Meredith and secretary and treasurer Rev. F. R. Maunsell, reminding landlords of their 'sacred duty' on what was to prove the eve of the great calamity. The appeal was headed 'An appeal to the landed proprietors and others in the district of Castleisland' and it highlighted how important it was for the poor that the cost of meal should be reduced:

> The Relief Committee recently appointed for the parishes of CASTLEISLAND, KILLEENTIERNA, DYSART AND BALLINCUSHLANE, beg once more respectfully to address the several Landed Proprietors of the District and all those to whom God has graciously afforded means to contribute to the relief of people on the very verge of FAMINE.
>
> A solemn and imperative duty lies upon such to come forward freely and liberally – a duty for the discharge of which they are responsible to Almighty God. The necessity is extreme, the call, therefore, upon those who are bound to meet it is most urgent.
>
> Indian Corn Meal – now the principal resource of the poor – and all other Bread Stuffs, have reached a price which makes it impossible for a labouring man – even if in full employment – to sustain a family; whilst under existing circumstances – no public works being as yet in progress – he is rendered altogether unable to purchase food almost at any price.
>
> Unless, therefore, the most speedy and effectual means are instantly adopted to cheapen FOOD and to counteract monopoly, the most disastrous consequences must necessarily ensue.
>
> The Committee being fully and fearfully convinced of this, hesitate not to repeat that it is a sacred duty imperative upon all who are interested in the district – Landed Proprietors and others – cheerfully and heartily to meet the present dreadful emergency – to stay the progress of destitution, and to afford effectual relief to their poor brethren in this their time of difficulty and distress.
>
> Remember – *'It is more blessed to give than to receive.'*[74]

Over two months later Rev. Maunsell wrote an open letter appealing to the people of England for assistance and condemning the manner in which English newspapers reported from Ireland. 'We call loudly on our sister island to help us ... We appeal to you as friends,' he wrote.

> We are fully and painfully aware for we have seen and read some of the clever but most severe and ungenerous articles put forth in one or more of the leading journals of the day touching the misery and distress so awfully prevailing in this our afflicted country; we have observed the bitterness wherewith they have almost mocked at our calamity; we have marked the untruth conveyed in many of those articles.[75]

Maunsell's letter was a powerfully worded appeal to English people 'to stretch out a generous hand to rescue unhappy thousands and to alleviate one of the most awful afflictions with which the Almighty ever visited a nation'. He believed that 'very few, if any, of our English friends can form an idea of the actual state of poverty and destitution' and told them that the government's response was inadequate and that famine already existed:

> The fact is undeniable as it is appalling – the poor are literally bordering on starvation!! This we aver! Of this we are eyewitnesses! – and their condition is now reduced to so low an ebb that we feel it our imperative though most painful duty to call loudly upon our sister country to help us – to bury in oblivion all unkind feelings or expressions which may have been manifested or expressed by but a few amongst us and to 'overcome evil with good'.[76]

Maunsell believed that 'of all nations under heaven, England is the last that would wish to see Ireland, or any of her sons, perish through famine':

> Ireland – which has stood beside her in all her battles both by land and sea, has given her many of her bravest captains and her ablest statesmen, and who will again, we hesitate not to affirm, stand beside her in every righteous cause of conflict that may arise.[77]

The publications which Rev. Maunsell specifically criticised were *The Times* and *The Spectator*. The general attitude of *The Times* is illustrated in comments such as this about news of distress from Ireland: 'It is possible to have been told the tale of sorrow too often ... The sufferer becomes an inveterate suppliant and expectant.'[78] Ironically, a week before Maunsell's letter, the *Post* carried verses from the satirical magazine *Punch* graphically illustrating the attitude which he decried, with accusations that the Irish poor were spending funds donated from England on weapons. The fact that the verses were reproduced without any comment by the *Post* would seem to indicate its approval of the tone:

> *Och, Paddy, my honey, we've given you money*
> *And we freely came down with the dust, did we not?*
> *And now you enjoy it, the way you employ it*
> *Is in laying it out in powder and shot.*
>
> *In want and starvation you cried to our nation,*
> *To relieve you we pinched our own indigent sons;*
> *You gained your petition – to buy ammunition,*
> *Pikes and cutlasses, bayonets, pistols and guns.*
>
> *Against us thus arming, your conduct is charming,*
> *To the friends that you found in your season of need,*
> *Sure, Paddy my darling, at Englishmen snarling,*
> *'Tis rare grateful boy that ye are then indeed.*
>
> *So shout for O'Brien, the young Irish lion,*
> *While pursuing your mighty magnanimous course,*
> *Our alms 'gainst 'our honour', the Sassenach donors,*
> *You convert into weapons of 'physical force'.*[79]

Tarbert and Ballylongford

In early October the *Madagascar*, a forty-four-gun frigate under Commander Burney, arrived in Tarbert, accompanied by the war steamers *Stromboli*, *Pluto* and *Swallow*. Their commanders were Fisher, Lowe and Bryant respectively. The *Madagascar* carried Indian meal and had a capacity of 1,200 tons. It had a company of Royal Marines on board and it was stationed at Tarbert until September 1848. The steamer *Alban* and a sloop-of-war, the *Dido*, were also expected to arrive in Tarbert. The *Post* carried a full report from another newspaper on the prompt and effective deployment of twelve man-of-war steamers and other vessels for the distribution of Indian corn around the west of Ireland.[80]

Not all locals appeared to benefit from this so-called 'prompt' response. As had happened in March, Fr Daniel McCarthy was once again the person to whom the poor resorted *in extremis*, as reported in the *Chronicle*:

> One of the most formidable arrays of human misery ever witnessed in this country was to be seen entering Ballylongford on yesterday, Tuesday, from the northern part of the parish (Asdee) and it must add to the terror of shopkeepers. After arriving, they marched to Lislaughtin Abbey, residence of Fr McCarthy … setting forth that their pinching want was already beyond endurance and they could not be expected to hold out any longer … A curate remonstrated in so sympathetic a manner with this, to all appearances, infuriated assemblage, that it had the desired effect and all returned peaceably to their foodless cabins.[81]

One of Fr McCarthy's parishioners, probably aided by the priest himself, wrote a heartfelt plea to Sir Richard Routh, who was chairman of the Dublin-based Poor Law Commissioners. She was Ellen Frawley and she and her husband, John, had a family of girls. John was employed on the public works and this was their sole source of income. Ellen wrote that on 7 November John had gone to work as usual and at the end of the day, 'when not being twenty or thirty yards distant from where he worked during the day in perfect health, he fell suddenly on the road a lifeless corpse'.[82] She told Routh that she was left 'with her young children, deprived of husband, father and the only means of her support in your employment, in one moment of time'. Ellen appealed for some relief 'for a much and truly distressed family … as objects deserving the kind consideration of all Christians'. She asked Routh to send his reply to Fr McCarthy. The reply was written over Ellen's letter, informing her that Sir Richard Routh did not have any fund for the relief of widows or other persons in distress and advising her to apply to Listowel board of guardians.[83]

Although the cause of John Frawley's death is unknown, it happened while he was employed on public works, and in other places such deaths caused outrage. The first deaths from starvation began in early October 1846, and that of Denis McKennedy in Skibbereen, Co. Cork, around 25 October was particularly shocking because he died while on the public works.[84]

Fr Daniel McCarthy wrote in a personal capacity to the lord lieutenant on behalf of his parishioners, and his letter was published in the *Examiner*:

> Lingering sickness and malignant fever, the consequences of starvation, are making frightful ravages among my unfortunate people. I did hope as a member of the relief committee and with the aid of the Government to be able to effect some immediate good and thereby avert famine and preserve the machinery of society intact, but I find by sad experience that my efforts have been fruitless and my hopes blasted. Under the present regulations of the Board of Works, the one-fourth of the heads of families (the average of which are from six to ten in number) cannot be employed. Your lordship can then easily perceive the consequences; I shudder even at the thought.
>
> Patience is a virtue; they have given proofs they possess it to an extraordinary degree; but when goaded by hunger and maddened by the shrieks of their starving children, they will consider forbearance a folly and patience a crime.
>
> I do then solemnly but humbly implore your Lordship in the name of common humanity and as you wish for the preservation of peace and order

for which this locality has been ever remarkable, to come speedily to their assistance and cause such immediate arrangements to be made as may give them the necessary means of existence.[85]

The *Examiner* introduced the letter as follows: 'Will the government bestir themselves? Will the following appeal make no change in the present order of things, when in the midst of staring famine, hope is held out but to bring disappointment and human patience in human infirmity fast approaches the limits of human endurance?'[86]

The editor of the *Chronicle* also referred to a private communication from Fr McCarthy, in which he wrote: 'We have had some deaths from starvation. The piercing and heart-rending appeals of the hundreds who are unemployed and consequently starving in this district are beyond description.'[87] The editor added his own views, attempting to draw international attention to the crisis:

> We can add little to the touching picture which our old friend has here given. All our communications from his district are appealing. The resident gentry are overborne by the pressure of want which collapses the gaunt frame of the people, while the majority of the absentee proprietors who have neither humanity nor wisdom to 'discern the signs of the times' are dead to the voice of human suffering. If the *Times* instead of libelling the resident gentlemen of Ireland, would concentrate public opinion against the conduct of those men, it would go far in redeeming its own character, and forcing from very shame, those hereditary incubi to do their duty. We trust that if the *Times* do not, his great and successful rival the *Daily News* will arouse the indignation of England and of Europe against this heartless class.[88]

The *Post* was also well disposed to Fr McCarthy and his efforts on behalf of the poor and hungry. It described him in these terms:

> Rev. Daniel McCarthy is not one of your brawling demagogues who are too often found among the Romish priesthood … but a sensible plain man

worthy of fulfilling his responsible duties and enjoying the respect of all parties who has on all occasions shown himself anxious to preserve the peace of the country and to uphold the rights of prosperity.[89]

Within a few days, Daniel McCarthy again expressed his personal sense of despair at the unfolding calamity, a sense of helplessness that must have been widespread among clergy, members of relief committees and government officials as the year ended. Once again, he met a crowd of hundreds of people walking to Ballylongford in search of food:

> I have further to inform you that on Wednesday last in the discharge of my duty, I met some hundreds of the people from the western portion of this parish, particularly from the lands of Asdee, Killelton and Clounaman, marching in a body towards Ballylongford crying out that they were arrived at the last extremity and that they would slaughter and should have food for themselves and starving children. After a long remonstrance with them the poor people retired, hoping for some immediate relief. The people looked to me. I have nothing in my power; all I could do I did. If the landed proprietor of this portion of the parish acted in the same spirit of giving employment to his labourers that the other proprietors are daily manifesting, it would save me the pain of being witness to this frightful demonstration.[90]

Lieutenant H. N. Greenwell, government inspecting officer, forwarded the memorial of Fr McCarthy to his superiors with this observation: 'Mr McCarthy's description is not overdrawn, the most frightful distress prevails in his district, which can only be relieved by at once sanctioning the drainage and other works presented for at Listowel on 30 November.'[91]

Lieutenant Greenwell had arrived in Kerry as inspecting officer in September 1846 and he remained until September 1847. He was the first of a number of resident government inspectors sent to Kerry to supervise the public works and to liaise with local officials and Dublin officials. Greenwell reported to the secretary of the Commissioners of Public Works in Dublin,

Mr Walker. Inspectors were members of the local committees and exercised authority over them, particularly with regard to the preparation of lists of those in need of relief.[92]

Initially Greenwell was responsible for the whole county; later Captain Douglas Labalmondière was appointed for the south Kerry area. Greenwell's report of 14 November gives an illustration of the nature of his duties in late 1846. On the previous Monday and Tuesday he had gone to Tralee to meet the relief committee and to issue tickets of work to those selected for the public works. On Wednesday he had gone to Killarney to brief Captain Labalmondière about south Kerry. On Thursday he was in Listowel inspecting various works. Friday was devoted to Tarbert, meeting the relief committee and inspecting various works. He went to Abbeydorney and Ardfert on Saturday, to deal with complaints against stewards on the works.[93]

Ballybunion

The Wreck of the Sea Lark

The schooner *Sea Lark* of Limerick under Captain Hutchins was one of three ships that set out from Tarbert in late November 1846. The others were the screw-steamer *Senator* and the schooner *Kate*. The *Sea Lark* carried a cargo of seventy tons of flour for the firm of J. N. Russell in Tralee.

On Friday 20 November the ships ran into a severe storm and all three got into difficulty, as they did not have time to lower their sails. The *Kate* managed to reach shelter at Kilcredan, while the *Senator* was driven onto a high bank in the Cashen area. The Ballybunion coastguards under Joseph Dexter went to the aid of the *Senator* and remained with it to protect the cargo. The *Sea Lark* ended up on Ballybunion strand, keel upwards, with no coastguards available to assist. The crew had been working on deck and had been washed overboard. On Saturday morning the ship was still intact and large crowds had gathered. The *Chronicle* reported that the ship 'was boarded by myriads of the country people whose first work was to lacerate her sides in order to effect the business of destruction and plunder with more ease and effect'.[94] The *Post* gave a graphic account of the incident 'from our correspondent', which may contain some exaggeration, especially with regard to the numbers present:

> During the night the news went through the country all along the Shannon that a vessel laden with flour was wrecked at Ballyeagh and before 9 o'clock on Saturday morning over a thousand persons arrived with horses and cars to carry away the anticipated plunder. At this time the tide was ebbing and the *Sea Lark* was lying keel uppermost in the water. So impatient were the people on shore to come at the cargo that they rode out on horseback with their hatchets to commence the attack. At this time Mr Christopher Julian, J.P. of Tullomore with a small party of police and the coastguards were on board the steamer [the *Senator*] for her protection within sight at about a quarter of a mile's distance, but could not attempt to do anything for the helpless *Sea Lark*. So stout was the little craft that it was a full three hours before a breach was effected in her side. Subsequently six holes were made at intervals in each side and four near the keel through which the bags of flour were extracted. The scene was most awful when the first bag was got out, as the people almost came to blows with hatchets, knives etc. for the possession of it. There were 70 tons of flour on board, more than three-fourths of which was carried away on Saturday. On Saturday night, Mr Russell's agents arrived on the spot from Tralee, as did also a strong police force under Mr Bolger, brought for the protection of the steamer. On Sunday morning about 4,000 of the peasantry assembled and the work of spoliation went on in the face of the police. About 9 o'clock, fifty of the 77th Depot, under the command of a Captain, arrived, but too late to prevent plunder. Just before the arrival of the military, several arrests were made of parties carrying away the flour in the most open and daring manner and no less than thirty persons were caught in the very hull itself.[95]

In the wholesale plunder of the wreck, in the words of the *Chronicle*, 'the most unscrupulous robbery was committed not by labourers or small farmers alone but by men of apparent wealth and respectability'.[96]

The *Limerick Chronicle* stated that 'this is not a common case of stealing from a wreck but one of the systematic plunder of property in the open day'.[97] When officials came on the scene they saw the flour being taken away, and were startled to find that 'instead of showing any symptoms of fear, the people became insolent, even menacing. Their numbers – upwards of 3,000 – gave the people confidence and they used their power with the most reckless disregard to order and to property.'[98] The incident was described in terms of a military operation: 'The position of the plunderers, having command of the cliffs, gave them complete control over the authorities. They remained in this condition until the arrival of a party of the 77th on Sunday morning when order was restored and about fifty persons arrested.'[99] The body of a cabin boy named O'Brien was found inside the hull of the *Sea Lark*. Captain Hutchins was drowned, as were the other crew members, two of whom were named Meskill, one McCarthy and one Looney.[100]

One immediate result of the loss of the flour was an increase in flour prices in Tralee. It was also noted that the ship was not insured and that the ratepayers would have to bear the cost. The *Chronicle* had nothing but praise for Mr Russell as a grain merchant, and was sympathetic to his financial loss, saying that he provided competition, kept up a regular supply and kept prices down in Tralee.[101] According to the *Post*, five people were arrested but 'no person could be got to identify the persons who first commenced the work of plunder, though it is notorious that they are known to many respectable parties in the village [Ballybunion]'. Its correspondent added: 'Comfortable farmers, I have heard, were the most forward and successful robbers on the occasion.'[102]

The threat to public order evident in the sight of hundreds of desperate people massing along the roads and the thousands reported in Ballybunion at this incident, was a reminder to property owners, farmers and shopkeepers of the kind of social upheaval which might ensue were the food crisis to continue. Although incidents such as these seem rare enough in newspaper accounts, the warning that 'hunger will break through stone walls' was frequently heard.[103] There was concern in Tralee when a signed public notice outside the church asked people to gather and 'march for food and employment'.[104] The signature was torn off before magistrates and police arrived to take down the notice. There were occasional reports of isolated attacks such as the killing of 'a beautiful cow of Mr Williams of Blennerville', when the crowd threatened to slaughter every cow in the country unless they got employment.[105] 'Insubordination of labourers' caused public works to be suspended in Milltown in early December.[106]

It is surprising that there were not more attacks on property and on farms, and it seems that the appeals of the clergy had a particularly potent influence on crowds. This was in spite of the fact that all that the clergymen could promise was that they would appeal on behalf of the people to the authorities to provide work. At some stage, people must have realised how ineffectual these promises were.

Ballyheigue Area

In October 1846, as part of the restructuring of relief in accordance with government policy, a new relief committee was set up for Kilmoyley, Ballyheigue, Rattoo and Killury, with Major Pierce Crosbie of Ballyheigue Castle as chairman and William Pope of Causeway as secretary.[107] Pope soon resigned because of sickness in his family and his inability to carry out the duties of the office. He added an ominous postscript to his letter: 'The people are famishing and only a few employed at 8d a day, they are beginning to slaughter the cattle.'[108]

Fr Eugene McCarthy, PP, attended a meeting in Abbeydorney about public works and spoke, as the report put it, 'in a very low tone, which indicated much modesty'.[109] It was more likely despondency or despair which affected him, as he told the meeting that 1,500 men had been 'disemployed' the previous night by the superintendent, Mr Cashman, on the orders of his superiors:

> Mr McCarthy spoke of the prevailing distress in the neighbourhood and said that the men had to go four miles morning and evening to work on these roads, while in operation, and that four of the labourers yesterday had to quit

their work and retire to their beds from weakness. Only he did not like to say anything that would be calculated to excite the people, he could state facts that would astonish the gentlemen.[110]

The result was that the county engineer, Mr Stokes, promised to open up all the public works at his disposal.[111]

The First Deaths from Starvation

1846 closed with some heart-rending reports of deaths from starvation in Kerry. Among the first deaths were those of two men from Corkaguiny. John Botend of Ballineanig 'fell on the new road there making [*sic*] and expired immediately'; the inquest verdict was that 'he came by his death from hunger and cold'.[112] John Browne of Kilquane was walking the thirty-mile journey from the Tralee workhouse to his home, most likely having been refused admission, when he fell on the roadside. He was taken to a farmer's house at Kilcummin but expired a few hours later. The verdict was that he had died of fatigue and weakness.[113]

The *Post* became as outraged as the *Examiner*, noting that 'famine and gaunt hunger [are] becoming daily more visible in the faces on the streets'. It asked: 'Are the authorities intent on driving the people into acts of desperation and violence?'[114] Its editorials became even stronger in December, and one was very direct in allocating blame:

> Starvation is already stalking through the land, seizing on its victims here and there … We contend that Lord John Russell, the Earl of Bessborough and their colleagues must be held guilty of the death of every Irish peasant who during this fearful season may fall a victim to starvation.[115]

Two weeks later the *Post* wrote:

> The famine, gaunt, lean and hollow-eyed, is stalking through the length and breadth of our county. Nay, hunger has already selected his victims from the

patient peasantry of Kerry. Strong men and women, the fathers and mothers of families have yielded up their lives to the demon of starvation. Yet this is the crisis in which the Whigs have chosen to maintain the principle of political economy. Famine may bring desolation and death to the cabin of the Irish peasant but the 'paternal Whigs' will not interfere with private speculation by opening the government depots even in the most distressed localities for the sale of food. The *Chronicle* writes that in Dingle – that most wretched district of a wretched country – the Indian meal is heating in government stores. Again the marines cannot pace the deck of the *Madagascar* in Tarbert Roadstead from the offensive smell of the pent-up supplies. Yet at that moment and in these localities, the people were famishing from the want, not so much of money, as of provisions.

Where is this state of things to end? When will the government step in to aid the local charity of the county? These are questions put by every thinking man and the general reply is that if something is not done soon it will be too late. The starving multitudes will become demoralised and the bonds of society will be dissolved by the pressure of famine. To what state may not our country be brought by the weakness and mal-administration of the Whigs? Oh, that some strong mind held the helm of the state during the present crisis.[116]

As evidence of deaths from starvation, the *Post* reported that six fathers of families in a village near Killarney were dead or dying, two people had died in Dingle and three in Kenmare. 'Where is this state of things to end?' asked the paper.[117] A woman who was walking with her child from Dingle to Tralee died on the way. In far-off Ventry, there were twelve deaths, five of them from starvation. A gentleman in Tralee was asked to help a particular family and he decided to visit the home to verify the truth of what he had heard. What he found appalled him: the 'unshrouded corpse' of a child lay on a table while the mother was 'pressing another child, almost dead of the cold, to her bosom to try and infuse warmth into its body'.[118] The child's body had been in the house for five days for want of the price of a coffin. Twenty-one people died in Tralee workhouse in the week leading up to 19 December, a death rate that would normally occur over two months. The *Post* wrote: 'the poorhouse is so overcrowded that disease and death are making fearful havoc among the inmates'.[119]

The first named children who died from starvation were two brothers named Michael and James Mitchell. Michael was aged seven and James was three months old. They died in the house of Cornelius Harnett in Castlegregory where they had received shelter, but it is likely that they had been walking with their mother and two other children from west Kerry towards the workhouse in Tralee. This is the report on the inquest held by coroner Francis Twiss on the Mitchell brothers:

> It appeared from the evidence of their mother that the elder child had had no food for several days prior to his death and that the younger also had been for days without any nourishment, owing to the complete drying up of its natural sustenance, the consequence of hunger in herself. Cornelius Harnett stated that the mother of the children applied to his wife on Saturday last for lodging which she gave her for charity. She had then four children with her and before any food could be prepared for any of them, Michael died on the hearth; on Sunday evening the infant also died – both, he had no doubt, from want of food. A post-mortem examination of both bodies was made by Dr Busteed of Castlegregory. No sign of disease was to be found on either, both were wretchedly emaciated but the younger more especially; and not the least trace of food was to be discovered in the stomach or bowels of either. In his opinion they both died of starvation. The jury returned verdicts accordingly.[120]

On Christmas Day 1846 the *Examiner* reported on the inquest on Michael Connell of Tralee, a widower aged between forty-five and fifty. He was a skilled man, a weaver, and one of many craftsmen whose lives had changed when the poorer classes, on whom their livelihoods depended, were devastated. Connell had three children aged between five and twelve. The children had been sick for weeks and their only means of support was the money an old woman could beg for them, 'for the last weeks not averaging a pennyworth in the day'. The family had passed several days without food:

> Beside the corpse on a miserable wad of straw lay two children almost gasping with hunger, the third child being out begging having left its sick bed. The poor man breathed his last on Wednesday leaving his attenuated and skeleton frame and the pallid countenances of his three children to attest to the fact of famine having made its ravages in this town. Mr Justin Supple, coroner, at his own expense provided a coffin.[121]

In early January 1847 one of Michael Connell's children died. Other deaths at this time were those of Stephen Geary, a man named Purty and a woman from Dingle who, 'having got a pennyworth of bread from a charitable person in this town [Tralee] dropped before she could eat it'.[122] *The Tablet* reported these deaths but believed it was 'almost a mockery of the frightfully appalling destitution which exists in this county to be particularising and chronicling a few instances of death from starvation, when numbers are daily dying from this cause, unnoticed and unheard of'.[123]

In appealing for donations towards the suffering poor of Kerry, *The Tablet* commented: 'The reader will see that on the ground of corporal suffering alone, Kerry has ample claims on their charity; and therefore we entreat them to make the next week, as far as their slender help can do anything, a good week for Kerry.'[124]

But there were to be no good weeks for Kerry for years to come.

4

'A CHILL FEELING OF DESPAIR'

JANUARY–JUNE 1847

We are in utter despair for the poor people of this county. Hourly destitution is becoming – not more extensive, for that is impossible – but more torturous, more fatal. Hundreds are dying and the living are but crawling skeletons.

Kerry Examiner, 23 February 1847

Tralee

The *Kerry Evening Post* began its seventy-third year of publication with an ominous editorial: 'Gaunt famine stalks the length and breadth of our island; disease and death follow in its train. All the land is steeped in poverty, want, misery and wretchedness. Here downright starvation seizes on its victim, there fever cuts off the starveling.'[1] The paper took a staunchly providentialist view, just as Charles Edward Trevelyan, the assistant secretary of the Treasury in London, and many others did, stating: 'The fact is that this visitation, dark and deadly though it be, has come from the hands of the Almighty Disposer of events. Man, evil man, has had no hand in bringing on this calamity – it has come directly from the good God.' It issued an exhortation to readers: 'Let us all unite in the cause of the starving poor' and looked to the year ahead as 'the most eventful in our country's history, if our anticipations are borne out'. It urged all classes to help the destitute poor 'so that they may be preserved alive to participate in the blessings that promise ere long to visit our now famine-stricken land'.[2] Ciarán Ó Murchadha has described the period from January to June 1847 in Ireland as 'the first full cyclonic blast of a national famine, during which mass death from starvation, disease and exposure to the cold occurred on a truly apocalyptic scale.'[3]

The Tablet also anticipated further disasters:

> Still this hideous famine. Still death, slow death, falling upon thousands. Still fathers, mothers, sons, daughters, grown children and infants looking helplessly and hopelessly on each other while the gaunt monster whose arms embrace them as with bonds of iron and who within them begins to live as they begin to die, drains drop by drop the life that God has given …
>
> Still we say these calamities continue and would to God that were the end of our story. Alas! It is only the beginning; the end is not yet. As yet God has but sounded the prelude of his judgments. It is the overture we have been listening to; for the hideous drama itself the curtain has not yet been drawn up.[4]

Over 20,000 people were receiving food daily from the stores of the relief committee of Tralee. 'Our streets are thronged with beggars,' wrote the *Post*, 'pale emaciated creatures hardly able to drag their limbs after them, while not a few impostors are to be found who do not hesitate to divide the charity of the benevolent with the really destitute.'[5]

On 4 January a crowd of 300 labourers gathered in Tralee demanding employment. The language of reports reveals the fears of the townspeople: the incident was described as an 'outbreak' and 'a tumultuous irruption' and the men were 'armed with spades and shovels'. The labourers appealed for help to the parish priest, Dr John McEnnery.[6]

The incident was repeated on the following day, when a crowd of 400 labourers protested, breaking into the bakers' shops 'from which they took every morsel of food they could find'. Then, 'as each shop was rifled, a wolfish struggle took place amongst the crowd'.[7] Fr McEnnery pleaded with them not to break the law as it would not help them or their starving families. 'The

Rev. gentleman's words, for the first time perhaps, went unheeded by the excited crowd,' recorded the *Examiner*.[8] They passed him by and went to the stores of the relief committee where they were resisted and prevented from getting food.

Word then spread that there was food on the vessels in the Canal Basin and they rushed there 'to seize on the provisions in the ships'. The master of one ship tried to move it to the middle of the basin to prevent the crowd from boarding it, but they managed to hold it by a rope. Then they turned their attention to some bags of bacon which they found on the quays, but George Day Stokes, JP, chanced to come along and he addressed them, promising them work if they remained peaceful for two days. 'After many entreaties and considerable difficulties, he prevailed on them to disperse.'[9] Stokes later told the board of guardians that thousands of pounds' worth of property would have been taken away had he not come on the scene. Another ship with a cargo of flour owned by John O'Leary of Killarney was attacked in the Basin and the crew of six was overwhelmed.[10]

Dr McEnnery delivered a powerful sermon in which he condemned attacks on property, but laid all the blame for the crisis on the government, declaring it 'imbecile, inefficient and corrupt'.[11] He warned that the people were literally starving, that they were willing to work but could get none, and that violence was bound to ensue.[12] McEnnery vividly described the debilitation and weakness which he had observed: 'If you put your hand on the arm of a young man, you will find no flesh, no muscle, nothing but a handful of bones. I have never seen such a wasting of flesh and shrinking up of muscle. The least attack of sickness must destroy these people ill-prepared to contend against its ravages, and they are the victims of famine even though they may die of other diseases.'[13] McEnnery worked closely with the Protestant rector Rev. Anthony Denny, and when the latter was ill from fever, the priest, in an unprecedented intervention, asked his congregation for prayers for his recovery. Rev. Denny, who was born in the town in 1807, was rector from 1831 to 1861. He was very active in relief during the Famine and was much respected by all creeds and classes in Tralee.

A letter in the *Chronicle* stated that 'deaths from starvation have taken place on our streets and many have died from this cause in their houses'.[14] It was signed 'one who would like to see all do what they can for the destitute' and the writer lamented the fact that very few individuals and mercantile firms of Tralee had come forward in January 1847 with subscriptions of £10 and over. The contributors were:

Messrs Donovan	£30
Messrs Russell	£20
Mr J. Mulchinock	£20
Mr J. Russell	£15
Mr Lumsden	£10
Sir E. Denny	£100
Mr M. O'Connell	£50
Dr McEnnery	£30
Miss Denny	£30
Miss D. Denny	£30
Lt Col. [J. Day] Stokes	£30
Mr W. Stoughton	£10
Mr J. Lynch	£20
Mr Drummond	£20
Rev. A. B. Rowan	£20
Mr F. Crosbie	£20
The Misses Foley	£15
Dr Alton	£12
Mr Jeffcott	£10
Mr G. Day Stokes	£10
Mr P. T. Foley	£10
Mr James O'Connell	£10
Rev. Barry Denny	£10[15]

Twenty-seven people died in Tralee in the week leading up to 16 February, according to prayers said for them at Mass, but there were many others who died and whose names were not on the prayer list.[16] The *Post* reported:

> Dysentery is most fatal in this town. Death is rife in every alley and lane in Tralee. Six deaths are reported to us as having occurred yesterday in the Old Quarry. On Wednesday five persons died of dysentery in the Rock. In two days since our last publication, the mother and father of a family, who had been in health last week, fell victims to this disease. We were ourselves aware of the heartrending circumstances of this case and the circumstances were most pitiable – the wife was dead and lying in the same wretched bed while the husband was receiving the last rites of the Roman Catholic Church.[17]

In the week of 10–17 February, seventy people were reported as dying in Tralee district from starvation, dysentery, fever and other effects of destitution.[18] In the last three weeks of February there were seventy-eight deaths in the workhouse, an average of twenty-six per week. In the week of 10–17 March, forty-three died in the workhouse and the total for the previous four weeks was 150. In the row of houses on the Tralee side of Blennerville bridge, there were eleven deaths in one week from 'the combined effects of starvation and disease'.[19] Another report went: 'On Thursday night last three bodies passed through this town in a donkey's car to the graveyard at Rathass to be interred without coffins!'[20] The exclamation mark denoted astonishment at this departure from burial norms. A 'poor countrywoman' who came to Tralee to buy three coffins was approached by two suppliers vying for her custom: 'no respect was shown to the poor bereaved woman, but a greediness for gain most shameful on such a melancholy occasion'.[21] Newspapers noted that many funerals took place with only very few people attending.

Another harrowing case at this time was that of Mary Kennedy. She died at Derrymore, west of Tralee, and an inquest was held on 27 March at which her sister, Catherine Moriarty, gave evidence. Catherine stated that, after being several days without any food, Mary and three children had been sent to Tralee workhouse from Inch by the parish priest, Fr George O'Sullivan, who provided transport for them on a horse-car. They were refused admission to the workhouse and the carman, Denis Sears, did not bring them the whole journey back but left them at Derrymore. They obtained shelter overnight there from a man named Jeremiah Flynn. They continued walking home, sleeping out of doors the next night, and by morning, Mary and one of the children, Daniel Griffin, had perished. The inquest verdict was death by starvation.[22]

Another inquest was held on 29 March and, tragically, it was on Catherine Moriarty herself; she also died of starvation. Catherine seems to have taken responsibility for the other two children after Mary's death. This was the account of an inquest witness as reported in *The Cork Examiner*:

> John O'Donnell deposed that he yesterday saw the deceased Catherine Moriarty and two children with her by the wall where she now lies; did not speak to her but spoke to the boy that was with her, who told witness she could take no food. In about two hours after, saw her, at which time she was not dead; the two children came to the house of witness after nightfall and told him she was dead; he put the children into a house of his and gave them some straw for a bed, and went to where she was and found her dead.[23]

Some people resorted to shocking ways of finding money to enable them to either bury their dead or simply stay alive themselves. Nine people stood begging outside the church in Tralee, with coffin lids as receptacles to show that the money was for a burial.[24] A woman begged while she carried her dead child strapped on her back, resisting all attempts to take the baby from her, saying that it was the only way she could get money to bury the child.[25] A man laid out his dead mother on a street in Tralee, while he stood beside her, begging for money to bury her.[26] One stark report stated: 'A man dropped dead in Castle St. today. An inquest was held on him and a verdict of "died of starvation" was returned.'[27] Tralee had become thronged with beggars, much to the alarm of residents: 'Notwithstanding the crowded state of the workhouse, mendicity is greater in our streets than ever it was and it is increasing.'[28] Other reported incidents included the robbery of six sheep from a Tralee butcher, the skins of which were found the next day; seventy-three stolen geese found salted in a house at Farmer's Bridge; and three heifers stolen and skinned in Causeway.[29]

Public Works

The Board of Works was accused of 'culpable neglect' by the Tralee relief committee, whose members were indignant at the limited employment sanctioned for relief works. Not even one-sixth of the needy labourers were employed, 'leaving five-sixths of the destitute population to struggle without employment against the rigours of mid-winter'. One man said that 'it seemed as if they wanted to test how far the endurance of starving people could go'. There was great confusion and delay, and officials were not capable of carrying out their onerous duties, with the result that 'starving creatures had to go to their desolate hearths unrelieved and the consequence is that famine and disease have claimed their victims in our very streets'.[30]

The committee exempted Henry Stokes, county surveyor, from criticism, saying that all parties acknowledged his 'wonderful exertions' and hoped that the arrival of a new engineer, Mr Bevan, would have a positive effect.[31] The *Post* had earlier excluded Stokes from its withering criticism of public works provided in Tralee, stating that he suffered 'destitution of help' and that his 'exertions and almost multiplication of himself into the various places where he is required are all but superhuman'.[32]

Colonel John Day Stokes drafted a letter requesting more aid, in which he stated that the relief committee was supplying 3,400 families with meal at cost price, funding it with their own donations and a loan of £3,000 from the bank on their own sureties. They had set up a soup shop, managed by the ladies committee, from which 950 quarts of soup a day were being sold at half price to those who had tickets.[33] Stokes argued that this practice could not continue and work would have to be provided for the destitute.

The *Examiner* was opposed to the system of task-work on the public works because 'the lazy will not work, the weakly [*sic*] cannot, and those who might be inclined to do a fair day's work do not see the use of exerting themselves to have others reap the benefits of their labours'. One labourer complained to the *Examiner* of the irregularities in the system, saying that 'comfortable farmers' in the area were getting employment on the public works and that they were thereby 'taking the food out of his children's mouths'.[34]

In early 1847 two more inspecting officers were appointed to Kerry: Captain Stuart RN was appointed to the Killarney area and Captain Herbert RN to Kenmare. Captain Labalmondière then took charge of Tralee and the barony of Trughnanacmy. H. N. Greenwell became responsible for Listowel and the baronies of Iraghticonnor and Clanmaurice, and his journal shows that, in late February 1847, he was also responsible for Dingle and the barony of Corkaguiny. Captain Labalmondière, reported from Tralee for the week ending 16 January 1847:

> I find everything in the works in the neighbourhood of Tralee (barony of Trughnanacmy) is in greatest disorder; there [*sic*] crowding in on the works in all directions and if any attempts are made to quit them engineers are threatened; and no doubt exists that if they were turned off, a popular *émeute* [riot] in Tralee would be the result. I shall remain here until I have introduced some kind of order and system.[35]

On 23 January Labalmondière compared his experience in Tralee with that in south Kerry, illustrating the type of administrative detail which had to be attended to:

> There is a more turbulent and discontented spirit discernible among the labourers in general than I have met with anywhere in the south of Kerry, which constituted my late district. Very much of my time is now occupied in receiving innumerable applications for check clerkships and examining applicants. I think I am obtaining a very superior class in this neighbourhood.
>
> I have found that in consequence of the system of task work not having been properly acted upon in the neighbourhood of Tralee, gangers not on the

relief lists have been kept on, and these men not working themselves, yet at the end of the week sharing in the money gained by such task, has had the effect of reducing the daily wage earned by the actual labourer. Of course I stopped this.[36]

Following the instructions of the commissioners, Labalmondière proceeded to lay off 20 per cent of workers, prior to the transfer to direct gratuitous relief through soup kitchens, but the relief committee expressed doubts about this policy, saying that there was no employment available for those laid off.[37]

At a meeting of Tralee relief committee in late March, Colonel Stokes proposed a system to ensure that members shared their responsibilities more equally, admitting, however, that the poor attendance of members at their first meeting did not augur well. Rev A. B. Rowan felt obliged to remind the members that 'without a resolution on the part of every member to do his duty, the people should starve or have recourse to acts of violence'.[38] As was the case with the board of guardians, the workload appears to have been falling on a small number of dedicated members of the relief committee.

In light of the critical situation, Stokes issued an appeal to all who had income from land, professions, commerce and trade to donate a sum of not less than £25 to the relief committee. An example was set by Sir Edward Denny, the pre-eminent landowner of Tralee, who lived in seclusion in England and left the management of his Tralee estate to his brother: he donated £1,000, while £100 was donated by each of the following: George Day Stokes, Rev. A. B. Rowan, Messrs Donovan and Colonel John Day Stokes himself.

A new Poor Law Relief Commission was established in early 1847 and *Punch* published a satirical farewell from the outgoing commissioners, entitled 'The last dying speech and confession of the Poor Law Commissioners':

> *Farewell good friends, if we may call*
> *One man among you friend,*
> *Assembled to behold our fall*
> *And view our shameful end.*

If you would know what brought us here
Your eyes this day before,
'Twas being cruel and severe
And hard upon the poor.

Administrators of the laws
Respecting them, ordained,
Against them each oppressive clause
With all our might we strained.
With hearts as hard as any flint
We parted man and wife;
And did so far their diet stint
It scarce supported life.

We wouldn't listen to their groans
And cries for want of bread;
Instead of meat we gave them bones
To crack, on which they fed.
We answered by 'the workhouse test'
The suppliant for relief;
That is to say we did our best
To treat them like a thief.[39]

In late January the board of guardians of Tralee appealed for an advance of £3,000 to meet their expenses 'in consequence of famine prices of all description of food'.[40] The board had never anticipated 'the pecuniary difficulties in which they are now placed' and could not 'have foreseen the awful calamity with which it has pleased God to visit this country'. Without an advance from the public purse, the guardians said, the workhouse would be closed 'and the unfortunate inmates, nearly 1,200 in number, must be thrown upon the roads to perish'.[41]

By March the board was effectively bankrupt and their cheques were not being honoured by the bank. Colonel Stokes, Captain Fairfield, Captain Chute and John Lynch declared themselves willing to become personally responsible for a loan of £2,000 from the Provincial Bank, if William Denny, John Hurly and other guardians agreed to join them. Rates on property rose dramatically through the year. Mr William Chute, the rate-collector, came in for a great deal of criticism, especially when the debts of Tralee Union rose to £4,000. He promised to bring in £1,400 over the following weeks. Stokes was appalled that Chute had collected only £12 in rates in Tralee in a week and he believed that the workhouse would have to close. At a board meeting in April he said, 'If we cannot get more money than we do at present, our case is hopeless; we cannot go on.'[42]

John Lynch was equally vociferous in his opposition to Chute's sluggishness in collecting rates, charging him with not carrying out his responsibilities with due diligence and with conniving in 'a game of delay' with ratepayers. Chute had some supporters who appealed for him not to be 'rough-handled' and pointed out that the times had altered so much that people who formerly would have been ashamed at not paying their rates promptly were now asking for more time.

As the meeting continued, with the grandees of Tralee discussing the rates issue, there was a poignant reminder of the pressing needs of the people when they were interrupted by the medical officer, Dr Alton, who said: 'There is a man at the gate who says that his wife and daughter are dead outside and that he has no assistance to bury them. They are in coffins and he hopes that you will direct that some of the paupers should dig a grave for them.' The board agreed and resumed their discussion.[43]

At a board of guardians' meeting in March, Stokes had proposed that in view of widespread opposition to payment of rates, a resolution should be passed urging all ratepayers to support the collectors; unless the rates were collected, he said, the destitute would starve. Some members took objection to this form of 'dictation' to landowners and the modest proposal was defeated by eight votes to six. In March there were 1,330 people in workhouse accommodation and the average weekly cost of each pauper was

2s 4d. The Poor Law Commission gave instructions under seal that no more admissions were to take place until numbers were reduced to fewer than 1,000, stating that their order should be widely promulgated.[44]

Constrasting Lives

The town jail was also a concern. It had accommodation for between 120 and 140 prisoners but there were 361 incarcerated, with four prisoners in every cell and sixteen in the larger ones. Of that number, 205 were awaiting trial and twenty-six were lunatics. Dysentery and fever were said to be raging in the prison despite regular whitewashing and ventilation.[45] Dr Francis Crumpe, the prison doctor, wanted timber sheds to be built to provide extra accommodation but the money was not available.[46] Crumpe later described the prison conditions of 1847 in graphic terms:

> Circumstanced as our gaol is, built on a flat from which there is no fall, and the hospital small and ill-ventilated, the sewers and necessaries become quickly choked up. The crowds of poor, starved wretches, hurried in droves to gaol for some petty thefts generally perpetrated for the purpose of being committed to gaol to be saved from death by starvation, were quickly taken off by death from disease. These also quickly fell victim to fever and from them it spread among the healthy classes in the gaol, who heretofore enjoyed good health and never suffered from starvation. The hospital soon became overcrowded though my call for more accommodation was urgent long before it was attended to.
>
> In this horrid den those labouring under local disease, those ill from fever, those dying, and the dead from fever and dysentery, were promiscuously stretched together. So insufferable was the atmosphere of the place, so morbidly fetid and laden with noxious miasma, notwithstanding constant fumigation … that on the door being opened I was uniformly seized, on entering, with most violent retching; and it is singular that I should be so affected, who dissected so much, have opened so many bodies, performed so many operations, and see often such forms of loathsome disease; yet the fact is so …

The mortality was enormous, deaths often taking place a few hours after admission; but this occurred in the most exhausted and worn-down subjects. A few cases were seized with vomiting, throwing up large quantities of black stuff from the stomach; some few were jaundiced all over, but generally speaking the form was mild, commencing with chills and wearisomeness, followed by heat of surface, slight headache, quick pulse, white tongue and loathing of food. By confinement to bed and simple drinks, these symptoms subsided in a very few days, sometimes from three to five, often without any medicine, being succeeded by a ravenous appetite which it was most difficult to regulate and control. Relapses and re-relapses were most frequent, diarrhoea generally setting in which no treatment could check. Had these cases occurred among previously healthy well-fed subjects, in private life when proper ventilation could be preserved and airy apartments procured, recoveries would be more frequent. Many of the gaol guards were attacked; none of these died in gaol, they were well-fed and had better apartments. In the female department cases of fever and dysentery were comparatively few, more cleanliness of person being enforced among them and they were not so crowded together.

So foul was the atmosphere, so cadaverous was the smell that I could not make post-mortem examinations, nor was there any accommodation to do so, though the bodies were numerous and often no claimants for them. From one post-mortem which I saw in the military barrack and from the symptoms and appearances – slight minute ulcers on the mucous coat of intestines – I am convinced that the same appearance would be found in all these fatal cases where diarrhoea succeeded fever. Strong, healthy, robust persons with local disease who would insist on going to hospital *contrary to all advice* were quickly attacked by the same fever which their fellow patients had and soon fell victims. I do not know of any circumstance which is a stronger proof of the contagiousness of the disease than the nurse-tenders being attacked.[47]

Crumpe, who was a gifted, pioneering surgeon, wrote to Lord John Russell in March 1847 predicting that the population loss from famine and emigration would ultimately be two million, the number now generally accepted. He advised Russell not to introduce gratuitous relief through the food kitchens on the grounds that it would encourage a return to early marriages and therefore an increase in population. The letter, with which the *Post* fully concurred, read in part:

> My Lord,
>
> A vast diminution of the pop. of Ireland has already taken place, but erroneously calculated at 250,000. This does not include the vast number interred without clerical ceremony at night, and without coffins. The prevalence of disease, dysentery, and fever is now more rife than ever – in fact we are only at the beginning of the end – and mortality unfortunately is every day on the increase. The tide of emigration has already set in and from the vast number emigrating and preparing to emigrate from this country, which may be taken as a sample of the impulse which is now stimulating the peasantry of Ireland, it may well be calculated that a diminution of the population from both causes, death and emigration, will take place before the summer sun attain[s] its highest meridian, exceeding TWENTY HUNDRED THOUSAND SOULS.
>
> Now, my Lord, if your intended provision for indiscriminate out-door relief in Ireland takes place, without some restriction, the result will be not only the annihilation of landed proprietors, of farmers, of all classes, in fact the wretched poor themselves, by encouraging those hasty and indiscriminate marriages to which the Irish are so addicted, so that the diminished population will soon be increased more than ever, and entail perpetual misery on this devoted land.[48]

As March turned into April, the *Examiner* reported that weekly deaths in the town averaged thirty; the situation was truly dire. A whole family of five or six died when they all fell ill at the same time and were unable to help each other. A woman's body lay on the street covered by a cloth and a woman and child begged beside the corpse. A woman with a baby crawled under an arch in Denny Street and they were rescued by a curate, Fr Enright, who found them lodgings. The bodies of two brothers went five days without burial and were eventually taken to the graveyard without coffins.[49] In Boherbee, a father lost three children in one day, after another had died some days earlier.[50] The jail and the workhouse were centres of pestilence and fever, and beggars thronged the streets. 'Familiarity with such sights as these is producing in many minds a horrid apathy towards human suffering,' reported the *Examiner*.[51] 'Scenes of deep misery are of daily occurrence around us,' wrote the *Post*, 'death of almost whole families and coffinless burials.'[52]

The *Post* continued to remark on the number of beggars (some of whom the paper saw as opportunists) in the town: 'Dead and dying are seen hawking about on every corner; mendicancy of every class – the deceiver and the starving jumbled together in undistinguishable confusion – besets every decently dressed person.'[53]

The condition of the graveyards gave rise to concern and Dr Alton told the board of guardians that Rathass graveyard was not very far from the workhouse and that there was danger of contamination from it, as 'effluvia of the graveyard in a prevailing wind will be wafted over the workhouse'. In Clogherbrien graveyard, cows and horses were feeding, and 'the bowels of an infant actually protruding, not only presenting an object offensive to the view and harrowing to the feelings, but offensive to the organs of smell'.[54] The outcome of this discussion was the employment of gravediggers at the graveyards of Rathass, Clogherbrien and Annagh; these were referred to as 'a kind of graveyard police' and they were paid eight pence a day to ensure that graves were dug deeper.[55] Relief committees were given the power to provide coffins out of rates and the *Post* was hopeful that people 'would be spared henceforth those heart-sickening scenes of daily occurrence in rural graveyards of this and an adjoining county – to hear of no more uncoffined dead nor of human bodies any longer torn and fed upon by dogs and pigs'.[56] It was observed that it was not uncommon in homes near graveyards for a dog to come into the house with a human limb in its mouth.[57]

Describing his visit to Rathass graveyard as 'a duty he would not willingly undertake again', Dr Alton said: 'It is most revolting to see the body of a child, rather grown, dragged quite out of the coffin and lying on the yard totally uncovered, with one leg and one thigh taken off and devoured by dogs which nightly prowl about this yard.' Alton also said that mourners attending funerals (few as they were) were in danger of contracting disease and that with the approaching summer, there was 'a positive danger of plague'.[58]

The problem was not so much shallow graves but a shortage of space, with recently buried bodies being taken up and left uncovered when a new burial took place. Rev. A. B. Rowan was alarmed at the burial of bodies without coffins in Kilgobbin and feared that 'plague and pestilence' would follow famine if the practice continued.[59] Every graveyard in the county was described as overflowing.[60]

Lord Robert Clinton, son of the Duke of Newcastle, offered his services to the British Association for the Relief of Extreme Distress in Ireland and Scotland (hereafter British Relief Association) on a voluntary basis and was assigned to Counties Galway, Limerick, Clare and Kerry in early 1847. The association was set up on 1 January 1847 in London by a group of wealthy bankers, including the philanthropist Baron Lionel de Rothschild. Its agent in Ireland was Count Paul Strzelecki, originally from Poland, but who became a naturalised English citizen in 1845. Strzelecki was an explorer and scientist who had spent many years in Australia. He offered his services to the association without payment and he is regarded as a great humanitarian and a heroic figure of the Famine. He particularly wanted the funds to be used to help children, and took pride in the fact that the association could feed one child for one-third of a penny per day.

The work of the association was originally mainly focused in Donegal, Sligo and Mayo, but it was later extended to a wider area and had a very direct and measurable effect wherever it was in operation. In Abbeydorney, for example, sixty-six families received support from its funds.[61] The association was entirely philanthropic with no element of proselytism or attempts at conversion associated with it, but because it availed of government officials and channels it was associated with the government.

Clinton took over the large stores of the former distillery owned by John F. Eagar at Ballymullen as a food storage centre: similar stores were established at Milltown and at Tarbert, where Clinton was based.[62] One of Clinton's reports corroborates the shocking details given above about the condition of Tralee's graveyards. Writing from Galway on 17 March 1847, he noted that he had not seen any destitution there equal to that of Schull or Skibbereen, continuing:

> At Tralee, they are however in a wretched state; their deaths were twenty-seven last week in the poorhouse, and as many or even double that in the town. I have never been about that town without meeting a funeral or funerals at any hour. At a churchyard or old burial ground two miles from the town the scene is more like a collection of stones to be taken up for macadamising than a decent cemetery. When I passed it on the morning of the 9th I saw two coffins lying anyhow on the open ground; and upon inquiring I heard that they had been dug up because there was not room enough for present emergencies and that the old bones would be taken out and the fresh corpse would take their place until its room should be wanted.[63]

It is likely that Clinton was referring to Clogherbrien graveyard.

A visitor was shocked at the scenes he encountered in Tralee in May 1847 and recorded that 'a country gentleman in Tralee remarked to me that the distress was so great that it was quite beyond their means of relief and they were now so accustomed to seeing people around them perish from starvation that they did not mind [i.e. notice] it at all.' He witnessed a disturbing scene, apparently from his hotel room:

> While I write this note there is a child about five years old lying dead on the main street of Tralee opposite the windows of the principal hotel, and the remains have lain there several hours on a few stones by the side of a footway like a dead dog, no one seeming to think it anything uncommon and this in a Christian country and on the estate of a rich, unencumbered landlord who

> draws about £12,000 a year out of it but whose subscription for the relief of his starving tenants was paltry in the extreme. Nothing but a Poor Law can reach such a man.[64]

The landlord referred to appears to be Sir Edward Denny, who had in fact made substantial contributions to relief. The author signed himself 'C.A.'

In April a man stated that he saw 'an emaciated and famine-stricken group' of five children lying on the flags of Denny Street in Tralee. 'So fearfully had hunger told upon them that they could not move or stand without assistance. Attenuated forms, they presented no appearance of life except an occasional listless movement of the eye.'[65] The children had come from Dingle and had been refused entry to the workhouse because it was full.

Given the widespread death and starvation throughout the country there was a dramatic change in government policy in early 1847. The public works were deemed to have failed, and a new strategy of direct food relief was adopted. The Society of Friends (Quakers) had successfully operated soup kitchens in the west of Ireland to prevent starvation and the government now decided to adopt this method of 'gratuitous relief', as it was termed. The Temporary Relief Act or Soup Kitchen Act was passed by parliament in February 1847. The inefficient and cumbersome public works were to come to an end in stages during March and April, pending the setting up of soup kitchens. But the transition period turned out to be a time of great administrative delay and inefficiency, and in many areas people were laid off the works before the soup kitchens were set up, leaving the most needy facing death by starvation. The *Chronicle* anticipated that the cessation of public works in Kerry would be the equivalent of 'a sentence of wholesale death upon our people' and urged the relief committees to 'bestir themselves' and called on 'landlords and every man interested in the peace – the social salvation of our country – to be at their posts'.[66]

An indignant correspondent, who identified himself only as 'a member of Tralee relief committee', wrote to the *Post*, protesting at the decision to dismiss people on the public works. He accepted that the committee had not been doing its best, that some members were poor attenders and that all the administration fell on a few members, but he believed that even if the committee had been working day and night, it could not meet the deadline for providing the necessary outdoor relief through the soup kitchens in the time allowed. He castigated the bureaucrats responsible for the decision:

> The poor may perish – everyone may suffer from disorder and confusion, but it is right that the public should be informed that the responsibility does not rest with the relief committee but with the persons at a distance who can loll in their well-stuffed official seats and write curt and uncivil letters to urge impossibilities and probably decide the fate of many a starving fellow creature.[67]

He had 'one pert official' in particular in mind, the 'well-paid and insolent Mr Stanley', who was the secretary of the Relief Commission.[68]

A poem entitled 'The Curse of the Whigs' also pointed to the politicians as the source of the problems of Ireland:

> *Go forth to the fields, they are bare and untilled,*
> *Tho' with hunger and sickness the cabins are filled;*
> *The famine is sowing for next year fresh seeds,*
> *See thousands of acres producing but weeds.*
> *And ask ye what cause to such ruin has led –*
> *To a present so fearful – a future so dread?*
> *And the rich man who toils not, the poor man who digs,*
> *Will answer: 'The Curse – the Black Curse of the Whigs'.*[69]

One of the fears of the authorities was that the public works had made people disinclined to cultivate their fields because they had become dependent on government support. In January the newly appointed engineer of the Board of Works in Tralee, Mr Bevan, had warned of the apparent apathy on the part of tenants, and his words revealed the widespread anxiety that they had despaired of tilling their fields in the wake of the crop failure: 'It is a well ascertained fact that east, west and south, the cottier tenantry and small farmers have determined on not cultivating their small holdings during the approaching spring, preferring the prospect of an immediate return for their labour in the public works.' Bevan encouraged landlords to lead the way in providing seed and promoting the cultivation of a greater variety of crops and asked why Kerry should not have fields of beans, carrots and parsnips, just like Wiltshire.[70]

This fear that the land would not be cultivated dominated discussion in Tralee in March. Tralee relief committee issued a public notice, which exhorted all classes to do their duty.[71] It was signed by the secretary of the committee, Colonel John Day Stokes, and would appear to have been written by Rev. A. B. Rowan. The notice gave advice on what practical steps ought to be taken by each social class in the county, and it was an attempt to bolster the morale of each class and to instil a measure of hope for the future. The immediate ending of public works was going to bring a new challenge and it would appear from the notice that apathy, despair and inertia were regarded as the main danger, after the appalling winter.

The specific advice to landowners reminded them of their paramount interest and duty to cultivate the soil and to begin 'a judicious distribution by loan or otherwise of seed or labour or both, as required'. The farmer was told that 'now that spring is advanced, the farmer is bound to God and his fellow creatures to engage in cultivating the soil and in his other ordinary farming engagements'.[72] Labourers were advised to prepare for the end of public works and to seek employment. The clergy were encouraged to use all their influence to impress on the people the need for immediate exertion in tilling and planting and to remind them that the displeasure of God 'would punish indolence or despair just now with aggravated suffering hereafter'. The notice made this appeal to all classes:

> Any apathy now will bring not only its own peculiar punishment in a future season but also leave the people of this country to suffer under the consequences of their own neglect, without that sympathy and assistance

which is now afforded to lighten a mysterious dispensation of Providence, but may justly be withheld from any recklessness or indolence of man.[73]

This public declaration was hailed by the *Examiner* as 'an excellent address' and it was seen as a sign of a determined effort to raise the morale of the people as spring advanced.[74] The *Post*, in an editorial headed 'Seed Time', also endorsed the 'most admirable address'.[75]

An announcement had already been made that 20 per cent of labourers on public works were to be laid off by order of the Treasury, a decision which Tralee relief committee deplored. Their opposition became even more strident in May when the members were incensed at the lack of any response from the Board of Works to their earlier protests at the ending of public works while soup kitchens were not yet in operation. They resolved:

> That the Tralee relief committee in considering the impossibility of completing in this extensive district the necessary arrangements for the distribution of gratuitous relief within the term specified for discontinuing the employment of the labouring poor, hereby repeat their protest against any such proceeding; and feel compelled to disavow all responsibility for any disastrous consequences which may result from a proceeding so peremptory and ill-advised.[76]

In May the committee went ahead and acquired and fitted out three additional stores in the Tralee area for distribution of relief: one in Rock Street, one in Castle Street and one in Blennerville. It also decided to whitewash all houses under £10 valuation in the lanes of Tralee – whitewash was made with lime and was believed to be a kind of disinfectant.[77] There was alarm a few days later, when a rumour spread that 'a large body of the disemployed labourers from the country districts were to congregate in Tralee'. Troops and police were alerted but the only incidents that occurred were that some 'starving wretches' went into bakers' shops and took away enough bread to satisfy 'their present craving hunger'.[78]

In the midst of all the sombre and despairing reports of unprecedented suffering, life went on as normal for some in the upper classes. A charity ball on a grand scale was held and a fine bullock, which had been fed by William Talbot Crosbie of Ardfert, was killed by Mr Benner of the Blennerhassett Arms Hotel for the assizes in early March.[79] In Ballyseedy in June there was an extraordinary celebration when Henry Blennerhassett reached the age of twenty-one. This celebration seems crass and insensitive to modern sensibilities, and is a reminder of how difficult it is for us to understand the prevailing attitudes of Irish society in 1847 and the gulf that existed between social classes. At the east gate of Ballyseedy house a bonfire was prepared with no fewer than 220 large rails of turf:

> Between the bonfire and the venerated entrance was a beautiful arch exhibiting rich festoons of laurel and other evergreens commingled with a rich variety of the choicest flowers from the exquisite parterre surrounding the noble residence. Spanning the festive arch was a silken tablet bearing the Blennerhassett arms and inscribed with various mottoes and devices germane to the occasion. Those who have seen the stately elms and other tall ancestral trees which surround this spot like so many warders may well conceive the Rembrandt picture which this night presented when the blazing bonfire with its numerous tar barrels had flung its full blaze over the leafy coronal above … At the southern gate too was a beautiful arch, rivalling in the tasteful combination of leaf and flower that already described.[80]

The lavish banquet provided for tenants included the meat of six bullocks and thirty-five sheep and ten tons of bread. Drinks included 120 gallons of whiskey and six tierces of porter. (A tierce was approximately forty-two gallons.) As evening closed in, the tenants and tradesmen gathered in front of the house, headed by four men bearing flags with slogans such as 'Long live our landlord' and 'Ballyseedy for ever'. They set out in a procession to Tralee, lighting their torches at the bonfires. 'In the deepening gloom of the night, the glittering of the hundred torches had the most beautiful effect, as they marched through Boherbee and round by the barracks to return by the south gate.' The houses of Boherbee were ornamented with green boughs and arches spanned the streets.[81] This route must have taken the revellers past the workhouse, but there appears to have been scant consideration among them for the deepening gloom of the inmates of that institution.

Similar celebrations were repeated in July when the twenty-first birthday of Rowland Bateman of Oakpark was celebrated.[82] Tenants led by a fife and drum band rode in procession through the town and up to the Rock area of town, where triumphal arches had been erected and houses were festooned with flowers and branches. Dinner tables for 200 guests were laid out in a great tent and the fare provided for this 'right-Irish festivity' was itemised as follows: six sirloins of beef, six saddles of mutton, eight legs of mutton, six rounds of beef, six rumps of beef, six spicy ribs of beef, eight shoulders of mutton, eight bacon hams, ten pies, fifteen puddings, twenty barrels of porter, punch, wine and ale, 'and every variety of viands which the season can afford'. The young master gave a speech in which he promised to live among his tenantry because he believed that the country would never prosper if landlords were absentees. He issued this injunction to absentee landlords: 'I warn them from this place to pause in their suicidal career – to live more amongst their tenantry.' Celebrations continued with a dance, the beautiful airs of the Irish composer Carolan, and the hobby horse making mischief. There was a huge bonfire to light up the night sky and men bearing torches marched in from the surrounding hillsides; a beautiful display of fireworks followed, which, 'as they descended in a luminous shower amid the trees, presented a perfect resemblance to the fireflies of the Tropics'.[83] Rowland Bateman's hopes for the family estate were not realised; the Bateman estate in Oakpark was among the first to be sold under the Encumbered Estates Act.[84]

There were truly two worlds in Kerry as elsewhere in Ireland in 1847, as Woodham-Smith observed: 'The Irish people starved and died in one world, the Irish landowning class inhabited another.'[85] Woodham-Smith stated that most landlords believed that, once they had fulfilled their obligations by providing employment, supporting relief committees and forgiving some portion of the rent, they had done all that could be expected.

Tralee Workhouse

The darkest days of that bleak, black year of 1847 were in the early months. Under the heading 'An hour in the board-room', the *Examiner* reported on the time set aside for interviewing workhouse applicants in Tralee workhouse. The first to come in was a boy who was initially thought to be paralysed, as he had to be supported by two others. In fact, it was exhaustion that had weakened him. Next came a fourteen-year-old boy with a baby in his arms and four other children with him. He broke down as he told the board that their father had died that morning and their mother a week before. 'It was truly heart-rending to look at the destitute orphans. Every member of the board felt it was so. The chairman [John Lynch] said it was better to be dead than alive and witness such scenes.'[86]

Even worse cases came next before the board, and disturbing imagery was used to describe them: 'The appearance of several large families from Castlegregory was truly shocking; it was something inexpressibly worse than the ordinary condition of lank, tottering skeletons – the parents, the children, even including at the mothers' breast had the rank, clammy appearance of exhumed corpses.' The report concluded: 'Taking the applicants altogether, we believe a greater variety and diversity of squalid loathsome misery was never before collected, a greater crowd of gaunt withered skeletons never crawled and tottered over so narrow a stage of life and in so short a period as the board-room during the hour of admission.'[87]

By January 1847 the workhouse in Tralee had 1,060 inmates and many applicants were being rejected: 'It was painful to witness the despairing looks of the wretched creatures as they retired'.[88] Dr Alton was always concerned at the health risks posed by accommodating more than 1,000 people in the workhouse, which was its official capacity. His stance was supported by the Poor Law Commissioners, who wrote to the board of guardians advising the members 'to be earnestly guided by the advice of their medical officer and steadily to refuse, however distressful it may be to their feelings, to admit applicants until the number of inmates is compatible to their health'.[89]

Although Dr Alton continued to insist on a cap of 1,000, Colonel John Day Stokes argued that the building could hold 1,072, probably because of some modifications. He reminded the board that 'deaths from starvation were of daily occurrence outside the workhouse and that starving wretches were now claiming admission to the house'. He put this stark dilemma to the board of guardians: 'There is a chance of disease if more paupers are admitted and positive danger and almost a certainty of starvation if rejected.'[90] His motion to admit 1,072 was accepted, although it ran contrary to the advice of Dr Alton and the commissioners.[91] The commissioners expressed their disapproval of this, but the *Post* said that the guardians had the support of public opinion for their decision.[92] However, a message was sent to parish wardens, particularly those in Corkaguiny, from where seventy-eight paupers had been admitted in one day, that they were to send no more paupers to Tralee, as it would be 'only adding to their misery, as the house being now crowded to excess, further admittance will be impossible'.[93]

The newspapers resorted to ghoulish imagery to convey the horror of the scenes witnessed when paupers came before the board to seek admission: 'Our imagination could not have conjured up anything so wretched, so spiritless, so woebegone as the groups of ragged, pale and emaciated beings who tottered into that board-room. Had they lain in the grave and been galvanised into mimic life their appearance could not have been more appalling. Alas for our people, where will all this end?'[94] Dead bodies were being stored in every corner of the workhouse and the police were called in to clear away a group of squatters who had taken over the workhouse yard after being refused admission; they were forced to eke out a living on the open roads and in the streets of the town.[95]

Inmates of the workhouse were required to work. For example forty girls under fifteen years of age were employed at plain needlework for three hours daily; twelve of these did 'fancy work'. Some were employed scouring and cleaning. Boys were instructed in tailoring for four hours daily and in baking for one hour daily.⁹⁶ They also worked on the land near the workhouse. Occasionally inmates of good standing who found work as servants were allowed to leave the workhouse in their workhouse clothes, but this was always noted as a departure from the regulations and a special favour.

Disciplinary issues and sanctions are frequently documented in workhouse records; the punishment applied in Tralee workhouse was usually confinement in a special room called the refractory ward. There are no records of physical punishments; instead the ultimate sanction was to be discharged from the house. One woman who was eventually discharged was Jane Linehan, whose name came up frequently in the records, such as in February 1845 when she was disciplined for 'making a noise in the dining hall and for being refractory'.⁹⁷ On 14 June 1846 Jane received twelve hours of confinement for refusing to work and for being abusive to the matron; on 15 June she received the same punishment for refusing to work and cursing the assistant matron. At the board meeting the next day, it was resolved that:

> … considering how many times Jane Linehan, a pauper, has been punished for refractory conduct in this house and the utter hopelessness of reforming her and considering her an able-bodied pauper capable of obtaining work outside this institution and so supporting herself, the board in justice to other paupers and for the due discipline of the house, feel it incumbent to direct that she be immediately discharged.⁹⁸

Other women discharged were Mary Mulchinock, Julia Bailey and Bess Breen for stealing soap, along with Catherine Crowley and Deborah Higgins for stealing shirts.⁹⁹ Two men who went to Tralee town on a pass and returned intoxicated were placed in confinement for twelve hours. When a pauper named Charles McCarthy was confined for refusing to obey an instruction, two others, John Brien and Michael Grogan, 'violently rescued him'. 'The board, thinking it necessary to preserve the due subordination of the paupers to the officers placed over them, and all discipline in the institution, felt it their duty to direct that the said Michael Grogan, as more culpable than the others, be discharged forthwith.' As in the case of Jane Linehan, it was explained that Grogan was able-bodied and so deemed to be able to survive outside the workhouse.[100] It is noteworthy that the board chose to justify and explain the decision to discharge individuals; it seems to be an indication that they felt a sense of accountability for their decisions.

Desertion of children became such a common occurrence that the board asked for a list of parents who had departed from the workhouse leaving their children behind, with a view to prosecutions being taken.

The following offences are recorded in the manuscript sources, with the number of hours in confinement as punishment in parentheses:[101]

Myles Sullivan – exciting the paupers to insubordination (12)
John Moriarty – refusing to work (12)
John Sayers – boxing with a fellow pauper (12)
John Tangney – going into town without a permit (12)
Richard Morris – refusing to obey schoolmistress (8)
Mary McCarthy – going into hospital and telling two children that their parents were sent to the fever hospital, at the fright of which one of the children died (12)
Mary Lynch – going into hospital without business (8)
Cornelius Connor – stealing a loaf of bread while it was being conveyed to the sewing room (8)
Peggy Touhy – returning drunk from a pass (8)
Joan Brosnan – violent language to a fellow pauper (4)

Other disciplinary actions include the confinement of Mary Griffin for eight hours for beating another pauper: she was later discharged for throwing food at a fellow pauper. Arthur O'Leary and Thomas Behane received nine hours confinement for 'viciously breaking twelve panes of glass in the workshop'.[102] Three men scaled the wall of the women's quarters and were charged with desertion of their families. A man who was found with bread obtained from his wife, who was in the workhouse, was prosecuted, and his wife and family were discharged from the house.[103] Other offences and hours in confinement were: abusive language to schoolmistress (8), making away with workhouse clothing (8), playing ball in the dining hall (8), striking a fellow pauper (8), refusing to pump water (12), going to the hospital without leave (6), throwing milk in a fellow pauper's face (12), pulling up turnips and bringing into the house to boil (8), concealing a dish of stirabout that was the breakfast of another pauper (6), bringing chips of timber for firing into the sick ward (6), going into the kitchen to smoke (6), a male pauper going into the female yard without leave (6), and striking and abusing the master (12).

However, health issues presented much more serious problems than indiscipline in the workhouse at this time. An 'intractable form of diarrhoea', with symptoms similar to dysentery, prevailed in January 1847.[104] Dr Alton advised thorough ventilation and later recommended that perforated zinc panels be used instead of glass in the windows. He also advised that four paupers should be employed 'daily and continuously' on whitewashing the whole building with lime.[105] Dr Alton's warnings that increased numbers would lead to higher mortality rates in the workhouse were borne out in the early months of 1847. He explained that overcrowding 'must engender and keep up disease of a contagious nature and cause diseases in themselves non-infectious to assume that character. An overcrowded state of the house, independent of generating impure and noxious air, leads also to a want of personal cleanliness and order so necessary to preserve the health of a number of individuals congregated together.'[106]

Weekly deaths in the workhouse were listed until early 1847, with full names and causes of death given. The National Library of Ireland (NLI) manuscript copy of the board of guardians' minute book, which begins on 26 October 1846, records the following numbers of weekly deaths in Tralee workhouse from 10 November 1846:

10 November: 3 deaths
17 November: 9 deaths
24 November: 7 deaths

1 December: 7 deaths
8 December: 13 deaths
15 December: 15 deaths
22 December: 13 deaths
29 December: 25 deaths
5 January: 20 deaths[107]

In the week leading up to Tuesday 12 January 1847 the number of deaths recorded was eighteen. Those who died were:

Daniel Howard, child – diarrhoea
John Thomas, infant – measles
James Hynes, young child – diarrhoea
Mary McCarthy, young girl – diarrhoea
Patrick Enright, adult – consumption of lungs
Thomas Leahy, aged man – dysentery
Patrick Bailey, child – measles
Mary Sullivan, adult – consumption
Patrick Flynn, infant – measles
William McGuire, infant – effects of variola
James Currane, aged pauper – dysentery
Jeremiah Moran, infant – rubeola
Biddy Hanafin, girl – gangrene in both feet, sequelae of measles, general debility
Biddy Carroll, infant – measles
John Mahony, adult – dysentery
William Barden, infant – sequelae of measles
Patrick Griffin, aged pauper – diarrhoea
Denis Shea, consumptive blind man – self-inflicted wounds

The medical officer added more details of Denis Shea's death: he 'attempted self-destruction by inflicting two external wounds nearly dividing the windpipe quite across … From the effects of these wounds as well as general decline he died on the 9th.'[108] Denis Shea (or O'Shea) was a tailor aged about sixty, and his shocking death by suicide caused the Poor Law Commissioners to ask for a report to be sent to them. Perhaps it was the circumstances of his death which caused the commissioners to inform the board of guardians that it was 'not necessary to insert in the minutes the names of the paupers who died in the house'.[109] This advice may have been issued in order to prevent any future press reports on the circumstances of deaths in the workhouse, Shea's death having been reported in *The Cork Examiner* on 15 January. This message from the Poor Law Commissioners marks a significant turning point in workhouse records; no longer were individual deaths in Tralee workhouse recorded by name and circumstance. Instead, only the total number of deaths for the week was recorded. It can truly be said that from mid-January 1847 onwards the workhouse dead were no longer individuals but statistics.

The Economics of the Workhouse

The workhouse was a major institution in Tralee and it played an important part in the town's economy, as it was supplied by a large number of local businesses. These businesses benefitted greatly from orders for supplies, although there were acute difficulties with receiving payment at times. Moreover, there were many positions of employment on the staff of the workhouse.

However, efficient management was hampered by the poor attendance of guardians at meetings, by inefficient and inadequate staff, by the ever-rising numbers applying for entry to the workhouse and by the lack of funds. In 1846 William Chute withdrew from a contract to supply milk, saying he was frightened by the sharp increase of numbers in the workhouse. The board considered this 'a violation of good faith' and believed Chute was 'acting collusively with another' in order to obtain a higher price.[110] They were better disposed to Mr Latchford, however, when he applied for compensation for his losses because of a contract he made in May for the supply of oatmeal, which had soared in price between May and October. The board accepted his argument and awarded Latchford £30 in compensation for his loss, although they were obliged to explain their decision to the Poor Law Commissioners.[111]

The minutes of the board of guardians contain regular estimates of the cost of maintaining an individual pauper for a week; this varied from 1s 6d in September 1846 to 2s 6d in January 1847 and 1s 8d in September 1847. These estimates appear regularly in the minutes and the amount was seen as a measure of the efficiency of the management of the house – the objective was to keep the cost as low as possible. The master's list of requirements for one week was as follows: 4,400 pounds of bread, 60 pounds of meat, 2 cwt of salt, 14 pounds of barley, 1,400 quarts of milk, 1 pound of arrowroot, 4 tons of coal, 1 stone of 'dipt' (dipped?) candles, 4 pounds of mould candles, 12 stones of soap. The following were also ordered to be procured: 150 yards of grey frieze, 150 yards of moleskin, 250 yards of linen for shirting, 6 gross (i.e. 864) horn studs, 50 girls' handkerchiefs, 3 pieces of linsey woolsey, 100 yards of white twilled calico, 1 large tin vessel for conveying milk, 6 razors, 6 spades, 6 shovels, 6 pickaxes and 1 chisel. Workhouse officers required 2 small tin kettles, 2 ewers and basins, and 3 knives and forks.[112]

At the beginning of June 1847, the master ordered these supplies: 2,600 pounds of bread, 180 pounds of meat, 5,400 quarts of milk, 2 cwt of salt, 3 pounds of tea, 1½ stones of sugar, 7 pounds of loaf sugar, 1 stone of barley, 2 pounds of arrowroot, 12 bottles of porter, 7 pounds of dipt. candles, 2 pounds of mould candles, 1 ton of coal and 12 stones of soap.[113] Supplies ordered on 1 December 1847 were: 150 worsted shawls, 1,500 yards of linsey woolsey, 1,100 yards of twilled calico, 500 handkerchiefs, 1,500 yards of corduroy, 1,500 yards of sheeting, 350 yards of check, 250 yards of frieze, 350 yards of tweed for vests, 500 pairs of blankets, 300 pairs of men's shoes, 300 pairs of women's shoes.[114]

Among the workhouse suppliers were the following businesses:

John Hanrahan (clothing and bedding materials)
John Lumsden and Co. (cloth and bedding materials)
Cornelius Murphy (shoes)

Thomas Barton (milk)
John Latchford (meal and flour)
Timothy Devane (straw)
John Lee (turf)
William Huggard (baker)
T. McCowen (solder for water pipes)
T. McMahon (horse hire and barrels of lime)
Michael Isten (conveyance of paupers)
P. R. L. Byrne (printing)
Thomas Payne (building)
D. Falvey (tables)
Thomas Donohue and Co. (Indian meal)[115]

One important supplier was Edmond Stack, who provided bread for the workhouse. By early March 1847 he was owed £835 and he wrote that he could no longer supply the workhouse and would have to direct his solicitors to take action to recover what was due to him.[116] A month later, *The Cork Examiner* reported that Stack was owed £1,000 and a Mr Hanrahan was owed £500 for clothing. Stack demanded immediate payment, but Hanrahan did not press his case, recognising the financial difficulties of the board.[117] In response to this, the Poor Law Commissioners approved the proposal by a number of guardians to give personal guarantees to the manager of the Provincial Bank, Mr P. Stewart, in respect of a loan of £2,000.

One method of saving money was for the workhouse to employ an inmate as its own baker, one William Huggard, who was given extra daily rations of half an ounce of tea and three ounces of sugar.[118] Huggard's bread was sampled by the board and declared to be 'far superior to the bread now furnished by the contractor', yet a later decision provided for better quality bread to be given to workhouse staff.[119]

In March the board appealed for a loan of £3,000 from the government in order to survive, stating that if this was not received, either an assistant commissioner would have to take over the management of the workhouse or else it would have to be closed.[120] The board then had debts of £4,237. A rate had been struck in February and again in March, which theoretically could have brought in £8,803, but in reality landowners were not paying their rates. The support which was finally given by the government was a weekly sum of £130, enough to tide the board over from week to week, but still an amount which caused 'painful regret' to the guardians. They stated that they believed that it would be impossible to keep the house open and that 'this is a position into which it is unwise to coerce them, as not only have they been day after day pressing the collectors to the most energetic and rigorous measures for the collection of the rate, but have sought even on their own personal credit to obtain, however and wherever they might, a sum of money to enable them to maintain the house and to afford the relief now more than ever necessary'. They went on to say that it might be necessary for the guardians to leave the house to the management of the commissioners.[121]

In June 1847 Edmond Stack was still owed £553 and was threatening immediate proceedings. He was given a cheque for £300 but was asked not to cash it for three months. Members of the board were acutely aware that suppliers to the workhouse were in extreme financial distress themselves: they informed the commissioners that 'the guardians do not exaggerate the case when they state that they will be actually driven, against their will, from the performance of their proper duty at the board by the pain, day after day of having to refuse the importunate demands of creditors of the board, some of whom they know to be almost on the verge of bankruptcy'.[122] Some suppliers angrily pointed out the anomaly that they were required to pay rates to the union, while the union owed them large sums of money.[123]

In May a printed appeal from the board to the government inspector, Captain Labalmondière, was included in the minutes. The board wished to inform him of the actual state of the funds of the union:

> The Union is deeply in debt and this house is only kept open by weekly advances from the Poor Law Commission. Under these circumstances the board of guardians beg leave to impress upon the attention of the government the

very great difficulties in which this Union is placed and how extremely onerous the collection of rates will become. In addition the board thinks it necessary to draw attention to the state of the electoral division of Tralee. The town of Tralee in which the workhouse is situated is so encumbered by paupers who have continued flocking into the town in the past and present seasons, and who have become entitled to relief permanently, that the mass of pauperism already existing is thereby so swelled that the rates are now becoming excessive.[124]

The letter went on to specify Dingle and Corkaguiny, as well as the electoral divisions of Brosna, Castleisland and Ballymacelligott, as 'notoriously in a very distressed state'.

One important economic issue arose in the autumn of 1847, leading to a course of action that is deeply shocking to modern sensibilities. There was deep antipathy among the authorities at all levels to the prospect of the able-bodied destitute being provided with outdoor relief, as it was believed that this would encourage idleness and dependency. A circular to boards of guardians stated that 'the evil which is to be most guarded against is the necessity of granting outdoor relief to able-bodied men'.[125] In order to prevent this, such men were instead to be offered places in the workhouse, as a way of testing their destitution; to be eligible for entry to the workhouse one had to have neither property nor possessions. This was 'the workhouse test' and if they refused a place in the workhouse, it was proof that they were not truly destitute. Extra workhouse accommodation was to be acquired but, where this was not feasible, extra places within the workhouse were to be made by clearing out the infirm, widows and the elderly, who would then be provided with outdoor relief.

This policy 'of forcibly emptying of the workhouses of certain categories of inmates' caused enormous problems.[126] Those poor people had to be destitute in the first place to be in the workhouse and so had no land, no possessions and no homes to go to, and outdoor relief provided none of these necessities, only food. Woodham-Smith described Tralee Union as 'the immense distressed union' where 'the workhouse inmates had no clothes to put on, no shelter to which to return, for landlords customarily took advantage of destitute persons being forced to enter the workhouse to pull their cabins down'.[127] When there was a proposal to give departing inmates a money allowance, Tralee Union could not even afford a halfpenny a day for adults or a farthing (a quarter of a penny) a day for children, such was the state of its finances.

There was a further problem with this policy: when the helpless and infirm were turned out of the workhouse, they would then use part of their food allowance in exchange for lodgings, and the result was that 'the cabins became crowded with ill-fed, ill-clothed, and sickly people and epidemic disease found victims prepared for its attack'.[128]

Another strategy for creating room in the workhouses was also adopted: women who claimed to be deserted wives (but may not have been) could be expelled along with their children, unless they gave evidence against their husbands. Ó Murchadha refers to these policies as 'stratagems' which 'reek of bureaucratic cynicism'. Even the very classification of 'able-bodied' was cynically defined to include people who were 'absolutely destitute, famished, barely clad ghosts'.[129]

A major financial overhead for the union was the workhouse staff. There were frequent changes of staff, and there were six different masters in the main workhouse during the Famine period. When the school master, John Hurly, indicated in August 1846 that he wished to resign, he was offered an increase in salary to £25 per annum. The nurse tender, Anne Neill, was regarded as very efficient and when she applied for an increase, her salary was raised from £10 to £15 per annum. An assistant nurse tender was appointed at a salary of £10 per annum.[130] In July 1846 the porter, Cornelius Leyne, resigned after a series of accusations against him: he had borrowed money without returning it, and he had taken coats, trousers and shoes from inmates and pawned them. Fifty handbills were printed and posted around the town announcing the vacancy for a porter.[131] Ten men applied and Thomas Walsh was appointed.[132]

The following quarter-salaries were paid to officers of Tralee Union in mid-1847:[133]

THE GREAT FAMINE

Clerk	£15. 0. 0.
Master	£15. 0. 0.
Assistant Master	£6. 5. 0.
Matron	£7. 10. 0.
Assistant Matron	£1. 10. 0
Medical Officer	£12. 10. 0.
Apothecary	£6. 5. 0.
Roman Catholic Chaplain	£10. 0. 0.
Protestant Chaplain	£7. 10. 0.
Schoolmaster	£6. 5. 0.
Schoolmistress	£3. 5. 0.
Nurse tender	£3. 15. 0.
Assistant Nurse Tender	£2. 7. 0.
Porter	£2. 10. 0.
Revisor	£15. 0. 0.

In May 1847 Michael Condran, the assistant master of the workhouse, wrote to the board with a series of accusations against the master. He was what is now termed a whistle-blower. He began by stating that several paupers had come to him with 'gross cases of peculation and fraud … sanctioned and connived at by the master of the workhouse'.[134] He cited the following practices of the master: removal of large quantities of meat from the workhouse to his father's house; allowing numbers of platters of stirabout to be conveyed out in the wash taken from the boilers; paring the loaves of bread sent in by the contractor, alleging that they were overweight, and distributing the parings to 'a junior class of paupers' as their midday meal; withholding from pauper children aged two to six one naggin of the three naggins of milk allowed to them; retaining a pauper on the books although he had given him a pass to be outside; and regularly entrusting a key of the serving room to a young pauper and allowing him to distribute the food, contrary to regulations.[135]

It seems that the board members did not object to these practices, many of which may have saved money. Perhaps the master was able to justify his

'A CHILL FEELING OF DESPAIR'

actions in the light of the fact that a substantial saving had been achieved in the cost of providing for each pauper. The guardians' response was to state that the master 'stands high in our estimation as a man of integrity'. However, they also accepted that Condran 'had done nothing more than his duty' in making a formal complaint, so both men remained in their positions.[136]

Some staff misdemeanours were also recorded in the minutes. When the nurse tender returned from town at 10 p.m. one evening and found the doors locked, she verbally abused the master. She resigned soon afterwards. On another occasion, the schoolmistress was reprimanded for having her daughter sleeping with her in the house.[137]

All of these financial and administrative matters dominated discussion at the weekly meetings of the Tralee board of guardians.

Listowel and Surrounding Area

In Listowel in January there were three or four funerals every day. The death rate was regarded as higher than during the cholera epidemic of 1832–3, but according to the *Post* the difference was that whereas that epidemic 'slew its victims indiscriminately, the WHIG PESTILENCE is consigning the poor only to their last resting place'.[138] A government inspector, Commander Stuart, reported on 20 February that the Listowel relief committee 'is working with the government but exceedingly given to political discussions'. Stuart urged the necessity for soup depots to be established, as there were none in an area that had 6,000 inhabitants. Stuart's general impression of the county is interesting: 'Kerry generally consists of brown reclaimable bogland and blue mountains. If the people were set about draining, I may say with truth, it would feed twenty times its present inhabitants.'[139]

In April four people were found dead on the roadside and Fr Mahony attended a woman named Daly, who lay 'stretched in fever on a wisp of straw in a dyke' with her twenty-four-year-old daughter lying dead beside her. Fr O'Connor attended a family named Pelican 'though none would approach this hovel of pestilence and death', and he also blessed a woman who died on a Listowel street, bringing him into close contact with 'putrid fever'.[140]

The *Examiner* commented: 'If the Almighty God does not interfere, our unhappy country will be a grave, its people dead and no priest to intone a nation's requiem. Thus are our poor clergy doomed to take on themselves all the burden, all the solicitude and encounter all the dangers of contact with plague.'[141]

There was 'great popular dissatisfaction' in Listowel at the ending of public works.[142] The state of the town was described as follows: 'Fever-smitten paupers are thronging into that town, in the streets of which, on the roads and in the fields surrounding it, they are to be seen stretched under the canopy of heaven.'[143] The precarious position of officials was apparent in a brief report on the death of Edward Stokes, who was paymaster of the Board of Works; his conscientious work 'saved many a famishing wretch from the horrors of starvation', but he fell victim to fever in the course of his duties near Listowel.[144]

At the spring assizes in Ballybunion, two men were convicted of taking breadstuffs from the ship *Skylark*, which had been wrecked on the strand in November 1846. They faced the statutory sentence of either three years in jail or fifteen years' transportation.[145]

In mid-January H. N. Greenwell was somewhat optimistic about the general situation in north Kerry and wrote:

> Nearly all the labourers are now working by task-work and earning from 1s to 1s 6d *per diem*, they are consequently contented and better satisfied than heretofore and would continue tranquil and obedient if constant work were provided. Farm operations are still suspended but if my informants be correct, there is a determination on the part of the respectable farmers to commence field work very shortly, in fact before the usual time. There is a considerable quantity of corn still remaining in the country.[146]

Greenwell's final remark about the amount of corn in the area points to one of the great issues of debate with regard to the unprecedented events of 1847: the export of corn throughout this time of greatest starvation and hardship. His optimism about the situation was not to last, and he became acutely aware of mismanagement and corrupt practices in the system of public works. On 23 January he complained about the administration of the public works in the Abbeydorney area, saying that it was 'without system and with irregularity' and that attempts to induce people to follow the rules and regulations were 'quite unavailing'.[147] Greenwell reported as follows on the barony of Clanmaurice:

> It is almost impossible to come to any arrangement with some of the committees in Clanmaurice, nearly all the members being farmers, or persons having but a slight concern about the immense sums being now expended, and desirous of providing in any way for their own or their friends' support, quite regardless of the claims of those really destitute.
>
> The gentry are very few in number and with one or two exceptions, quiet, indolent persons, unwilling to act in any way likely to draw down on themselves the ill-will of the people.
>
> It is not to be expected that any great assistance will be given by relief committees towards scrutinising the lists and otherwise decreasing the numbers of labourers now employed on public works. As the members generally are too much wanting in moral courage to stand firm against the entreaties and threats of an excited people and many also are so ignorant as but slightly to understand the great importance of weaning the people from their present unprofitable and demoralising work.[148]

On 6 February 1847 Greenwell stated that distress was on the increase in spite of the large sums being expended on relief; dysentery and fever were becoming more virulent and although 'in this part of Kerry no well-authenticated death has as yet been published', the lack of food had weakened the destitute and left them more vulnerable to diseases. In reality, despite Greenwell's claim, people had already died of starvation and disease. He continued to be critical of the relief committees of Clanmaurice (with the exception of that in Listowel itself), saying that they were composed of 'very objectionable persons' and that it was very difficult to obtain relief lists from them and to ensure that relief reached the most destitute. Clearly, officials such as Greenwell were under pressure from superiors to keep the lists of those in need of relief as short as possible:

> A most common practice is, on a requisition being made, to fill in the sheets with a number of persons in comparatively comfortable circumstances, and then on forwarding the sheets to represent, and frequently with truth, that a number of really destitute have been omitted, and hoping by that means to get work for all.
>
> Two or three Committees have also refused to fill in the forms as required, not possessing the courage to make a selection, alleging as an excuse that the general destitution was so great, that it was impossible to make any distinction. The consequence has been that several poor persons have been struck off when we were reducing the number to that required by the engineer.[149]

On 6 March 1847 Greenwell gave a very critical report on Ballybunion and the irregularities he found there:

> This district is in a most neglected and unfortunate condition; the chairman of the Committee, Geo. Gun rarely resides at B.Bunion [sic] and during his absence a temporary chairman is elected; their books have never been complete, the Govt. instructions are not attended to and farmers even now make up the lists of labourers putting on their own friends and leaving out the destitute; one farmer, David Costello, a member of the committee, made a collection on the road five weeks ago from the starving labourers to purchase a horse for Mr Scollard the R.C. coadjutor [curate] and now sends in lists of substitutions to be made signed by that gentleman and the P.P., Mr Walsh, which after enquiry I find, if acted on, would have thrown the destitute out of employment and given work to persons comparatively better off.
>
> I cannot place entire confidence in any statement that I receive from them as their meetings are one day held in B.Bunion and another in Gunsbro

[Gunsborough] and without the presence of secretary or chairman, but signed by persons self-elected to fill those situations.

It is absolutely necessary that a change be made as quickly as possible, as the existence of the present committee is prejudicial to the interests of the poor and subversive of their confidence in the Govt. Having had experience of their conduct, I would most strongly recommend that all farmers be excluded from the committee to be newly formed, and also that Jer. Scollard, their present secretary, and the Revd J. Scollard R.C.C. be excluded, both being exceedingly violent men and who, having already impeded, would, I am confident, impede the other members in the execution of this duty and give anything but a cordial assistance to the exertions of the Govt.[150]

In further comments Greenwell spoke about the growing outrage throughout the countryside:

Insubordination is becoming more general; parties from Ballylongford and Ballybunion having entered Listowel during the past week, and although prevented from committing violence to persons and property, displaying a spirit and determination rarely witnessed in the inhabitants of this area, near the causeway; also the labourers and the populace have become rebellious and discontented, having on one occasion driven the steward appointed by the engineers off the road, and put another man, by their own election, in his place.

The position of the engineer is difficult and dangerous, there are no resident gentry, no police, the people have no confidence in the members of the Committee, with the exception of the parish priest, Mr Eugene McCarthy, whose authority is uncontrolled, and whose exertions are all directed to the cramming of labourers on the roads, irrespective of the advantages to be derived thereby. The relief committees in Clanmaurice are without exception inefficient and sufficient proof has already been given that in the statements of several no confidence or reliance ought to be placed.[151]

Notwithstanding these criticisms and concerns, in early March H. N. Greenwell expressed some optimism about Listowel Union, writing that the public works were proceeding with 'regularity and order ... and destitution is not so general'. The poor, he wrote, 'took advantage of the fine weather to set a few cabbage plants'.[152]

Tarbert and Ballylongford

Commander Stuart, the government inspector, described the Tarbert relief committee as 'the best managed I have seen throughout Kerry', but also noted that 'at present they are greatly embarrassed by 600 men being discharged from the public works'.[153] There were only two small soup depots serving an area of 18,000 people around Tarbert. Stephen Sandes was chairman and Thomas O'Connor secretary of the soup committee. The latter wrote to the Relief Commission on 23 February:

> I am directed by the Ballylongford soup committee to again solicit your attention to sad condition of this parish and to state that the soup fund in aid of which His Excellency the Lord Lieutenant was pleased to give a donation of £86 is totally insufficient to arrest the progress of famine and that deaths are daily increasing.
>
> This committee having felt the importance of maintaining their funds were for some time past selling soup at the cost price and for the last week in consequence of the great increase in destitution have been dispensing it gratuitously in extreme cases but the applications of the famishing have become so numerous and the relief which in consequence could be afforded by one boiler (the two boilers expected from government having not yet arrived) so comparatively valueless that the committee are painfully obliged to discontinue gratuitous aid and confine themselves to the sale of soup at 1d for three pints. I am therefore directed to lay these facts before you and to state that three-fourths of the labourers being for the last three weeks without employment and on the public works, it is the opinion of the committee that unless relief be immediately afforded a great portion of the people of the parish will inevitably perish.[154]

The soup committee had £95 10s in January 1847, to which was added £86 from the lord lieutenant and donations from P. Cheevers, resident magistrate (£2), Charles L. Sandes (£5) and the Honourable Mrs Massy Yescombe (£5).[155] The *Post* reported that Mr and Mrs Thomas Sandes of Sallowglen gave 'a noble example' by feeding 150 children with rice and Indian meal boiled together, and the same number of old and infirm received rice and soup. They were putting their own health at risk in doing this: 'Although the greater number of these people came from fever houses, Mrs Sandes was not deterred from ministering to their wants.'[156]

Lord Robert Clinton of the British Relief Association wrote from Tarbert on 4 March, saying that he awaited the arrival of the *Rob Roy* and that he could sell its cargo in one week. Twenty vessels had come up the Shannon from Limerick on the previous day, whereas the usual number was seven or eight vessels; but still the price of meal had risen sharply and merchants were selling it as fast as they could. He visited the Tarbert relief committee and he 'dampened their hopes' for a grant of money or food when he learned that they had £1,300 in hand; he believed that the committee had adequate funds to meet the needs of the poor.[157]

In what was headlined as a 'Death Census', the *Examiner* reported on the scale of deaths in some north Kerry parishes in the six months from October 1846 to March 1847.[158] The information was provided by parish priests and it was read out by John O'Connell, son of Daniel, at a meeting of the Repeal Association. The report does not indicate where the meeting was held but it was most likely in Conciliation Hall in Dublin, the headquarters of the Repeal Association. Fr Daniel McCarthy reported that there were 780 deaths in Ballylongford and Tarbert between 1 October 1846 and 1 April 1847, an increase of 300 per cent from the same period a year before when 260 died. Over half of these deaths were from the effects of starvation, and several people were buried without coffins. He advised that the distribution of free seeds and payment for daily work for a period of two weeks was the only way to prevent more starvation. There was no emigration from the area 'for want of means'.[159]

Fr James Walsh of the nearby parish of Lisselton reported that there were 120 deaths between 1 October 1846 and 1 April 1847, an increase of 500 per cent on the previous year, when twenty-five died. Over eighty of the 120 deaths were from starvation. He had recently buried three bodies without coffins, and 'all died of perfect starvation'.[160]

Fr John Long was parish priest of Murhur, which is in the Moyvane area. He stated that 180 had died between October 1846 and April 1847, but this number excluded children, of whose deaths no records were kept; those who died of starvation numbered about 105. Long wrote that the present state of his parish was awful, and he gave details of some deaths: a family of eight died almost unknown to people, because they lived in a remote area; eight more people died by the ditches, four of whom were buried without coffins. He had serious concerns about the imminent lay-offs from public works and the delayed beginning of gratuitous relief through the soup kitchens:

> Of the number who died of hunger I administered last rites to eight of them in my own house, seven of whom died shortly after. Perhaps I ought also acquaint you that before the famine, my parishioners were honest, exemplary and religious. I am sorry to say now that theft and robbery and nightly burglary are beginning to appear among them and the dismissal of the poor from the public works will increase these dreadful crimes. The outdoor relief cannot be in operation for five weeks.[161]

Fr J. Scollard was a curate at nearby Lisselton. He wrote of the deaths of several persons from starvation, observing that they were 'members of families who have hitherto lived in opulence and comfort'. His parish had 3,000 heads of families whose only income was from the relief works.[162] This is an indication of the fact that after the labourer and cottier class had been devastated, the classes above them were the next most vulnerable. Craftsmen such as shoemakers and tailors whose businesses had relied on the poor were also soon reduced in circumstances, and they were disadvantaged when placed on public works, as they were unused to manual labour.

In May James Alexander provided John Sandes of Tarbert with half a ton of Indian meal and 400 biscuits donated by Limerick Quakers for the children of Tarbert Wesleyan day school. Miss Sandes of Pyrmont received three hundredweight of rice and four hundredweight of biscuits for the children of Tarbert infant school.[163] The work of James Alexander on behalf of the Limerick Quakers covered north Kerry as there were no Quakers based in Kerry.

Ardfert

A sense of desperation had taken hold of the Ardfert area by this time. Fr Francis Moore, curate of Ardfert, stated in January that he knew whole families who were living on boiled seaweed for days on end.[164] John Goggin of Ballinfriar (Ballinprior), who worked as caretaker on the Crosbie estate and owned a gun, was asked by Thomas O'Brien and Denis Flynn to shoot their donkeys so that they could feed themselves and their families. He did so, and the *Post* noted that they hoped to save themselves for a short while by eating 'this loathsome and disgusting food'.[165] Captain Robert Mann wrote a report on Ardfert, stating that 'the revolting food caused sickness, on which an inquiry was held'.[166] John Mitchel, the nationalist leader and journalist with *The Nation* newspaper, referred to such incidents as commonplace during the Famine: 'In some hamlets by the seaside, most of the inhabitants being already dead, an adventurous traveller would come upon some family eating a famished ass.'[167]

In Ballyrobert townland, numbers of people were reported as 'living on crows', shot for them by farmer Maurice Carmody.[168] Dr Thomas Mahony, a surgeon, wrote from Ardfert to the editor of the *Chronicle*, criticising the lack of press attention on the acute distress in the area:

> Good God, Sir, what is to become of us when we behold these phantoms of what were once men, those living skeletons, those mere outlines of the human form, crawl every morning from their wretched cabins to their work, when they can obtain it, and return in the evening to regale themselves and their families on a few turnips.[169]

The editor of the *Chronicle* responded and apologised for not having the reporters or resources to cover Ardfert and the many other 'scenes of want, woe and desolation' in all parts of the county.[170]

Captain Mann's report on Ardfert described it as 'a very distressed locality' with a village of about 600 souls and a relief committee responsible for about 11,800 people in Ardfert, Abbeydorney, Killahan and Kilflynn.[171] The committee had raised £350 for relief. There were three commons areas in Ardfert with a pauper population of 1,000 squatting in them. Captain Mann promised to supply the committee with twenty tons of meal as soon as he received the money for it from the committee, and he urged his superiors to provide a soup boiler for Ardfert and for other areas with the same requirements. Mann confirmed that Ardfert's problems as a very distressed locality 'arose out of a sudden suspension of work and employment on the public roads before other means of earning money was provided'. Mann was told by a medical man in Ardfert that death and disease had extended to an alarming degree due to 'insufficient food and raiment', which caused dysentery, colds and fever. He visited the churchyard and saw for himself the truth of that statement.[172]

The *Examiner* acknowledged the work of the priests of Ardfert, where 'distress is becoming truly frightful and is daily increasing'.[173] Fr Jeremiah O'Sullivan, PP, and the curate Fr Francis Moore were engaged from morning to night in attending the sick and dying, and in almost every case the cause was exhaustion and starvation. Two men named Michael McQuinn and Patrick Lyne had died of starvation on 22 February. The paper concluded: 'We are in utter despair for the poor people of this county. Hourly destitution is becoming – not more extensive, for that is impossible – but more torturous, more fatal. Hundreds are dying and the living are but crawling skeletons.'[174]

By March distress in the Ardfert district 'had reached a most afflicting extent'.[175] Fr O'Sullivan gave some statistics on deaths for the six months from 1 October 1846 to 1 April 1847, the height of the Famine: approximately fifteen people each week died in Ardfert and twenty each week in Kilmoyley. The total number of deaths was 910. Of these he estimated that about 416 (nine each week in Ardfert, and seven each week in Kilmoyley) had died as a result of famine and destitution.[176] Two more who had died of starvation in Ardfert were named as Patrick Lawlor and Tom Cournane. Eight men were given the last rites on 13 March and four of them were dying of 'actual starvation'.[177]

In May Fr O'Sullivan wrote: 'My curate the Rev. Mr Moore and I have been obliged to give the last rites of the church sometimes to persons on the public roads. It is my opinion that half the poor in my parishes will not survive the present year.'[178] The *Examiner* noted the zeal of the two priests and the sad state of Ardfert, saying that the dying were tottering up to the door of the priests' house to ask for the last rites: 'In whatever direction the duty of the parish obliges our reverend pastors to go, they find the same doleful evidence of destitution, hunger, thirst and nakedness and sorrow and despair. This is a sad and lamentable state of things in Ardfert.'[179]

In May Fr Moore wrote to the editor of *The Tablet* appealing for help:

> May I ask you in the name of charity to use your influence to procure some aid for this afflicted district. The enclosed which I send from *The Nation* newspaper will give you but a faint idea of the state of the poor here as their sufferings are incredible – fever, dysentery and dropsy are in every quarter of the parish.[180]

At least one English parish was moved to respond: Rev. Henry Whedall of St Peter's in Leamington sent £4 in response to Moore's appeal, wishing that it were more, but believing that 'in various ways, our congregation has done nobly'.[181] Fr Moore responded with gratitude and told Rev. Whedall that his money went to the family of a man named Reardon, whose two children had died of starvation the previous week and had been buried without coffins.[182]

One witness to the Famine in the nearby Banna area was Dr David Moriarty, who had been elected president of All Hallows College in Dublin in June 1846, having previously been vice-president of the Irish College in

Paris. Moriarty was born in Lixnaw and he served as Bishop of Kerry from 1854 until his death in 1877. He suffered from consumption and in July 1846 he was obliged to move to his mother's home in Banna in the hope that rest and the invigorating sea air would improve his health. His mother, Bridget Stokes, came from Listowel and had moved to Banna following her husband's early death in 1827.[183]

Moriarty was in Banna throughout the long winter of 1846–7 and some of his letters from there have survived. However, they contain surprisingly little information on the events in the Banna and Ardfert locality at this time of crisis. The letters were to his deputy, Fr Woodlock, in All Hallows College, and referred mainly to administrative matters in the college, as well as his own health. For example, in a letter of 10 March 1847 he advised that the senior students should be spoken to as grown men and equals in intellect while the juniors should hear 'a considerable dose of humbug and endearment'. The letter ended:

> I have been going on very badly with stomach and bowels for the last fortnight. The easterly winds too crept through me like quicksilver. It was by far the most trying weather I had until within the last three or four days. All here are well. The poor are going fast to a better world. There was not so much mortality from cholera.[184]

Fr Moriarty wrote another letter on 20 June and it was entirely concerned with college matters. This apparently indifferent attitude towards the dire situation in Ardfert is puzzling, unless David Moriarty was too unwell to give his attention to events occurring around him, not having any priestly duties in the area. However, he later noted that he had seen Dr McEnnery, parish priest of Tralee during this time, always surrounded by a body of poor beggars, and he was well aware of McEnnery's charitable activities. Perhaps Moriarty's attitude is an indication that the deaths were occurring at a remove from him, among another social class. It appears that it was not only landlords who inhabited another world from the poor, as Woodham-

Smith wrote, but that some senior clergymen were also detached from the worst aspects of the Famine.

Many landlords provided private relief services, often with their wives organising distribution of food rations. William Talbot Crosbie was the landlord of Ardfert, one of very few resident landlords, and he had set up a soup kitchen in his residence, Ardfert Abbey. Crosbie, who also had land in Abbeydorney, and his wife distributed 600 quarts of soup each week; some of it sold at a penny a quart, more at a halfpenny a quart. He personally paid for the soup to feed fifty people gratuitously. His wife sent from England a large quantity of blankets for distribution among the poor, as reported in the *Post* under the heading 'Private Benevolence'.[185] Crosbie said that he was 'severely oppressed by the want of those destitute persons about him, and that it [was] beyond his power to relieve them'.[186] Ardfert also benefitted from Quaker charity, receiving six bags of biscuits and six barrels of Indian meal from the secretary of the Quakers Auxiliary Relief Committee, John Beale.[187]

In May relief works in Ardfert were being suspended, in accordance with government policy, and an anonymous letter-writer to the *Examiner* stated that 379 people had been denied aid and identified some of those by name. The relief committee of Ardfert, Abbeydorney and Killahan, of which Crosbie was chairman, was charged with 'a neglect not merely culpable but inhuman in times like these'.[188] The whole population of needy people had been thrown out of employment, with the exception of about thirty men, and they were consigned to inevitable death, according to the *Examiner*. Soup was being provided, but Fr Moore did not think much of its nutritional value, saying that one man who had got a quart of soup collapsed in the street and was only revived when Fr Moore gave him some bread.[189] The priest requested that instead of soup, people should be given one pound of meal, but this was rejected by the committee, which a correspondent of the *Examiner* characterised as being composed of the chairman and 'his myrmidons'.[190] In the heated atmosphere, the correspondent also implied that the funds of the committee were not being properly applied and asked for audited accounts to be produced. The committee was accused of 'gross and wilful neglect'. The anonymous writer ended with the warning: 'I tell them again to beware, for on their heads will be the blood of fathers, mothers and helpless children in this locality.'[191]

One issue was whether certain people obtaining relief were correctly entitled to it, and it was felt by some members of the committee that Fr Moore was naive in pressing the claims of some applicants. These committee members believed that his compassion was being manipulated by fraudulent and undeserving claimants, and that he was being duped. The *Post* captured the opposing values of the priest and the ratepayers, and the opposing demands of charity and financial husbandry, when it praised Crosbie and the Ardfert committee for 'being charitable without being lavish, open to a real case of destitution, but wary and stringent against fraudulent attempts to obtain rations, giving as those who feel for the distresses of their poor neighbours while they remember that they themselves must pay for the charity which they dispense'.[192] This stance reflected the prevailing feature of all official relief during the Famine; such support as there was could be only for the 'deserving poor', and those deemed undeserving had to be excluded by all means available.

On 12 June the *Post* reported on a meeting of the Ardfert, O'Dorney (i.e. Abbeydorney) and Killahan relief committee, which was addressed by Lieutenant Greenwell. He told the committee that the poor would have to be supported by the rates system and that a rate of 2s 6d in the pound would be a fair rate to meet these demands. George Rice argued that that rate was too high and that the names of undeserving people had been included on the relief lists 'quite promiscuously and incorrectly' and that instead of 420 names there should be only 250.[193]

There were also revelations at this meeting as to the reasons why Abbeydorney people were quite content with Crosbie's actions as landlord, while their counterparts in Ardfert were not. The Abbeydorney tenants agreed to a system of 'voluntary assessment', which meant that the tenants paid a tax of 4d, which yielded a total of £75; the principal landlords, Crosbie and Lord

Listowel, matched this sum, paying £52 and £23 respectively, giving a total of £150 to relief funds. A government grant in aid of an equal amount brought the figure to £300. Greenwell expressed himself satisfied with that outcome, saying that £300 would feed the destitute not just for three months, but for a whole year. He asked the committee to lodge the £150 in the bank as soon as possible and he would then do the necessary paperwork for the government grant, and would visit Captain James Murray Home in Listowel 'that very night' on the matter.[194]

The outcome of these arrangements in Abbeydorney was that Crosbie was hailed as 'a bright example to Kerry'. The *Chronicle* declared: 'Let other landlords follow the example of Mr Crosbie and other ratepayers that of the farmers of O'Dorney.' It described Crosbie as 'ever active in the advancement of his tenantry and the improvement of his property'. Every able-bodied man in Abbeydorney parish was employed, according to the *Chronicle*, at a rate which would enable him to earn 1s 6d per day and that work was not on 'useless roads' but on increasing the productiveness of the land, 'thus adding to the wealth of the country'.[195]

It seems that William Talbot Crosbie was adept at steering a course that was in his own best interest as a landlord as well as in the long-term interest of his tenants. He was ever alert to government grant schemes, as shown in the fact that his application for aid under the Landed Property Improvement (Ireland) Act of 1847 was the highest in the country and the only application from Kerry. He applied for £15,269 9s 3d, an amount equivalent to approximately two million euro today. He was also an early applicant under the Labouchere scheme, which allowed for drainage works by landlords to qualify as relief work, 'the good effects of which', noted the *Post*, 'have been most apparent in his district'.[196]

The favourable arrangements made in Abbeydorney contrasted with the situation of tenants in Ardfert who were paying 3s 10d in rates; they could have had the same happy outcome, wrote the *Chronicle*, were it not for the 'mischievous … and factious opposition' that existed towards Crosbie.[197] The *Post* had never wavered in its support for Crosbie, stating on 5 June that 'he has been devoting his entire time to the cause of the poor in his district and we have heard it generally remarked that his conduct at this trying crisis is most praiseworthy'.

It is difficult to reconcile this praise for Crosbie with the accusations that were levelled against him by the anonymous correspondent in the *Examiner* of 4 June, but it does not mean that the harrowing descriptions of distress were not accurate. However, it does seem that the attacks on Crosbie were exaggerated, a fact acknowledged even by the *Examiner* when it eventually stated: 'Mr Crosbie has in our opinion fully exonered [sic] himself and the committee.'[198]

Fr Moore and Fr Fitzgerald of Abbeydorney were also happy to exonerate Crosbie, but there was a sting in the tail of this controversy. Fr Moore had written to the relief commissioners about the complaint that Ardfert people had been denied aid because of the gross and wilful neglect of the relief committee, and he published their reply to him, which stated that the delay in extending relief to Ardfert and Kilmoyley 'appears to have been occasioned by the culpable inactivity of the committees'.[199] This provided a measure of vindication for the complainants, as noted in Fr Moore's accompanying letter to the *Examiner*, which asserted that it was 'confirmation of what I stated in O'Dorney about the neglect of some members of the relief committees'. The reply of the commissioners was republished in the *Post*, albeit with the observation that its first publication showed 'but little taste' on Fr Moore's part. According to the *Post*, the delay in providing relief was caused only by 'a most praiseworthy desire' to fully assess the validity of the claims for it.[200]

Ballyheigue Area

Lieutenant Greenwell was not alone in recognising the influence of Fr Eugene McCarthy of the united parishes of Ballyheigue, Killury and Rattoo during this period. In January 1947 the *Examiner*, when recording the 'very deplorable condition' of the labourers in the Ballyheigue district, reported:

> Our informant stated that the men on several of the works had not received their wages for *more than a fortnight*!! This treatment of the wretched labourers is most inhuman. It must be caused by a want of sufficient staff officials or by those employed neglecting their duty. The relief committee of Ballyheigue should take care to represent this grievance and all others of a similar character to the Board of Works and Government. Much praise is due to the Rev. Mr McCarthy, P.P. who has got an independent relief fund which enables him to keep a tolerably fair supply of provisions.[201]

An official of the Board of Works took offence at the implied criticism of its response to the crisis, acknowledging Fr McCarthy's 'vaunted liberality' in establishing a relief fund, but writing that 'it was unnecessary to praise the reverend gentleman at our expense, as his humanity is duly appreciated in Ballyheigue'.[202] The anonymous official defended the actions taken, which included providing two bags of meal costing £20 that were paid for by an unnamed local publican. He added that the relief committee had opened shops for the sale of meal in Ballyheigue and Kilmoyley, and that labourers had been paid every week. The *Post* carried a statement authorised by the pay-clerk of Ballyheigue district that labourers had been paid regularly every week.[203]

Nevertheless, the *Examiner* repeated its claim in February, citing a reliable informant who claimed that several men on the public works 'declare that they had not received a single penny of their wages for three weeks!! and that he saw several of them who crawled in the morning to work lying on the roadside completely exhausted'.[204] The paper was appalled at this 'cruel and inhuman negligence' and demanded an investigation. The labourers were paid the following day.[205]

There was also criticism of Fr Eugene McCarthy in February when an anonymous letter-writer accused him of victimising a man named Dooling who had converted to Protestantism. The letter stated that Dooling was employed as a steward on the public works and that he was of exemplary character, with a large family of dependants. The letter ran thus:

> Fr Owen, as he is termed, could not permit this opportunity to pass without exhibiting himself. This *hero* calls upon the poor labourers not to 'work with the Devil'!! They, not from principle, but lest they should be, as they said, scandalised before the flock by the threats and curses of this abusive, violent and ignorant priest, obey the tyrannical call; he withholds the rites of his office from some of the humble persons who resist and as a member of the relief committee brings into play his influence among the respectable Roman Catholics, who should indeed know better, to drive the poor man from the works.[206]

The letter-writer, who signed himself 'A Protestant, Rattoo', praised the engineer Mr Samuels for refusing to dismiss Dooling, and the *Post* stated that it considered Fr McCarthy's action unworthy of a minister of the gospel.

The incident afforded an opportunity for the *Examiner* to charge the *Post* with bigotry and call it 'a vile rag' for publishing the 'loathsome saliva of bigot vipers'. The paper dismissed the accusation against Fr McCarthy as 'the *ipse dixit* [baseless assertion] of an unscrupulous, unprincipled scribbler, the snarlings of a cur that should be spurned with the foot'.[207]

These early months of 1847 were desperately difficult times for the poor of Kerry and there are some heart-rending reports that give a sense of the horrors endured. On 28 January Oliver Moriarty, who was secretary of Ballyheigue and Kilmoyley relief committee, wrote to the Poor Law Commissioners about 'this dreadfully distressed district'. He wrote again on 6 February:

> I beg to remark that with the exception of one or two we have not received any aid from absentee landlords and this district is about twelve miles in extent with about six thousand individuals actually starving, already many have met an untimely end by dysentery, fever or brought on by want.[208]

Rev. J. P. Chute wrote in early February that 'nothing can so aid in alleviating the misery of the poor particularly at this season of the year, as a large supply of soup. Two boilers, of sixty gallons each, would be sufficient, one for each parish.' Michael O'Halloran, secretary of the Farmers' Fund Committee of Killury, reported that the committee had raised £100 'for the purposes of relieving the poor of this parish, than whom there can hardly be anywhere persons in greater want of relief'.[209]

On 16 February the *Examiner* carried a report on the situation in Ballyheigue, including yet another drowning of a woman trying to gather seaweed for food:

> In Ballyheigue generally we have been informed, the greatest misery and destitution prevails. The clergymen of this extensive parish, we are told, have had to attend each week, for a few weeks past, not less than sixty or seventy persons, ill of fever and dysentery or dying of starvation. The following are particular instances of destitution which occurred in the locality in the last week: three men who died of starvation were interred without coffins. A woman was drowned in endeavouring to gather seaweed – the only food to be procured for herself and her wretched family. And lastly three women were discovered on the public works disguised in their husbands' clothing whose place they endeavoured to supply, the latter having been attacked by the prevalent disease, dysentery. It is useless to comment on these facts. We have been recording similar instances of extreme suffering, of squalid living wretchedness as occurring in almost every district of this county until we experience a chill feeling of despair at the many repetitions.[210]

In all coastal areas, edible seaweeds such as dilisk (dulse) and carrageen moss were intensely harvested and limpets (or *báirneach*) were eaten also; rocks were 'picked clean' and 'beaches were stripped bare of the tidal crop'.[211]

The public works on a new road in the Kerry Head area were causing further problems, the *Examiner* stated, because neither the old road nor the new road were passable and therefore farmers were prevented from bringing seaweed and sea sand to their fields as they usually did.[212]

Oliver Moriarty wrote again on 26 March 1847, describing the continuing distress in Ballyheigue and Kilmoyley:

> Such is the destitute state of this district where there is but one resident proprietor, that if relief is not extended without delay, the worst consequences may be dreaded; it should be known that though situated on the west coast we are deprived of every advantage in the way of fish; [word unclear] that this locality [is] dependent entirely, from the facility of sea manure, on the potato crop as means of subsistence, is now left in the worst position from the circumstances of there being very few able to assist in alleviating the misery of the inhabitants of a thickly populated and extensive district.

He requested 'a larger grant than under the circumstances the district would be entitled to'.[213]

One source of funding was the Society of Friends (Quakers) of Limerick, who sent a donation of £30 to Rev. J. P. Chute for the poor of Ballyheigue.[214] A list of subscriptions to the relief committee there shows that the £30 donation made up over one-third of the total amount of £77 19s 6d. It stands out from the smaller sums ranging from £5 to under £1 and it came from James Alexander, the Limerick Quaker.[215] Rev. John Fitzgerald Day of Ballymacelligott received supplies from the Quakers of Cork for the children of the schools in his area: in July he received ten hundredweight of Indian meal and four bags of biscuits, and in December four barrels of Indian meal, three bags of biscuits and a box of American clothes.[216]

In May 1847 a rumour circulated that a large crowd was to assemble in Ballyduff and proceed to Ballyheigue Castle 'with the view of laying hands on the engineer of the Board of Works, Mr Samuels, to whom it erroneously attributed the stoppage of employment'. A force of policemen under Mr Fletcher and soldiers under Major Clarke went to Ballyduff but found that it was a false alarm and there was no such activity in the village.[217]

Major Pierce Crosbie of Ballyheigue Castle told a reporter that he never saw anything so promising as the condition of the potato crop. It is a fact that the crop of 1847 did not fail, but its yield was very low because there had been so little planting.[218] Crosbie chaired a meeting of landlords in Listowel to discuss a system of improvements to their estates, which would provide employment for labourers. Among the works considered was a 'stupendously useful project' of draining the lands near the rivers Brick, Feale and Gale.[219]

By March 1847 'Ireland's road network had become a gigantic construction site', with over 734,000 people working six days a week on outdoor relief.[220] The works provided did not always prevent deaths. In January the *Chronicle* reported that on a road near Causeway, labourers 'were falling to the earth from want of food'.[221] Their hunger was reflected throughout the general populace. That same month a group of men stole two heifers from Timothy Connor of Sandford and the hides and offal were found the next day by a nearby stream.[222] In February a travelling pedlar from Clare died of starvation in Causeway and was buried without a coffin.[223]

Civil disorder loomed as people became desperate. In mid-February a crowd of 300–400 people marched to Causeway from Kilmore, Clahane and Ardoughter demanding employment and wages of 1s 6d a day from Mr Samuels, the engineer in charge of the district. The *Post* reported:

> When they found that Mr Samuels would not comply with their demands they went off to Ballynoe and drove off four cows, the property of Miss Pierse; they then went to Killury Glebe and drove away five cows belonging to the Rev. Richard Plummer. His men resisted this invasion of their master's property but were beaten off by the lawless mob. At this stage of the proceedings, Rev. Eugene McCarthy came up and prevailed on them not to slaughter the cattle as was their declared intention, by promising they should get the work they asked for. Afterwards, the Rev. Plummer and Fr McCarthy, accompanied by Mr Samuels, went on to the lands referred to and set the people to work. This step produced quiet and the cattle were returned to their several owners uninjured.[224]

In re-publishing this account, the *Examiner* added:

> We think it right to add that we were in the neighbourhood of Causeway since the above mentioned occurrence and heard several persons speak of it

but we heard no mention whatever of seizure of cattle though we did hear the strongest testimony borne to the patience and honesty of the poor people of Causeway and Ballyheigue and particularly those living in the direction of Kerry Head.[225]

The Nation carried a further report from 'a provincial journal', noting that the districts of Rattoo and Killury were even more desperate than Ballyheigue:

> Our informant states that these two districts contain about 13,000 inhabitants, of whom at least 9,000 are in a state of utter destitution. On yesterday morning seven funerals with at most a half dozen persons attending each passed his place. At least sixty persons have died from actual starvation in these two districts. He adds it could not have been otherwise for numbers are without employment and those employed cannot possibly live if wages and food continue as at present. A few days ago he entered a labourer's house and found a family, six in number, sitting around their only meal for the day – a basin of gruel – which was not sufficient to satisfy one person. Another family's food for one day consisted of two salt herrings. The people are completely exhausted.[226]

The source of that report was the *Examiner*, which went beyond simply reporting to make the following accusations:

> Such is the heart-stricken account we have received. The relief committee of these two districts we are informed, is extremely active in relieving distress and as provident and enterprising as they can possibly be, with the limited funds at their disposal. The amount does not exceed £150. This bespeaks a cruel neglect, an inhuman apathy, on the part of some, at least, of the landlords enjoying and *enforcing* the rights of property in these localities. We know that they are nearly all absentees spending their time away and squandering money which should be applied to save the lives of their starving tenants. Trinity College also has property there: we should like to know the amount it has contributed to the relief fund.[227]

The *Examiner* went on to state that there was an urgent necessity for the landlords of the area to purchase and provide seed for the next crop. April was 'seed time', and the *Post* perceived that 'a confidence is returning to the minds of the farmers'.[228] However, it also published some sombre verses, which captured the despair of the poor:

> *There's wrath upon our smitten soil,*
> *Want glares from out a nation's eyes*
> *And stalwart arms inured to toil*
> *Hang feebly down – weak woman cries,*
> *While her pale infant closely prest*
> *Seeks vainly nature's due supplies*
> *From its worn mother's milkless breast.*[229]

5

'WHAT UNDER HEAVEN ARE THE PEOPLE TO DO?'

July–December 1847

Now we come to the momentous questions: How are the people to be fed? How is property to be preserved?

Kerry Evening Post, 13 October 1847

In the summer of 1847 there were significant but misleading indicators that the worst of the crisis had passed. The blight did not recur that year, but the potato harvest was small because planting had been so limited. In historian John Kelly's words: 'In the public mind, the healthy 1847 potato crop had become an unofficial demarcation point. The famine was over and it had had an unexpectedly happy ending: the Irish people were learning how to help themselves.'[1] There was even a government declaration in August that the Famine was over.[2]

In a study of the newspapers in Co. Waterford, Eugene Broderick has noted that 'coverage of the famine in the local newspapers ceased from June 1847'. He believes that this was because a certain fatigue had set in among readers and editors and that a respite from the tragic reportage of early 1847 was welcomed 'with alacrity and gratitude'.[3] Coverage in the Kerry newspapers did not cease, but there was certainly a sense of palpable relief that the acute crisis appeared to be over.

'WHAT UNDER HEAVEN ARE THE PEOPLE TO DO?'

Amendments to the Poor Law

A major change in government policy regarding relief came in August 1847, with the strong support of Charles Trevelyan, chief secretary of the Treasury in London and head of administration of British Famine relief in Ireland. Trevelyan played 'a pivotal role in managing the day to day provision of government relief' through the Famine years.[4] Following the maxim that Irish property must pay for Irish poverty, responsibility for funding all future relief measures was transferred to the Irish Poor Law system, in other words to the ratepayers of each union. At a national level, the Irish Poor Law Commission was separated from the English Commission and, generally speaking, the Westminster government withdrew from financial responsibility for the relief of the destitute in Ireland. This coincided with the official declaration that the Famine was over and with a dramatic falling-off in financial support as 'donor fatigue' took hold in England. Under the new laws, each board of guardians was to become much more efficient in collecting the rates due and to use the money to fund workhouses and outdoor relief. This put enormous pressure on the guardians, the ratepayers and on the finances of the unions of Tralee and Listowel.

Several acts of parliament were also passed, amending the Poor Law Act of 1838 in various ways. For example, the original act had expressly prohibited any relief outside of the workhouse, but the 1847 amendment allowed this under certain conditions. Outdoor relief meant the distribution of food, usually cooked meal, as raw meal might have been sold by unscrupulous recipients. If the workhouse was full, people could now receive food locally; local 'relieving officers' would compile lists of those applying for relief and these would be examined by the guardians. The principle of the 'workhouse test' was strictly enforced, whereby conditions in the workhouse were made as unattractive as possible, so that entry would always be seen as a last resort. There was great concern that able-bodied adults would abuse outdoor relief, and sometimes the sick and the old were discharged from the workhouse so that the able-bodied could be offered places in order to test if their distress was genuine.

Another legal change was the introduction of the notorious 'Gregory Clause', which meant that occupiers of more than a quarter acre of land would not be eligible for any relief, as they were not deemed to be destitute.[5]

Shortlived Hope

There were clear signs in the local newspapers of August 1847 that the crisis was perceived to be over, and that people were starting to resume their normal seasonal activities of previous years. The *Post* was once again railing against the practice of profiteering, observing that 'no sooner have the potatoes shown themselves in our markets than those harpies the forestallers are to be seen at their old occupation – just as the rapacious sea fowl follow a scull of pilchers'.[6] Races were held on the strand of Ballyeagh on the Cashen in mid-September and the *Examiner* stated that, after the melancholy character of the previous eight or nine months, it could not complain about poor people indulging themselves in their favourite recreation.[7] There were regattas in The Spa near Tralee and on the Killarney lakes, and a rowing contest in Dingle.[8] A bonfire was planned in Castleisland to mark the election of Mr Herbert to parliament, but this proved very divisive as he had many opponents in the area; a riot was deemed imminent until the 'popular and patriotic curate' Fr Edward O'Flaherty intervened to make sure the bonfire did not take place. Not to be deprived of recreation, the people promptly revived the bonfire initiative, this time in the guise of an expression of gratitude to the clergymen of all persuasions 'for their untiring exertions during the year to support the people'. The clergymen were the rector, Rev. Maunsell, Fr O'Leary, parish priest and two curates, Fr O'Flaherty and Fr John O'Connell. The absence of any spirit of bigotry was acknowledged and 'great good feeling prevailed during the night and the merry dance was kept up until the appearance of Aurora's blushing face'.[9]

Another reason for a sense of some improvement in affairs was the disbandment of relief committees, the publication of their 'final reports' in the press and the departure of the inspectors who had been appointed in the autumn of 1846. Their work was now done and the crisis was over, or so government officials and local public figures wished to believe. Newspapers carried many expressions of gratitude to Lieutenant Greenwell and Captain Labalmondière from the various relief committees with which they worked. An editorial in the *Post* praised Labalmondière as follows:

> His manner, which is always unobtrusive, is characterised by a fairness and decision which give great effect to his opinions; at the same time we have never observed any wish on his part to interfere in the slightest degree with the opinions of those gentlemen members of different boards whose zeal and activity he must, we are assured, fully appreciate … We predict his future career will afford him opportunities of distinguishing himself.[10]

The relief committee of Ballincuslane (near Castleisland) thanked Labalmondière in these terms:

> During the late period of unexampled calamity, on every occasion you have exhibited a strong feeling and interest in the wants of our locality and while anxious to co-operate in any measures calculated to confer real benefit upon the afflicted poor, you have afforded an example of unflinching integrity in checking whatever might have tended to abuse and of decision in carrying into effect the judicious regulation as well as the benevolent intentions of the government. Be assured, Sir, you take with you our very best wishes and heartily praying that in whatever sphere you may henceforth be occupied the Almighty may bless and crown your labour with success.[11]

From the Tralee relief committee, the parting address was more attuned to the bureaucratic and practical difficulties that had arisen in the cumbersome and unsatisfactory administration of relief. It was signed by chairman George Day Stokes and treasurer Rev A. B. Rowan:

> None can be better aware than we are of the complicated and harassing duties you have had to discharge or of the embarrassments and confusion inevitably

attendant upon the working of such a system as that under which relief was administered, and it is due to you to say that we always found your aid most ready and effective in reducing such matters to order.[12]

Labalmondière's reply to the Tralee address also acknowledged the difficulties that arose in Tralee, although he suggests that they were mainly at the beginning of his time there:

> Your own untiring exertions, of the extent of which a better testimony than mine is borne by the working of the relief measures in this large and populous district, have combined with the courteous attention I have always received from you to render that a comparatively easy and a pleasant duty which threatened in the outset to be difficult and irksome. The recollection of the past season of sorrow will always bring with to my mind a remembrance of the kindness I have received during my sojourn in Kerry.[13]

Douglas Labalmondière (1815–1893) went on to have a somewhat illustrious career after 1847. He retired from the army on half-pay in 1850 with the rank of lieutenant colonel and joined the London Metropolitan Police as a superintendent. He received a royal award, the Companion of the Bath (CB) in 1851 as a reward for his policing of London's Great Exhibition, and went on to become the first assistant commissioner of police from 1856 to 1888, with responsibility for administration and discipline. He was acting commissioner for three months in 1869.[14]

There were also many tributes to Henry Nicholas Greenwell from the relief committees of north Kerry. The Lixnaw chairman, John Gibson, for example, praised his 'unwearied exertions in co-operating with us in our endeavours to relieve the destitute of this neighbourhood and the assiduity and urbanity with which he always discharged his duty'.[15] Oliver Fitzmaurice, chairman of Duagh committee, thanked Greenwell for his 'very able advice and assistance and the gentlemanly, efficient and impartial manner in which he has discharged the onerous duties imposed upon him whilst among us'.[16]

Greenwell left the army soon after his work in Kerry and then emigrated from his native Durham, settling eventually in Hawaii, where he established a coffee business that still thrives today.[17]

The relief committees were presenting final reports in advance of the implementation of the new Poor Law Extension Act, which transferred the responsibility for all future relief to local ratepayers. As the Tralee relief committee dissolved itself, there were generous tributes to its chairman, George Day Stokes, who was said to have devoted 'his undivided time and attention to the complex and multitudinous affairs' of the committee, often working from 6 a.m. to 10 p.m.

However, as all these changes were taking place, the *Examiner* was already sounding a warning note: 'We fear that this may not be the end.'[18] The warning was justified. In a sign of official recognition that the crisis was not over, two new Poor Law inspectors were appointed: Captain Thomas Spark in Listowel and Captain A. J. Hotham in Tralee. The last months of 1847 brought more desperate conditions for the poor, as acknowledged by a fundraising initiative in England, which was endorsed by Trevelyan. This was a Queen's letter read in all churches appealing for funds for Irish relief. A similar letter read in churches on 13 January 1847 had raised £172,000, but on this occasion only £30,000 was raised.[19] Donor fatigue had taken hold in England, sustained by *The Times*' argument that the poor in Ireland did not deserve any more charity.[20] One of its editorials made these declarations:

> England is called upon for more. We are treated like those rich Italian pastures where, Virgil tells us, more grass grows in the night than the cattle can eat in the day ... The poor of this country received much less alms and hospitality last winter in consequence of the drain for Ireland ... The evil of dependence is one which is sure to increase ... The Celt is propped up on the British donkey.[21]

Another major reason for the change of attitude in Britain towards the crisis in Ireland was the steady stream of impoverished Irish people arriving at its ports, raising the spectre of 'England positively invaded, overrun, devoured, infected, poisoned and desolated by Irish pauperdom'.[22]

Tralee

The Tralee board of guardians was concerned at the financial burden placed on it by the Poor Law Extension Act. In a memorial to Lord John Russell the board asked for Irish citizens to be treated as 'co-subjects of the same crown', thereby invoking the spirit of the Act of Union of 1801. The memorial made the case that Ireland was not being treated as an equal part of the United Kingdom of Great Britain and Ireland and that while decision-making became increasingly centralised, financial responsibility was being passed to Irish property owners. Their concern is borne out by the financial figures of the time. Ó Murchadha notes the £8 million spent on relief in Ireland compared with the £20 million in compensation paid to former slave owners in 1833 and the £69 million spent on the Crimean War; furthermore, much of the £8 million spent in Ireland was intended as a loan and a great proportion was spent on administration and salaries.[23] Kinealy estimates that a 'derisory' amount of £10 million was spent on relief in Ireland, the equivalent of approximately 0.3 per cent of annual gross national product.[24]

The following memorial was sent by the Tralee board of guardians to Prime Minister John Russell, using his official title of First Lord of the Treasury:

> That as the awful calamity wherewith the people of Ireland have been afflicted was of divine dispensation, beyond man's causation and control and as the legislative Union professes to connect Great Britain and Ireland in one common fortune; memorialists respectfully submit that advances made under the 'Temporary Labour Rate' and the 'Temporary Relief Acts' by an Imperial parliament out of an Imperial treasury to save a people, co-subjects of the same crown, from famine shall be an Imperial debit and ought not to be exclusively charged to Ireland.
>
> That while as guardians of the poor we are determined by all means in our

power to administer relief to the destitute in full accordance with the law in spirit and in letter, nevertheless we should but inadequately discharge our duty did we hesitate to declare as our unanimous and conscientious conviction that in the present embarrassed state of the country, repayment even of Ireland's legitimate proportion of such advances, if sought to be immediately enforced, would not only fail to be effected but would most assuredly immediately lead to the total destruction of the tenant rate-payers as a class and to the pauperization of an entire people.

Memorialists therefore most humbly hope that Ireland may be altogether released from repayment of such advances or, in accordance with the terms of the 7th article of the Union, be only charged with her own fair proportion thereof, repayment by moderate annual instalments from and after 1st January 1850.[25]

Captain A. J. Hotham of the 75th Regiment, one of the replacement Poor Law inspectors, wrote a report from Tralee on 5 November, following a meeting of the board of guardians that he attended. He stated that the books on which relief provision was based were in such disarray that they would have to be completely remodelled, but nevertheless the board decided to use these books anyway, accepting that the relief might not reach the most needy people. On the issue of releasing inmates from the workhouse, Hotham noted the difficulty that 'some have been in the house so long that they have no house to return to and scarcely clothes to put on'.[26] For this reason it was proposed that adults leaving should receive an allowance of one halfpenny a day and children one farthing a day to secure clothes and shelter. This was to be a strictly temporary measure.

Hotham also reported that the meeting had been interrupted by 'a tumultuous assembly chiefly from the town of Tralee bearing a black flag with the words in white on it "Flag of Distress" who, making their way to the workhouse, broke open the gates of the enclosure but committed no further violence'. The military and police were called for and the ringleaders were arrested, whereupon the crowd dispersed peacefully.[27]

Hotham identified the relieving officers as the source of many problems, but allowed that they were 'overwhelmed with applications' and that 'everyone who received relief under the former system thinks himself much aggrieved if his name is not returned under this'. Hotham agreed that the leaders of the group who broke into the workhouse were far from personal poverty, but he qualified this by adding that 'it must be confessed that the shades of Irish poverty are so nicely defined as to require a very careful and experienced observer to know where the correct line should be drawn'. He also noted the main shortcoming of the board of guardians, namely that members spent too much time in debate rather than administration of relief. Being aware of their own ineffectiveness, they were pleased when Hotham told them that he would be resident with them for some time to come.[28]

Another shortcoming of the Tralee board of guardians was the continued difficulty in collecting rates, which were required for the administration of relief. In September Colonel John Day Stokes was irate, saying that it was 'quite unsatisfactory' that out of a potential £14,000 due, the rate collector, Mr Chute (who had a salary of £800 a year), had collected only £416 over a two-week period.[29] It was not simply a case of incompetence on Chute's part. The men employed by Chute were often unreliable and fraud occurred, with one collector for example using the money to travel to America. Another example of Chute's difficulties was demonstrated when he visited a Mr Murray in Fenit to collect the rates and was hit on the head by a stone.[30] A few days later Chute returned with sixty men of the 77th Regiment, a party of police, Magistrate Drummond and County Inspector Hawkshaw, and he succeeded in obtaining the £54 due.[31]

Similar actions were necessary throughout the county. In October a party consisting of thirteen policemen and forty-four soldiers marched to the districts of Castlehill and Cugera near Castleisland to collect rates. They were led by Magistrate T. A. Dillon, Sub-Inspector Wyse and Captain Balfour. They were confronted by a party of 300 men, armed with pikes and spades, who were incited by rich farmers to throw stones. Dillon proceeded to read the Riot Act and cattle were confiscated, ten men were arrested – the rates were paid soon afterwards.[32]

Two incidents took place in November that give a graphic insight into social conditions. In Blennerville, a group of desperate people went into a potato field after harvest to gather any small potatoes that were left behind. The owner, Kean Mahony, arrived on the scene with a loaded gun to confront them and a heated discussion took place. A man named Flynn raised his spade, according to him not in a threatening way but just to place it over his shoulder and depart, but the owner believed he was about to be attacked and fired a shot. Flynn was wounded in the shoulder and was taken to the county infirmary where his arm was amputated by Dr Crumpe. Mahony was attacked by the crowd and fled to the police barracks to surrender himself and to seek protection. Flynn was described as 'a most inoffensive lad', and the *Post* said that 'the strongest feelings of indignation have been incited' against Mahony 'for what everyone pronounces a wanton and murderous attack on a neighbour's child for the sake of what – the gleanings, if we may appropriate the word, of the potato field – should be open to all to gather'.[33] At Banna, a man and woman went into a field 'and commenced rooting the tillage in search of potatoes'; the sons and servants of the owner came to them and an altercation followed.[34] The man was struck on the head by a stone and later died of his injuries; a coroner's court returned a verdict of wilful murder.[35]

Tralee Workhouse

Conditions for the destitute in Tralee were still desperate and there was huge pressure for workhouse places. The workload on the guardians was also having an effect on their attendance: only two attended a meeting in late September: Colonel John Day Stokes and his brother George. Three people were required for a quorum, but efforts to find a third man failed and the meeting was abandoned.[36] People continued to gather around the workhouse on Tuesday every week, the day of the board meeting, to appeal for entry. These impoverished applicants were usually weak from hunger and exhausted from having walked great distances.

In September a crowd of about 100 people had marched through the town from the Blennerville direction carrying a black flag. The number had increased to 500 by the time they reached the workhouse. Some people entered the kitchen and seized the food which was being prepared there: hominy (coarse meal mixed with milk or water).[37] In early November another attack on the workhouse (the one described by Hotham on page 159) took place when a crowd of 200 people carrying a black flag broke down the front door and the military were called in from Ballymullen Barracks. The people initially refused to leave and offered 'passive resistance to the power of the law' as the *Post* expressed it.[38] The prevailing attitude towards relief is clear from that paper's comment that 'such has been the demoralizing effect of the temporary relief system among the labouring classes that we could perceive, even among that small number, many who could have no claim for public alms'.[39]

Another incident took place two weeks later when the workhouse was attacked by a group of 'worthless ruffians who are always found ready for any mischief' as they were described by the *Post*.[40] While hundreds of people were queuing peacefully to apply for admission, the men, who were armed with clubs, incited the crowd of applicants and broke the windows of the workhouse attempting to get inside. Some of the guardians came down from the boardroom and engaged in one-to-one conflict with the attackers. Colonel Stokes, Mr Sealy, Mr Hickson, Charles Fairfield, John McCarthy and W. Thompson were among the guardians who resisted the assailants. Fairfield was bitten in the hand, cut in the face and severely bludgeoned before the leaders of the violent group were restrained with the help of some of the waiting applicants. The *Post* was outraged at the fact that gentlemen were subjected to personal violence and reported that a military guard was requested for future board meetings.[41]

The ringleader of the attackers was named in the *Post* as James Tangney; Pat Kavanagh and John Ahern were also named. All three were described as known troublemakers, although Tangney was actually in employment. Ahern was 'a well-known disturber of the peace' and Kavanagh, 'a notorious vagabond', had been dismissed from the workhouse for repeated misconduct.[42] The three were convicted of assaulting the police and received sentences of two months in jail or a £5 fine. Unable to pay the fines, they were committed to the county jail. 'Tangney who had displayed great effrontery during the trial appeared quite crestfallen when the sentence was announced and pleaded in an undertone that he had been in liquor.'[43] At the trial, Charles Fairfield commended the 'quiet and orderly demeanour of the mass of poor people present' during the incident but warned that the guardians would not continue to attend board meetings if their lives were at risk.[44]

Unfortunately, the main source of information on this incident is the *Post*, and its bias is evident in the descriptions of the men as motivated more by wantonness than by want. It could be that they were not the blackguards depicted in the *Post*, but rather men motivated by a spirit of solidarity with the destitute, outraged at the scale of suffering the people were enduring and driven to a desperate attack on the administrative centre of relief operations in Tralee to vent their frustration.

In the face of scenes like these, it is not surprising that a spirit of despair prevailed in the newspapers, among the members of the board of guardians, and even among the clergy. On one occasion in September, when only two out of the fifty guardians attended the weekly meeting (as mentioned above), the master of the workhouse decided the fate of the many applicants who attended.[45]

'How are the people to be fed? How is property to be preserved?' asked the *Post* in a strongly worded editorial, focusing on these 'momentous questions' and the insuperable dilemmas facing the country.[46] The answers to these questions would decide 'whether Ireland shall again be the scene of desolation, misery and death it presented last winter and spring and continue in the depressed and almost bankrupt state that it is in now, or rise buoyant from its misfortunes, the condition of its people improved, its resources developed, its industry fostered and its wealth increased'.[47] The *Post* believed that property owners were over-taxed and that it was the government's responsibility to provide food for the people. The government had laid responsibility for the support of the poor on the property owners, but they were unable to provide this support: 'is it not then the duty of the government to take upon themselves the office which they had in vain deputed to another?' asked the *Post*. It called for 'the peddling paltry policy of 1846–7' – i.e. government reluctance to provide direct relief – to be abandoned and for food depots to be established all over the country on a massive scale: 'Let us have no more parade of cold political economy to serve English interest at our expense, while famine cuts off tens of thousands of lives.'[48] Calling on all classes to 'pull together', the *Post* ended its editorial with the plea: 'We in Ireland are almost paralysed. Government as the most powerful agent in the commonwealth should take the first place in the movement forwards.'[49]

The haphazard attendance of the guardians continued throughout the final months of 1847. However, on 10 August there were thirty-five guardians present at the usual board meeting because that meeting concerned the election of relieving officers for the various districts. In October/November the board met for nine consecutive days for the purpose of examining the relief lists.[50] It also met on five days in late November in order to deal with the volume of applications. Hotham stated that the board members, who were busy farmers and traders, had 'an extraordinary pressure of duty and an inability as yet to contend with it'.[51] It was usual for them to conduct their meetings while a mob assembled outside the room and threw stones through the windows.

As the number of applicants rose throughout 1847, additional accommodation was acquired in other parts of the Tralee Union; these buildings were known as auxiliary workhouses. In November the board advertised for tenders for 'renting houses in or near Tralee for the accommodation of about 400 children belonging to the workhouse schools [*sic*] together with suitable rooms for the officers in charge'. The notice was signed by Thomas O'Connell, clerk of Tralee Union.[52]

The first of the auxiliary workhouses was an old distillery in Ballymullen, which had been offered by John Frederick Eagar for seven years at a rent of £150 per annum. After two years, there was an option to end the lease with six months' notice.⁵³ This building had already been used as a storehouse in 1847 by Robert Clinton of the British Relief Association. 'After a lengthened discussion on the report of the committee appointed for the purpose of inspecting the several premises offered for increased workhouse accommodation, the board agreed to take the Ballymullen distillery for that purpose from Mr John Eagar at a rent of £150 per annum.'⁵⁴ A committee was set up to select a person to make repairs to the building to make it suitable for female paupers, to order clothing, bedding and other necessaries, and to employ the staff required.⁵⁵

At the board meeting of 7 December a sub-committee reported that all male children were being moved that day to Ballymullen branch workhouse, which had cost £1,000 to fit out. Verandahs had also been completed in the main workhouse, as a result of which there was on that day accommodation for 300 paupers in the main workhouse – 150 of these places were reserved for applicants from the Dingle area. Dr Alton objected to the admission of 300 people, saying that there was clothing for only eighty-six people and that the area reserved for new inmates was damp and would cause illness to spread. The board discounted his objections and voted to admit the 300 applicants.⁵⁶

By 1849 there were auxiliary workhouses in Rock Street for able-bodied men and boys, in Blennerville for women nursing children, in Ballymullen for women and girls, and in Castleisland for young women.⁵⁷ The building in Rock Street was an old brewery owned by Mr Chute and had accommodation for 700.⁵⁸

By early December 1847, with the expansion of facilities, there was workhouse accommodation for 1,800 in Tralee Union area and outdoor relief was provided for 5,000 people, while 2,300 children were being fed in the national schools by the British Relief Association.⁵⁹ However, this expansion appeared to have little impact on the overall state of the poor; if anything, their situation appeared to be worsening. 'The principal event of the past week,' wrote Hotham on 14 December, 'is the fast increasing destitution; whole districts of the country seem to have become masses of paupers. The relieving officers in two instances were plundered of their meal and in others had to give some to able-bodied men to be a guard and protect the remainder; and one relieving officer, frightened at his duty, has resigned.'[60] By the end of the year Tralee board of guardians, responsible for an area with 90,000 people, was feeding approximately 7,000 people in the workhouse and in outdoor relief, and the British Relief Association was feeding 3,000 children in the schools. A despairing Hotham wrote: 'but yet that really seems to have no effect'.[61]

In a passionate and moving speech to the Tralee guardians, Colonel John Day Stokes proposed that a separate union should be established for Corkaguiny and that a workhouse should be built in Dingle to accommodate applicants from that distant area and help ease the burden on Tralee Union.[62] There was a growing realisation at national level that the size of the Tralee Union area was inflicting great hardship on the destitute of the Dingle peninsula and on Tralee Union as a whole. Stokes described the scenes that the guardians witnessed outside Tralee workhouse each week:

> Most of you were present on the last and preceding day of meeting and saw hundreds of paupers from those windows, and many of them with children on their backs and others by their sides, from the most remote districts, mostly without clothing in a state of half starvation, dripping with wet and shivering with cold, seeking for admission here – a place which the people of the country dislike and into which nothing but starvation drives them. Those poor people – whose condition no language of mine can describe – we were unable to admit, not from want of inquiry into their claims, not from want of sympathy with the crying urgency of their case, not because we were not convinced of the necessity of affording them relief and shelter but for want of room. The Dingle guardians then present were requested by the chairman to go down and signify to those poor people why they could not be admitted. They said, 'We will not do so. Were we to tell those poor people to attempt to crawl back, we would be answerable for their lives on the streets and on the roads.' This is not the first time, nor the fifty-first time that we have witnessed similar scenes.[63]

By the autumn of 1847, given the ever-increasing mortality rate in the workhouse, the commissioners had changed their policy on burials and advised that the burial of paupers in the workhouse grounds was 'objectionable' and should be discontinued.[64] They recommended a new burial place outside the workhouse 'on sanitary grounds', which 'should be at least a quarter of a mile from the workhouse and from any town or public institution, and in a sufficiently exposed situation to prevent the accumulation of malaria and that each grave should be five feet deep'.[65] John Lynch proposed that the new burial place might also serve the general public of Tralee, but the board disagreed and the discussion was closed; 'no further step was then taken in the matter'.[66]

The *Post* had earlier proposed that a new cemetery for use by all classes should be acquired outside the town, since 'our present graveyards are crowded to excess'. It commented indirectly on the changed attitudes to the rituals of death by noting that feelings of reverence towards the dead had been 'most grossly outraged this past melancholy season in every part of the county for want of room in the several graveyards to receive the remains of our famine-slain peasantry'.[67]

In 1849 a Mr Quill offered an acre adjoining the workhouse for use as a burial ground for £110, but this was rejected as too expensive.[68] Eventually, a new workhouse graveyard was opened in Ballybeggan and it is known today as God's Acre.[69]

Listowel

A short account written by a visitor to Listowel shows that appalling scenes were still occurring in the town in the second half of 1847. John O'Kelly, who was staying in Culloty's Hotel, saw positive signs, but could also see that the people of the town were still suffering: 'I have not witnessed here so much wretchedness and famine-stricken objects of charity as I have perhaps in wealthier localities, but to be sure there are to be seen, as elsewhere, many miserable creatures, the very specimens of hunger.'[70]

As autumn turned to winter, one Listowel correspondent identified only as 'Catholicus' was in despair and believed that the crisis was deepening:

None but an eye-witness can imagine the hard wretchedness and maddening hunger that is borne with by the generality of the people in this locality. The malignant typhus too is progressing and burning up the last principle of vitality in the famished bodies of its victims. What under Heaven are the people to do? Are they to trample upon their manhood and in idiotic dotage lie down and die with the fruit of God's earth before them? Then if they assemble under the black banner of their misery and ask for food, who is to give it to them? There are in this barony *thousands absolutely starving*.

Hundreds are living in this parish on one bad meal in the twenty-four hours, hundreds of every age and sex are daily to be seen re-digging the land in quest of roots of any sort to satisfy the cravings of hunger. The poorhouse is now full and the country is swarmed with companies of beggars. Still there is no outdoor relief given and I should imagine the guardians are in no hurry to give it. The general opinion is, in which I fully agree, they are not doing their duty to the poor. The landlords, whether resident or non-resident, are not doing their duty to the poor ... For if they did, the people would not be rotting as so much carrion before their eyes. These gentlemen have their rents paid up – they care nothing then for the poor man's sorrow. They care not for the country's ruin, for they feel it not. They hear not the imbecile blasphemies of the hungry father as he calls upon Heaven to give food to his starving children, for they are without his reach.

These gentlemen landlords are enjoying the pleasures of life in listless indifference whilst their country and people are falling in ruins around them. But no wonder, for 'Nero fiddled whilst Rome burned.' ... If the people are not fed, this county, hitherto so peaceable, I fear will not long continue so. Already symptoms have appeared in this locality that may be ghastlier in results than those of the fever or the famine. And if once the temple of society be upturned, anarchy and bloodshed will be erected in its ruins.[71]

The newly appointed inspector for the area, Captain Thomas Spark, was in conflict with the board of guardians in Listowel because of pressures on workhouse accommodation. His report of 9 December depicts the tragic and incredible dilemma, whereby sending 200 starving people away from the workhouse was deemed an act of humanity, because to admit them would have increased the likelihood of disease and deaths among those already in the workhouse:

> Above 200 applicants for admission into the workhouse were necessarily rejected, after coming, some of them, twenty miles with their miserable families, many of them in a famishing state and the guardians very humanely ordered them a meal of bread to sustain them to endure their journey home. Their names were entered in the application and report books of the relieving officers present ... I beg to remark that in the teeth of this report the rural guardians urged strenuously that further admissions should be granted from the crowd of applicants clamouring outside, which I insisted most positively against, on the ground of humanity even, and I carried my point.[72]

The disastrous ineffectiveness of the relief system is clearly shown by the fact that providing 'a meal of bread' for desperate, starving people who had walked twenty miles and faced the same walk back was seen as 'very humane' treatment.

In justice to the landlords of north Kerry, some did respond to the crisis by forming bodies such as the North Kerry Reproductive Committee and the Kiltomy Reproductive Employment Committee. The former was an initiative to raise funds to meet 'the crying necessity' of providing employment for the poor, 'for come what may the people must be fed'.[73] Landlords attending a meeting in Listowel, chaired by William Talbot Crosbie, included James Murray Home, George Hewson, Oliver Day Stokes, Stephen E. Collis, Stephen C. Sandes, Robert Leslie, John Sealy and Thomas O'Connor. Their proposal was once again the drainage of the rivers Feale, Gale and Brick, a project that would also enhance the value of their land as well as provide employment. A sum of £22,000 was estimated to be the cost of this project.[74]

In the Kiltomy initiative, George Hewson, Goodman Gentleman and James Murray Home were prominent, and they called a landlords' meeting in Lixnaw. Home stated that their aim was to devise some means of employment for the poor in the coming winter with the double objective of preventing starvation and keeping the rates down by reducing numbers in the workhouse. The aims of the two bodies overlapped and William Talbot Crosbie also spoke at the Kiltomy meeting. One of the difficulties in Kiltomy was that there were many landlords with smallholdings and short leases, and most of these did not respond to invitations to attend the meetings. Crosbie was one who had only a small holding in that area, but he declared himself willing to provide employment 'to the uttermost'.[75] He praised the spirit of self-reliance shown by the organisers and hoped that every electoral division would follow the Kiltomy example. The *Chronicle* welcomed these landlord responses to the crisis, praising the views of Crosbie and Home and anticipating the best results from the meetings.[76]

Castleisland

A meeting of landlords and ratepayers was held in Castleisland in September 1847. It was convened by Rowland Bateman of Oakpark, Tralee, and the chairman was Charles Fairfield. The object of the meeting was to find some means of employing the starving poor. Many Protestant and Catholic clergymen were present, including Rev. Macintosh and Fr O'Leary. An unnamed reporter began by stating that language was inadequate to describe the condition of the people now that all relief had ended:

> Up to this, owing to the untiring energies, the intelligence, zeal and efficiency of the relief committees, the woes of these unfortunate creatures were in some degree mitigated; famine in their regard was, so to say, deprived of its sting. But what is their position just now? Unaided, unfriended, desolate, not knowing whither to turn, or to whom to apply for relief, able and willing to work yet nobody to employ them, their mental and physical energies are completely paralysed! They appear stupefied even to the level of the brute creation!! But how calmly consider the future! Verily it is not in man to consider without instinctive horror the awful calamities that appear looming in the distance.

> Only imagine whole families, numbering several thousands, without the smallest earning, without a rood of land to supply food, without shelter from the approaching winter, without a covering save a few rags which leave them almost in a state of nudity, without a hope on earth save in the Almighty, and you have an exact picture of the misery and desolation which pervades this locality, but more particularly on the mountainous districts of the Ballincuslane electoral division.[77]

The *Chronicle* praised the work of the Catholic and Protestant clergymen for consoling drooping spirits and afflicted hearts and for saving many lives. It believed that the rack-rented farmers had no further resources to support the poor and that it was up to the landlords to rally to their aid by providing work. It recorded how Rev. Macintosh told the meeting that masses of people were living on cabbage and some did not even have that. Fr O'Leary described a people whose 'moral sense had been blunted by the past' and he advised every landowner 'to put his shoulder to the wheel'.[78]

After long discussion, resolutions were passed encouraging all landlords to avail of government loans to employ labourers on improvements on their estates. Those who committed themselves to providing these works were: G. Stokes, C. G. Fairfield, Rev. William Blennerhassett, H. A. Herbert, Lady Franks, John Bateman, Colonel Drummond, E. Harnett, Sir D. Roche, Bart., and Messrs Twiss. A sub-committee was appointed to meet regularly and point out to other landlords any opportunities for employing labourers on their lands, 'to awake them to a sense of the urgent necessity existing'.[79]

These measures did not appear to be enough for many of the destitute. Daniel Collinson, on behalf of the labourers of the united parishes of Ballymacelligott, Novohal and O'Brennan, appealed directly to the lord lieutenant, Lord Clarendon, in what the *Chronicle* saw as 'a very remarkable' address:

> We respectfully submit to your Excellency that the extent of the said united parishes is about twenty-two miles in circumference and contains a population

of about 5,000 souls, of whom over 3,000 lived this summer on outdoor relief. That one half of these, by reason of their extreme youth, old age or infirmity are utterly helpless and dependent on the other for support; that the other half by the late visitation of Providence and the calamity of the times are, in their turn, destitute and now merely live on the bounty of others. All are now destitute. That in addition to the rest, we have lately learned with the utmost dismay that the outdoor relief, whereby we all now merely exist, is to be soon withdrawn and no other to be substituted.[80]

The labourers saw their prospects as a choice between death by starvation, or death by musket ball or by grief in some penal colony if they were to resort to violence. However, they described themselves as 'poor but peaceable' men who thought it 'virtuous and honourable to live by the sweat of our brow, whereas we consider it disgraceful to our character to live on the bounty of others'. They simply asked for either a continuation of outdoor relief or for work to be provided for them. The reply they received was that the lord lieutenant could not sanction either request, and they were advised to apply to the board of guardians for relief.[81]

It is worth acknowledging here one man whose work in Castleisland was remembered over eighty years after the Famine: John Williams, who was prepared to visit the sick in their homes and who would often carry a dead body on his back and bury it himself. 'In him and in his son Henry was the blood of heroes and gentlemen,' wrote T. M. Donovan.[82]

Tarbert

Tarbert was an important port and market town and a centre for storage and distribution of Indian corn. The ordnance store was being enlarged to accommodate 110 additional troops to guard the provisions depot and patrol the areas near the town. The port was very busy, with twenty-one vessels recorded there on one day in December, and the frigate *Madagascar* was still in the bay. The *Post* commended the Limerick merchant John Norris Russell for his plan to build new stores, a mill and a new slipway, with the support of the landlord, young Robert Leslie. These projects were expected to provide valuable employment in the years ahead.[83]

Despite this, social disorder threatened in the area, and there were several raids for arms in the Kilflynn and Duagh areas in December.[84] The abundance of foodstuffs in Tarbert led to a plan by people described as 'evil-minded incendiaries' to plunder the provisions stores of a corn merchant named Spaight on the fair day.[85] Fr Daniel McCarthy received advance notice of 'the wicked and insane designs of the peasantry' and condemned it from the altar on the Sunday before. He said that he had been their pastor for twenty-three years and they had always been a peaceable and industrious people; he had always been a faithful subject of the crown and he hoped that they too would continue to be. The fair passed off peacefully, sales of stock were brisk and prices were high. The *Post* was pleased to commend Fr McCarthy 'as an example of the benefit that may be conferred on the country by the exertions of a constitutionally-minded priesthood'.[86]

Ballyheigue, Causeway and Ballyduff

Some of the roads built as Famine relief projects were described as roads to nowhere, roads with no practical benefits, but some in the Ballyheigue area are still in use today. A total of 114 miles of road were built in the baronies of Clanmaurice and Iraghticonnor during the Famine. A public notice in the *Chronicle* of 14 August 1847 gave details of road projects, including two in the Ballyheigue area. One was described as 'a new road from Ballyheigue to Listowel, between Ballyheigue Strand and Ballincrossig'. This road was five miles, five furlongs and sixteen perches long and cost £4,500, of which £3,348 had already been spent. Called the Line, it is still in use today. John Ball had recommended it in his report of April 1846, accurately stating that it would serve several parishes. The second road was 'from the top of Drinagh bog to the village of Tiershanahan'. This road was three miles, one furlong and fifteen perches long and cost £1,600, of which £1,199 had been spent. This road is the one in use today from Dreenagh to Tiershanahan Cross.

Other roads mentioned in the *Chronicle*'s report are a new road from

Kilmoyley church to Ballinoe mill (one mile, five furlongs and sixteen perches) and a road near Causeway 'from Feean's Cross to Mahony's house' (one mile, seven furlongs and eleven perches).[87] These two are not as easy to identify today.

On 27 November the *Chronicle* recorded that a letter from Fr Eugene McCarthy was sent to the board of guardians in Listowel stating that 'while the greatest destitution prevailed in his parishes, nothing was done by the guardians to carry out the law therein; that this destitution was enhanced by the eviction of 150 families by an ex-officio guardian; that none of the landlords were giving employment'.[88]

Major Crosbie of Ballyheigue Castle was quick to respond: 'If he alludes to me, I deny that a single person was turned out or evicted on my property.'[89] In fact, Fr McCarthy seems to have been referring to William Gough Sandes, who had land in the Ballyduff area. Sandes confirmed this when he said that 'he supposed that he was referred to'.[90]

Major Crosbie also replied to the accusation of Fr McCarthy that the landlords were not giving work:

> I have laid out a good deal of money myself under Mr Labouchere's letter. I have also applied for £2,606 under the Landed Property Act. I am from hour to hour expecting an answer. My letter is before the Treasury. I have forty or fifty men at work every day myself. I am not bound to support those on other properties. It is enough for me to support my own and that I will do to the utmost of my power.[91]

The *Post* took the side of Major Crosbie and pointedly asked of Fr McCarthy: 'Has the reverend gentleman used his influence to induce the rich farmers of his extensive parishes to give any employment to the people? We trow he has not.'[92]

Fr McCarthy was tireless in supporting the starving people of the area during the dark year of 1847. He organised a fund whereby strong farmers could help those most in need, and he ensured the distribution of Indian meal in Ballyheigue and Kilmoyley; he kept pressure on the authorities to provide relief measures, writing to newspapers to castigate the landlords and to appeal for aid to the board of guardians.

A letter from Fr McCarthy to the commissioners has survived among the parliamentary papers. It is dated 19 December 1847 and gives a poignant account of the hardship of the people of his parishes in those desperate days. The number of destitute people in need of relief in the three parishes was estimated by Fr McCarthy as 6,000. His letter made the case for those unable to make their own appeal, and in it he advised the authorities to send an independent investigator to assess the reality of the situation, rather than rely on information from the board of guardians, mainly composed of landlords who had vested interests:

> In your letter of the 30th ultimo, you are pleased to state that the 'Commissioners trust that the steps taken on the 18th by the board of guardians (Listowel Union) will be found effective in relieving the destitute in the Listowel Union.'
>
> There is as yet no relief for the poor of these three parishes – Rattoo, Ballyheigue and Killeery [sic]. In the latter some widows and poor had gotten something about ten or eleven days ago. Everybody remarks 'It is Providence alone is keeping the poor alive.'
>
> In September last there was a list taken by the now relieving officer of 977 who had no means whatever of support at that time, and that list [has] been given by persons on oath to give a list of the poor, each in his own farm, and that list was for Killeery alone. There were then, at least, as many more for Rattoo and Ballyheigue, i.e. a total of entirely destitute in these three parishes of about 4000 souls in September last; the number must be now 2,000 more and no relief.
>
> In my letter of the 13th through the Under-secretary's office, I had committed a mistake in stating that the Rattoo poor were relieved; I have been since assured that they had not.
>
> I am quite convinced that the Poor Law Commissioners and the

Government have the best wishes for the relief of the poor; but in those remote districts, the Government and Commissioners can know nothing of us. Some of our Guardians are absentees, and had long since left their poor to do for themselves.

If the Commissioners were pleased to send a trustworthy person of their own, who without favour or affection, or irrespective of the smiles or frowns of the Guardians, either rural or ex-officio, would visit all the hovels of the destitute in this district, and take a list of the starving inmates and report on all the different cases, what an appalling catalogue of wretched sufferers would be laid before them.

I would presume on imploring of the Commissioners to do something for those thousands of poor here, who are daily pining away by a slow and lingering death.[93]

Another short letter, dated 20 December 1847, was sent by Fr McCarthy directly to the lord lieutenant, accompanied by a memorial from the poor of the area of the united parishes. These two items of correspondence were sent on to the Poor Law Commissioners. The letter read:

The destitute poor who had been in attendance at Ballyden [sic] yesterday have requested me, as chairman, to forward the accompanying memorial setting forth their grievances. I take the liberty of assuring your Excellency that it is not possible to give any idea of the state of suffering of, at least, 1,000 wretched families in these parishes of Rattoo, Killeery and Ballyheigue.[94]

The memorial focused specifically on the impact of the Gregory Clause, which stated that occupiers of a piece of land of over a quarter acre were not eligible for admission to the workhouse or for outdoor relief; they would have to give up the land, a desperately final decision and something which was abhorrent to many of the poor. James S. Donnelly wrote that the Gregory Clause 'became a by-word for the worst miseries of the disaster – eviction, exile, disease and death'.[95] Another historian wrote that the clause was 'one of the most draconian measures ever passed by a British parliament. Together with the requirement that landlords pay the rates for holdings valued at less than £4, it gave them a free hand in systematically clearing their estates of small holders who by necessity were in need of some poor relief.'[96]

The memorial read, in part:

> That if this law should be strictly carried out, your unfortunate memorialists will be driven into the open air without shelter, like beasts of the field; that in addition memorialists are informed they will be called on to give *eight hours work* in the day as an equivalent for any food they may receive, and that this is in consequence of directions received by the board of guardians from the Poor Law Commissioners, the relieving officer having stated on this day that he should *see us on the roads at work* before he could give us relief.
>
> That your poor memorialists most earnestly, but humbly, entreat your Excellency to give directions that they may receive relief without being obliged to surrender their holdings, as in the event of their doing so they will be left perfectly houseless, and lose all prospect of ever being able to support themselves or their families by their honest industry; and further to direct the Poor Law Commissioners to withdraw the directions as to labour in return for food, as, in fact, from their very destitute [state] they are not able to work, nor could they in this inclement season with their miserable clothing stand out.[97]

It is likely that Fr McCarthy had a major part in composing this appeal, and there are clear indications of a people at the end of their tether. The trenchant arguments are supported by today's historians. Ruán O'Donnell has written that:

> Far from spurring landowners to more responsible estate management, the 'Quarter acre' amendment [the Gregory Clause], enabled the gentry to rid themselves of unwanted tenants. While this outcome won favour with economists and undoubtedly benefitted many landlords, the methodology employed seemed unduly harsh in the context of a famine. With no automatic

right of return from the workhouse, the misery of homelessness was added to that of starvation and destitution.[98]

O'Donnell also cites evidence that Lord John Russell acknowledged privately that the Gregory Clause 'was little more than an instrument of landlord tyranny'.

Captain Spark's Support for Fr McCarthy

The general attitude by officials to appeals such as Fr McCarthy's was to treat them with suspicion. They assumed the appeals were exaggerated in order to elicit as much aid as possible. On this occasion, however, the parish priest's description of the situation received support from an important local official, Captain Thomas Spark. He wrote to the commissioners on 24 December 1847, commenting as follows on Fr McCarthy's letter:

> I beg to observe that, although there may be some excess in the reverend gentleman's representation as to the numbers, I consider the distress in those parishes to be very great indeed, as it is also in other parts of this Union, and particularly along the whole of the western coasts. I believe there is no part of Ireland where destitution and wretchedness prevail more. There is no employment in prospect, nor at present afforded by the proprietors and farmers in the districts to which I allude.
>
> The measures to afford outdoor relief in this Union are, however, now organised, (not a moment having been lost since the arrival of the order) and I trust in time to save the poor from the calamities to which their destitute state would otherwise subject them during the present winter; yet I fear the extent of destitution will greatly exceed any local or legal power of relief the board of guardians can command to meet it, unless all the *large* landed proprietors *at once* come forward to aid the poor labouring classes, by affording them employment under the Acts of Parliament passed for that benevolent purpose by the Legislature.[99]

Captain Spark wrote again a day later – Christmas Day 1847 – with a humanitarian appeal, reinforcing the particular requests of the people in the memorial, and pointing out the hardship imposed by the conditions covering public works. He specifically requested that the requirement that people must work eight hours a day in order to receive relief be reduced to four hours a day, since the labourers were already so weakened by hunger and ill-health that eight hours' work was beyond their capability:

> I believe the distress of many of the holders of upwards of a quarter of an acre to be as great as that of those who are occupiers of smaller allotments, and who are therefore entitled to relief, which the former are by law shut out from. The demand of eight hours labour each day is in accordance with the Poor Law Commissioners' directions; but I see great difficulties in the way of exacting it, particularly at this season of the year. I believe a modification of this regulation to be necessary; at the same time I would most earnestly recommend that *some* degree of labour should be required, perhaps *four* hours is as much as can be expected at this season from half-clad people, on one pound of Indian meal *per diem* to sustain them.[100]

The response of the Poor Law Commissioners to Captain Spark's pragmatic proposal of four hours' work per day was obdurate, offering only the most minor concession. The reply showed how wedded the authorities were to the idea that a 'test of destitution' was essential, and that eight hours' work a day was to be 'strictly exacted':

> In reference to your remarks as to the amount of daily labour required from each able-bodied pauper, I am to acquaint you at the present season of the year the Commissioners would not object to the period for a meal in the course of the day being included in the eight hours; but the Commissioners think that, otherwise, eight hours' work should be strictly exacted from every able-bodied man as a test of destitution.[101]

THE GREAT FAMINE

This eight hours of work did not take into account the weakened physical state of the labourers or the fact that they were also obliged to walk to and from the place of work, which could be far away from their homes. Little wonder that many died by the roadsides where they were meant to be working and that public works, instead of being a solution, were in themselves a cause of deaths.

The commissioners also replied directly to Fr McCarthy, expressing their view that existing measures would be adequate to save lives and stressing their guiding principle that 'the law is imperative' and that a 'test of destitution' was essential – as if the people had not been sorely tested already:

> Adverting to your letter of the 19th instant, on the subject of distress existing in certain parts of the Listowel Union, I am directed by the Commissioners to inform you that they have now received Captain Spark's report on your letter, and also on the memorial from the parishes of Ballyheigue, Killeery and Rattoo, which you forwarded to his Excellency the lord lieutenant.
>
> The Commissioners are assured by Captain Spark that the measures for affording out-door relief are fully organised; and the Commissioners entertain a confident hope that these measures, in conjunction with such employment as may be given by the landed proprietors in the Listowel Union, will be found adequate to save the poor of the district from the calamities to which the present pressure of severe distress would otherwise subject them.
>
> With reference to the two points urged in the memorial, viz., the refusal of the relief to persons occupying more than a quarter of an acre of land, and as regards the requiring [of] a task of work from the able-bodied as a condition of their receiving relief, the Commissioners desire to observe that the law is imperative in prohibiting relief to persons holding more than a quarter of an acre of land; and as regards the requiring a task of work from the able-bodied recipients of relief, the Commissioners have given the subject their fullest and most anxious consideration, and they do not think that this test of destitution could properly be dispensed with.[102]

The last correspondence for 1847 between Captain Spark and the commissioners dealt with the nature of the public work assigned to able-bodied paupers, anxious to know whether it would be 'bona fide laborious, so as to be a test of destitution'. Spark had referred to fencing and stone-breaking for roads and also sweeping the streets of Listowel. The commissioners were dubious about the street-sweeping and queried whether that work would be 'a mere cloak for idleness'. Spark responded somewhat tersely that cleaning was necessary previous to laying the stones down and concluded: 'If this is made a cloak for idleness, it will be the fault of overseers, and I shall recommend them to be dismissed.'[103]

There were numerous bureaucratic pressures on men like Spark who had a good knowledge of the area and who worked diligently at providing relief and at urging guardians and landlords to take their responsibilities seriously. Spark was often as equally frustrated by the responses of the Listowel board of guardians as he was by the orders of his superiors, as would become apparent in his dealings with them in 1848.

The Role of the Clergy

One Presbyterian visitor to Kerry in 1855 had an acerbic view of the typical priest in the county:

> The Kerry priest is a curiosity. Passion, anathema, cunning, the horsewhip, scowl and terror are weapons of his warfare. It is not uncommon to find him bound to keep the peace towards Her Majesty's subjects by the penalties of the law. His reign there is absolute.[104]

The priests of Kerry had close bonds with the people and there is abundant evidence that they performed Herculean tasks during the year of 1847. News items in the local press show that they provided immediate humanitarian assistance while also communicating with the press, with the national authorities and with local officials. For example, as Christmas approached in 1847, the priest of Duagh appealed to the Listowel board of guardians on behalf of the 13,500 destitute people in his district.[105] The priests were also involved in the local relief committees and in mediating peace in situations of potential conflict. They rallied the people into action and strengthened their resolve at critical times. Above all, they provided spiritual comfort to the people. For many of the starving, their only consolation in their agony was that they would receive the last rites from a priest. Catholic clergy were more numerous and more prominent, but Protestant clergymen were also actively involved in relief work, as readers of the *Post* were reminded when it praised Rev. Maunsell of Castleisland for securing relief funds in England and observed that 'the Protestant ministers of Ireland have distinguished themselves in every locality by their benevolence and philanthropic zeal'.[106]

The obituary of Rev. Anthony Denny of Tralee in the *Irish Ecclesiastical Gazette* in 1891 paid him this tribute:

> He will be best remembered as the friend and succourer of the sick and needy during the terrible famine of 1845–48. In the days of the cholera visitation, Mr Denny was to be seen constantly beside the beds and at the graves of the stricken poor, ministering to their spiritual necessities and with his own hands tending to the sufferers. There are few households in Tralee to which sickness or sorrow came where he will not be long remembered.[107]

Revs Maunsell, A. B. Rowan, Denny and Chute were indeed very active in providing relief in and around Tralee.

There were examples of high levels of co-operation between the Protestant and Catholic clergy in Kerry during the Famine years, which seemed to augur well for the future, as shown when Fr Eugene McCarthy thanked Rev. Dr Spratt for his contribution of £15 to the poor of Ballyheigue and assured him that he would 'do nothing without the concurrence of the Protestant clergyman of my parishes'.[108] Rev. Fitzmaurice Sandes, curate of Aghavallin near Ballylongford, paid the ultimate price for his humanitarian work: he died in February 1847 after an illness of a few hours, believed to have been a victim of typhus contracted while providing comfort to the sick and starving.[109]

Rev. Archibald Macintosh was rector of Ballincuslane and there was an excellent relationship between him and the priests of Castleisland as they worked together on the relief committee; he commended the priests for carrying out their duties with great credit.[110] Early in 1847 Rev. Macintosh acknowledged subscriptions received for relief in his area, including £10 from Abraham Beale on behalf of the Society of Friends, £10 from the Peas and Rice Fund, £40 and two boilers from the Irish Relief Association and £5 from Mr George Twiss.[111] In 1848 Macintosh attended a meeting of tenant farmers in Castleisland, arriving with the ailing parish priest of Castleisland, Jeremiah O'Leary, leaning on his arm. The meeting was held to appeal to landlords to provide work for the poor. O'Leary described the scenes they had witnessed over the previous two years: 'hundreds dead in the dykes and ditches and some of those not properly buried'. He believed that unless reproductive employment was provided by landlords, 'nothing but the most ruinous consequences must otherwise be the result for every class, from top to bottom'. When Rev. Macintosh spoke it was to praise Fr O'Leary's work on behalf of the poor and to acknowledge the peaceable, honest and patient endurance of the people.[112]

The sudden death of Rev. Macintosh in November 1848 came as a great shock. He was aged forty-six and died at his residence in Kilmurry; he had been healthy and active only a week before, when he visited the cabin of a sick family near where he lived. The *Post* speculated that he caught a malignant fever during the visit, and he died within days.

> To the poor of his immediate neighbourhood his loss will be severely felt and by the inhabitants of this town [Tralee] his memory will be long remembered with respect and affection as their faithful minister for many years until advanced by his bishop to the rectory of Ballincuslane where his exertions had just completed the erection of a church.[113]

There was a telling news item from Tralee at Easter 1847: the priests were so occupied in ministering to the sick that the Holy Week ceremonies were suspended. Care of the destitute took precedence even over the most sacred rituals of the church year; charity took precedence over liturgy.[114]

In Tralee in May a young priest, Thomas Enright, died of fever, 'victim to the heavy duties which in common with so many others of the priesthood he had been called on to discharge at the bedside of the fever stricken poor'.[115] He was the priest who had rescued a woman and baby from a lane in Denny Street a month earlier. He was one of six to eight priests of the diocese suffering from fever at that time, and Fr Kieran O'Shea names four other Kerry priests who died of fever contracted in the course of their ministry between 1846 and 1849. They were Fr Jeremiah Falvey, Glenflesk; Fr John O'Donoghue, Kilgarvan; Fr Patrick Touhy, Castlemaine; and Fr Michael Devine of Dingle, who died of cholera in May 1849.[116]

A most generous and surprising tribute was paid in Tralee church one Sunday by parish priest Dr McEnnery towards his Protestant counterpart, Rev. Denny, rector of Tralee, who was ill with fever. During Mass, Dr McEnnery asked for earnest prayers from the congregation for the health of Rev. Denny, praising his 'zeal in the cause of the poor, regardless of religion'. Surprising too was the response of the people: there was 'an immediate burst of fervid feeling from the entire body of the chapel, as gratifying as it was novel'.[117] The *Examiner* expressed the hope that this was a sign of greater unity among the Christian churches.

However, there were also many examples of bitter sectarianism in Tralee and north Kerry, with frequent recriminations between individual clergymen of Protestant and Catholic denominations.

The *Examiner* always showed a keen recognition of the work of the priests and an awareness of the risks they faced in the course of their duties. It proposed a fund to support priests whose incomes had greatly reduced, saying that it was a certain fact that many of them were in deep distress. The distress alluded to was financial, but the clergy must also have suffered from emotional and spiritual distress. The priests were described as 'an exemplary body' and the *Examiner* stated that their 'devotion, zeal and reckless disregard of self' had won the admiration of even their enemies:

> In these days of affliction the chamber of contagion has become almost the residence of the Catholic priest – if he escape its influence, he lives to witness in some adjoining hovel the father, mother and the children stretched on the wretched bed of filthy straw, on the bare ground, some of the wretched family dying, others of them dead, and none to remove the latter until decomposition has at length commenced its foul work and the stench of the grave is perceptible in this house of sorrow and suffering. None dare, none will, enter to give even a drink of water … Ah, there comes the priest. The gaunt peasant points out the poor abode that contains so much of all that our common nature shrinks from; the minister of heaven bends as he enters the lowly dwelling and there, unawed, he stands in the midst of the harrowing scene around him and unsubdued by its terrors and its horrors, he bends his ear to receive the confession of the occupant of the bed round which the contagion forms a deadly atmosphere …[118]

However, this proposed fund does not seem to have progressed any further.

The work of religious sisters and brothers did not receive detailed attention in the pages of the press, but the annals of the Presentation Convent in Listowel show that the sisters there were deeply concerned for the welfare of the children they taught. The recorder wrote at the end of 1846: 'The prospects for the coming year are appalling. May God assist his own and help us to relieve the loved children.'[119] In March 1847 the twelve sisters of the community began to feed the children, with numbers starting at thirteen but rising rapidly to 250. The children received bread, milk and a mug of boiled rice every morning. Also that year the nuns distributed 31,000 breakfasts in Listowel. They received funds from the Society of Friends and from local clergy and £80 came from Cardinal Franconi, prefect of the Congregation for the Propagation of the Faith in Rome.[120]

The annalist of the Presentation Convent in Tralee described these scenes of 1847:

> The famine that threatened in 1846 arrived at its height in this year … A

frightful dysentery swept off thousands. The Poor Houses crammed to excess, out of which the dead were usually taken off on a dray and thrown without coffins into one common pit. In some localities the dead were left to de-compose on the wayside until fear of putrefying the site obliged public officers to consign them to the earth ... Never was any country so prostrate.[121]

She recorded a daily occurrence for the parish priest:

> Dr McEnnery could never appear abroad that he would not almost instantly be surrounded by crowds of famished men and women tottering with disease and the ravages of hunger strongly marked on their ghastly faces. It was truly an appalling sight to see the chapel yard crowded every morning to surround and almost seize him for relief.[122]

After the death of Dr McEnnery in 1861, Bishop David Moriarty paid this tribute to his work during the Famine:

> I saw him then surrounded, pressed up and almost dragged asunder by the starving poor, he himself pale and staggering with weakness from excess of fatigue. I will never forget that sight. In that seething sea of misery, buffeting its waves and almost overwhelmed by them, saving from death at the peril of his own life, he appeared to be the greatest and the noblest man I ever looked on ... Then indeed he was a giant in charity.[123]

Souperism in Ballybunion

There are many references in Kerry newspapers to 'soupers' – people who converted to Protestantism in return for food – and priests would often claim that these converts were insincere and would have death-bed returns to Catholicism. Clearly, there was a kind of competition for souls, but this was not just an Irish phenomenon. There were regular reports of prominent English converts to Catholicism and even a report from Germany, which stated that the last descendant of Martin Luther had become a Catholic.[124]

A strong element of triumphal gloating was evident in these reports.

The Tablet carried an editorial on the practice of souperism by evangelical Protestants, describing it as 'a very old, a very foolish, a very wicked manoeuvre' and coining a new verb from the parish of Ventry, where a Protestant crusade had been carried out for years. For *The Tablet*, such missions were designed:

> ... to take advantage of the present famine to *Ventryise* as much of the country as they can; to buy up souls for hell wherever there is an opportunity; to make the child's agony a means of damning the father and the mother; to use the husband's 'wolfish' and hungering madness for the perdition of the wife; to set a man's empty belly against a wavering conscience and to make the poverty of thousands, which by the divine law is the best preparative for heaven, an equally efficacious preparative for hell ... The famine is too good a thing to be allowed to slip through the fingers ...
>
> Once more hired distributors of relief ... are to be let loose among the people with food in one hand and the mutilated word of God in the other to make converts whose new creed will last only to the next harvest.[125]

In June 1847 Rev. John Stamer wrote an account of an incident that occurred when he walked through Ballybunion with a hundred converts on their way to Sunday service in Lisselton. They were attacked by a jeering mob, who threw stones and sods of turf at them. At Lisselton the mob continued its barrage against the windows of their church and attacked some animals, cutting off the ears of a donkey and beating a cow until it was nearly dead.[126] Stamer's account was corroborated by Mr Dennis, a landlord, and by a visiting member of the church. Another such incident took place in September.[127]

The *Examiner* carried an alternative perspective on the original incident from the correspondent who signed himself 'Catholicus'. He described Rev. Stamer as 'this pugnacious little parson' and his followers as 'this soup rabble'.[128] He stated that the minister had lately received money from England, which had acted 'like opium on the mind', and it was because of this money that 'a few debauched and outcast men [became] followers of his soup heresy'. As regards Mr Dennis, the writer had this to add: 'It would be well if, instead of marching under the banner of hypocrisy and bigotry at the head of the unfortunate serfs starved into Protestantism, he would give them work and food and would in these times of famine and misery, allow these wretched people to worship God as their fathers worshipped.'[129] This was the tenor of many reports on religious rivalries.

Rev. Stamer (1803–89) was from Co. Clare. His approach to his mission was shown in his comment in an English newspaper:

> I have no doubt that a large portion [of Ballybunion] would become Protestants if I could only procure any kind of house ... The influence of the priest is much weakened not only by his curses but also by his blessings, for the converts he cursed some months since in their crops and in their children are now as well and happy as ever they were ... whilst the diseased cows which he had been blessing and saying masses for are all dead ...[130]

But even bitter rivals sometimes agreed: Rev. Stamer, described as 'a Protestant gentleman remarkable for the zeal in which he propagates the religious opinions in which he believes' and Fr Mahony, parish priest of Listowel, described as 'equally zealous for his own religion', came together in 1849 to sign a petition on behalf of state prisoners, and this was seen as a good omen.[131]

There were frequent attacks of stone-throwing and window-breaking on the newly built Presbyterian or Scots church in Tralee, with the *Examiner* stating disingenuously that these were not sectarian in nature but just normal blackguardism.[132] In Ardfert there was alarm at the desecration of the burial ground near the Protestant church when skulls were taken from graves and smashed into pieces, which were then thrown into a person's house.[133]

Catholic Curates

The work of curates during the Famine has not been fully acknowledged, and Thomas P. O'Neill has written that the policy of not allowing them to be members of relief committees was a great mistake. He quoted this comment by Lord Monteagle, referring to the area near Foynes and Glin, Co. Limerick: 'Without them – and here they are labouring like tigers for us – we could not move a stroke'.[134] O'Neill points out that curates had youth and energy and were usually more familiar with and closer to the circumstances of the families in their parishes.[135]

In December 1847 Fr J. O'Connor, a curate in Listowel, spoke about 'the frightful mass of misery' that was to be seen throughout Listowel Union. He had witnessed a family living on one meal of turnips in twenty-four hours and a man who had not the strength to leave his cabin to appeal for help. He accused the board of guardians of taking no steps to relieve the people and of 'being culpably neglectful of the duties entrusted to them'. He also said that 'there was an apathy among them bordering on disrespect for the lives of the people and of disregard for the faithful discharge of the most important duties ever confided to man, the preservation of the lives of God's creatures'.[136] These were strong accusations and he was warned by the *Post* that his position would be 'anything but an enviable one' if his charges were disproved.[137]

When his fellow curate Francis Newton Hurly was later transferred from Listowel to Castleisland, his parishioners presented him with a parting gift of £15. They also paid an impressive tribute to his work, regretting the loss 'of one so gifted and so good, one whose ear and heart were ever open to us and whose sympathy was as lively on behalf of the poor child deprived by an over-scrupulous relieving officer of her little portion of meal, as it was ready to seek the redress of grievances'.[138]

The work of the clergy in general during the Famine years was described by the humanitarian Count Strzelecki in evidence to a parliamentary committee. Strzelecki was expanding on his opinion that a sense of fatalism had enveloped the people, a sense that there was 'a curse upon the land' which affected 'both priests and people, depressed them morally, and slackened the ties of common and usual influences':

> [Priests] do their utmost, but I have seen their faith not a little shaken by the appalling circumstances by which they are surrounded, and the extraordinary misery to which they themselves are subject. In some instances, where priests were confined with fever, I found in their cabins nothing available beyond stirabout for their own sustenance; there was no tea, no sugar, no provision whatever; in some of their huts, the wind blew, the snow came in, and the rain dripped … [They suffered] distress as great as that suffered by any of the poor people; there was no difference between them.[139]

In 1850 the *Examiner* raised concerns about the low income of curates, saying that one had an income of only £8 in 1849; the average income was £15 and the maximum for any curate was £30. Out of this he had to meet expenses of clothing, lodging, food, drink and sundries and the keep of a horse. A priest with £30 a year would have a weekly income of 11s 6d, about half of what a skilled carpenter or stonemason would earn. It proposed that a fund be established in the diocese in order to raise this 'starvation income'.[140]

In her assessment of the responses of various groups and individuals to the tragedies of 1847, historian Mary Daly concluded as follows:

> More could have done more to save lives during that terrible year, but responsibility does not lie solely with the government; greater humanity and activity on the part of landlords and land agents would have helped. Farmers should have shown greater sympathy to their starving cottiers; Catholic clergy could have been more pro-active and grain traders less greedy. Politicians such as O'Connell and Young Irelanders could have devoted less time to squabbling over political issues and more attention to the condition of the people. It is easy to be wise after the event.[141]

However, on the evidence in the newspapers of Kerry and of official documents, many of the clergy of north Kerry gave selflessly of their time and energy and little blame can be assigned to them. The deeds of many of them were heroic and should be recognised as such. Fortunately for their parishioners, men like Eugene McCarthy and others continued to be strong advocates of their people for the following traumatic years, until a gradual improvement in conditions began to take hold.

6

'GRAVES CALL TO YOU FOR VENGEANCE'

1848

> *I assure you that it was a great comfort to me, after seeing the terrible destitution of the country, to witness so many little children, happy, healthy amidst the dreadful desolation which surrounded them ...*
>
> Captain Hotham, Poor Law Inspector, 16 January 1848, on the work of the British Relief Association

On the first day of 1848 the *Dublin Evening Packet* reflected on 1847 in this editorial:

> That the year which has just terminated will be chronicled in history and handed down to posterity as one of the most disastrous in the annals of Ireland must be readily admitted. It has been a year of trials unexampled, of sufferings unprecedented and of privations for which no parallel can be found in the records of any country in the world enjoying the blessings of domestic peace. *Annus mirabilis* it may well be called, but alas, the wonder must be blended with sorrow and shaded deeply with the gloomiest tints of melancholy colouring. Whether as a punishment for past transgressions, or it may be, a salutary warning for the future, Ireland has been scourged with a whip of scorpions and no class or order of her inhabitants has escaped

Tarbert House today. (*Author's collection*)

Rev. Dr John McEnnery, parish priest of Tralee. (From *The Diocese of Kerry, formerly Ardfert* by Fr Kieran O'Shea)

Opening page of the journal of Lieutenant H. N. Greenwell, 18 September 1846. (*Courtesy of Maile Melrose*)

Henry Nicholas Greenwell *c.* 1847. (*Courtesy of Maile Melrose*)

Above: Ballyseedy House today. (*Author's collection*)

Right: William Talbot Crosbie of Ardfert Abbey. (*Courtesy of Tommy O'Connor*)

'Famine in Ireland', an image dating from *c.* 1850. The caption reads in part: 'The scene here represented is from the description of eye-witnesses, but the more revolting features are omitted.' Printed by Hullmandel and Walton from an original by A. S. G. Stopford. (*Courtesy of the National Library of Ireland*)

The ruins of Listowel workhouse after it was destroyed during the Civil War, 1922. (*Courtesy of Michael Guerin*)

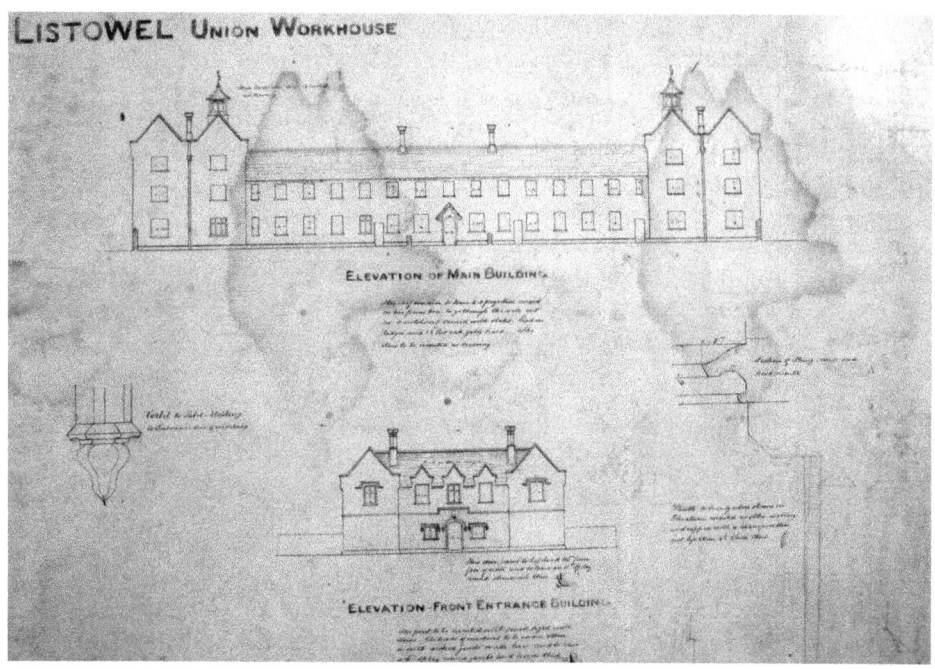

Plans of Listowel workhouse and its entrance building.
(*Courtesy of the Irish Architectural Archive*)

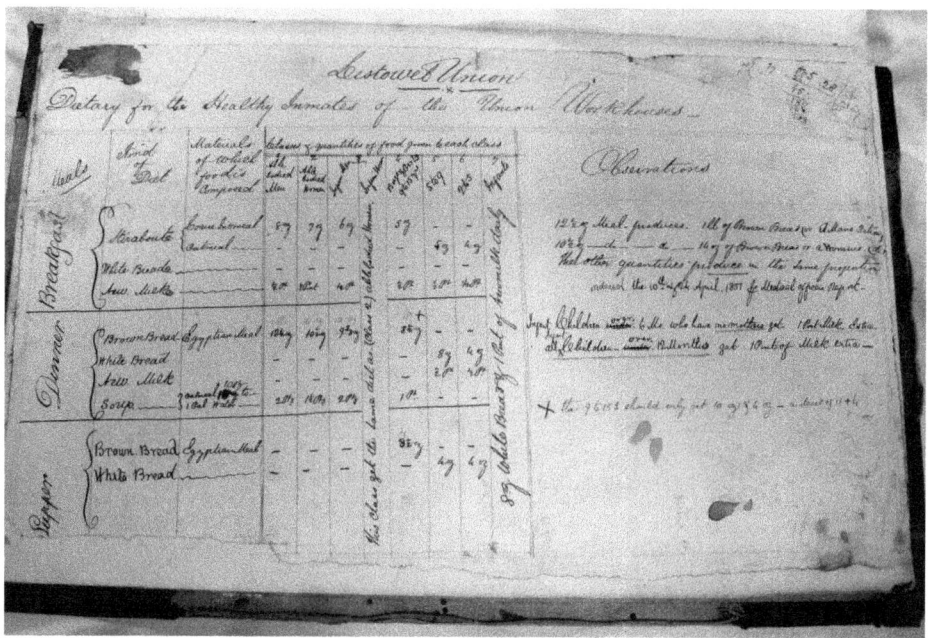

'Listowel Union: Dietary for the Healthy Inmates of the Union Workhouses', 1851. Supper was provided only for children under fifteen. Infants received eight ounces of white bread and one pint of new milk daily.
(*Courtesy of Kerry County Archives*)

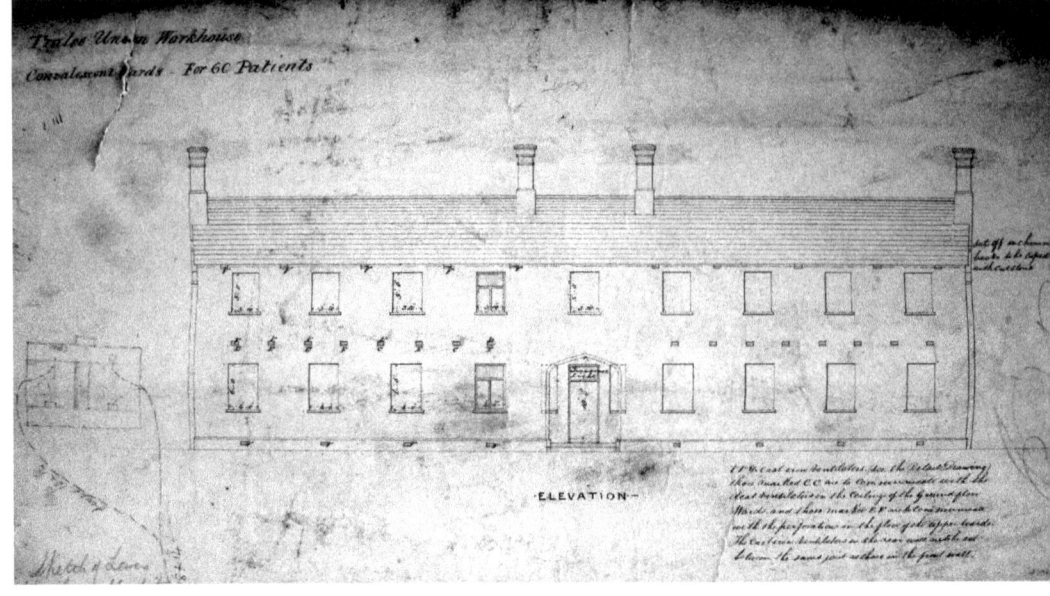

Plan for a 'convalescent ward for 60 patients' at Tralee workhouse: front elevation. The small openings were for ventilation. (*Courtesy of the Irish Architectural Archive*)

A page from the minute book of Tralee board of guardians, 24 May 1851, when there were 7,197 workhouse inmates. The abbreviations refer to auxiliary workhouses. (*Courtesy of Kerry County Archives*)

Tralee workhouse graveyard at the rear of Áras an Chontae, County Buildings, Rathass. The inscription at the base of the Celtic cross reads: 'Known to God, 1847'. (*Author's collection*)

Clogherbrien cemetery today. (*Author's collection*)

A detail from the memorial window to Fr Jeremiah (Darby) Mahony, PP, in St Mary's Church, Listowel. (*Author's collection*)

the dreadful, the tremendous infliction. The visitation has fallen heavily if not equally upon all. While the poor perished by myriads, many who were once rich but are no longer so fully participated in the general woe and the chastisement has been sweeping, unsparing and indiscriminate. That no human prudence could have averted the calamity which fell upon Ireland in the autumn of 1846 and has more or less continued down to the present day everybody will acknowledge. The potato failure cannot be attributed to the neglect of man.[1]

A comment by a leading churchman in February 1848 is revealing. Dr Slattery, Archbishop of Cashel, in a letter written to Archbishop Murray of Dublin, gave his insight into the effects of the Famine in Munster:

God help the people, they are in a worse state than they were last year, though under the name of getting outdoor relief they are actually starving and in rags, yet insufficient as that relief is, it will absorb the entire rated property of the district if it continues for any time, and continue it must, as there is no employment for those who are able and willing, but who will soon be unable to do so even when they get the work. When or how this state of things will end the Lord only knows. In the meantime extermination goes on under the protection of the law, and everyone who sympathises in any way with the unfortunate victims is held forth as an abettor of crime and of murder.[2]

In another letter Archbishop Slattery wrote of the toll that the crisis had taken on his health:

In truth I am completely stricken down by my own personal difficulties together with the deplorable condition of our unhappy people – the very heart is almost gone out of me and my most anxious desire is to make way for someone else possessing energies adapted to the trying times upon which we have fallen.[3]

THE GREAT FAMINE

When Queen Victoria visited Ireland in 1849, Archbishop Slattery refused to meet her and took no part in official receptions, as a protest against what he saw as her indifference to the suffering of the Irish poor.[4]

Despite the prevailing gloom at the turn of the year, in the spring of 1848 there were hopes that the potato crop would be free of blight, since the disease had not appeared the previous year and the distress among the poor in the winter of 1847 was caused instead by the very small crop. These hopes were dashed in August when a blight 'as virulent as in 1846' appeared in the west of Ireland particularly.[5] In the areas affected, such as Tralee and north Kerry, this was the fourth year of food shortages, exacerbated by widespread disease, which placed a crushing burden on the most destitute.

Tralee

Captain A. J. Hotham had arrived in Tralee in November 1847 and soon experienced some regrets about the extent of the workload he had taken on his shoulders. In January 1848 he summarised for his superiors what he had said to the board of guardians in Tralee:

> I reminded the board that two months ago, on my arrival in Tralee, great destitution prevailed in the union; that the meetings of the board were invariably interrupted by large mobs of distressed people seeking for admissions into the house; that the house was full; that the relieving officers had been appointed but were utterly untrained and nothing was done towards bringing outdoor relief into operation and that under these circumstances and foreseeing the enormous mass of business which must fall upon them, I had determined in every way in my power to assist them.[6]

Hotham then listed all that had been done since his arrival: the workhouse had been 'cleared' of all infirm persons and widows with two or more legitimate children and their places had been given to the so-called able-bodied; another building capable of holding 900 had been hired and fitted out (Ballymullen auxiliary workhouse); verandahs of the old workhouse were enclosed, fever sheds made secure and the capacity of each dormitory was written above the door to prevent overcrowding; 'the children had been turned out of the house' (perhaps meaning they had been transferred to Ballymullen); clothes and utensils had been 'examined' and general repairs had been completed in the store and other departments; outdoor relief had been implemented; and relieving officers had begun to understand their duties. He then told the board that he had been acting more as a paid vice-guardian than as an inspector, and that he was doing work that was properly the responsibility of the board. He concluded by telling them that he was not justified in co-operating with them so actively and that 'the time was now coming when they must be prepared to take the whole burden on their own shoulders'.[7]

Hotham had sympathy for the arduous work of the relieving officers who spent two days a week travelling to and from board meetings, some of them from over thirty miles distant; another day was spent at a committee meeting in their districts leaving only three days for dealing with applications and visiting applicants' homes to investigate claims. 'The extreme size of this Union,' he wrote, 'renders their duties very severe and puts them to considerable expense. Two are threatening to resign.'[8]

Hotham described the duties of the relieving officer for Ventry, who travelled thirty-three miles to Tralee on Monday with his accounts; he waited for the board's orders on Tuesday when it met; returned on Wednesday and distributed relief on Thursday; he attended a guardians' committee meeting in Dingle on Friday and spent Saturday receiving applications, visiting applicants' houses and investigating their circumstances. Hotham was deeply involved in matters concerning the setting up of a separate union and separate workhouse for the Dingle area and spent much of his time on that issue.[9]

Tralee Workhouse

Abuses grew persistent in the workhouse throughout 1848 and culminated in the dismissal of the master and matron. The scale of theft of food and clothing was described by Owen Lloyd, Poor Law inspector, as 'wholesale plunder', and he recommended raising the height of the perimeter walls to prevent all communications between inmates and friends outside.[10] Lloyd recommended changes in management of the workhouse and 'an increase in restrictions on the paupers so as to make the house more distasteful to them and consequently more efficacious as a test of destitution'.[11]

The guardians eventually passed a motion that 'in consequence of gross neglect and inefficiency, the entire staff should be dismissed'.[12] Their failings were summarised as follows: the house was carelessly managed; books were not kept up to date and for five weeks, while the master was ill, no books had been kept; property had been lost and wasted by the neglect of officers; and rations had been acquired for 287 more people than were in the house. On a single day, sixteen people were charged with theft from the house. Eighty-six paupers were reported as absconding with workhouse clothing, and ninety people were admitted, all but ten of whom had to be provided with footwear, which it was believed they would soon sell in exchange for inferior shoes. It was first proposed to leave them barefoot, then to provide them with wooden shoes made in the town jail, as they would be cheaper than leather shoes.[13] The guardians had by then apparently lost confidence in their own administrative ability and asked Lloyd to select the new master and matron from among the applicants; he chose Hugh Falvey and Margaret O'Sullivan.[14]

'Honest John Lynch' of Tralee Exposed

Terrible occurrences continued in and around Tralee during 1848. Mr Shea of Liscahane near Ardfert died 'from want of food'.[15] He left a wife and three children behind; he had made repeated attempts to enter the workhouse but was refused.

In an exchange at a board of guardians' meeting concerning the health needs of Tralee, board member John McCarthy said that every day he was in the town he was followed by fifty, sixty or a hundred paupers, who never complained of want of medicine but of want of food. In contrast John Hurly said that he had never seen Tralee looking so healthy and so few needing medical relief.[16]

In April the parish priest, Dr McEnnery, was concerned about violence and cautioned the poor of the town not to be misled by 'the apostles of anarchy' into actions that would be 'as foolish as they were criminal'.[17] Hunger still drove people to desperate measures: a large body of men attacked a bread shop at the corner of Denny Street and 'they set about devouring the plunder with great greediness, being evidently without food for a considerable time'.[18]

Undoubtedly, the most sensational event in Tralee in 1848 was the dramatic revelation of a massive fraud perpetrated by John Lynch, one of the town's most respected and popular men, acclaimed as a defender of the poor and the oppressed. His conscientious work as chairman of the board of guardians during the appalling winter of 1846–7 was very much appreciated and when his term had ended in March 1847, the members tendered him their unanimous thanks:

> ... for his valuable, efficient and indefatigable exertions while chairman of this board and at a time when the pressure on the board was excessive and the duties connected with it not only onerous, but from the diseased condition in which many of the paupers presented themselves, attended with considerable danger of contracting disease.[19]

Among many other public roles, Lynch had been the secretary of Tralee Savings Bank since its foundation and the bank actually operated out of his own house in Bridge Street. His annual salary from the bank was £60 a year and his competence and integrity had never been challenged. But when a depositor attempted to withdraw his funds in April 1848, the bank chairman, Rev. A. B. Rowan, discovered that the bank did not have assets to cover the amount. He went to his colleague and friend John Lynch to clear up what he believed to be an accounting error. Lynch immediately broke down and confessed to a system of fraud that he had been practising on the depositors over many years, resulting in a total amount of over £30,000 being embezzled by him. Apparently crushed with remorse, he won some sympathy initially by confessing everything and by explaining how the fraud operated, but this sympathy gradually eroded as the scale of his brazen fraud became clearer. Having publicly and frequently denounced landlords and others for their greed and lack of concern for the poor, the hypocrisy of John Lynch was on a grand scale. He was ultimately sentenced to fourteen years' transportation for his crime.[20]

The Work of the British Relief Association

In the Listowel Union area, in the period from October 1847 to July 1848, the British Relief Association made a total grant of £2,712 12s 3½d. This was spent as follows: relief of general distress: £60; rationing children at school: £2,400; clothing children at school: £252 12s 3½d.[21] The association's distribution of clothes and food in the Listowel Union area covered twenty schools and 6,309 children over twenty-three weeks. The clothes distributed were:

> Boys: 430 jackets, 300 waistcoats, 430 trousers, 435 shirts, 420 caps.
> Girls: 25 bibs, 95 gowns, 817 petticoats, 817 chemises.[22]

In the Tralee and Dingle areas, 3,098 children in forty-eight schools were provided with relief by the association over twenty-nine weeks. The total amount expended was £1,361 15s 3d, made up of £1,110 on rations and £261 15s 3d on clothing. The clothing was itemised as follows:

> Boys: 500 jackets, 350 waistcoats, 500 trousers, 500 shirts, 500 caps.
> Girls: 1,040 petticoats.[23]

Captain Spark in Listowel reported that schools were 'crowded to suffocation on account of the relief provided by the British Association' and he was reminded by the commissioners that food should be given only to children who were previously enrolled in the schools.[24] Children in Ballyheigue schools were beneficiaries of this aid, as adverted to briefly by Fr McCarthy in an application for support for an assistant teacher for a national school in Ballylongane townland, where the attendance had increased.[25]

In general, wherever the British Relief Association distributed food and clothing, the numbers attending school rose dramatically. Captain Hotham received £200 from the association to feed schoolchildren between the ages of six and fourteen. 'Children are already, on hearing of this, flocking to the schools so that I shall have serious difficulty in preventing them from being overcrowded,' he wrote. He recommended that the number of national schools should be increased immediately.[26]

Other schools in north Kerry which benefitted from the funds of the British Association were the following: Aughrim schools in Moyvane (£25), Erasmus Smith school in Ballybunion (£27 5s), Brosna (£19), Listowel (£21) and Kildare Place school in Sallowglen, Tarbert (£59).[27] One telling feature of the association's work in Kerry was that Captain Spark made a personal donation of £100 to the charity, of which he was the local administrator, and this provided seventy gowns, 792 petticoats and 792 chemises. Another individual donation was from a Miss Hewson, who donated £20, which also provided gowns, petticoats and chemises.[28]

The work of the British Relief Association was a ray of hope in the gloom of 1848. Count Strzelecki's inspired initiative of feeding and clothing children through the schools had a wonderful effect. Captain Hotham wrote this informative tribute to the work of the British Relief Association in his district on 16 January 1848:

> I saw about fifteen schools and the result was highly satisfactory. You are acquainted with the difficulty in general experienced in Ireland of granting any money without entailing a train of abuses in its distribution, but I think the system of our schools here is as free from abuses as any system of the kind possibly can be. I assure you that it was a great comfort to me, after seeing the terrible destitution of the country, to witness so many little children, happy, healthy amidst the dreadful desolation which surrounded them and I sincerely wished in my heart that the subscribers to the Association's funds could witness the real good, almost unmixed with evil, it has caused.[29]

Lord Robert Clinton, agent of the association in north Kerry, set up a large food kitchen in Tralee and an auxiliary store in Milltown and he praised the landlord there, Sir William Godfrey, and the local parish priest, for their great zeal, energy and generosity. They assisted Clinton's efforts by transporting a cargo of meal to Milltown and providing a meal store free of charge. He wrote: 'I wish I could find more members of relief committees imbued with the same liberal feeling towards their neighbours.'[30]

The invaluable work of the association unfortunately came to an end in the summer of 1848, by which time it had spent over £470,000 in relief in Ireland. By then it had simply exhausted its funds; what is now called donor fatigue had set in, particularly in Britain.[31]

Listowel Union

The Correspondence of Captain Spark

A good deal of information on the issues involving Listowel Union can be learned from the reports of Captain Spark to his superiors in Dublin. Referring to the amount of correspondence and government reports generated by the Famine, John Mitchel wrote that the poor were 'slaughtered by stationery'.[32] Certainly there was an incredible amount of correspondence to and from officials such as Captain Spark all over the country.

On 18 February 1848 Spark wrote of his inspection of the southern and western parts of the Listowel Union, where he was dissatisfied to find that the able-bodied paupers were receiving rations for work which mainly involved improving road-fencing rather than stone-breaking, which he favoured. There was a shortage of stones because there were few quarries and farmers were not supplying stones as they used them for drainage. There was also a shortage of hammers. Spark found these problems in Kilmoyley in particular, where he stated that 'here, and indeed in all the most western portions of the Union, a great degree of the most abject wretchedness appears among the numerous cottiers and no sort of employment is yet afforded by the landlords and farmers. The land is in too wet a state to be worked for cropping.'[33]

Spark referred to the relieving officer for Kilmoyley, James Cooke, who had been ordered to resign by the commissioners because he had allowed some names to be added to his lists of people in need of relief on the recommendation of individual ratepayers. Cooke had admitted this, but Spark supported him, saying that he found him 'most actively and satisfactorily doing his duty'.[34] Cooke was allowed to continue as relieving officer, but not for long, as a more serious scandal led to his dismissal in 1849 (see page 221).

Rather than receiving detailed instructions from his superiors, it appears that Spark was devising his own administrative procedures, as he sent them proposed job descriptions for the various officials involved in providing outdoor relief for their approval. This was his description of the duties of a relieving officer:

> The relieving officers on having their application books revised by the guardians, and the amount of provisions sanctioned for each impotent pauper, shall issue to each a week's allowance by an order on the storekeeper; but when an able-bodied pauper, whose claim has been admitted by the guardians, makes application, he is to be furnished with an order to the overseer in charge of working party according to subjoined Form A.
>
> In case of extreme and urgent necessity the relieving officer may issue an order for temporary relief on the storekeeper, marking all such orders 'Special'. In issuing this and all other orders on the storekeeper, care is taken to write the amount in full as well as in figures.
>
> On the next board day the books will again be revised and the expenditure book examined, and any improvident or unauthorized distribution will be charged to the relieving officer.[35]

Spark included further descriptions of the duties of storekeepers and overseers, along with samples of various forms which were to be filled in, and this description of the duties of the head overseer, which gives a picture of the bureaucracy of relief:

The head overseer of the district is to point out to the overseer in charge of the stations at which the working parties are severally to be employed; he is also to point out the nature of the work to be done, the manner in which it is to be performed and the daily task to be required from each labourer, which should not be less than what could be performed by eight hours fair labour from the individual according to his age and strength. He is to visit each station once a week for the purpose of ascertaining the total amount of work done and its value, and certify the same to the guardians at their next meeting; he is also to pay particular attention to the conduct of the persons employed and to report any irregularity.

It is supposed that stone-breaking by task-work will be the best mode of employing the able-bodied; a portion in quarrying, some in breaking, and others in spreading. It will be necessary that the stones, and those quarried and not broken, should not be removed that week, in order that the head overseer may ascertain, by actual measurement, the precise amount of work done during the week. One third of the number employed in breaking stones will be the number employed in quarrying; the stones quarried, but not broken, must be measured and taken into account – and thus may be ascertained the numbers employed in breaking and quarrying respectively.

The head overseer will in this way be a check on the overseer's issue of orders on the storekeeper.[36]

On 31 March Spark noted that a letter had been sent to the board of guardians from Fr Eugene McCarthy, who was continuing his work as an advocate of his parishioners. According to Spark, Fr McCarthy represented 'very strongly the distress existing in the western districts of Rattoo, Dromkeen and Ballyheigue among persons not entitled to relief'.[37] The relieving officers all declared that, with the exception of Ballylongford and Abbeydorney, there was very little employment available for labourers and that relief should continue to be provided.[38]

Relief was scheduled to end on 7 March 1848, as the government did not want to sustain a policy which might become a permanent drain on the exchequer. Spark recommended that it should be extended until 18 March, because the wet weather prevented farmers from offering any work to labourers. He advised that the electoral divisions of Ardfert and Abbeydorney could be excluded from the extension, because 'labour for all is laudably being provided by proprietors and farmers'.[39] This appears to indicate approval of William Talbot Crosbie's actions as landlord. Spark also recommended that, as a saving, all single, able-bodied men over eighteen and all married men with only two children should be excluded from relief. The commissioners agreed with this last recommendation but stated that they could not exclude specific electoral divisions. Spark continued to recommend repeated extensions of the relief deadline, finally securing it until May 1848. However, the fear persisted that able-bodied men would become idle if relief was too easily available and Spark wrote about an occasion when 300 men in Ballylongford refused to do drainage work when offered it and were consequently struck off the lists for relief. He wrote on 3 March 1848: 'The people generally will not work so long as they can obtain food without it.'[40]

Civil disobedience also continued into 1848. On 18 March Spark reported that the grainstore for Kiltomy district in Lixnaw had been broken into for the second time in two weeks and that ten sacks of Indian meal had been taken away. One man was arrested for having an unexplained quantity of meal in his house and Spark in exasperation commented that 'nothing can be worse than the character of that people of that village and district, who are, it appears, noted nightly robbers and marauders'.[41]

Spark was also unsympathetic to the appeals of a man from Ballylongford who wrote a letter to the lord lieutenant saying that large numbers of people there were 'dropping with famine and distress'.[42] He went to Ballylongford in early February to investigate and found that only three or four elderly people had died there since Christmas and that they had obtained relief. He claimed that there was plenty of work available for able-bodied men, but many of them refused to work because 'they prefer idleness and shun labour under any plea, in order to get the outdoor relief'.[43]

Other matters that arose in the voluminous correspondence between

Captain Spark and the commissioners reveal a great deal about administrative procedures. Among the matters arising were the appointment and dismissal of staff, and the purchase of spinning wheels, wool, flax and reels for the women of the workhouse. Spark devoted a great deal of attention to the question of how best to provide food for those entitled to outdoor relief. He drew up detailed costings for four possible options, detailing the pros and cons of each: baked bread made from Indian corn meal, stirabout or porridge, raw meal, and wetted or steeped meal. He was concerned that if raw meal were distributed it would be sold, as it was a marketable commodity, whereas steeped meal could not be sold. He recommended steeped meal and the commissioners agreed to this.[44]

Listowel Workhouse
There are no surviving records from the Listowel board of guardians in Kerry County Archives for the crucial period of 1846 to late 1848. The minute books for the period May 1840 to November 1845 have survived, but there are no available records from then until November 1848. Therefore, although the Listowel workhouse opened on 13 February 1845, there is little information available on it prior to 1848. What is known is that the workhouse was situated on a six-acre site and had a capacity of 700. The building cost £5,980 and the fittings cost £1,276.[45] Sleeping galleries were added later to create another 100 places.

An inspector named Denis Phelan investigated the conditions in the workhouse in February 1848 and his report gives an overview of conditions.[46] He found the house and yards unclean and the grounds impassable in places because of water and mud. The inmates were 'moderately clean' but there was a shortage of straw for bedding and ventilation needed to be improved. Nursing and care of infants was unsatisfactory, and although Phelan accepted that this was normal in workhouses, he attributed it to the ineffectiveness of the matron. The medical officer attended regularly, but the infirmary was overcrowded and Phelan recommended that patients with skin diseases should be moved elsewhere. Smallpox and measles were present in the house, but not to an alarming extent and vaccinations were used when required. There were twenty-six cases of fever, mostly caused by influenza, but only three were serious.

Each pauper received stirabout made from 3 ounces of rice and 3 ounces of Indian meal for breakfast, but Phelan regarded this diet as too expensive, with Indian meal costing £9 a ton and rice costing £19 a ton. He recommended that the stirabout should consist of three parts meal to one part rice.

Phelan found that the management of the workhouse was inefficient, with the master being very young and new to the position. The matron was well intentioned and a person of integrity, but lacked the qualities of mind and body required for the position. Both had inherited a poor system of management from the previous incumbents. A building being prepared for the accommodation of paupers was found to have water lodged under the floorboards and Phelan ordered building work to be stopped until proper drainage was installed. He also recommended that heads of families applying for relief should come before the board to be examined, rather than applying to the local relieving officer, whose decision might be swayed by favouritism.[47]

Captain Spark had also dealt with the Listowel workhouse during his time as Poor Law inspector. One of his reports included the recommendation that a vacant old mill near Listowel should be used as an auxiliary workhouse to cater for the larger numbers seeking accommodation when outdoor relief ceased. The mill had seven floors and would be capable of keeping 600 inmates.[48]

The *Examiner* praised Captain Spark's attention to the affairs of the Listowel workhouse in glowing terms:

> Captain Spark, the Poor Law Inspector for the Union, has won golden opinions for himself by the very great improvements which he has introduced into the general management of the workhouse since his arrival in Listowel. The gallant officer is, we understand, possessed of the most humane and kindly feelings towards the poor, at the same time that he observes all due strictness in the discharge of his public duties. Indeed the conduct of the inspectors of

the several Unions in this county is most satisfactory and praiseworthy. They are all gentlemen of great intelligence and possessing great knowledge of the practical details of business.[49]

However, there was criticism of workhouse conditions from some of its guardians. Kerry Supple said that 'the general complaint among ratepayers was that the paupers were pampered. His wish was that the poor should get sound and wholesome food but he objected that they should be better fed than the farmers who would be obliged to pay for that food.' Captain Spark was willing to adapt the diet of the workhouse in order to make savings but reminded the guardians that dysentery was prevalent and that medical advice would be required before any change was made.[50]

The basic workhouse diet was prescribed as follows: adults were to have two meals a day: a breakfast consisting of 8 ounces of stirabout and half a pint of milk, and a dinner of 3½ pounds of potatoes and a pint of skimmed milk; children had three meals: a breakfast of 3 ounces of oatmeal and half a pint of new milk, a dinner of 2 pounds of potatoes and half a pint of new milk, and a supper of 6 ounces of bread.[51] When potatoes were not available, more stirabout made from Indian corn or oatmeal was the substitute.

As with the Tralee workhouse, mass resistance occurred on a few occasions in the workhouse. For example, in February 1848 when a large group of paupers rushed into the dining hall and took the bread, those for whom the bread was intended were furious and attacked the robbers and a riot ensued. The police were called and five people were arrested.[52] Captain Spark blamed the inexperience of the assistant master for the handling of this and other incidents, saying he was no more than a boy and had been appointed because his father was one of the guardians. In fact, the assistant master was aged twenty-four and one guardian defended him, saying, 'If he were as large as the colossus of Rhodes, he could not control such an excited people as the paupers must have been'.[53]

The acute administrative crisis of Listowel Union is seen in its plea for more support from the government in February 1848. The board of guardians stated that there were 1,002 inmates in the workhouse and its auxiliaries, and that 22,373 people were being supplied with food as outdoor relief. This amounted to 'an alarming total of 23,375 out of a population, according to the census of 1841, of 78,757' and a weekly expenditure of £780 on food alone. Union funds intended to last for twelve months would be exhausted in four months. Almost 30 per cent of the union's population was dependent on the food rations provided, and applicants for relief had risen 'to the overwhelming numbers of 32,373'.[54]

Tributes to Captain Spark

In early autumn Captain Spark was transferred to Scariff, Co. Clare, and was replaced by Captain Hart. Spark's departure was widely regretted, with the *Examiner* praising his 'charitable and humane disposition and actions towards and on behalf of the poor of the town [Listowel] and of the inmates of the workhouse'.[55] This 'gallant Englishman' left a very positive impression on all with whom he had engaged in the difficult year he had spent in Kerry, as expressed by the editor of the *Chronicle*:

> Of the manner in which Captain Spark discharged his duty we have had personal knowledge and gladly avail of this opportunity to record our sense of his urbanity and philanthropy as a Christian gentleman. It was through his instrumentality that so large a measure of relief was administered to the north of the county, a mode of relief which from all we can gather, would under similar surveillance, be the greatest boon which the benevolent could bestow on the poor of this country.[56]

Spark's private charity and administration of the funds of the British Relief Association drew praise in a public statement by the Catholic clergy of north Kerry, a fact which the *Chronicle* saw as proof that, contrary to some assertions, there was widespread gratitude and appreciation of 'the munificent charity of the people of England'.[57] The clergy addressed Captain Spark as follows, believing that he was leaving Ireland altogether:

> As the ministers of those for whom you have intensely felt and humanely acted, offering you our gratitude, deep and heartfelt:
>
> We made your acquaintance as a public officer in fearful and calamitous times when the continual sight of fever and famine had paralysed the actions of the strongest minded – and we cheerfully bear testimony to that active humanity and Christian charity with which you performed your duties as an officer and soothed and relieved the misery of your fellow-man. Your private charities are known to have been extensive, distress and sorrow never appealed to you in vain. In the distribution of the grants of that benevolent body, the British Association, your assiduity and deep anxiety called forth the admiration and gratitude of all, while your own Christian benevolence free from all sectarian prejudices, silenced every slander.
>
> May length of days and every blessing in a more favourable country be yours. Farewell then, very dear Sir.[58]

The parish priests who signed the tribute as 'your very sincere friends' were D. Mahony, Jeremiah O'Sullivan, Eugene McCarthy, Daniel McCarthy, James Walsh, Timothy Hartnett, Jeremiah O'Connell, John Long and Thomas Fitzgerald; the curates were Florence McCarthy, Thomas Moore, John Mawe, John O'Connor, Martin McMahon and Daniel Houlihan.[59]

Captain Spark replied graciously:

> I shall retain an enduring remembrance of the kindness I have received and of the cordial co-operation I have met with from yourselves and all your reverend brethren in carrying out the benevolent measures of the British Association and of the government in affording relief for eight months of a trying season to nearly eight thousand poor children through the medium of the schools … I pray that threatening calamities to the poor of your flocks may by God's mercy be averted.[60]

The board of guardians had also paid tribute to Spark and he thanked the members for:

… tendering to me in such marked and handsome terms their approval of my conduct whilst inspector of the Union. I shall always feel grateful that my endeavours to carry out the Poor Law in the spirit of benevolence on which they are based has won for me their good opinion and friendly regard.[61]

These warm, unforced tributes went beyond polite formalities and it is noteworthy that corresponding tributes do not appear to have been offered to other inspectors in the county. They indicate a genuine appreciation of the efforts of Captain Spark, who like his predecessor in Listowel, Lieutenant Greenwell, was seen as compassionate and conscientious.

As it happened, Captain Spark's work in Kerry was not over in 1848; he subsequently returned to take up the position of inspector in Tralee and later in Dingle, where he continued to work closely with the guardians, often in situations of conflict.

Dissolution of Listowel Board of Guardians

By the autumn of 1848 the financial state of Listowel Union was disastrous and an order came from the commissioners dissolving the board. The *Post* paid tribute to the work and constant attendance of William Sandes Jr, who had been chairman of the board since its establishment.[62] But two weeks after his arrival in Listowel to replace Captain Spark, Captain Hart reported to the Poor Law Commissioners that 'for a very long period your rules and regulations have not only been a dead letter but they have also been systematically violated in a most flagrant manner' by the Listowel board.[63]

The board was dissolved in October and the union was administered for a year by paid vice-guardians. This temporary arrangement was applied to many unions all over the west of Ireland, in cases of mismanagement or insolvency. The first men named as vice-guardians were Captain Hart (who became a major in December),[64] Mr Austin and Captain Routh, with James Smyth later replacing Routh. The *Post* welcomed the fact that the new vice-guardians immediately set about reforming the system of jobbery or favouritism, which, it claimed, was practised by the outgoing board, which contained many farmer-guardians. The *Post* claimed that they had unduly influenced the selection of those on outdoor relief.⁶⁵

However, the *Examiner* regarded Hart's arrival as a calamity, reporting that one of his first acts was to cram 1,189 people into the workhouse, which had accommodation for only 750. Some inmates had not changed their clothing in five days and some had no bed clothing; the stench was described as deadly and disgusting. The paper warned Hart that 'a Poor Law inspector should be a man of compassionate and tender feelings, the friend of the poor, the advocate of their cause, the barrier between them and their workhouse oppressors, but above all he should not be himself their greatest oppressor and their most heartless tyrant'.⁶⁶

Landlord Clearances
All over Ireland, the crisis of the Famine led to huge clearances by landlords of tenants who were unable to pay their rents. Fr Mathias McMahon sent a long letter dated 9 April 1848 to *The Nation* about conditions in the Ballyheigue/Causeway/Ballyduff areas.⁶⁷ Fr McMahon, who was ordained in Killarney in May 1847, was a man whose pen would champion the rights of the people and scourge landlordism in north Kerry for many years to come. This letter was a tirade against local landlords, and it revealed a good deal of interesting detail about the landlords of the area.

Fr McMahon's defence of his people is of significance because, as well as being a curate in Causeway, it seems that he was also a native son, born there in 1820. Fr Eugene McCarthy, also born locally, was the parish priest, and these two articulate leaders made a formidable combination during their short time together. Fr McMahon was soon transferred to Ballybunion, from where he continued to write to the press. He ultimately became parish priest of Boherbue, Co. Cork, where he was a leading figure during the land agitation of the 1880s.

The letter opened with a general attack on landlords, describing them as 'determined upon utterly extirpating the peasantry' and appealing for a stop to be placed on the 'murderous proceedings of these "thugs"'. Fr McMahon went on:

> The landlords of Ballyheigue, Killury and Rattoo may, with one or two exceptions, be classed as the very worst in Ireland. In greediness and inhumanity they appear to be emulous of one another. It would be hard to decide which is the severest in exacting impossible rents, which most unscrupulous in exercising all the means of legalised ingenuity for the ruin of the poor man. Upon these parishes the curse of absenteeism lies heavy. There is but one resident proprietor, a Mr Crosby [*sic*], not the most indulgent of landlords, and I am told about to clear a populous village. The absentees draw from us some £8,000 a year. Out of that sum they contributed only £90 to meet the horrible distress of last year. One of these worthies, a Mr Oliver, never saw his estate here. The industry of his tenants is encouraged by having the rents raised in proportion to their own improvements at every new letting. Two more of them, Thomas Anthony and William Stoughton, Esqrs, visit their properties at long intervals, to do no other good, as far as I can learn, than gratify their caprice or see their books cleared. The latter gentleman came here last summer. The only benefit his serfs derived from his arrival amongst them was an extensive eviction …
>
> Another of our landlords, a Mr Gun, is a sort of a half-absentee. He is sometimes in England, sometimes in Rattoo. Last summer when his presence was most required, he went off, instead of labouring to relieve the distress around him, like a true Irish landlord, he fled in base and unchristian abandonment of that most sacred duty.

Fr McMahon repeatedly used the word 'extermination' for the actions of local landlords, stating that they had made no allowance for the circumstances of tenants and the 'crushing calamity of the last two years'. He cited some specific instances of landlord evictions:

> Extermination to an extent truly awful has already taken place here. On the 23 December last, twenty-three families numbering about a hundred and twenty souls were evicted on the property of William Stoughton. One of these poor people, the mother of eight children, the youngest only six months old, died, according to the verdict of a coroner's inquest, from fright brought

on by dwelling in a cold hut hastily constructed of her own furniture, exposed to the worst inclemency of the weather for four days.

Over thirty ejectment processes were some time ago issued by the agent of T. A. Stoughton. He is to bring the sheriff, I understand, one of these days, to turn out nine families. Gregory's Clause got him possession from the rest quietly. The holdings were given up because the miserable occupants had nothing to eat. Some few more were thrown out on the property of Mr Oliver. Within the last twelve months or so, twenty-five families numbering one hundred and fifteen souls left the property of a Mr Sandes, a middleman. 'He did not turn out anyone' – so he was lately reported to have said; not he, good man! He only applied to them the gentle pressure of rackrent, starvation and threatened imprisonment. Distraint and Gregory's desolating clause have removed one hundred and fifty families, numbering six hundred and fifty souls, from the property of a Mr Mason, another middleman.

The letter also gave an account of the priest's daily experiences which was a powerful cry from the heart on behalf of his people:

Imagination can scarcely conceive the state of our poor; even in Ireland of the plagues, it is astounding. They have neither employment, nor clothing nor food. At almost every step one meets on the roads the hideous spectacle of human beings in the agony of hunger, walking in a living death and that, oh! that, in a land of plenty and which they have a far better right to possess than the brigand government who oppress or the vile tyrants who destroy them. Deaths by starvation and burials without coffins are of common occurrence and likely to be more so.

Fr McMahon was still in Ballybunion in 1859 and he had lost none of his patriotic fervour and passion when he wrote about English rule in Ireland:

She is no longer dominant in the world. Her decrepitude and imbecility is declared by her own senators, and patent to foreigners who scoff at her pretensions to supremacy and look upon her loud talk about fleets, defences etc. as the insane swagger of a spent bully. English 'civilisers' laden with the plunder of nations and the guilt of centuries, are shrieking in the helplessness and terror of guilty consciences at the near prospect of that retribution which they know and feel that they so richly deserve.[68]

Justin Supple and the Young Ireland Rebellion

The spirit of Young Ireland was strong in Tralee in 1848. The nationalist Young Irelanders had broken away from O'Connell's Repeal Association in 1846, because they considered it too moderate in its demands. Young Ireland and its leaders, such as Thomas Davis, John Blake Dillon and Charles Gavan Duffy, espoused a more radical policy of independence for Ireland. Anger and dismay at the extent of the suffering endured by the Irish people during 1847 inspired many political activists and ordinary people to challenge the policies of the Westminster government and fuelled the discontent with the Act of Union that was ever-present. With the emergence of more radical leaders, including John Mitchel, an armed insurrection became a real possibility, fomented by a strong sense of grievance at the government's policies towards Ireland during the Famine.

In 1847 Gavan Duffy and William Smith O'Brien formed the Irish Confederation as a separate organisation and it promoted the establishment of Confederate Clubs around the country. The Irish Confederation initially espoused self-government and non-violence, but the French Revolution of February 1848 became an inspiration to the members and there were widespread rumours – and, for some, fears – of violent rebellion.

As early as April 1848 in Tarbert there was general talk of rebellion and pikes were being prepared; notices were posted calling on the people 'to stand well prepared for a general rising'.[69] There were reports of conspiracies to shoot landlords, and these ignited fears of a breakdown of the social order. A *Chronicle* editorial was headed 'Crime in Kerry', but it began reassuringly: 'Let not our readers be startled by this ominous heading.'[70] It continued: 'Crimes against God and society, of a dark character, will exhibit themselves at intervals.' The paper referred to a plot by one man to shoot three landlords near Ballylongford (George Wren, W. S. Sandes and Thomas O'Connor), which had been foiled by the intervention of the parish priest, Fr Daniel McCarthy, who received an early warning of it. The *Chronicle* also cited a conspiracy to murder Frederick Mason of Kilmore near Ballyduff, for which eight men were arrested and two of them committed to jail awaiting trial.[71]

In June a group of about eighty people gathered in the sitting room of Dan Browne in Upper Castle Street, Tralee, under a portrait of John Mitchel. They were first addressed by Justin Supple, solicitor and coroner, who became president of the Confederate Club which was formed that night. Browne was a shopkeeper and publican and those in attendance were described as 'merchants' assistants and artisans of the humbler class'.[72] Supple expressed his delight that there were no gentry present and that the movement had begun with the people. He roused the audience by saying that the people were suffering from the effects of English misrule and domination and that the time had come 'when the bone and sinew of the nation must right itself':

> We are the bond slaves of a faction. How long are we to remain so? Are you prepared, men of Tralee, to bow down under the iron heel of English oppression ('No, no' and cheers). To have injuries inflicted upon you, calumnies heaped upon you, and fraud perpetrated against your properties, your lives, your liberties? (cheers) Are you prepared to see your poor starving people – to see half a million or a million yearly of your countrymen – whose graves call to you for vengeance – from Corkaguiny to Skibbereen – hurried into eternity by starvation in the land that bore them, not a coffin to cover them, devoured by dogs – are you prepared for a repetition of this?[73]

Supple went on to say that peaceful agitation, petitions and constitutional efforts had achieved nothing and were all futile. 'Let there be no such thing as Young Ireland or Old Ireland. Let our watchword be the name of Irishman. Every Irishman should make common cause, for the time is come when distinctions of creed should be done away.'

The Confederate Clubs were not illegal and when Sub-Inspector Wyse and other policemen entered the room they received tremendous cheers. Wyse sat at the top table and heard speeches extolling John Mitchel, who had been openly advocating a rebellion and in May had been sentenced to fourteen years' transportation for sedition. 'Mitchel may be manacled and driven into exile but his spirit still hovers over this country,' said a Mr Kenefick.[74]

In July more arrests took place around the country, and the Irish Confederation was declared illegal, provoking the long-anticipated attempt at armed rebellion. That began and ended at Ballingarry, Co. Tipperary, where William Smith O'Brien led a small group in a badly organised military engagement. This was a failure as a rebellion, but one historian stated that 'as revolutionary theatre, it was a gesture against death and despair, evictions and emigration'.[75] O'Brien was sentenced to death, although this was commuted to transportation to Van Diemen's Land (Tasmania). He was released in 1854 and pardoned in 1856; he then retired from political life.

The rebellious spirit of 1848 was evident in both north Kerry and west Limerick, beginning with an armed raid on mail coaches a mile south of Abbeyfeale. Abbeyfeale is in Co. Limerick but it is very close to the Kerry border and its hinterland includes places such as Brosna and Duagh in Kerry. The attackers included a group of young men of Duagh, who had earlier in the day attacked the home of Mr Fitzmaurice of Springmount, searching for arms. The leader was a local insurgent named 'Danny Dan' Harnett, a follower of Richard O'Gorman of Dublin. The latter was a close friend of John Mitchel and an organiser for the Young Ireland movement in the Limerick area, who was reported as being near Abbeyfeale at the time of the raid.

The *Post* wrote of the 'alarming intelligence' that a body of about 200 armed men attacked the two mail coaches where they met *en route* to and from Limerick. Robbery of Her Majesty's mail was then a most serious offence. The raiders were described as well dressed, with tweed coats cut in shooting-jacket style, and were armed with guns, pikes and common pitchforks. They offered no violence and, having seized the mail, marched away in a leisurely fashion towards Brosna. It was not an attack for plunder and the men declared to the coachman: 'We want to free our country and stop the communications.'[76] The raiders later told the local postmaster that they wanted only official communications such as warrants and proclamations rather than private mail, and he was invited to a remote location to retrieve all other items. *The Cork Examiner* was concerned at what the raid might portend and referred to the raiders as 'banditti' but acknowledged their 'great politeness … and high sense of honour and delicacy'.[77]

Immediately after the Abbeyfeale incident, an armed group – possibly the same men – arrived at the home of Rev. Edward Norman of Brosna and demanded arms. When he told them that he possessed no weapons, they departed peacefully. Later on another armed group arrived and the same scene was repeated. The armed groups behaved 'with great civility', but there was one shooting incident when a scripture reader, who lived nearby and was believed to have weapons, was fired on.[78] Many years later Norman claimed that the insurgents were warned by their leader that if he or his wife were harmed, the leader would shoot those responsible. Norman was attempting to show that he and his wife were popular among the people.[79]

When extra police were drafted into Abbeyfeale after the raid, shopkeepers and others showed their support for the rebels by offering them 'passive rebellion, most inconvenient to the police', by refusing to deal with them. (This was in effect a boycott, but the term had not yet been coined.) The police responded by taking the supplies they needed and leaving payment on the counters.

The *Post* said that most of the raiders were from Duagh, a locality that had always been 'most ripe for disturbance'. Arrests had been made and the armed group, which had taken refuge in the hills, was 'fast breaking up like a wreath of snow in the sun'.[80] There was support for the rebels in Tralee, as noted in the *Post* in August, after the Ballingarry affray:

> On Saturday evening it would be easy to single out the disaffected in this town by the smiles with which their faces were wreathed. On Sunday however their spirits got a great fall and the news on Monday night of Mr Smith O'Brien's arrest altogether knocked them up.[81]

A reward of £300 was offered for the capture of Richard O'Gorman, and there were reported sightings of him a few miles outside Castleisland. Head Constable Hogben was searching for him when a party of local men surrounded him and took his warrants, watch and purse, and then released him.[82]

A considerable amount of military activity, and great waves of rumour and speculation, took place around Abbeyfeale throughout August. Even as late as 27 September there were signs that the authorities in Abbeyfeale were on high alert, and soldiers of the 88th Depot were stationed there amid reports that O'Gorman, Harnett and others were in the area and planned an uprising.[83] Harnett was reported as being outside Newcastlewest at the head of a large group of men.[84] The *Post* published a letter written by Morgan John O'Connell in which there is a passing reference to the areas of Abbeyfeale and Duagh, where 'the most stupid of all the recent stupid attempts at rebellion has just taken place'.[85] In the aftermath of the Abbeyfeale mail robbery, two men named Hughes and Bourke were sentenced to seven years' transportation.

The rebellion of 1848 had serious consequences for Justin Supple of Tralee. He was arrested in dramatic circumstances on the basis of a letter from him that was found in the papers of the arrested leader William Smith O'Brien. The police raided his home at 3 a.m. and took him 'from the connubial bed'. He was treated with every courtesy by the police, who searched the house for weapons but found none. The arrest was for 'treasonable practices and on suspicion of being guilty of high treason', but no incriminating papers were found.[86] Supple was the second prominent solicitor and public figure to be sensationally arrested that year in Tralee, John Lynch being the other.

Supple spent two months in Tralee jail. A petition was organised for his release but this did not have an immediate effect. The editor of the *Chronicle* supported the petition, saying that Supple should be acquitted of all 'troublesome designs'.[87] Eventually, following an appeal from the parish priest, Dr McEnnery, Supple was released on bail in October.[88] He appears to have resumed his former duties as a solicitor, acting on behalf of the board of guardians, for example, and by the end of 1849 he was once again acting as coroner.[89] He did not curtail his political activity and later became a prominent speaker at Tenant Right meetings around the county.

As for the Repeal movement and the Young Ireland movement, the *Post* welcomed the year 1849 with verses in which they were consigned to history:

> *What's become of the Clubs and Repeal?*
> *Of the rifles, rebellion and pikes?*
> *The Young Irelanders all turned 'Tailers,*
> *Lord John Russell can do what he likes;*
> *We hope they won't hang Smith O'Brien –*
> *That poor bottle of small frothy beer –*
> *And we hope they won't think of trying*
> *Any more of those blockheads this year.*[90]

7

'THE POOR ARE SINKING'

1849

We do contend that these evictions are not only justifiable but unavoidable – nay more, that they are of great advantage to the public and the poor.

Kerry Evening Post, 14 April 1849

1849 was yet another year of great distress, especially in the west and south of Ireland, with homelessness now added to hunger and disease. Mortality rates in the four provinces for 1847 and 1849 show how severely Munster was affected, with an increase of over 10,000 deaths in the latter year:

	1847	1849
Munster	82,496	92,737
Connaught	43,045	44,958
Leinster	59,208	60,360
Ulster	64,586	42,472[1]

The *Kerry Evening Post* began the year with an editorial reminding readers that it was the oldest provincial newspaper in Ireland and stating that 'the destinies of Ireland hang in the balance and should the scale of her misfortunes be weighted but a little more, she must sink into a helpless social anarchy'. In the same edition, it identified the two great issues that threatened the country as free trade and a disastrous Poor Law. It also carried verses touching on local and international concerns, from the frequent flooding of Tralee to the travails of the papacy:

> *We wish every person in town*
> *A happier year than the past*
> *That is if the flood doesn't drown*
> *Ourselves and our houses at last;*
> *'Tis a beautiful washer of streets*
> *But it drenches us all front and rere*
> *And makes the poor lie in damp sheets*
> *But we wish them a happy New Year!*
>
> *The country more wretched is growing,*
> *The Union is deeply indebted;*
> *The poorhouse choke-full to o'erflowing*
> *There's a Rate! 'don't you wish they may get it.'*
> *The payers are paupers without,*
> *The paupers within have good cheer.*
> *So they'll stop where they are beyond doubt,*
> *And we wish them a happy New Year.*
>
> *What's become of the Pope – gone from Rome?*
> *What's become of our friend Lamartine?*[2]
> *Many monarchs are found 'not at home'*
> *And have proved most 'uncommonly green'.*
> *His Holiness finds 'tis no joke*
> *Through a 'Red Revolution' to steer*
> *So in London we're told he's bespoke*
> *A 'cheap furnished house' by the year.*
>
> *Little business is done in our shops,*
> *Roguish tenants are cutting away,*

And we fear many fields will want crops,
And that no traffic will pay;
Our prospects are dark – but we hope
That the gloomy horizon may clear,
And that all (not forgetting the Pope)
May yet see bright days in this year.[3]

A striking fact about the Famine deaths as reported in the sources cited here is that few names of victims of starvation were recorded. Inquest reports did sometimes shed light on tragic deaths and the inquest on a man named Michael Driscoll was one such instance. In late December 1848 a letter to Listowel Union vice-guardians from coroner Francis Twiss and Fr Eugene McCarthy was noted in the minutes.[4] It stated that at an inquest on Michael Driscoll, the jury returned a verdict of manslaughter against James Cooke, relieving officer for Ballyheigue. The vice-guardians, Major Hart and Mr Austen, resolved to visit Ballyheigue to investigate the circumstances. Following their investigation, in January 1849 the vice-guardians called for Cooke's resignation, citing inefficiency and incompetence. Cooke resigned a week later and John Connor was appointed to act in his place.[5]

The circumstances of Michael Driscoll's death were recounted in shocking detail in the *Post*. The inquest jury laid a charge of 'death from starvation and of manslaughter against the relieving officer … for not affording relief, though called on repeatedly to do so, to the deceased, his wife and six children'.[6] The newspaper report gave some moving details of the family's desperate situation:

> So wretched-looking objects as the poor family presented could not be seen; they were nothing but skin and bone and they had nothing to feed on except tops of turnips, which they used to collect after the but[t] roots were removed, and stumps of cabbage. On this sort of food they have been living for months past.
>
> On the post-mortem examination, the lungs, heart and liver were found

in a perfectly healthy state, the stomach contained no food of any kind, the intestines contained some barley and some turnip tops in an undigested state and the whole frame was quite emaciated. It appeared in evidence that about six weeks since the relieving officer was told by a member of the relief committee there that Driscoll and his family were in the greatest distress as he often saw the children going through the fields where turnips and cabbage were growing, collecting whatever they could, on which they existed; however this had no effect on the relieving officer.

The deceased left home and was about six weeks begging. He returned to the house on the day before his death so worn out from starvation that he lay in bed on Friday and had nothing to eat but cabbage stumps and turnip tops. He got up on Saturday to go for relief to the meal store not more than a mile from him but was so weak he could not go on and was obliged to return. In the course of that day a man passed close to the hut of this poor man and his wretched family and met the wife there who told him her husband was very bad and that she feared he was dying from hunger. The man went to his house and brought about a pint of milk with him and gave it to Driscoll, a part of which he could then only take, and when his wife was about warming the remainder for him, he seized the vessel and drank it off. When this man first went to the house, poor Driscoll could scarcely speak but when he drank the milk he could speak very well, being so much relieved.

Our correspondent further remarks that this is no way for our unfortunate fellow creatures to be treated where there are officers paid for administering relief to those who require it. About a fortnight before the death of poor Driscoll, his wife and son went to the house of the relieving officer, as they said, to notice him to come to their house (if such it could be called) and see how they were situated; but this appeal of theirs had no effect on him. On Thursday last the son of Driscoll went to the meal store and begged some meal for his mother and family (his father being then dead) which he was refused, although, as it was shown on the inquest, the relieving officer knew him. Now when the country is so heavily taxed for the relief of the distressed, is this the way the really poor should be treated and that by a paid officer?

Perhaps the verdict of the jury will have the effect of making other officers pay better attention.[7]

After the forced resignation of James Cooke, a succession of other men held the position of relieving officer for Ballyheigue in 1849: Mr Griffin (at a salary of £50 per annum), Mr Williams and Mr Patrick Edgeworth (at a salary of £40 per annum).[8] In December the unnamed relieving officer (presumably Mr Edgeworth) was suspended. This followed criticism of him by the guardians for not taking 'a store at Kilmoyley for distribution of meal as directed' and for ignoring an order not to employ a man named Griffin to cart meal to the depot.[9]

The number of articles pawned or redeemed throughout north Kerry was taken as an indicator of conditions among the poor. In January Major Hart of Listowel reported that Bridget Donovan was the only pawnbroker in his area and that she had stopped taking in items because of lack of storage space. He stated that great numbers of the poor were much in want of clothing, and that there was no Sunday wear. Tralee Union had six pawnbrokers, with one of them based in Castleisland: they were Michael Neligan, James Mahony, John Carberry, Christopher and John Ruttle and Mrs Ruttle. Their stores were reported as 'filled with wearing apparel of every description, home-made clothing materials, feather beds, bedding and tradesmen's tools of every kind'.[10]

The Sudden Death of Major Crosbie

In April Tralee Union reported to the Poor Law Commissioners that 'the people are dying by dozens of starvation and disease'.[11] A notable death took place in May, that of Major Pierce Crosbie of Ballyheigue Castle, and it was announced as follows in the press:

> It is with feelings of great pain that we announce the demise of the respected gentleman whose name stands at the head of this obituary – much increased by the awful circumstances under which this melancholy event took place.

On Saturday last, Major Crosbie went in his usual health to see his labourers who were cutting turf and while on the bog about two o'clock he fell in a fit, whence he was brought to Ballyheigue Castle in a state of insensibility from which he did not recover and he expired about nine o'clock that evening.

As a landlord, a grand juror and a magistrate, Major Crosbie enjoyed the respect and esteem of all classes in this county in which his family have ever been popular. In his own neighbourhood and among his own tenantry, his good qualities will not soon be forgotten.

Major Crosbie was about fifty-six years of age when thus suddenly called away. He has left a large family to mourn his loss. He will be succeeded by his only son by his second wife, Miss Sandes, Mr James Crosbie, now in his 17th year. By his third wife, Miss Wren, who survives him, he has left seven young children. By his death the greater number of the territorial families at this side of the county will be placed in mourning.[12]

This tribute indicates that Pierce Crosbie was giving some employment on the bog. However, his heirs were in financial difficulty, as shown by an advertisement in the *Post* in June for a sheriff's sale of stock, farming implements, household furniture and green crops.[13] Many of the estate workers were doubtless affected by this sale and by the fact that the son and heir, James Crosbie, was a minor.

It later emerged that a Tralee merchant, Mr McCowen, held an insurance policy on the life of Pierce Crosbie, probably as security for a debt and that it was cashed by him.[14] Mrs Crosbie and her children were not entirely dependent on the estate, as another advertisement informed the public that she would continue to run her grocery, wine and spirit store in Bridge Street, Tralee, 'in the same manner as in the lifetime of her husband'.[15]

Tralee Workhouse

The great philanthropist Count Paul Strzelecki, who was the agent of the British Relief Association, visited Tralee workhouse in 1849 and wrote in the visitors' book:

> I have much pleasure in bearing testimony to the efficiency with which I found the workhouse on my morning visit. The dietary, the appearance of the people, cleanliness of the ward rooms, and particularly the infirmary, fever and dysentery hospitals deserve the most just tribute of praise.[16]

Strzelecki has been described as working 'tirelessly for three years on behalf of the sick and starving poor, a task for which he refused any payment'.[17] His Polish name always presented difficulties of spelling and pronunciation, and the *Post* referred to him as 'Count Skreterky'.

Despite Strzelecki's favourable evaluation, there were regular reports of sexual scandals in Tralee's workhouses, usually between staff and adult female inmates. John Hurly, master of Ballymullen branch workhouse, was accused of seduction in 1849. An inmate named Kitty Cournane gave evidence to the board that Hurly had struck her with a rod and then made sexual advances, 'making a hand of her' as she described it. Warned that she was on oath, she told Mr Denny:

> Mr Hurly said to me that if I did it with him, I would not be a bit the worse for it; he did not offer me any money but he said he would be kind to me. He told me the reason he wanted me upstairs was to do it with him, and he said I would not be sorry for it if I did … I told all this to my mother and she would not let me stop in there any longer. My mother told it to Mrs Howard, the porter's wife.[18]

Dr McEnnery gave evidence that while he knew that Hurly was a drunkard, he believed that 'he never tampered with these women' and would never be guilty of 'that abominable crime of seducing a female for another party'.[19] Kitty Cournane subsequently withdrew the accusation, probably under duress, but Hurly faced other charges such as drunkenness, purloining workhouse flannel, and enabling his wife to steal milk from the children's rations, and he was dismissed.

Sectarianism

Sectarianism was a problem throughout north Kerry in 1849, with reports of various discreditable incidents. One was in Tralee, where it was reported that a man named John Connell, who was dying of cholera, wished to return to the Catholic faith, which he had left years before. On hearing this, one of the Tralee priests, Fr Enright, went to attend to Connell. However, when he arrived it was made clear to him that the man did not wish to see him, so he retired. A noisy crowd then gathered outside Connell's house, apparently to intimidate him into returning to the Catholic faith, and even when the dying man rose to tell them that he wanted no priest 'as Christ was his priest' they were not deterred. Eventually magistrates were called to clear the street.[20] On another occasion a preacher at St John's Church of Ireland in Tralee was shouted down by a mob. This incident was condemned by the priests of the parish.[21]

In March Rev. Stamer of Ballybunion wrote that the house of John Sheehy, a convert to his church, was maliciously burned down, leaving the family beggared. Stamer wrote that Sheehy received no sympathy from the community but was jeered and mocked afterwards by his Catholic neighbours.[22]

Another incident, which led to a long correspondence, was one involving Thomas Dooling (also named Doolan and Dowling in the sources), who was a convert to Protestantism and active in promoting his new allegiance in the Cashen area at the mouth of the River Feale. The following summary is taken from the *Post*, which sympathised with Dooling's position. After being evicted from the Trinity College lands, Dooling was taken as a tenant by Oliver William Mason of Killahan and Aghamore. Fr John Mawe was the curate at Killahan and he visited Mason's farm – in what was described as 'a crusade' by the *Post* – to denounce Dooling and to warn him against proselytising. Mawe stated that he received verbal abuse from Mason but issued no threats. He then proceeded to denounce Mason's insolence from the altar on the following two Sundays, without specifically naming him. A week later, a house owned by Mason was maliciously burned down. Fr Mawe denied any responsibility for this occurrence, but the *Post* had no doubt that the burning was a result of the priest's condemnation and likened the affair to that of Major Mahon of Strokestown, Co. Roscommon, who was assassinated after being denounced by a priest. The *Post* appealed for freedom of conscience, condemned Mawe for 'hounding on his congregation against an unoffending man' and advised him to spend more time ministering to his dying flock.[23] In his account of events, Mawe denied any culpability and suggested that an 'unprincipled underling' of Mason might have caused the burning of the house – which Mawe described as a crumbling old thatched cottage – without his master's knowledge.[24]

The newspapers were not blameless in the reporting of such incidents and they sometimes inflamed passions. The *Post* had earlier published an inflammatory piece of verse entitled 'Popeland'. The poem of twenty stanzas satirised aspects of Roman Catholic practices, such as the rich design of church interiors, the Latin used at Mass and the fact that the priest had his back to the people:

> *In Popeland once I saw a Church*
> *The sweet bells chimed away,*
> *To call in worshippers of God*
> *Upon his holy day.*
> *But in that Church such gaudy glare*
> *It grieved me to behold,*
> *The walls were like a showman's board*
> *Bedecked with paint and gold.*
>
> *The Popeland church was carved and decked*
> *With bauble glittering bright,*
> *'Twas like a well-filled baby house,*
> *The silly child's delight.*
> *Here stood a little ark of wood*
> *And there a roodscreen carved,*

The eye was feasted there, no doubt,
But ah! the soul was starved.

I saw in Popeland Church
A priest stand up to pray;
His back was to the people turned
He faced the other way.
A cross was broidered on his back,
A cope hung from his head;
He muttered on but none could tell
A word of what he said.

He bowed and rose and sawed and crossed,
A hundred times at least,
He turned him west and north and south,
And often to the east.
The Popeland congregation seemed
To think it mighty fine –
Poor silly folk, to deem such stuff
Could please the Power Divine.[25]

When there was a dramatic altercation between two priests in 1850, the *Post* could hardly conceal its glee in reporting 'a boxing match between a well-known agitating clergyman and his coadjutor in which the latter had suffered so severely that he had to come into town yesterday with a pair of black eyes'.[26] It refrained from identifying the priests or the place, but said it happened about ten miles from Tralee towards the setting sun. The matter was under diocesan investigation and the *Post* speculated that the parish priest would be removed from the parish, which it said would please his parishioners 'as they had been suffering the severest tyranny at his hands'.[27]

Cholera Epidemic

Cholera had been spreading across Europe in 1848 and came to Ireland from Britain. It was first reported in Belfast in November–December 1848 and spread throughout the country, arriving in Limerick in March 1849. Unlike typhus and dysentery, the cholera epidemic was not related to the Famine. It affected all classes of society but of course the destitute and debilitated were more at risk and less likely to be able to fight it off.

Fear of cholera generated a wave of panic. The main symptoms were vomiting and diarrhoea, and it was transmitted by contaminated water and food. Death resulted from dehydration and usually occurred very quickly. Doctors of the time did not understand how it was transmitted and there was a debate about whether it was contagious.[28] Ó Murchadha states that the effects of cholera caused 'a unique dread and terror ... which could cause parents or siblings to shrink in revulsion from stricken family members' and even led to victims being driven out of the family home.[29]

There was an expectation that it would arrive in Kerry before long and in April the *Post* exhorted its readers, 'for the last time before the fatal epidemic now ravaging the adjoining counties with such virulence appears among us', to 'PREPARE FOR THE CHOLERA'.[30] A fatal case was reported in Brosna in late April and the same issue of the *Post* had news of the death of Sir Arthur Blennerhassett of Churchtown House near Beaufort, who was one of the first to die of cholera in Kerry. He was aged fifty-three and had been in Tralee on the previous Saturday; on his arrival home he was attacked by cholera and was dead within twenty-four hours.[31]

In Tralee, preparations for the arrival of the cholera epidemic were discussed by the board of guardians. Fever sheds and a wing of the hospital were being prepared to receive patients; a wing of Castleisland fever hospital was likewise prepared.[32] 'The epidemic is spreading itself indiscriminately all over the country,' wrote *The Cork Examiner*, 'and the characteristic of the Kerry peasantry for generosity and sympathy is fast disappearing.'[33]

By early May twenty deaths were being reported in Tarbert, although approximately forty people had also recovered from the disease. Among the dead were Mrs Luby, Mrs Quinlan, Patrick Quill and James Harold. An investigation was ordered into a report that the bodies of several recipients of outdoor relief who had died of cholera were left unburied for days.[34]

One hundred and ten cases of cholera were reported in Tralee workhouse in early May, and fifty of those proved fatal. To protect themselves, the guardians moved their weekly meetings to the courthouse instead of the boardroom of the workhouse.[35]

The *Post* described how the disease first 'affected the more destitute classes in our lanes' and then made inroads in the workhouses, where 'its ravages became at once of the most deadly danger, cutting off in those refuges of destitution, some two hundred persons, chiefly of the worst constitutions and those most reduced by poverty'.[36]

During May the epidemic appeared to subside, but the respite was brief:

> On Wednesday [23 May] this bright hope was dashed to the earth by the fearful intelligence that several persons in the most respectable rank of life and residing in the most open and airy part of the town (along the canal) were simultaneously attacked by cholera. Fear at once took the place of hope and Wednesday night fell upon Tralee in gloom and woe. Three deaths occurred during the night and every hour of the day brought the intelligence of a spirit passed into eternity and of a new victim laid on the plague-bed of sickness. Yesterday was a day of increasing gloom and widespread mourning ... We cannot dismiss this painful subject without bearing our warmest testimony to the almost superhuman efforts made by the clergymen of all denominations and the medical men generally in this town to come at and discharge properly the largely increased professional duties thrown upon them by this fearful visitation.[37]

Two prominent and very active clergymen died of cholera: Fr Michael Devine of Dingle and Rev. Robert Conway Hurly, rector of Killiney, near Castlegregory. Captain Davis of the schooner *Harmony* died in Blennerville.[38] Constable Mahony of Blennerville was one of three policemen who died.[39]

In late May the *Post* listed some of 'the more respectable parties' who died of cholera in Tralee: Mrs John Blennerhassett of Day Place, who had been recently widowed and who left a three-year-old daughter, 'now doubly an orphan'; Mrs John Busteed, also of Day Place, 'a woman in the prime of a life spent in works of love and charity'; Miss Agnes Day, sister of the rector of Kilgobbin; Mrs Ruttle, wife of the pawnbroker and 'mother of four interesting children'; Anne Beecher, eldest daughter of the matron of the county infirmary; Mrs Brereton, 'trustworthy and efficient matron' of the county jail for almost thirty years; Isabella McCarthy, whose father, John, ran a classical school in the Square; Robert Nash, aged thirty, son of the rector of Ballyseedy; Michael Crosbie, 'a man of high integrity and honour'; Thomas Delahunt, a publican, of Ballymullen; and John O'Donnell, a shopkeeper on Bridge Street.[40]

Another list of names appeared in the *Post* a few days later, with this comment: 'Gloom and fear are still brooding over our town and the voice of mourning is heard in our broad ways and in our narrow ways, in our streets and our lanes'.[41] This list included Mrs Lumsden of Denny Street, known for her charity to the poor, who attended her funeral in large numbers; Rev. John Byrne, a retired Methodist clergyman; Miss Elizabeth Gorham of Prince's Quay; Hugh Raymond, aged seven; Barbara, the daughter of William Busteed; William, the five-year-old son of Charles G. Fairfield, a member of the board of guardians; and four-year-old Elizabeth Leahy.

The cholera epidemic was frightful but of relatively short duration and the medical officer, Dr Lawlor, reported that the special cholera hospital was closed down on 18 June, by which time it had admitted sixty-six males and ninety-three females; of these, thirty-eight males and fifty-three females died.[42] The national mortality rate of those who contracted cholera during the epidemic was calculated at 42 per cent, but this is regarded as an underestimation.[43] The number of deaths in Ireland caused by the cholera epidemic has been estimated as 30,000.[44]

There was a palpable sense of relief in the Kerry press that the epidemic was not as devastating as had been anticipated. Francis Crosbie of Ballyard House, clerk of the peace for Kerry, as a gesture of gratitude for being spared, donated £3 15s towards the maintenance of a boy who had been orphaned during the epidemic.[45]

There were touching examples of individual charity during this time. For example, in Boherbee, Tralee, a widow who was on her way to bury her daughter without a coffin passed by a group of boys who were busy getting a bonfire ready for the traditional celebration of St John's Eve, known as 'bonfire night'. They responded by offering the money they had collected for their bonfire to buy a coffin and then 'kindly assisted the poor woman in burying her child decently'.[46]

In June the need for additional burial space in Tralee was addressed again by the board of guardians and a suitable site was sought. A spacious plot was taken 'adjoining the old graveyard of Rathass at a rent of £10 a year'. There was a proposal to make this available 'to all the humbler classes' but ultimately it was decided 'to confine it to the use of the unclaimed dead of the workhouse, the several charitable institutions and the county prison, to be extended at the discretion of the board to those who may die on the outdoor relief lists'.[47] A 'neat gravedigger's cottage' was proposed at the edge of the plot adjoining the road and gravel paths and trees were to be added 'to give the place a decent and reverent appearance'. The *Post* hailed this development because 'it will not only secure decent interment for the deceased pauper but it will also relieve in a great measure the pressure for room caused by the late excessive mortality'.[48]

Black '49

There were signs of hope for all the crops of 1849 and a sense of a return to normal life for some people at least. Queen Victoria's birthday was marked by a volley of shots in Ballymullen Barracks square in mid-May. The *Examiner* carried the headline 'The Deplorable Year 1848, The Auspicious Year 1849' and it welcomed 'with gratification the multiplied proofs of better times with which we are surrounded. All descriptions of the crop are healthy and abundant.' It went on to reflect on the trauma of the previous years, believing that the worst was over:

After all, may not the late visitation of Providence – the potato disease – be for the ultimate advantage of the Irish peasantry who have survived the horrors which it entailed upon the entire country? We may be excused for saying that we think it will, as we have evidence already in support of this opinion.[49]

However, on 21 September the paper reported that 'the potato crop is rapidly hastening towards destruction ... There is now no denying it.' The crop failure of 1849 was worst in southern and western counties, and Ó Murchadha states that 'over a great part of the country, in fact, 1849 proved to be even worse than the year already referred to as Black Forty Seven'.[50] Kinealy also refers to 1849 as 'Black 49', a fourth successive year of shortages.[51] It certainly was another appalling year for many of the people of north Kerry.

Fr Eugene McCarthy described the plight of the poor in his parishes in a letter of 22 May 1849 to the central relief committee in Dublin. There is a great sense of his anxiety and urgency in the letter:

> I beg to state for the information of the Central Relief Committee that the condition of the poor in these three parishes under my care, Ballyheigue, Rattoo and Killury, is for the last four or five days truly alarming; they are receiving only half rations and are to be confined to half rations in future. On yesterday there was no relief given, nor is there any expected on this day. It is now 6.00 p.m. and there is no meal as yet arrived. Whether all this be in pursuance of the 'orders to slay' as the proprietor of the *Freeman* would term it, I will not take it upon me to assert, but the officials at the gruel depot have assured me on this day that they have received orders from the authorities to confine the poor to half rations in future.
>
> The poor are sinking in consequence of this arrangement, and my coadjutors and myself had been obliged within this week, and even on this very day, to attend to some poor widows and others at the very depot who had come a distance of some seven or eight miles off in expectation of some relief.
>
> The acting relieving officer, whom I had called on this day, assured me that

there had been issued in outdoor relief in these three parishes about twenty tons of meal weekly and that no one person was given more than one pound of meal *per diem* and all under nine years of age received only half a pound. This will enable the committee to form an idea of the vast numbers on the relief list. In fact almost all the people are on the relief list; and what must be the state of suffering of a whole people who are two days in succession without any relief at all and who are by the authorities cut down to half rations in future?

The relieving officer had also assured me that the average of deaths in these three parishes was about thirty weekly but he took no account save of those who had been calling for coffins. Several had been known to conceal their deaths from the relieving officers so that the average of fifty or sixty deaths weekly would be something nearer the truth and all died of dysentery, cholera and starvation. In short I don't think that there is anywhere that I have read of, and I have read about Connaught and elsewhere in the *Freeman*, a greater amount of misery and suffering in every possible shape than in these three parishes of Ballyheigue, Rattoo and Killury.

PS. Even the Poor Law Inspector of this Union, Listowel, had admitted that in no eight parishes of the Union had there been so much destitution as in my three; and he had ordered one third of the rations of the union in '47 and '48 for the children of my national schools, although in the ratio of the number of parishes, I was only entitled to one eighth or one ninth rations. This is further proof of the extreme destitution of this barren district of mine.[52]

The central thrust of this letter is supported by other evidence from the early months of 1849. In February William Pope chaired a meeting of ratepayers in Causeway, which forwarded a petition to parliament for a change in the Poor Law system. It stated that poverty was making its way to the very doors of the higher classes, that the better class of farmers were emigrating and that the labourers were almost annihilated from destitution, nakedness and exposure to the winter cold. Rates in Killury (or Dromkeen) were 13s 4d in the pound, not including the county cess and the labour rate, and there was no possibility of paying this. The number on outdoor relief was about 2,000 and it was rising daily.[53] Landlords William Gun, John Pierce, Justin Rice, Kerry Supple and W. G. Sandes wrote in November that the high rates in their areas of Killury and Rattoo would lead to bankruptcy and ruin.[54]

An anonymous writer from Listowel was critical of two major landowners, Lord Listowel and Sir John Benn-Walsh, the former for not giving employment on his estate and the latter for refusing to give a site for a school in Irremore. He wrote that even artisans were being obliged to seek 'the plague-ridden shelter of the poorhouse' and concluded with an apocalyptic prediction:

> The state of the country is appalling. Here and in the neighbouring parishes of Lixnaw and Irremore, fever and dysentery are making ghastly havoc. The people are dying and will die in hundreds. The government will make this doomed land one vast graveyard and the folly and imbecility of its landlords will erect in it many a red sepulchral monument upon which posterity will read, inscribed by the finger of the avenging angel, their country's desolation, their own and their people's ruin.[55]

Evictions and Extermination

On a farm near Causeway seventy-four families (approximately 370 people) were evicted by order of the Provost of Trinity College, and their houses were knocked down. The landlords were Pope of Causeway and Rice of Bushmount, and before them, it was in the possession of Stoughton, but they were all sub-letting from the ultimate owner, which was Trinity College, Dublin. The *Examiner* reported that 'it speaks volumes for the deplorable condition to which the unfortunate poor of Ireland are reduced, cast out of their wretched homes, fathers, mothers and children, to beg or starve or be fed at public expense, and all this that the votaries of Mammon may fatten and prosper … In truth, comment is unnecessary; such deeds speak, trumpet-tongued, their own atrocity'.[56] With accounts of similar evictions coming from south Kerry, the *Post* took exception to the *Examiner's* reporting, defended the rights of property and approved of the evictions if they were carried out because of non-payment of rent or absence of legal title:

> That evictions are not [*sic*] daily occurring in the south and west of Ireland we do not attempt to deny; but we do contend that these evictions are not only justifiable but unavoidable – nay more, that they are of great advantage to the public and the poor. Although well aware of these facts, the radical press in this country has not hesitated, for factious purposes, to hold up every exercise of the rights of property as a direct breach of its duties. Thus, the exchange of an insolvent tenantry for one capable of cultivating the land and paying rent is reprobated as heartless extermination … Before the *Examiner* hazarded the use of the expression 'atrocity' he should have given the details of these ejectments – whether brought for non-payment of rent or non-title; and so enable the public to judge whether such observations are justifiable, or whether they are not gross libels on landlordism in general, and the managers of the properties in question in particular … If then a tenantry become so reduced in circumstances as to be unable to pay their rents, or even to till the land and so increase the food and capital of the country, and afford employment to the labouring classes, our contemporary will not surely insist that they are to be left, like a dog in the manger, in the possession of farms which they can neither cultivate nor pay for … The cry of 'get rid of the insolvent proprietors' is every day ringing in our ears and is then the greater evil of insolvent occupiers to be left untouched? Yet that is the obvious meaning of the indiscriminate attacks upon the owners of property in this country.[57]

In response, the *Examiner* revealed the circumstances which led to the cruel mass evictions. Its editorial began: 'It is melancholy to reflect upon the perverted ways of the world. There is no act of inhumanity, no "atrocity" that is or can be perpetrated by individuals or classes – man against man or men against men – that will not find apologists, interested or voluntary, some to justify, some to palliate.'[58] The editor asserted that, regardless of issues of rent or title, 'unhousing families by wholesale, under the wretched pretence, the paltry plea, of non-payment of rent or insufficient title, is what should not be tolerated in any Christian, in any civilised country on earth'. He exonerated the agents and officials who were obliged to carry out the evictions and blamed instead 'the system which the fell spirit of Irish landlordism has generated'. This was followed by an explanation of how high rents and the practice of having many tiers of middlemen gave rise to the eviction problem:

> High rents, which few can afford to pay by the mere produce of the soil cultivated by the head tenant's capital and hired labour, obliged the latter often to introduce a number of poor under-tenants denominated 'squatters', whose presence and existence are tolerated or connived at by the head landlord or his agent as long as these squatters are found useful as auxiliaries to the middleman to enable him to pay up his rent when the landlord's necessities require him; but should the middleman or sub-middleman or under-sub-middleman, as the case may be, feeling that he is unable longer to hold out, surrender or fly, it is then discovered that the remaining poor are valueless – they must be got rid of – they 'owe arrears' – their 'title is bad' – or the landlord 'knows nothing of them' – 'he set them no land' – crash come down the thatched roofs to the amazement and the grief of the wailing mother and her hungry, half-naked children, out they must go, for no shelter is left to tempt them to return, and thus, as is sometimes the case, one thousand individuals are suddenly cast out on the world and at the same time cast on the well-taxed mercy of the overburdened payers of the grinding poor rates.[59]

If it was absolutely necessary to evict families, the *Examiner* offered a practical suggestion to alleviate their hardship:

> Compensation should be given to the ejected, which by its amount would pluck the evil from the deed and console and appease and fully satisfy the wishes of the poor people who were content to depart for an equivalent adequate to the sacrifice which they were called on to make. Nothing short

of this can justify the vile and heartless system of eviction carried on in this county and in other parts of the kingdom.⁶⁰

On 25 April *The Cork Examiner* wrote, in reference to the state of the whole country, that 'human tongue and human pen are utterly inadequate to convey an idea of the horrors which abound. It is not the curse of a single affliction; it is a congeries of evil. It is not famine alone; the super-induced and subsequent realities are enough to affright the soul of the strongest'. As an example, it published a letter from Fr James Walsh of Lisselton, who wrote that there were over 500 deaths in his area over the previous four months. One dying man came for shelter and the priest gave him a space in his own cowhouse, where he died an hour later. A travelling woman whom he had sent to the workhouse was sent back to him because another form signed by the relieving officer was required; she died within hours and was buried without a shroud or a coffin. Fr Walsh ended his letter with this question: 'Would not our gracious sovereign shudder at such a melancholy picture – her own image, likeness and fellow creature thus brutally slaughtered by our so miscalled governors?'⁶¹

Such was the despair at the state of the country and at government policy that even the arch-conservative and unionist *Post* was tempted to question imperial rule and support Repeal, believing that under current policies, one-third of the population would soon be in receipt of indoor or outdoor relief. This was written two weeks after the *Post* had sought to justify evictions:

> Unutterable facts are accumulating fast to warn us that the approaching summer is likely to be one of greater horror and misery than we have yet seen. Disease is cutting away the population at a rate not easily estimated and the people, under pressure of their wretchedness, are degenerating into brutality. The poor are buried by stealth uncoffined and at night. Parents bury their children in gardens and bye-places to hide the fact of their death, *in order that their miserable pittance of meal might not be stopped*. The dogs are turning into beasts of prey and we heard a few days since of a dog horrifying

'THE POOR ARE SINKING'

a parcel of men at a smith's forge by rushing amongst them *with the head of a child in its mouth*, which no doubt it had scraped out of its shallow hasty grave. It is evident we must bear a famine with all its horrors and miseries, but we must bear it with the bitter aggravation of being *called* an *integral* part of the empire, the most civilised in the world, whose executive deals to us the rules of political economy instead of bread ... There is strong temptation in the dealings of our rulers with our miseries to raise the wild cry of Repeal. Desperate as such a resource might be, it could scarcely be worse than the lingering destitution to which every interest in society seems destined under imperial rule.[62]

The Cork Examiner sent a reporter to Kerry to investigate reports of evictions. Trinity College as proprietor was responsible for the eviction of 127 families, or approximately 635 individuals, in north Kerry, where college-owned property was leased to landlords such as Stoughton, Pope and Rice. Among the evictions were these in the following townlands: Ballinascrena (35 families), Ballinvranig (16 families) Knockavuhig (15 families), Acres (11 families), Corabally (13 families), Cloarbougher (9 families), Derryreagh (15 families), Beendhuve (7 families), Crotto (2 families) and Maulin (2 families).[63] With alternative spelling, Ballinbranhig, Knockavaghig and Corbally are listed today as part of Rattoo civil parish, while Crotto is partly in Kilflynn and partly in Kilfeighney parish; Acres is in Kilconly; Ballinascrena and Derryra are in Killury civil parish; and Maulin is in Ballyheigue.[64]

The reporter from *The Cork Examiner* concentrated on Knockavuhig, where he saw the unroofed and recently vacated cottages, and then saw smoke coming from some huts on the roadside. These huts were about five feet long and three feet high and were made of old timbers and sods of grass. In these huts there were three evicted families, two named Leahy and one named Halloran. John Leahy had held four acres of land from Pope, who held the land under Stoughton, who held it under Trinity College, according to the middleman land rental system. Leahy paid £4 a year in rent and was one year behind when he was evicted by order of the solicitor of Trinity

College. He was receiving one and three-quarters of a stone of meal every week to feed his family of five.

The reporter crouched down to enter the hovel through the opening which was three feet high and operated as both door and chimney: 'On the damp earth was shaken a little straw, on which lay some eight or nine sickly-looking children, their faces as black as those of Negroes from the turf smoke. I have often seen pigs better littered.' He went on to visit families named McCarthy, Hanrahan and Boyle, some of whom lived in makeshift huts situated even more deeply within the bog.[65]

Outrage at such incidents was felt by officials of the highest rank. The lord lieutenant, Lord Clarendon, wrote to the prime minister stating that he did not believe 'that there is another legislature in Europe that would disregard such suffering as now exists in the west of Ireland or coldly persist in a policy of extermination'.[66] Edward Twistleton, Chief Poor Law Commissioner, resigned in March 1849 in protest at 'the indifference of the House of Commons', saying that he refused to administer a policy that he saw as extermination. He condemned Treasury officials who had 'steeled their hearts entirely to the sufferings of the people of Ireland' in the belief that it was 'the law of nature' that destitute people should die. A humanitarian, Twistleton stated his deep conviction 'that it is part of the system of nature that we should have feelings of compassion for those people and that it is a most narrow-minded view of the system of nature to think that those people should be left to die'.[67]

The *Illustrated London News* of 15 December 1849 also strongly condemned government policy, writing that 'calmly and quietly from Westminster itself, which is the centre of civilisation, did the decree go forth which has made the temporary but terrible visitation of a potato rot the means of exterminating, through the slow process of disease and houseless starvation, nearly half of the Irish'.[68] Sidney Godolphin Osborne, a clergyman and philanthropist, visited Ireland in the summer of 1849 and expressed his views very powerfully: 'I have no hesitation in adding my firm conviction that very many have been done to death by pure tyranny … I cannot get rid of a very strong impression I entertain that there has been a disposition to look at the difficulties of the crisis in these respects as so great that there was a sort of tacit determination to let things take their course at any cost.'[69] Osborne did not visit Kerry, but he did refer to Listowel Union in a letter to *The Times*:

> Within the last few weeks God only knows how many thousands of gable ends, monuments of house havoc, how many sites of dwellings but lately wholly levelled I have passed. I can hardly say where this mad indiscriminate war on habitations has prevailed most; it seems almost universal in this part of Ireland ... I am prepared to assert that a very large amount of bygone, nay, now-acting eviction is carried out in a wanton unfeeling spirit towards the evicted and on grounds of mere selfish expediency most disgraceful. Since I began this letter I have been informed that within this last fortnight 137 houses were levelled in one district in the Listowel Union.[70]

The Cork Examiner welcomed Osborne's fierce condemnation of the clearances:

> The rage for eviction, for uncivilising, as it were, the population is a moral taint, a contagion of inhumanity which must be extinguished wholly and absolutely and without reference to other considerations; and if positive law will not do that, we must only accumulate upon the guilty parties such a force of opprobrium as will have the same effect. The practice may be extenuated by circumstances, excused never. There can be no compromise which includes in its terms a permission to take away life, no political necessity which renders it impossible for people to live on in the land of their birth.[71]

Christine Kinealy has written about the 'hidden agenda' of the British government in respect of these large-scale evictions, which, although deeply shocking and inhumane, were actually within the law. Landlords were empowered by official policy and prevailing attitudes to the rights of property owners and it suited the government's long-standing desire to improve the structure of land-holding in Ireland to allow such clearances of tenants with small holdings, a policy described as social engineering: 'the government was able to use the chaos caused by the Famine to facilitate a number of social and economic changes'.[72]

The newspapers often carried poetry of a pastoral or romantic nature, but in May a poem with dark, graphic imagery was published, showing how wealth and poverty, excess and deprivation co-existed. In general, the voice of the poorest of the poor is not recorded in any newspaper, but this writer empathised with them and conveyed their desperate condition when hope died and desolation reigned. These plaintive stanzas were called 'The Cry of the Poor':

> *Look down on us, God! from thy throne upon high,*
> *Man heeds not the woes that his fellows endure;*
> *Of hunger, while plenty surrounds us, we die,*
> *And lean dogs grow fat on the bones of the poor.*
>
> *Around us the highway of pleasure is crowded;*
> *Ay, crowded, while we 'passing under the rod',*
> *Are thrust into grave pits uncoffined, unshrouded,*
> *Unwept and unpitied – look down on us, God.*
>
> *Around us fresh stimulants luxury craves;*
> *Wealth opens the portals of joy by a nod,*
> *While manhood and beauty fills thousands of graves,*
> *And childhood is withered – look down on us, God.*
>
> *There's wealth in this empire, yes wealth in redundance,*
> *Up springs the green harvest of hope from our sod;*
> *The wide world is teeming with joy and abundance,*
> *We starve and rats eat us – look down on us, God!*[73]

Perhaps it is an indication of the widespread experience of loss of life that a tragic incident in December at Glenderry in Kerry Head received only a few lines in one newspaper. Four men drowned while trying to salvage timber in a small boat. One was a father of eight and the others were single men; none was named in the report.[74]

Landlords, Rates and Rents in Listowel Union

As was regularly noted in the *Post*, the financial position of many landlords was very precarious, with pressure from very heavy rates and much reduced rental income. For many landlords, the choice was stark: ejecting tenants who were unable to pay rent or being ejected themselves. Large-scale clearances of unproductive tenants and assisted emigration were two measures taken by landlords. Clearances involved the consolidation of holdings and the levelling of houses to prevent tenants returning to them. The government had introduced the Encumbered Estates Act in 1848, which helped landlords in deep financial trouble to sell their whole estates, albeit at a greatly reduced price.

Landlord and guardian Peirce Mahony spoke at a Listowel board of guardians' meeting about the intolerable burden of taxation which faced landlords and gave the example of St John Blacker who, he said, had spent thousands in Ballylongford in the previous eighteen months and the result was that his valuation of the land was £6,469, out of which he was obliged to pay £5,206 in rates.[75] 'Is not that enough,' asked Mahony, 'to deter him and others from continuing their efforts to improve the country through the employment of the people?' Mahony also cited Killehinny, where the valuation was £2,637 and the rates on it amounted to £3,330, and Dromkeen, which was valued as £4,485 and yet £5,347 was demanded in rates in 1849. A rate of 14s 8d in the pound was applied to Dromkeen, Rattoo and Killehinny. 'We cannot work out impossibilities,' said Mahony.[76]

Mahony was an expert on financial affairs and he was scathing about the wasteful expenditure of public money by Listowel Union during 1848, when it was run by two vice-chairmen rather than by a board of guardians; he claimed that the total Poor Law expenditure in Kerry in 1848 was £97,000 and of that, over £50,000 was spent by Listowel Union.[77] He told the board that the cost of distributing outdoor relief of £1 12s was £1 7s 6d. He also suggested that to encourage home produce, paupers should be given barley meal or oatmeal instead of imported Indian meal.[78] One of Mahony's suggestions about practical instruction for farmers on how to improve butter production was taken up by the government.[79]

A scheme known as rate-in-aid was introduced in 1849 to assist unions that were in the deepest financial difficulties. It involved the levy of a rate of 6d in the pound on all unions in June 1849 and a further 2d in the pound in December. The money raised was to assist the worst-off unions in the west and south. It was welcomed by unions which were in financial difficulty, but greatly resented by the successful ones. The *Post*, on behalf of landlords, took grave exception to the scheme, stating that 'it is now plain that rate-in-aid is Roman. Let the Protestants look to it: Rome will never co-operate with Protestants but to betray them.'[80] This religious argument was an unusual line of attack on rate-in-aid.

A high-level delegation from Listowel board went to Dublin to appeal formally to the lord lieutenant, Lord Clarendon, and met with him for over one and a half hours to explain their predicament. The delegation included Peirce Mahony, William Talbot Crosbie, St John Blacker, Meade C. Dennis, William Hickson and Charles G. Fairfield.[81] Their main request was for assistance through the rate-in-aid scheme. Not all members of the board of guardians agreed with the majority stance on the rates issue, however, and James Murray Home resigned as chairman of Listowel board on the grounds that the new board 'had reverted to the worst faults of the former elected board of tampering with the rates, delaying their signatures and setting at nought their own resolutions'.[82] Home's letter of resignation ended with the simple statement that the board should do its duty of setting a rate and confiscating the goods and chattels of anyone who failed to pay the rates. He concluded as follows:

'THE POOR ARE SINKING'

I will not sit as chairman of a board habitually to violate the law ... a board which procrastinates, hesitates, changes when it ought to act; a board, most of the members of which having been dismissed only thirteen months ago with contumely, which cannot learn that its duty is to carry out the law ...[83]

However, Home was soon persuaded to resume his position as chairman.

Listowel Workhouse

The financial problems of the Listowel board also affected the workhouse and resulted in a report that they could not meet the costs of food for the workhouse, as the Provincial Bank would not honour any cheques of the union beyond the cash held in the bank.[84] This may be understandable, as in December 1848 £789 had been collected in rates while £18,554 remained to be collected. By May 1849 the corresponding figures were £278 and £4,996, in July they were £1,154 and £10,387 and in September £438 and £7,282.[85]

While the vice-guardians managed the union, it was decided to begin admissions early in the day 'thereby doing away with all pretence for the gathering and crowding of paupers outside, increasing their distress, creating dissatisfaction and a disposition to riot when together after nightfall'.[86] Another decision recorded was that all dead inmates of the workhouse were to be taken out for burial at 6 a.m., apparently to conceal the number of deaths.[87] There was also a record of a claim by the guardians that a 'systematic plan' had been put in place by able-bodied paupers who had been struck off outdoor relief to present themselves at the workhouse, hoping by virtue of their numbers that they would not be admitted, and so would qualify for outdoor relief again; this was foiled by expanding temporarily the number of places in the workhouse.[88]

A reporter from the *Post* visited Listowel workhouse in July 1849 and was shocked to learn that 36 per cent of the population of Listowel Union was in receipt of outdoor relief at a weekly cost of £700, compared with 16 per cent of Tralee Union. Indoor relief in the workhouse was considered more economical than outdoor relief. The cost of outdoor relief was met by the rates, so the higher the number of people claiming it, the higher the rates. The editor was also appalled to learn that 210 families in the union were receiving relief because they had not been subjected to the 'workhouse test' due to the inefficiency of relieving officers; the families were allowed 'to quarter themselves on a public charity to which legally or morally they had no claim'.[89]

The reporter walked through the workhouses of Listowel and saw 'nothing to regret'. In the main workhouse a large number of women worked on spinning and winding linen thread, and had already made 5,000 yards of thread. There was a loom in the large room and elsewhere women worked at spinning wool. The workhouse was soon expected to become self-sufficient in clothing and bedding of wool and linen produced by the paupers. There was order everywhere and the children were cleaner and healthier than the reporter had expected. Mortality that week was seen as low, with only three deaths; there were seven deaths the week before. The average cost of keeping each pauper per week was one shilling.[90]

Positive Press for Some Landlords

There was some evidence of a general disposition among some north Kerry landlords to make abatements or reductions to their tenants in view of the difficult times and there were instances where landlords were praised by individual tenants and by the press. Peirce Mahony, for example, was described as 'a pattern to the landlords of Kerry' when he visited all his tenants and gave abatements of 30 per cent on all rents and forgave arrears of the majority of tenants. To those who could not retain or work their holdings, he 'considerately' gave £10 to enable them to emigrate to America with their families. Mahony planned extensive drainage works and brought in an English engineer named Webster to build kilns for making bricks and drainage tiles, and to build limekilns for the tenants.[91]

Assisted emigration was also widely used by another prominent north Kerry landlord, Sir John Benn-Walsh. He was praised by a Listowel curate, Fr

Daniel Huolahan [*sic*], for being 'a bright exception to the general rapacity of landlords'. According to Huolahan, when Benn-Walsh took on a new tenant, he did not demand rent for a year and a half, and made generous allowances for all improvements made by the tenant during that period. When some tenants, 'looking on this country as a doomed land', decided to emigrate, they received financial support from Benn-Walsh. 'What did Sir John do,' wrote Huolahan, 'but send down his kind and considerate agent, Mr. Gabbett from Dublin, to make his inquiries and the result is that any man wishing to go is sent out, an outfit procured for him, his passage paid, and all at the sole expense of Sir John.'[92] Sixty tenants had availed of this option at a cost of £400 to the landlord. Assuring readers that he had never met Benn-Walsh or Gabbett, Fr Huolahan wrote that they were models to others. He ended his letter: 'I understand Sir John is about to visit this country in a few days and never did monarch receive from subjects a more warm reception than this good man will receive from a grateful, contented, because a comfortable, tenantry.'[93]

Rev. Edward Fitzgerald Day was a landlord in Ardoughter, Causeway, and Richard Boyle was one of his tenants. The clergyman bought the property in 1845 and came into possession in 1846. Boyle praised him for his generosity, good feeling and practical wisdom. Among Rev. Day's actions were the writing off of a year's rent, payment of portions of tenants' rates, and giving employment to the value of £40 per week to tenants and to paupers. One result was that 'not a single pound of meal was required as relief' on his property. In springtime Day distributed seed to all who needed it, brought in an agriculturist from Dublin to instruct tenants and gave them implements such as hoes, rolling-stones and turnip-sowers free of charge. The *Chronicle* was impressed by these initiatives and as proof of their success it cited the fact that none of Day's tenants had absconded. It had simple advice for other landlords: 'Go and do likewise.' Edward's brother Robert, another clergyman and landowner, was also praised.[94]

In January 1850 James Crowley, Repeal warden of Benmore, Ballyduff, replied to a number of queries from the Loyal National Repeal Association's

Distress Committee, saying that the potato crop was rotting and would only last for another month, that the poor were selling 'all disposable articles, even bed-clothes and wearing apparel, to buy necessaries', and that lack of clothing prevented people from attending Mass. He estimated that there had been 952 deaths from starvation, that 419 people had emigrated and that 217 families had been exterminated, including three families in the previous week.[95] He claimed there was 'no employment in this parish whatever if we except the Rev. Edward Fitzgerald Day, who has given considerable employment on his property in the parish of Killury, beyond £4,000'. Crowley added: 'He gave to his tenantry and labouring classes plenty of seed for green and white crops at the commencement of spring.'[96]

St John Blacker was praised in some reports, although he would later be publicly condemned as an exterminating landlord. Blacker was from an Armagh family, but in August 1849 was reported as taking Ballydonoghue House near Tarbert as his permanent residence in order to devote more time and attention to his Ballylongford lands, with the help of his agent, Stephen Sandes. He arrived at his residence with his two sisters and they were welcomed with 'bonfires, triumphal arches and every other sign of a grateful people'.[97] He was lauded in the *Morning Post,* which asked: 'What could the most wealthy and enterprising English capitalist do more?'[98] Blacker was praised in the *Farmer's Gazette* for devising an improved way of sending packed butter from Tarbert to Liverpool at a cost of £3 per ton, instead of the £6 per ton it cost to send via Cork.[99] The *Post* described him as 'one of the best landlords in this or any other county'.[100] It regretted that enterprising landlords such as Blacker, who provided valuable employment, were 'grossly maligned by every nameless and malicious scribbler' in some quarters for paying low wages.[101]

In Kerry Head area, eight named tenants acknowledged 'our worthy, liberal and truly philanthropic landlord, Thomas A. Stoughton Esq. of Ballyhorgan' for abating three years' rent, amounting to hundreds of pounds, and making other allowances. 'Hurrah for a Stoughton forever', they wrote, and the landlord promised 'that he would see his tenants justified for ever'.[102] These reports suggest some news management on behalf of landlords, perhaps to counteract bad publicity. Other landlords who were praised were Henry Arthur Herbert of Muckross and Lady Headley of Aghadoe. Both of these had extensive landholdings mainly in south Kerry, but they also had land in the Castleisland and Brosna areas.

Throughout the 1840s Lady Headley dispensed charity in the form of clothing and money to her tenants, and this continued during the Famine years. In 1843 she distributed blankets, quilts, shirts and money to thirty or forty families in the Aghadoe area (near Killarney) and she was held up as an example to other landlords: 'Her truly noble heart can sympathise with the wretched and never turns a deaf or heedless ear to the petition of the distressed.'[103] She donated £50 to the local relief committee in 1846 and in 1847 was quick to reduce rents by a third, a gesture which was warmly welcomed.[104] In the area north of Aghadoe, she had tenants in Castleisland, Glounsharoon and Ploughlands. She retained the goodwill of tenants and of the press by continuing the reduction in the following years, and one paper demanded: 'In the name of common sense, why will others not follow the example of Lady Headley?'[105] It was pointed out that as a consequence of Lady Headley's generosity, not one of her tenants had fled. Her 'well-directed benevolence' led to her being lauded as 'one of the best landlords in the county'.[106] Peter Gray cites sources confirming that the Headley estate 'was well known for waste-land reclamation and the comfortable condition of its tenantry'.[107]

In February 1851, at a dinner in Lady Headley's honour, there was great goodwill towards her, although it was gently pointed out that her benevolence was also serving her own long-term interests. The occasion was the re-valuation of her estate by John Powell, which was done to the satisfaction of all parties. Fr Jeremiah O'Leary, PP, presided at the event in the Assembly Rooms in Castleisland, and there were genuine tributes from clergymen of all denominations and other speakers. Justin Supple of Tralee praised Lady Headley as giving:

> ... a noble and bright example and one which ought to be imitated by every landlord in Ireland. She has not squandered her income in Rome, London, Paris or Dublin but among her own tenants. Her re-valuation of the rents accepted that from the depression of the present times, tenants could not afford to pay the promised rents and so she reduced the rents. Her ladyship has not only acted nobly but wisely and I venture to say that at the end of four years she will have received more money than if she was to press them for the last shilling.[108]

Similarly, Henry A. Herbert was hailed in Brosna when 'his numerous respected and contented tenantry' organised a bonfire in his honour. Over 100 people attended a dinner and evening of music. An anonymous correspondent wrote: 'If the different landed proprietors of this unfortunate locality possessed Mr Herbert's kindness of disposition and business habits, the people would show nothing of the misery and habits they have undergone.'[109]

Newspapers also had some amusement at the expense of landlords, as in a satirical piece on Peirce Mahony, which described his visit to Killarney in 1849 in overblown imagery, in the style used for reporting the visits of dignitaries. (The lord lieutenant was in Killarney at the time and there was some public ceremony around his visit.)[110] Despite the paper having earlier praised him for his kindness to his tenants, this composition appeared in the *Post* and was an entertaining broadside at Mahony's pomposity. It was addressed to 'Peirce Mahony, the prince of jobbers', a description applied to him by Daniel O'Connell in 1832 when the two men were at odds.[111]

> May it please Peirce Mahony, we the inhabitants of Kerry, starved and well-nigh expiring, beg to shelter ourselves under the shadow of your mighty wings;
>
> Great Peirce Mahony, vouchsafe to become our representative in the Imperial Parliament on the next vacancy;
>
> Inimitable Peirce Mahony, make a railway for us to America;

Immortal Peirce Mahony, tell Queen Victoria when you are next speaking to her to come to Killarney and take a marine villa on the banks of Lough Leane;

Awe-striking Peirce Mahony, get a loan for us from the government for ten million and make them turn the last loan into a grant;

Peirce Mahony, Thaumaturge, stay the potato disease and keep away the cholera;

Peirce Mahony, the all-embracing, shower down upon us a few places in the customs, excise, post office, or the Four Courts;

World-wide Peirce Mahony, leave us a lock of your hair.[112]

8

'AN UNPRECEDENTED AND UNEXPECTED INFLUX OF PAUPERISM'

1850

I hardly think it possible that a more naked, hungry, sickly, emaciated set of human beings could be seen anywhere.

The Cork Examiner, 24 May 1850

Tralee Union and Boundary Changes

The pressures on the workhouses of Tralee and Listowel were intense by 1849. In Listowel Union in 1847 the workhouse population was below fifty per 1,000 of the population of the union; in 1849 this had risen to over 200 per 1,000 of population. In Tralee, the equivalent figures were between 50 and 100 per 1,000 in 1847 and between 150 and 200 per 1,000 in 1849.[1]

On 30 March 1850 Tralee board of guardians learned that a boundary commission appointed by the Poor Law Commissioners had recommended boundary changes in the Kerry unions. A few townlands from the Killarney area and nine electoral districts from the Listowel Union were to be moved to the Tralee Union. There was outrage among the Tralee guardians at this change, which brought Ardfert, Tubrid, Banna, Abbeydorney, Ballinorig, Kilflynn, Killahan, Ballyheigue and Kerry Head under their union. These places were seen as 'the very poorest parts of the Listowel district'.[2] As early as July 1849 there had been indications in the press of forthcoming boundary changes, but the scale of the changes came as a shock in Tralee, and especially because of the poverty prevailing in some parts of the transferred areas.[3] The *Examiner* took the view that the change 'must prove overwhelmingly disastrous to the already ground-down ratepayers of this district [Tralee]'.[4] Initially, there appears to have been little response from Listowel to the change, except for the board of guardians to lament the fact that William Talbot Crosbie of Ardfert Abbey would no longer be part of the union and to express regret at the loss of his expertise. It was suggested at a meeting of Tralee board of guardians that the influence of Lord Listowel and Peirce Mahony had been the cause of the transfer of 'the host of pauperism and contagion of the Listowel Union', but the two men denied any involvement in the decision.[5]

It was the financial burden of responsibility for the poor of the newly annexed districts that alarmed the Tralee guardians. According to the *Post*, 'the greatest wrong has been inflicted on the ratepayers of the old Tralee Union ... They are united to an extensive and impoverished district by which we may calculate that not less than 2,000 additional paupers will be thrown upon them for relief.' The paper asked: 'Is Tralee to be ruined that the plans of Poor Law officials may be carried out?'[6]

It was clear that it was having responsibility for the Ballyheigue and Kerry Head areas which was most resented, as they were seen as the poorest of the nine new districts. A protest meeting of Tralee ratepayers was held in the courthouse 'to protest against the annexation of the impoverished parts of the Listowel union' but the town's borough commissioners explicitly specified 'the proposed addition of the Ballyheigue district'.[7] The order of the commissioners was described as tyrannical and despotic, 'a *fiat* ... with all the force of a Russian *ukase*', obliging Tralee Union to take responsibility for the paupers of an area which stretched from Kerry Head to Feale Bridge, near Abbeyfeale.[8] At the meeting Rickard O'Connell spoke about 'this late oppressive order dooming this union to bear the burden of the pauperism caused to a great degree by the mismanagement of the paid guardians at Listowel'. Another speaker said that the effect was to give Tralee 'the most pauperised portion of Listowel union'.

The feeling among most of the guardians was that 'if the paupers of Listowel once find a footing within our borough, they will undoubtedly remain an incubus on us forever'. The *Post* welcomed 'the perfect unanimity of feeling and opinion' which was evident at the meeting.[9]

The *Chronicle* at first remained neutral, stating that the opposing views had been given an adequate airing in its columns and did not require an editorial opinion.[10] However, it later declared that the board members were 'fully justified in their dissent from the arbitrary *ukase* of the commissioners'.[11]

It was a cruel irony that after years of hardship, when their fate lay in the hands of unknown bureaucrats in Dublin and in London, the poor of the districts in question now appeared to be at the mercy of more familiar bureaucrats – the guardians and ratepayers of Tralee. The *Post* predicted the worst consequences of the refusal to accept responsibility for the destitute of the nine districts:

> What is to become of the paupers of the disputed districts in the meantime? The Listowel Board are rid of them by the Commissioners' orders and the Tralee Board will refuse all connection with them. Much suffering, nay, starvation and death, must be the first results of this change.[12]

A long and heated discussion took place at a meeting of Tralee board of guardians on the boundary changes. The issue was the financial support available to the newly transferred inmates of Listowel workhouse. John Sealy was in the chair and the following exchanges took place between John Hurly, solicitor and chairman of Tralee Borough Commissioners, and Captain Spark. Hurly said that the board did not have the funds to support 'a host of pauperism from other districts'.[13] Spark responded that there was £500 available in the hands of the treasurer.

> Mr Hurly: But there are numerous claimants for that trifle, and we met here today for the purpose of dividing that sum between contractors, to whom large sums are due.

Captain Spark: The preservation of human life is more important than anything. There are 1,200 people thrown upon you for support now and the Poor Law Commissioners require you to provide for them; and if you don't do so, the people will perish.

Hurly: I think nothing can be more important than to pay our contractors who will not further supply our houses if not paid. The Poor Law Commissioners when they sent these people should have sent money to support them. It gives this board and the ratepayers of this union quite enough to do to support their own.

Spark: These prospective considerations should not be placed in competition with the lives of the people. The people ought not to be allowed to die and mere matters of finance should not prevent the people's lives from being preserved.

Hurly: If they die, that must be attributable to the Poor Law Commissioners and not to this Board. The Commissioners send a parcel of people from the pauperised unions on us, without sending the means to support them; and this board has neither money nor credit to carry out the wishes of the Commissioners, and they send these people also without the least notice or intimation. On the contrary, this board was led to believe by the Commissioners' communication of 28 March that this union would not be divided at all.

Spark: You have had notice, sir. The relieving officers from these districts have been here the last board day and are here now, ready to give the people relief if you give the funds.[14]

Resolutions were passed stating that 'want of funds, exhausted credit, inadequate accommodation and an amount of debt exceeding £11,000' meant that Tralee Union could not relieve their own destitute, not to mention the paupers from Listowel Union.[15] As a temporary measure, and since the relieving officers of the disputed districts were present that day, the guardians offered them £27 to provide relief, but stressed that this was not to be seen as a precedent.

Hurly's position was supported by other guardians, with George Hilliard saying, 'it is impossible for us to give [relief]. Let the Commissioners give us the money and we will.' Mr Leahy timidly asked: 'But what will become of these 1,200 people in the meantime?' Hurly answered: 'The Listowel Union is now in a better position than it was to relieve these people. Tarbert being taken from them, even with these electoral divisions, Listowel Union would be quite regular and compact. It would in fact be a ring-fence.'[16]

Captain Spark said firmly that the Tralee board was legally obliged to give relief to the people of the new districts and that he would not be doing his duty if he did not 'in the most peremptory manner' inform the board members that it was their duty 'to step in and prevent the people from starving'.[17] The guardian Daniel de Courcy McGillycuddy asked him: 'But Captain Spark, what will our contractors do if we give all our funds for the support of these people?' Spark replied that their credit was not so low that contractors would refuse to be repaid by instalment, and went on to say that it was his duty to tell them that the people should not, at all hazards, be allowed to die. He called in the relieving officers who were waiting outside and asked how much was needed to supply outdoor relief in the disputed areas for a week and they said £26 would suffice.

Richard Chute said that they could not give money directly, as that could be seen as implying consent to the new arrangements, but would give it to Captain Spark for him to distribute it. Spark declined to co-operate on these terms, because it would be putting him in a false position and stated that 'he would rather give the money out of his own pocket than see the people starve'. Hurly said that he did not wish to place Captain Spark in any improper position, but the board would not be party 'to introducing the people of these districts with their filth and disease into the heart of the town'.[18]

The *Chronicle's* report went on: 'Captain Spark implored them in the name of humanity not to stand on technicalities about this terrible sum of £26 which would preserve the people's lives.' Richard Chute said that it was not about the sum of money but the principle. Leahy, who was the only member supporting Spark's case, asked again what would the people do and this exchange followed:

> Hurly: Let the Listowel people relieve them.
>
> Spark: They don't belong to Listowel now. There is a sealed order giving them to this union.
>
> Hurly: We will make them a present of it but we will not give it as a right.
>
> Spark: With every regard for Mr Hurly, that is not the way to meet the question.
>
> Chute: I think it is. This £26 will be followed by as much more every week and where is this to come from?

In response to Captain Spark's appeal for a spirit of humanity from the guardians, John Hurly gave a graphic account of what Tralee guardians had been through over the previous years, which explains, although hardly excuses, the position he and others adopted:

> Mr Hurly said they could not be charged with any want of humanity, for during the last three years they clung to their own people, braving disease and contagion in the house, on the stairs leading to this room and even in the room itself. They did not shrink from the discharge of their duties, under trying and perilous circumstances, at late hours and in inclement weather, struggling to support the poor and save the ratepayers as well as they could without aid or assistance from any quarter.[19]

Captain Spark acknowledged the truth of this and gave the board members credit for the efficient way in which they had carried out their duties. The outcome of this meeting was an agreement to provide the £26 required for one week's relief.[20]

A report in the *Post* counterpointed the scene outside the boardroom while the long discussion above took place, and made a direct comparison with the unprecedented scenes of 1847 outside the workhouse:

> We were not for some months past so forcibly reminded of the harrowing scenes of '47 as at last Tuesday's meeting of the Tralee Board. There were 500 poor creatures seeking admittance to the workhouse and there appeared to be the greatest suffering and wretchedness among them. No less than five or six children were reported to be dying in their mother's arms. Between three and four hundred were admitted bringing the number in the workhouse to little short of 5,000.[21]

The Tralee protests were rejected by the commissioners, whereupon the majority of the Tralee board of guardians resigned their positions. The guardians who resigned included James O'Connell, John Hurly, George Hilliard, Justin Supple, Daniel de Courcy McGillycuddy, Gerard O'Connor, John McCarthy, Maurice Dunne, Rowland Chute, Pierce Chute, Richard Jeffcott, John Keane and Curry Rae.[22] A rump of guardians from the Castleisland area continued to conduct board business.

As the person representing the Poor Law Commissioners, Captain Spark was obliged to defend their decisions. However, he had no answer to the complaints of the Tralee guardians that they were without funds and without credit and had received 'a host of pauperism and no money to meet it'.[23] All that Spark could say was that the Treasury was not responding to the requests of the commissioners, so it appears that the ultimate responsibility lay on the desk of the assistant secretary of the Treasury in London, Charles Trevelyan.[24]

At subsequent meetings William Talbot Crosbie of Ardfert made some conciliatory proposals, including the suggestion of a separate union for Castleisland. This was not acted on. The Tralee guardians who had resigned wrote to the commissioners that 'it was physically and morally impossible for any set of men' to manage the affairs of the union following the 'unprecedented and unexpected influx of pauperism', but that a grant of financial aid would induce them to resume their duties.[25] A grant of £1,000 was approved by the commissioners in May; this eased the immediate crisis and the Tralee guardians resumed their duties.[26]

Another reason the Tralee guardians resisted the new arrangements was because they would have to acquire more accommodation for the increased numbers by renting a suitable building and staffing it. This took some time, but by June a building was rented: 'Mr Riordan's store at High St, the last available one now, was reported ready for the reception of paupers and it was resolved to discontinue outdoor relief to the twelve hundred now in receipt of it.'[27] But the guardians of Tralee continued to express their resentment that they had been 'encumbered … with a host of sturdy beggars in perpetuity, whom nothing but time could relieve them of'.[28]

Although it is easy to be judgemental about the attitude of the Tralee guardians and ratepayers, there are many reasons for not rushing to condemn them. It is impossible today to understand fully the complexities of the issues and the many strains under which the guardians were operating. They felt a sense of duty to their ratepayers, and Tralee Union was 'overwhelmed by debt', with liabilities of over £10,000.[29] Even Captain Spark was refused credit when he wished to buy £10 worth of timber, probably for coffins.[30]

Tralee's Workhouses

Several properties in Tralee were acquired in early May for use as auxiliary workhouses; one of these was referred to as the Old Chapel corn store; three or four other similar stores were on offer to the board, and the *Chronicle* saw this as a sign of a depression in agriculture and in business.[31] This list of Tralee workhouses with the numbers of inmates was published in June, when the total number was 6,085: main house 1,125; Ballymullen 915;

Rock 1,028; Blennerville 223; James Street and Palmers 489; Old Chapel, O'Connell's and Waterloo 624; O'Leary's 428; Riordan's 421; Castleisland and auxiliary 832. There were hospitals in 'Riordan's store' and 'Waterloo Lane' with eighteen and eighty-three patients respectively.[32]

The stream of impoverished applicants to the workhouse continued, and a group of '377 creatures in their wet clothes had to be crammed into a loft in O'Connell's store which had not been used for twelve months'.[33] The board stated that 'notwithstanding our admissions this day exceed 500, there are vast numbers of emaciated and starving creatures in vain applying for admission, the board having no mode of relieving them'.[34] A reporter from *The Cork Examiner* was moved by the scenes he witnessed in Tralee:

> There were about 400 applicants, 338 of whom were admitted, many of whom were so far exhausted that they had to be taken immediately to hospital. I hardly think it possible that a more naked, hungry, sickly, emaciated set of human beings could be seen anywhere. All the men, or rather skeletons of men, were drafted to the Rock branch house, in their new clothes of course, at the separation of the board.[35]

The desperate state of these weak and demoralised people, who had endured so much hardship since the first failure of the potato crop, is truly shocking. Some may have walked to Listowel first, and on being refused admission there, continued walking the sixteen miles to Tralee. They were refugees in their own land. And the poor continued to die on the roadsides. Fr O'Connell found an exhausted man named O'Shea in a collapsed state in Ballybeggan and arranged for him to be taken to the workhouse, but the man died as they made the short journey; in fact he 'expired in the arms of the persons carrying him'.[36] A woman fell dead in Blennerville in November and her body lay on the roadside all day, with nobody willing to shelter it. The cause of her death was given as heart disease.[37] Another woman, named Roche, was found in an exhausted state at the gates of the Tralee workhouse and she died later in hospital. The reporter believed her death was from starvation.[38]

Some disturbing atrocities were also reported. In May a man and a woman were discovered to be offering human bones for sale in the town of Tralee. When suspicions arose that the bones had come from a burial ground, the two culprits were taken into custody but 'they seemed to enjoy the affair as if it were all fun, and appeared quite hardened and heartless as if accustomed to such horrid depredation'.[39]

Fr Francis Moore, curate of Ardfert, who had written in 1847 to *The Tablet*, wrote again in 1850, giving a revealing picture of the renewed distress and confirming the fate of many of the Listowel workhouse inmates. He stated that the number of deaths in one fifteen-day period in Ardfert and Kilmoyley had been higher than the number for the previous six months. One reason he gave for this was that the turnip crop was exhausted; another was the annexation of parts of Listowel Union to that of Tralee:

> Immediately on their separation, the Listowel guardians turned out of the workhouse the paupers of this district without waiting until the Tralee guardians could procure the necessary accommodation for them. So far are the farmers from giving them any relief that it is with difficulty that I can get the use of a stable or cow-house in order to administer the last rites of the church to these fellow creatures, so loathsome and offensive are their persons from diseases brought on by famine ... I can state with truth that their condition is worse at present than it had been at any former time.[40]

The letter provides confirmation of the plight of the desperate people rejected by Listowel Union and obliged to apply to Tralee Union, where they were equally unwelcome. It is also notable that by this time the farming class had little sympathy for the unfortunates, who were seen as dangerously disease-ridden. Newspaper reports reveal that there was little sympathy anywhere for these wretched of the earth.

Later in the year the rate-collector for the nine newly added divisions of Tralee Union was sharply criticised for not bringing in more money. The guardians told him that 'they had been feeding the paupers of those divisions for several months and now there were but three hundred pounds collected'.[41] The Tralee board of guardians seems to have been quite chaotic and dysfunctional in late 1850, with Mr Denny describing it as 'a perfect bear garden' and the *Chronicle* writing that the boardroom was 'a scene of disgraceful confusion'.[42]

The expenditure of Tralee workhouse was investigated in October 1850, and Dr Chute and Dr Alton were closely questioned by the guardians. In the previous six months purchases had included 156 pounds of tea, 1,655 pounds of sugar, 255 bottles of wine, 543 bottles of porter, 86 gallons of whiskey, 4,787 pounds of meat, 248 pounds of arrowroot and 496 fowl. When Dr Chute was asked why so much wine and meat were consumed in the Ballymullen auxiliary workhouse, where many of the inmates were children, the following exchange took place:

> Dr Chute: In Ballymullen a great deal of meat was used because those patients in ophthalmia, whose eyes had sloughed, required generous treatment.
>
> Mr Denny: Do you think that wine is necessary in ophthalmia?
>
> Dr Chute: When greatly depressed they require it and may thus become well in a day, whereas without nourishment they would become blind in two days. Many eyes have been saved by wine and generous diet.
>
> Mr Denny: Would not whiskey answer?
>
> Dr Chute: Many of them get whiskey too.
>
> Mr James O'Connell: If they have a drop in one eye, you endeavour to give them a drop in both eyes (laughter).
>
> Mr Supple: You visit farmers paying high rents. Are they able to afford themselves wine?

> Dr Chute: A man is obliged to treat a disease to the best of his knowledge.
>
> Mr Herbert: I am not finding fault with you but with the system.
>
> Mr Hurly: I suppose the next thing you will give them will be champagne.
>
> Dr Chute: If champagne would save the poorest pauper in the house, I would order it.[43]

The board was shocked at the 'enormous consumption' of meat, tea, sugar and alcohol in the workhouse, especially at a time when ratepayers were having difficulty procuring the necessities of life for themselves and their families. The outcome of the investigation was that the board greatly reduced the amount of meat and of alcohol to be ordered in the future.

Six months later Dr Chute protested at having his salary reduced by the board and described his workload:

> I have attended the hospitals in the several auxiliary workhouses with zeal and attention, travelling in all weather distances varying from four to six miles back and forward and as far as my exertions professional and otherwise could avail. I have successfully treated patients, hundreds who were attacked by, and for a long time labouring under, virulent ophthalmia which you are aware had spread to an awful extent through the branch houses, particularly Ballymullen, where all patients labouring under that complaint were sent from the main house and all other houses.[44]

As well as financial difficulties, scandals continued to be a recurring problem within the workhouse in 1850. Sexual advances by staff on inmates seem to have been accepted as an inevitable part of workhouse living arrangements. For example, in July 1850 the workhouse master in Tralee resigned just before he was to be dismissed for 'gross immorality'.[45] Six months later, when Thomas O'Connor, master in Tralee, was being investigated for having improper associations with female inmates, and Mr O'Sullivan the assistant master was facing other charges, this exchange about the number of workhouse pregnancies took place in the boardroom:

> Mr Hurly: Has there been any inquiry about the women in the Rock house in that interesting way [pregnant]?
>
> Mr Morphy: There are six or eight women with child in Dingle workhouse by one man – the porter.
>
> A guardian: Such things will occur in the best regulated establishments.
>
> Mr Hurly: Is it true that nearly every couple at the Rock house is with child?
>
> Captain Spark: Whose business is it to ascertain that?[46]

A guardian said that they had more important matters to discuss, but John Hurly was of the opinion that nothing was more important than the character of the officers of the union. Mr Supple urged them to postpone discussion of these issues and to direct their attention to 'the hundred unfortunate creatures who are below shivering in their wet clothes' appealing for admission. Mr Denny agreed, saying, 'We cannot turn them out on such a night like this.'[47]

Listowel Union

The *Chronicle* of 20 April 1850 reported on the proceedings of Listowel board of guardians, at which members were incensed that the Tralee board was refusing to take responsibility for the newly allocated areas. There was a stand-off between the two unions. Maurice Leonard stated that Listowel guardians 'sent 600 poor infirm persons away yesterday though they knew they were objects'. This meant that although their claims for relief were valid, the Listowel guardians could not accommodate them. This was because the workhouses were full and some paupers from the areas transferred to Tralee Union were still being accommodated in Listowel workhouses. Leonard and other guardians wanted them to be sent to Tralee to make room for Listowel's 'own' paupers. Meade Dennis put the case succinctly when he asked if it was 'humane to allow their own paupers to die while they relieved those of Tralee'.[48]

The Listowel guardians had concerns other than their stand-off with the Tralee Union. Listowel Union was in a desperate state in 1850, notwithstanding the redrawn boundaries. The Poor Law inspector, Mr Duncan, attended a board meeting on 2 May where numbers in the workhouse were recorded as 3,854. He informed members that that was 400 higher than was permitted by a formal sealed order of the commissioners. He stated that 'there were 1,500 applicants on yesterday, 254 of whom were ordered admission, but the master refused to admit them'. Duncan went on to say that 1,804 people had been admitted during the previous month and only 705 discharged. He anticipated that for the following ten weeks or so, until the harvest, there would be large numbers of applicants.[49]

In June, when there were 4,600 in the several workhouses of Listowel, Ballybunion, Ballylongford and Banemore, and 5,000 receiving outdoor relief, despair pervaded one newspaper report. The *Chronicle* did not mince its words in describing Listowel Union:

> This Union is in a deplorable condition. There are four thousand six hundred paupers in the house and its auxiliaries and five thousand receiving outdoor relief. There have been continual and wholesale evictions in almost every part of the Union. The mortality in the Union is great, the poverty greater. As fast as hundreds die away, hundreds of homeless, hungry, sickly skeletons fill up their ranks. It is unmanning to see crowds of them every board day applying for relief; many are received and many are rejected; and those after travelling many miles are obliged to drag upon their tottering limbs their almost lifeless bodies to some ditchside – and die. There are some of the board mercifully disposed – men who look upon charity not as an abstraction but

as a noble act – an emanation of the Deity. Among the number … none are more prominent than the chairman [Captain James Murray Home] and Mr. Leonard.[50]

It is difficult to obtain a clear perspective on all that was happening in Listowel Union in mid-1850, but it is clear that the 'ghastly havoc' which followed in the wake of the blight of 1845 was continuing to hit hard. Extreme hardship was widespread among the poor and chaos reigned supreme in the administration of relief. If the report above was accurate, and people were once more dying in the ditches, they were dying of poverty, but, apart from this report, the newspapers did not express any great sense of outrage at these tragedies. It may be that society in general had become inured to horror or imbued with a sense of impotence or fatalism. Further research would be required to understand fully all the factors at work, but it seems that the ultimate resolution came with time – and the utter annihilation of the poorest of the poor and the weakest of the weak.

While deaths were being recorded in the hundreds, there is a brief record of one individual death, that of Mary Purtill. She died by the roadside and an inquest was held in early 1850. The verdict was recorded in the minutes of the Listowel board of guardians. Cornelius Connor, relieving officer for Causeway, was found guilty of manslaughter by a coroner's jury in respect of Mary's death.[51] Mary had left the workhouse with her son on 21 January but asked to be re-admitted on 29 January. Connor first refused this request, stating that 'he did not think that persons who left the workhouse so recently could be destitute, and knowing from experience that applications under such circumstances must generally prove to be undeserving of attention'. Nevertheless, he admitted that he had learned on 2 February that Mary was truly destitute and he visited her to give her a ticket of admission to the workhouse. She proceeded towards Listowel but died on the way. Connor stated that he did not think she was so seriously ill and that if he had realised this, he would have given her provisional relief.[52]

Some members of the board of guardians took Connor's side, pointing out that he did not have an opportunity to present his case at the inquest. They stated that 'while they required vigilance, attention, integrity and humanity from their officers, they also desire to be permitted to extend to them justice and protection in return'.[53] They believed that Connor was 'a meritorious officer' who tried to carry out his instructions in the spirit and in the letter, and that the facts as presented did not do justice to him. However, Connor was dismissed from his post for neglect of duty, by order of the Poor Law Commissioners.[54]

The Cork Examiner was shocked at accounts of three other deaths from starvation in the same month, saying that they were 'a blot upon human nature'.[55] The information came from an anonymous letter, which said that an elderly man named Fenally had died in Clandouglas, Lixnaw, after being repeatedly refused entry to the workhouse. The two others were 'of tender years' and were named Buckley; they were also refused assistance from the relieving officers. The writer blamed the three deaths on the board of guardians and believed that there were likely to be more such deaths in remote areas that went unreported. It concluded that 'the Listowel guardians must be civilised into humanity. They must do their duty or the commissioners must do theirs.'[56]

Fr O'Connor of Listowel challenged George Sandes for refusing to admit a dying man named Griffin into the workhouse, revealing that this was the second such case he had dealt with. The priest was invited to a board meeting, where he was supported by the chairman, Captain Home, and some guardians. Home regarded the case as a grievous one and said that Sandes was in the wrong when he refused to allow the man to be admitted.[57]

Another death from starvation was that of a travelling man from Killarney. This revealing exchange about the man's death shows how some board members would have preferred to sanitise such deaths:

> Rev. Mr. O'Connor: No matter where he came from, as long as he is found in your Union, according to the spirit of the Poor Law, you are bound to keep body and soul together, if food can do it.

> Mr Duncan (Poor Law Inspector): Most certainly, Rev. Mr O'Connor is quite right, you cannot let any man die of starvation.
>
> Mr Harnett: That word in Rev. Mr O'Connor's report is too severe. I would wish it was out.
>
> Mr Rice: The word is too severe; the doctor said he died from want of food.
>
> Rev. Mr O'Connor: And, Mr Rice, what is want of food but starvation, and the literal meaning of starvation, want of food?[58]

While administrative controversies occupied much of the time and energy of the Listowel guardians, the affairs of the workhouse continued to deteriorate. John Pierse has estimated that between November 1848 and June 1852, 3,380 people died in the workhouse, 1,869 of whom were aged under fifteen.[59] In one week in March 1850 there were fifty-five deaths in the workhouses; of these, sixteen were children under two years of age, and eighteen were aged and infirm.[60]

The scale of deaths in the workhouse was a cause of great concern to some members of the board in early 1850, when an average of five people died of dysentery every day. The medical officer, Dr Gabriel Thorpe, believed that the diet in the house was one cause, because it was of a laxative nature, and he recommended that it should be replaced by soup. He also cited other factors, such as the intensely cold weather, scarcity of fuel, insufficient clothing and overcrowding in all parts of the house where the sick were lodged.[61] Mr Lynch, Poor Law inspector, attended the board meeting and reported his shock on visiting the workhouse hospital:

> On going into your hospital a most horrible sight presented itself to my notice ... I am only surprised the deaths were not more numerous. But bad as the state of things was, I was told by the matron, the master and the Catholic clergymen that there was a great improvement since yesterday.

'AN UNPRECEDENTED AND UNEXPECTED INFLUX OF PAUPERISM'

> There were ten children in one bed and eleven children in another, suffering under severe dysentery – actually dying! In the whole course of my experience of workhouses I never saw anything like that before. Your hospital is in a shameful state. It is full of dirt from top to bottom. There was no straw, no change of linen. I am only surprised that the deaths are not double. The doctor told me that there were in the hospital of the workhouse no less than 222, though it was only calculated to contain 140. But that does not account for ten and eleven in a bed. But he told me that there was no straw to put in the bed, where there were five children sleeping heads down and five heads up, and all in dying state. Surely you would not put ten children in a healthy state in the same bed. Several beds had eight, some five and none less than four children … Then they are left without breakfast till one o'clock, while there is no less, I am told, than twenty-three percent water in the milk.[62]

Lynch's account was supported by the chaplain, Fr Mahony, who said that he had just visited the infirmary and found that the sick paupers had not yet had breakfast. Mahony did not blame the master of the workhouse for this situation, but his subordinate, who had not carried out his duties:

> The paupers were lying on their beds without a drop of drink till half past one. There have been forty-five deaths for the last fortnight and eight yesterday. The eight days before that there were thirty-one deaths. In my parish where the population in 1841 was 7,072, there were not four deaths during that time.[63]

Dr Thorpe told the board that he was overwhelmed by his duties attending to patients with all manner of infectious diseases, risking his own life daily in ministering to them. His workload had expanded hugely and the board was continually adding to it. Thorpe described his duties:

> I have to come to the workhouse here and attend to 374 patients in all sorts of cases. I have to check the books, examine the state of the ventilation of

the house, attend the board when they require me, and other minor matters taking from 10 till 3 o'clock. That is as much as any honest medical man could perform.[64]

Maurice Leonard, solicitor and guardian, accepted that it was physically impossible for one man to carry out the duties required and proposed that Thorpe should have an assistant; Dr McCrystal was duly appointed. Leonard gave the following critical appraisal of the board of which he was a member, acknowledging that it had not served the ratepayers or the poor, as it should have:

> I have no hesitation in saying, from the gross mismanagement of your officers and the melancholy position in which those poor people are placed by the neglect of this board in some degree – and I must take my share of the blame – we should not hesitate for one moment in dismissing every single officer in this house with the exception of the very efficient person who sits here as clerk [Mr Phillips] … I ask any one of them if we as a body, since the 1st of October, have done our duty by the poor or the rate-payers?[65]

Leonard was commended in editorial comment in *The Cork Examiner*, which saw the shocking reports from Listowel as 'scarcely credible of a Christian country':

> We blush to own that even in quarters the most remote from the influence of public opinion, any of our countrymen should be found so deficient in humanity or in practical habits of business as the guardians of that union appear to be … Oh, is it not shameful, is it not a deep disgrace upon the country at large that any portion of the people bred upon the same soil with us should be left to die in such a manner? Our conclusion is plain from the circumstances mentioned that the guardians cannot possibly have administered their charge properly or at least cannot have exercised that vigilance which is felt to be the duty of those in a similar position here. We

fear that in other localities equally isolated, the dreadful state of things in Listowel union may not be without further example.[66]

In a peculiar expression, Dr Thorpe regularly reported his regret that 'he could not congratulate the board on a decrease in mortality'.[67] Thorpe, under great personal stress, listed the reasons for the high death rate. Chief among them was the fact that people were admitted in a 'wretchedly exhausted state … from their several diseases having been too long neglected'.[68] They were in such poor health that they could not be helped. Thorpe repeatedly told the board that he despaired of reducing mortality rates until better medical aid was provided *outside* the workhouse, as many people came in as a last resort and availed of the workhouse as their only way to access medical care. He listed the other factors affecting the death rate as: an epidemic of dysentery of a most obstinate and fatal kind and a peculiar kind of relapsing fever; severe overcrowding in all parts of the workhouse; the wretched and starved condition of those admitted, making them more susceptible to disease; want of clothes and warmth in cold weather; the secret introduction of improper articles of diet; want of personal cleanliness; and imperfect sewerage in the workhouse.[69]

Thorpe had no solutions to offer except 'a judicious and cautious extension of outdoor relief', a reduction of overcrowding and an improved diet in the workhouse.[70] Stirabout made from equal parts rice and oatmeal was regarded as an improved diet.[71] Thorpe's recommendations also included adding more wheaten flour to the soup provided.[72] He complained about the quality of the workhouse bread, having seen 'a loaf about the size of an orange, as hard as a hammer, black as ink and so composed as to be completely unfit for mastication and much less for digestion'.[73]

In late April 1850 there was accommodation for 3,462 in the Listowel workhouses, but there were actually 3,588 resident. Dr Thorpe was personally distraught as he reported to the board:

> The medical officer is distressed at being so often obliged to direct the

attention of the board to the state of overcrowding which has arisen since yesterday, which must be fraught with dangers to all the inmates in the workhouse and especially those recently admitted already broken down in constitution.[74]

As well as all these heart-rending issues, there was also a growing awareness that the arrangements for pauper burials at the Listowel workhouse were not satisfactory. Peirce Mahony believed that mismanagement under the vice-guardians led to timber intended for coffins being taken for other purposes, resulting in the 'ill-covered contents being devoured by dogs'.[75] It was at this time that the new pauper graveyard, Teampall Bán, was acquired near the workhouse.[76] The board instructed that burials should be in 'the newly consecrated burial ground adjoining the workhouse' and that 'care is to be taken to have such interments in a proper manner and with every respect for the dead'.[77]

George Sandes' Visits to the Workhouse

The board of guardians' minute book for Listowel frequently recorded irregularities and failures to carry out instructions, for which staff members were regularly disciplined and even dismissed. In one significant case, a serious complaint was lodged by Fr Cornelius Sheahan, curate of Ballyheigue, in which he expressed great unease about certain practices in the workhouse. His entry in the visitors' book, copied into the minute book, ran as follows:

> I have this day visited the house for the purpose of calling the attention of the board of guardians to the anxiety and unease of fathers and mothers at the unreasonable, unnecessary and very frequent visits of individual guardians to the workhouse and its auxiliaries. They cannot understand why any person, the officers of the house alone excepted when on duty and then accompanied by others, under certain circumstances would be so officious, were he not actuated by improper motives. Entering fully into their feelings as the pastor of a large number of them, I hope that the chairman, in whom so much

confidence is deservedly reposed, the deputy vice-chairman, in whom the poor have ever found a willing and efficient advocate, and the board of guardians will take such steps as will in future prevent the irregulated zeal of individuals from adding even unintentionally to the heavy load of misery and sorrow by which our poor in these ill-starred times [are] unhappily overwhelmed.[78]

The subject of this accusation of 'improper motives' for visiting children in the workhouse would have remained unknown had not George Sandes responded on the next page of the visitors' book, and his response was also transcribed into the minute book:

Considering that the statement on the other side refers personally to me, I beg to state that I have frequently visited the houses but never later than half past nine o'clock, that I have never gone through any of the houses at that or any other hour without an officer of the house or another guardian being with me and that the insinuations put forward on the other side are not justified by fact and have not the slightest foundation.[79]

In a sequel to this, on 4 April 1850 the workhouse chaplain, Fr Darby Mahony, PP, also expressed his anxiety, and put the following proposals to the board: that no member of the Visiting Committee should be allowed to make unaccompanied visits to the workhouse, that no visits to the workhouse should take place after 2 p.m. in the winter and 4 p.m. in the summer, and that the workhouse should be fully closed at 9 p.m., as specified in the rules of the Poor Law Commission, 'as the paupers are supposed to retire to rest at that hour for repose [and] they should be generally protected from intrusion'.[80]

The board rejected Fr Mahony's suggestions on the grounds that Fr Sheahan 'has not retracted the implications he made, and which Mr Sandes believes were solely intended for him'. The board pointedly stated that 'by Mr Sandes' frequent visits to this house, a great many abuses have been checked and we beg to thank him for his very active exertions in that respect'. This motion was proposed by Mr Moriarty and seconded by Meade Dennis.[81]

One example of how George Sandes' work was appreciated by his colleagues on the board was his investigation into the master, Matthew Hogg, which found that Hogg had stolen 300 quarts of milk to the value of £16 over a period of eight weeks. Hogg was dismissed.[82] Nonetheless, the protest of the clergy had some effect because two years later Sandes was aggrieved that he was prevented from visiting the auxiliary workhouse at Banemore.[83]

It is clear that the two clergymen had grave suspicions about the behaviour of George Sandes towards the young inmates of the workhouse. Sandes was aged about twenty-nine in 1850, but his scandalous career appears to have already begun. He was an autocratic chairman of Listowel board of guardians in the decades up to 1880 and he used his position as agent for a number of estates to prey sexually on the wives and daughters of tenants. His misdeeds became public in court cases taken against him. His career was summed up in this obituary in 1895:

> The iron of Mr Sandes' despotic rule had for well-nigh half a century entered into the very hearts of the people ... As chairman of the board of guardians, land agent and justice of the peace, his rule was all powerful and no petty governor of a half-civilised settlement in the farthest limits of the globe exercised a more irresponsible sway than he did.[84]

On another occasion, when Fr Mahony complained about physical violence towards inmates, he was told by Meade Dennis that his interventions were 'impertinent'.[85] There was a sequel to this in the Square in Listowel, when Fr Mahony approached Dennis, called him a coward and said he ought to be horse-whipped, raising his cane over his head to demonstrate how that should be done.[86] It was a simulated rather than an actual assault, but Dennis's response was to make strenuous attempts to have Fr Mahony dismissed as workhouse chaplain. The affair reached the national newspapers and, in a long account of his grievance, Dennis wrote that Fr Mahony deserved to be horse-whipped through the town and that he personally would carry it out.[87] Dennis was determined to pursue the matter in the courts but the affair came to an end with a full public apology by Fr Mahony, who admitted that 'in a moment of warmth and irritation' he had used 'insulting language' towards Dennis. The apology was welcomed by the *Post* as 'better late than never'.[88]

Famine Clearances

Large-scale clearances continued in north Kerry in 1850. One such example was in the Chapeltown area near Fenit in April when seventy families were evicted and the landlord Mr Denny was reported as seeking passage to America for them.[89] Fr Mathias McMahon, based in Ballybunion, wrote a powerful letter about landlord clearances in his area. He stated that 'the landlords here may be classed among the worst in Ireland. The most malignant fiend in hell could not evince more indifference for the sufferings of human beings.'[90] He gave specific details of clearances carried out by named landlords – St John Blacker, Meade Dennis, Mrs Harenc and Lady Burgersh – and stated that 'extermination, emigration, hunger and proselytism' summed up the state of the locality. McMahon showed an astute awareness of the power of the press in highlighting the grievances of tenants:

> Alas! that we can put no check upon the perpetrators of these calamities save that of public opinion. Yet it is some consolation to think that a fearless and powerful press will scathe and stigmatise them and hold them up to the indignant reprobation of the virtuous, the principled and the good the world over.[91]

James Crowley of Benmore cited an instance of families near Ballyduff being evicted:

> Inhabitants of this locality being much diminished in numbers are further discouraged in consequence of notices being served on many farmers in the parish of Rattoo to give up possession and quit their lands on the 25 March next. Their landlord here was heretofore considered liberal and kind-hearted,

as were all his most worthy family, notwithstanding his being an absentee. His tenantry are much disheartened, not knowing their fate and dreading eviction. It is most awful to reflect on the pauperised state of the country and the insensibility of absentee landlords to their private interests, as also to their loss of influence by a sweeping diminution of their tenantry.[92]

From this news report, the identity of the landlord to whom James Crowley is referring is unclear, but he does give specific details about 145 families, comprising 1,500 people, who were 'thrown houseless and foodless wanderers on the world'.[93]

In Lixnaw, on lands owned by Henry Petty-Fitzmaurice, Marquis of Lansdowne, 157 people were evicted in September. This incident has been described as 'a microcosm of the impact of that catastrophe [the Famine] on land tenure throughout Kerry as a whole'.[94] Twenty-three houses occupied by twenty-nine families were levelled, although the tenants were described as prosperous and well able to pay their rents. Two brothers named Quilter were evicted from Monument Farm, and among the other families were three widows and their children. There were carpenters, coopers, shoemakers and blacksmiths among them and over a hundred of those evicted were children. They were obliged to knock their own houses as they left and one man, the father of seven, was killed when the gable fell on him. The only compensation was £20 to be distributed among the twenty-nine families; this contrasted with £30 given by Sir John Benn-Walsh to one woman he evicted.

A letter from 'a Lixnaw man' describing the evictions was first published in *The Cork Examiner*. The writer was known to the editor and although he was not identified, the editor was satisfied that the information was accurate. He had, however, 'tamed down the letter to the limits of strict legality'. The condition of those evicted was desperate:

> Never was there such misery inflicted on any class of humanised beings, and what rendered the act doubly afflicting is the fact of their not being allowed a place for the night to shelter themselves. Hard would be the heart that would

not feel, whose chords would not vibrate with sorrow on beholding them, coming on night, sheltering themselves under the slender shade of a bush on the wayside from the inclemency of a long, cold, dreary night. Still they are to be seen on the roadside and by-ways under the shade of a few sticks covered over with a sop of black straw (even admittance to erect those revolting sheds is denied them). Good Heaven – what a sad state for created beings to be in! Alas how turned upside down are not the ways of Providence. Ah, would that the noble Marquis at the head of Her Majesty's government had seen here with his own eyes the desolation … They who on yesterday or so had good hopes of supporting themselves during life are now on the roadside, moving about like mad people, distracted, emaciated, worn out, a sad spectacle to behold.[95]

Audi alteram partem ('listen to the other side of the case') was the philosophy of the *Chronicle*, which on 28 September republished the letter, but also reported the perspective of the Marquis of Lansdowne. His case was set out by William Steuart Trench, the recently appointed manager of the Lansdowne estates. He claimed that Lansdowne had lost between £400 and £500 in the previous years. He had given very generous abatements or reductions of 25 per cent over the years, wrote Trench, and 'ample remuneration' for improvements, so much so that 'tenants here seemed to think that they ought hardly to put a spade into the ground without claiming an allowance for their improvement'. Trench claimed that Lansdowne had 'almost been improved out of his estate'. In light of this generosity, claimed Trench, Lansdowne might reasonably have expected rents to be paid up, but they were not. The majority of tenants owed three or four years rent and some owed five years. He stated, moreover, that many of those who had been evicted were from elsewhere and had settled on the Lansdowne lands as if they were a commons, trusting that 'his lordship's well-known munificence' would allow them to stay. Trench was unmoved by the pitiful state of those evicted and concluded:

> I trust that no outcry or attack of any kind shall prevent me from doing my duty faithfully and impartially between man and man – I never will consent to be the medium of cruelty on the one hand nor, on the other, will I stand idly by and see the estate of a noble proprietor confiscated by paupers, nor an unjust advantage taken of the tenderness and leniency of its almost too generous owner.[96]

The *Examiner* was perfectly satisfied with Trench's explanation and suggested that the Lixnaw tenants were 'unreasonably querulous, abusing the goodness of an excellent landlord'.[97] *The Cork Examiner* took a more caustic approach, under the headline 'Killing with Kindness', and examined in particular Trench's statement that 'his lordship's goodness had cast the tenants into a state of apathetic dependence'. This was 'thorough cant', it said:

> The idea is evidently borrowed from a school which has cherished the harshest and most contemptuous opinions of the people and which has sought to poison the public mind with the belief that kind treatment is thrown away upon them and that they must be lashed and scourged into exertion. The controversy which has arisen on the subject may at all events be considered to prove conclusively that Mr Trench will not create that state of helpless dependence which is the consequence of mistaken liberality. According to his principle, the Lixnaw evictions are calculated marvellously to promote the spirit of self-reliance.[98]

The Lansdowne evictions would resound through the speeches of those who championed the rights of tenants in Kerry in the years ahead. Gerard Lyne has done a thorough study of the complex story of the eviction, and concluded that there was enough evidence to indicate that Trench's position was at least 'open to question'. Lyne makes the point that the outcome was clearly very beneficial to the landlord, with 'a 100-acre rural slum with a teeming population of 157 souls replaced by a farm occupied by a single solvent tenant'.⁹⁹ In fairness to Trench, Lyne also states that these were the only evictions of any significance which he carried out during his time as agent of the extensive Lansdowne estates, which were mainly in the south of the county.¹⁰⁰

Alongside reports of the Lixnaw evictions, newspapers carried positive news about landlords. According to one letter-writer, Henry Herbert of Muckross was a good landlord, whose tenants in Brosna were given reductions of 25 per cent; a premium for the best turnips, best clover and best manure heaps; and encouragement for well-maintained farms. His visits to tenants were said to be kindly, paternal occasions of encouragement, rather than threatening visits of browbeating and bullying, which was the norm:

> He is cutting away and uprooting ignorance and indolence, instructing the people according to the exigencies of the times, and in their present prostrate condition, infusing into them vigour and hope and the people know this. In the present moral eclipse of the country, his tenants – to one's great delight – always present a beaming cheerful and sunny countenance, a thing pretty general some six or ten years ago.¹⁰¹

Tenants in Duagh celebrated the return of their landlord, Oliver Fitzmaurice, from Scotland with 'a brilliant illumination and an immense bonfire' and a night of music and dance.¹⁰² Another positive report on a landlord came from the tenants of William Stoughton in Ballinoe, Causeway, whose agent was John Pierce. The spokesmen for the tenants were Maurice Harty, Edward Connell and Timothy Driscoll, and they were grateful that Stoughton had remitted all arrears, reduced the annual rent by half and cut future rents by 25 per cent. His 'humane consideration of the tenants' difficulties' was acknowledged in a formal address.¹⁰³

Stoughton also received lavish praise from a tenant named Thomas O'Connor of Ballinclogher, Lixnaw, who wrote: 'We writhed alternately under oppression and distress, the necessary consequence of oppression, till June '49, when, to our great joy, our excellent landlord, Mr Stoughton, took that portion of his property out of the hands of those rascally middlemen.'[104] Stoughton reduced the rent of O'Connor's mother from £80 to £54 and gave similar reductions to all tenants. His 'benevolence, sagacity and Christian feelings' were praised by O'Connor, who contrasted him with the rack-renting landlord who only 'seeks to dispirit and depress the man who looks up to him for advice and aid'.[105]

Tenant Right League

By mid-1850 a new movement was beginning in Ireland: the campaign for tenant rights. The Irish Tenant Right League was formed in Dublin in the summer. It was also known as the League of North and South and its aim was to secure the 'three Fs' for tenants: fair rent, fixity of tenure and free sale. Although I have not discovered any statements by Fr Eugene McCarthy on the issue of the annexation of Ballyheigue and other areas to Tralee Union, or on the fate of the paupers rejected by Listowel Union, he was not inactive or silent in 1850. His support for this new movement was noted in the columns of the press. In July the *Examiner* reported on a meeting held in Causeway, at which 'a large assemblage of the farmers of Ballyheigue, Rattoo and Killury unanimously agreed to give all the aid in their power to the Tenant Right Conference in Dublin':[106]

> Through the well-directed and unsleeping exertions of the popular P.P. of Ballyheigue, whose name tells his patriotism and public worth, the Rev. Eugene McCarthy, the tenant farmers of his district have been brought together to proclaim their adhesion to the principles proposed by the Committee of the Tenant Right Conference about being held in Dublin. We cannot say more today than to urge on the other parishes of this county to follow without delay the example so nobly set them by the meeting in Causeway on Sunday last. There is no time to be lost.[107]

A local committee was established to collect funds and to collate information 'as to evictions etc. in this most wretchedly harassed locality'. The *Examiner* commended the initiative shown at the Causeway meeting and pointedly asked, with a barb towards the ratepayers of the county town: 'What is Tralee, the capital of Kerry, doing? It was expected that the inhabitants of that town and its locality would be foremost in legal patriotic exertions.'[108]

Fr McCarthy had always been a loyal supporter of Daniel O'Connell, whom he described as 'that great man – the greatest of the human race'.[109] He had sent regular contributions to the Repeal fund, and he was once again sending money to Conciliation Hall in Dublin, the headquarters of the Repeal movement; for example, he sent £1 15s 3d in October 1850.[110] As well as supporting O'Connell, he also promoted the rights of tenants. He wrote about the effects of clearances and new farming conditions in his large parish, and he lamented the change from tillage to pasture, which provided far less employment:

> Very many of the middle class gentry are possessing themselves of the land for the pasturage of cattle. One gentleman in this locality has over 1,000 statute acres of land in his own possession, with exception of (as I suppose) 120 such acres held by five or six farmers; on this vast extent of land were nearly 120 families exterminated since the commencement of the potato blight averaging probably 1,000 persons, many of whom are now in their graves and very many in the workhouse, and on this extent of surface, so depopulated, are a number of dairy cows, with a few herdsmen and milkwomen to attend to them. But they are not allowed to make sale of a pennyworth of milk for the convenience of the poor. Pigs and calves are latterly chosen in preference to the former most industrious and hardworking inhabitants.[111]

A Tenant Right League meeting was held in Listowel on 28 October and was dismissed by the *Post:* 'A sorrier demonstration we are proud to say was never made in any part of this kingdom in favour of that communist principle – Tenant Right – than that attempted to be got up by the tenant farmers of Iraghticonnor and Clanmaurice on that occasion.' It saw the meeting as 'a complete failure'.[112] A report in the *Chronicle* stated that 'under 3,000' people attended and it highlighted the absence of country gentlemen and the better class of farmers, adding that the atmosphere was sombre and the people were subdued and depressed.[113]

Two Listowel priests, John O'Connor and Francis Hurly, who had been involved in organising the meeting, were unable to attend as they were appointed elsewhere in the diocese just before the meeting. Although the *Post* described this transfer as a sinister act of 'ecclesiastical tyranny', it may have been a normal diocesan redeployment.[114] Two curates from elsewhere, Fr McMahon and Fr Foley, attended, as did Fr James Walsh, PP of Ballybunion/Lisselton, who was chairman of the meeting. He began by setting a moderate tone, saying that they had not come to invade the rights of either landlord or tenant: 'We only seek justice for the tenant and justice to the tenant will in the long run be found to be the best protection of the landlord's interest ... Our motto is "Live and let live".'[115]

Justin Supple gave a more impassioned speech, urging the people to assert their rights and to stand up to 'shoneen tyrants', some of whom he said were peeping out from the curtains of houses around the Square where the meeting was held (George Sandes, for one, lived in a house on the Square). He reminded them of the sundering of families that had occurred in the recent past and of the many people who died prematurely or were now in workhouses, which he termed 'bastilles'.

Supple provided a detailed list of recent evictions in specific townlands in north Kerry. He estimated that a total of 3,321 people had been evicted in the six months from January to June 1850, and said that they were forced to find shelter 'in quarries and under ditches'. He recited a list of evictions, giving precise dates for each: 'Let it go forth to the world from this platform that on the 25th January 1850, 150 human beings were turned out of their farms on the lands of Ahanagran. Not one tenant was left. All were thrown on the world's dreary common without a place to shelter them.'[116] He continued to list the numbers evicted between January and June 1850: 284 at Leensbawn, Faha and Bromore; 431 in Tarbert, Doonard, Kilfahadoge and Teeraclea; 303 in Ballybunion and Killehinny; 84 in Agoula; 32 in Ballylongford; 111

at Carrahoonaremela; 118 in Coolaclarig; 9 in Ballyduff; and in the month of June: 948 in Lenamore, Roonagra, Guranaclouna and Lislaughtin; 489 in Ahanagran, Rusheen and Rushy Park; and 354 in Ballylongford. The precise details cited are convincing as evidence. The appalling scale of the clearances is shocking and explains the vehemence of the response of men like Fr Mathias McMahon, who daily witnessed the consequences of the evictions: hundreds of homeless poor people surviving on the roadside.

The clergymen who spoke were deeply appalled by the scale of evictions. Fr Foley, a fine orator, declared: 'Our country is in a state unparalleled in the history of mankind, or rather I should say, that which was once our country has been cancelled from the map of the world (cheers).' Using poignant imagery, he went on to speak of a recent death at which he was present:

> Yes, my friends, no later than last night, the angel of death snatched another victim from the ranks of the people. A poor man – what was once a man, I should say, died in my arms from the effects of starvation. It requires no powers of oratory to give to this fact an exciting emphasis. It speaks volumes for itself, far better and more graphically than ten thousand speeches. Yes, he died in my arms of starvation! I ask you are we to tolerate this any longer? Are we to allow the stream of desolation to flow on and on till its waters overwhelm the last of our friends and relations and countrymen? If we do, God only knows whether we shall not be ourselves the sufferers next year.[117]

Fr Foley continued:

> Scenes every day present themselves to my eyes which enable me to assert unblushingly and unhesitatingly that the present relation between landlord and tenant cannot hold as it is much longer … Many of you have scarcely enough to eat while the landlords are spending the money wrung, as it were, from your very bones and sinews and blood in England or in the coffee houses and gaming houses of France.[118]

He went on to cite the recent eviction of 157 people on the Lansdowne estate in Lixnaw, where 'the crowbar was put in requisition and their houses were tumbled to the earth and their unfortunate inmates sent adrift'. During the eviction a man died, his wife and eight children were made homeless and 'the poor woman was for a time in that charnel-house above [the workhouse]. She took sick and is now half out of her mind, thrown on the roadside.'[119]

Fr Mathias McMahon began his address by telling the gathering that it was his first time to address a crowd on a public platform. His speech proved a match for his pen, as he launched an attack on the actions of landlords such as Mrs Harenc, who had turned out fifty-eight families and was about to evict another seventy-four, and St John Blacker, who levelled a village of twenty houses: 'Whole villages have disappeared before the hands of the exterminator by oppression most revolting. The people have been hunted like vermin and then crammed into the pest-house [workhouse].'[120] Fr McMahon later named Lord Listowel, Meade Dennis and Mr Raymond as other landlords who were 'the scourgers and destroyers of God's poor'.[121]

The Tenant Right movement of the 1850s had collapsed in disarray by the end of the decade, but it laid the foundations for the more successful Land League of the 1880s, spearheaded by Michael Davitt, leading eventually to a series of Land Acts that gradually transferred ownership of the land to the tenants. The culmination of this process was the Wyndham Land Act of 1903, by which the reviled landlord-tenant system came to an end. The pioneering work of men such as Mathias McMahon was remembered during the so-called 'land war' of the 1880s. He was then parish priest of Boherbue, Co. Cork, and when *The Nation* newspaper ran a series entitled 'Notable Irish Priests', he was one of the men profiled.[122] He died in 1888.

Souperism and Clerical Co-operation

Proselytism was frequently referred to by Fr McMahon of Ballybunion and his parish priest, Fr James Walsh, who wrote in 1850 to newspapers, including *The Tablet*, on the issue. Walsh gave details of the return of named soupers to their original Catholic faith, declaring that 'perhaps in no part of Ireland has the system of seducing the poor for their faith been carried on with so steady and persevering a hand [as] by a certain Rev. Gentleman in this way'.[123] He stated that Mortimer Mollineux and Norry Driscoll had married under Protestant rites but had lately returned to the faith 'from which they had been seduced by the vile mess doled out in the time of their wretched misery'.[124] The couple were married again under Catholic rites. Patrick Corridon, James Stack and a man named McMahon also returned to the Catholic faith.[125]

Walsh named Rev. Stamer as 'the reverend proselytising parson'.[126] Stamer responded that the named individuals were never fully part of his church and charge and counter-charge between these two clergymen appeared in the press. Stamer noted that during 1847, when he and Fr Walsh served on the relief committee, the latter had magnanimously stated: 'I assure you, Mr Stamer, that I would rather give employment to a person that reformed with you than to one of my own, lest I should be thought to persecute'.[127] Stamer regretted that the attitude of the priest had changed since then, as shown in his 'scurrilous and mendacious letter'. One of the barbs directed by Stamer was that the priest was engaged in celebrating 'that most unprofitable of all services, a Latin Mass for the Irish-speaking people of two parishes'.[128] One of the attractions of the Protestant services at this time was that they were conducted not in Latin but in the language of the people, which in 1850 in the Ballybunion area was clearly still Irish.

Walsh responded in a personalised and vitriolic letter saying that Stamer's brain must have been affected by the full moon and informing him that several named people returned to the Catholic faith on their deathbeds. Responding to the taunt about Latin, Walsh said that prayers were read in Irish before Masses and that the gospel was read in Irish and the sermon delivered in Irish.[129]

By contrast, enlightened and liberal religious values were exhibited at a dinner held in Castleisland in honour of John Sealy, the then chairman of Tralee board of guardians. The parish priest of Castleisland, Jeremiah O'Leary, believed that the people had passed through 'a fearful ordeal' but the terrible crisis was now nearly over.[130] He welcomed the renewal of social ties:

> The social community of Castleisland has been for years without meeting one another in that neighbourly and kindly intercommunion for which this locality had at one time been so remarkable; much less could such a meeting have taken place on account of the awful circumstances of the country. But he took that night's re-union as an unmistakeable sign of better times coming.
>
> He cited 'a facetious friend' who noted other signs of renewal, such as the young men 'goaling in the fields', dogs barking again near cottages and hamlets and people keening at funerals.
>
> The assemblage over which he had the honour to preside was composed of men of every party and creed but they had an identity of interest. He differed from many of them but they all loved old Ireland.[131]

Fr O'Leary paid tribute to John Sealy and also to the collaboration between the clergy of all persuasions 'during the four years of the famine'. His remarkable tributes were interrupted by cheers:

> I could not point out one Catholic clergyman who did more than the Protestant clergyman or one Protestant who did more than the Catholic. There was a generous rivalry between them to know who could do most good, each co-operating to assist the other. My solemn belief is that in Ireland – I may say in the empire – no body of clergymen at both sides more fearlessly or more faithfully discharged the duties placed on their shoulders …
>
> The clergymen at both sides I have seen aiding each other like children of the same father. It is a holy lesson to our people to love one another, when they see the clergymen of both persuasions hand and hand, going together in the promotion of the general good (cheers). It promotes Christian charity in the people at large. I could never see the charity of hating any individual on account of his maintaining his inalienable right to his own opinions, which none but the Lord can alter, by reason and not by force. If you want to force

your opinions down the throat of anyone, you only inflict an injustice. There is no part of Ireland where there is more kindly feeling among the several religious denominations than in the neighbourhood of Castleisland.[132]

Rev. Thomas Herbert of Killeentierna represented the local Protestant clergy and he reciprocated, paying tribute to two men who had given their lives working on behalf of the stricken people; they were Dr Philip O'Leary, a relative of the parish priest, and Rev. Archibald Macintosh, rector of Ballincuslane from 1836 to 1848. This prompted Fr O'Leary to remember his lost friend: 'Of Mr Macintosh, I will say he always went heart and hand with me. Living, I loved him as a dear friend, and lamented him in death. I think his death has left a vacuum in society which many a long year will not fill.'

It is clear that there was substance to the claim of excellent relations between all these clergymen on two sides of the religious divide in Castleisland at least.[133]

The Crops in North Kerry

There were signs of changed times in north Kerry farming in 1850. Archdeacon John O'Sullivan's diary of a journey with Bishop Egan through the area provides a revealing portrait of how the countryside had changed over the past years:

> 23 July 1850. This morning very wet in Listowel and the Causeway chapel being a good way from us, we had made up our minds for a very unpleasant day but it turned out to be the very reverse. On the new road to Ballybunion over the Cashen ferry and we arrived at the Causeway about twelve o'clock.
>
> Singular the change in the crops as we drove along. Instead of the potato, nothing was to be seen but beans and barley, beans and barley everywhere and in every direction, beans and barley. The area of barley we could easily comprehend but what they needed all the beans for was what we could not come at at all. We were informed that after they ground them and the flour

when mixed with barley or with Indian meal made very good bread. The poor cottiers seemed to value them as even alongside the cabins may be seen the small patches of beans that used formerly to be occupied by potatoes.[134]

The harvest of barley, oats and wheat was excellent in 1850, according to the *Chronicle*, but the potato crop was 'doomed' and the editor hoped that 'our people will no longer put their undivided confidence in that esculent but … betake themselves to the culture of parsnips, carrots, turnips, mangolds [mangels], cabbages, peas, beans, rye, bere, oats and flax'.[135]

Reliance on the potato remained widespread, however, so much still rested on the crop's success or failure. Confirmation that the year's potato crop had failed came from William Denny in Tralee in January 1851: 'Providence has thought fit to visit us again with famine. The staple food of the country is gone and I fear we have to look forward to another year of great distress.'[136]

A land steward in north Kerry wrote around the same time that there were fewer good potatoes in Kerry than ever before:

> The Fenit islands and other places along the coast that escaped blight in former years have suffered severely this year and those who were able to supply the market with good minion potatoes have not enough for seed. The minions are almost extinct. The only varieties that have escaped the blight are a variety called rattler and another sort called wellingtons, neither of which are equal in quality to the former minions.[137]

James Caird travelled the mail road from Tarbert to Tralee in 1850 and he made these observations:

> The country is high, bleak and unpromising. There are numerous huts along the road on the edge of the bog and from these an active traffic was going on by men carrying loads of turf on their backs to Tarbert for sale. Each load at present brings only a halfpenny. The poor creatures manage to go two or three times a day, according to their distance from town, bringing back Indian meal

with their money ... Within about two miles of Tralee, a great traffic was being carried on from the bog by donkeys in carts and with panniers and by people – men, women, boys and girls – all carrying burdens of turf on their backs to the market.

Caird concluded: 'That the people in this part of Kerry are suffering most severely from the consequences of famine, no one can doubt who travels along the road.'[138]

9

'TAKE FORTUNE'S TIDE – THE WORLD IS WIDE'

1851

The face of the country is hideous with ruins, whose gables, black and bare and pointing to the sky, would seem to call Heaven to witness the barbarities perpetrated on their unfortunate occupants.

Fr Mathias McMahon, curate of Ballybunion
The Nation, 15 November 1851

North Kerry Farming Society
It was ironic that the newspapers which carried reports of the Listowel Tenant Right meeting in 1850 also carried reports of an initiative on the part of landlords. This was the founding of Listowel Farming Society (later the North Kerry Farming Society). The aim of this society was 'to encourage an improved system of agriculture and ameliorate the condition of the farming and labouring classes'.[1] S. E. Collis was chairman, and Meade Dennis and William Hickson were secretaries. Lord Listowel was president and W. T. Crosbie, Lord Burgersh and Sir John Benn-Walsh were vice-presidents. The chairman of its second meeting was Colonel Henry Horatio Kitchener.[2] The Tenant Right meeting in Listowel and the formation of this society indicated a change in circumstances for the survivors of the Famine – albeit in contrasting ways.

The Farming Society became a very successful organisation and acted as a spur to improvement of farming methods and standards. The society held an annual exhibition and awarded prizes for the best animals and crops and for ploughing matches. There was even a digging match with a prize of £1 for the labourer who could dig 'in the best manner and shortest time, one statute perch of land, twelve inches deep'.[3]

However, the fact that the organisation was managed by landlords made it anathema to the *Examiner* and to people like Fr Mathias McMahon. The *Examiner* addressed those who had gathered to set up the new society:

> Honest gentlemen and good and worthy masters, what have you been doing these years back? Have you been asleep while death has been closing the eyes of thousands? And do you hope that your new 'Society' will awake the dead to life and give to the living new energies, fresh strength and happier firesides? How much have you yourselves contributed to aggravate the calamity which you now pretend to mitigate? How many houses have some of you who figure in this new work of 'amelioration' levelled to the ground and how many of the wretched inmates have you sent wanderers and beggars on the world? We fear that *Hypocrisy* and *Humbug* are joint promoters of this project. At all events it is not such societies that Ireland now stands in need of to improve her condition or diminish her miseries. If the present society can effect these objects it will prove a wonderful concern.[4]

The first public event of the North Kerry Farming Society was held on 4 February 1851, when 'a large concourse of the peasantry' attended to watch ploughing and digging competitions that took place in a field near Listowel owned by John Church. Nineteen ploughmen competed and at the evening dinner there were passionate speeches about the potential benefits of the society, which Captain James Murray Home saw as an opportunity of 'bringing together all classes connected with land and improving practical knowledge'.[5] There was great pride in the newly formed society, membership of which was confined to the landowners of the baronies of Clanmaurice and

Iraghticonnor. The society flourished and a telling response came from an envious farmer in the south of the county who wrote that 'north Kerry has got the start of us and is going ahead of us at such a pace that we shall be far distanced if we loiter any longer in the career of agricultural improvement and prosperity'.[6] Even the eminent Henry Herbert, MP, found that his application to take part in competitions was rejected, as he had no tenants in the north Kerry baronies.[7]

In other signs of progress, there was a welcome for a proposed sugar beet company that planned to set up factories in several locations around the country.[8] The butter export trade of north Kerry was becoming more organised, with direct exports from Tarbert and the appointment of a salesmaster in London.[9] Another sign of improving conditions was that there were fewer reports of distress and that approximately 3,000 people had left Tralee workhouse during the three months of summer.[10]

The society made preparations for an autumn agricultural show in Ballinruddery, and this went off very successfully, with prizes for the best animals on show as well as the ploughing and digging competitions.[11] But still, landlord-tenant relationships were far from amicable and there was one man who was not impressed by the new Farming Society. After attending the dinner at which Lord Listowel presided, he wrote to the press railing against the atmosphere of smug self-congratulation he perceived at the event. Fr Mathias McMahon was that man. He was incensed at the proceedings, as he wrote to *The Nation*.[12] He wrote as the champion of the poor and described the North Kerry Farming Society as:

> ... a landlords' scheme for keeping up high rents and at the same time sheltering our north Kerry exterminators from the public reprobation they so richly merit. Their extermination of the people is now, by a just retribution, recoiling upon them, in the shape of unprofitable lands and overwhelming taxation.[13]

The attendance at the dinner consisted mostly of landlords and one of the prizes awarded was a forty-guinea silver cup. McMahon declared with withering sarcasm that, in the custom of barbarians of old, 'a human skull fashioned into a cup would have been much more appropriate … a fitting ornament for the sideboard of an exterminator'. He went on to say that 'the face of the country is hideous with ruins, whose gables, black and bare and pointing to the sky, would seem to call Heaven to witness the barbarities perpetrated on their unfortunate occupants'.[14]

Emigration from Tralee

Annual emigration from Tralee before the 1840s was never more than 300 persons in any year; the number in 1837 was 286 and in 1838 it was only sixteen.[15] Cargo ships bringing timber from the United States and Canada found it profitable to bring passengers from Irish ports on their return voyages. Quebec in Canada was the destination of most ships from Tralee, a cheaper crossing than to the United States. Only two ships sailed in 1845, the *British Empire* bound for Quebec and the *John* for an American port.

The numbers departing from Tralee from 1844 to 1852 were as follows:

1844 – 222
1845 – 73
1846 – 1,861
1847 – 58
1848 – 308
1849 – 1,360
1850 – 354
1851 – 2,701
1852 – 2,926[16]

These figures do not represent all the emigrants from the county as the records are not comprehensive and many would have left from ports other than Tralee, but they give an indication of the trends. Full recording of emigrant numbers began in 1851 and Geraldine Lucid cites the numbers of emigrants from Co. Kerry as 8,732 in 1851, 8,893 in 1852 and 10,448 in 1853.[17] 'The desire to emigrate still rages about us', commented the *Post* in 1851.[18]

'Take Fortune's tide – the world is wide, has room enough for all' went a line of a poem in the *Post*, but there were also warnings to prospective emigrants about what faced them on arrival in America: no immediate support and no free passage to the interior.[19] Fr Hampston in Illinois, who was formerly a curate in Kerry, encouraged emigrants to travel to the far west where they could earn $100 a year with board and lodgings; 'this is being somewhat better off than being a landlord in Ireland', wrote the *Examiner*.[20]

The *Post* observed that in America many of the emigrants 'resumed the character which made or kept them knaves or mendicants at home' and quoted from a report in the *Daily News* of New York:

> How long is Ireland to pour forth these wretched crowds? *The moment these people arrive they commence begging.* The streets swarm with them. Looking around and finding that they are not followed by any police, they begin to swagger; they begin to tell you what fine farms and houses they occupied at home. They offer to work if you will offer them 4s or 5s sterling a day but they soon get tired. They rush to the alms house or the dispensary or the emigration offices to get relief, and within a few days become *ready to dispute with you the possession of the soil.* Really they are in many respects the curse of our land and we all know it. Very few live to old age; an old Irishman is a very rare sight in this country. Useful in some respects as they are, they have so degraded labour among us that Americans will no longer perform the work which they are willing to do. The Irish emigration is the American Sphinx.[21]

The concept of assisted emigration was adopted with success in many areas, not least in Kenmare under Lord Lansdowne. Henry Herbert, MP, received praise for sending thirty women from the Killarney workhouse to New Orleans; the cost per pauper was £4 13s, which included passage, clothing, provisions for the voyage and £1 on arrival. The women were grateful to

Herbert and they were described as kneeling down outside the courthouse in Killarney to say prayers of gratitude for him for contributing 'to remove them from the workhouse bastille to a land of promise and comfort'.[22]

In 1849 the Tralee board had been against assisted emigration on grounds of cost, saying that £750 to support 150 emigrants was too high. Another reason given was a principled objection to the emigration of 'the bone and sinew of the country'.[23] By 1851, however, policy had changed and thirty young women from Tralee workhouse emigrated from Cork to New Orleans. It cost £5 per head for clothing, provisions, passage money and a gratuity of £1 on arrival.[24]

William Denny proposed a similar scheme to Herbert's, citing acts of parliament to show that the board could borrow money to assist emigration and be repaid by the government over time.[25] He explained the benefits for the board in being able to reduce pauper numbers in the workhouse and therefore reduce rates, and benefits for the paupers in giving them an opportunity to break the downward spiral of their lives by leaving the workhouse. Denny had the support of Nicholas Donovan, and they promised to lend £200 and £100 respectively for such a scheme. Denny said he had no intention of removing able-bodied men, who, he hoped, would in time resume their work as labourers, but his target group was able-bodied women between the ages of seventeen and thirty, and widows with five or six children. These groups were regarded as unlikely ever to better their position and would be a constant burden on the ratepayers. Only those who had been in the workhouse for six or seven years already would be chosen, in order to prevent women coming into the workhouse purely to be selected for the emigration scheme. The women were to be chosen from the electoral divisions which Denny and Donovan represented as guardians, i.e. Clogherbrien, Ballinahaglish, Bartregaum, Doon and Tubrid. Denny had already identified fifty-seven suitable women from Clogherbrien and seventy-seven from Ballinahaglish.[26]

Denny's proposal was welcomed, as these responses indicate:

> Mr Hurly: There were four or five thousand in our houses before the

admissions of this day and it may be well to consider what would be the expense of sending out a thousand.

Mr Supple: Can you take that as a fair average of that class? Recollect all the old men who swell your numbers. If you could get rid of five hundred, you would do the Union a great service.

Mr Nash: A permanent one.

Mr P. Leahy: A further service will be this. If you send out a member or two of a family, they will bye and bye enable the other members of the family to emigrate.

Mr Supple: Mr Denny's proposition should be hailed with feelings of pleasure. These poor girls when they come into the house remain there year after year. If you can raise money in this way, and send them where they will be enabled to eat the bread of industry, and if they are industrious [and] provide for other members of their families, you will confer a blessing on them and a great advantage on the Union.[27]

By May fifty-six paupers had been assisted to emigrate by Denny at a cost of £4 14s each, whereas the cost of keeping each of them in the workhouse for one year was £4. For this modest once-off payment, the individual emigrant was raised 'from a state of idle and hopeless dependence in the workhouse to one of labour and independence in America'.[28] Nicholas Donovan sent out about twenty-five people from his land at Tubrid, many of them children.[29]

Listowel followed Tralee's initiative with a proposal by Maurice Leonard to borrow £650 to assist emigration.[30] A group of thirty-five women from the Kenmare Union and thirty from the Listowel Union emigrated from Cork on board the *Giffion* in June. They were 'good-looking, young and healthy' and were comfortably clad in cotton frocks and handsome shawls, with good shoes and stockings. Arrangements were made to have them looked after separately on board ship and no communications were allowed with other passengers; a government emigration agent recommended the levels of light and ventilation which would be best for them. They were to be given ten shillings on arrival, a sum that was regarded as inadequate. The *Post* was not impressed with the decision to send the women to Cork port and advised that emigration from Tralee port would have been more advantageous to the businesses of the county, more convenient for the emigrants themselves and less expensive all round.[31]

Concern about Nicholas Donovan's emigration scheme was expressed by the commissioners in a letter to the board of guardians.[32] The scheme meant that the board was to borrow money from Donovan himself to assist emigration, and would repay it with interest, but Donovan was accused of selecting only emigrants from his own estate, some of whom were not true paupers. Not only that, said his accusers, but he selected whole families rather than individuals, the point being that if individuals were chosen, they in turn would send money for others of their family to follow, making the scheme more advantageous to the union. In one case, it was claimed that James Stack, the father of a large family, was sent by Donovan to the workhouse solely to enable him to qualify for the scheme and that he left the workhouse the next day.[33]

Nicholas Donovan was summoned before the board of guardians where he put his side of the case to Thomas B. Hurly, who summarised the accusations. Donovan said that he followed the example of William Denny in selecting his own tenants, believing that that was their right as lenders of the money and that the union would not lose any advantage because of that arrangement. He explained that James Stack was extremely poor (albeit the owner of 'a miserable cow and horse') and his family comprised eleven people, all of whom were destined to end up in the workhouse in the long term, so that it was advantageous to the union to have them emigrated. He cited other cases to show that he was selecting paupers whose departure would most benefit the union, and said that Captain Spark approved and had helped with his selection.[34]

Two families named Driscoll and Kearney were emigrated at Donovan's own expense and he gave examples of other families whose emigration he had also supported out of his own pocket. In selecting the whole Commane family in the workhouse for emigration, Donovan said it would have been 'both impolitic and unchristian' to separate the young children from the older family members. He further revealed that all of the emigrants, about sixty or seventy, were sailing on his ship, the *Jeanie Johnston*, for £3 rather than the usual £3 10s. By the end of the meeting Donovan had said enough to convince the board to proceed with the emigration scheme without objection.[35] However, while each family from the Denny estate received £1 on landing in Quebec, those from Donovan's estate did not; perhaps he felt that he had been generous enough already.[36]

An emigrant woman from Killarney workhouse, who arrived in New Orleans under Henry Herbert's scheme, sent a letter to her mother in May 1851, enclosing a cheque and confirming that she would soon send for her two brothers to join her. The letter was published in the *Post* but the woman's name was not given.[37] Thade Sugrue, originally of Lahard, had written the letter for her, and he was delighted to meet so many from his neighbourhood arriving in America. She was extremely grateful to Herbert for giving her and her friends the means of getting established there, rather than having to beg like other emigrants. She reported sadly that many of her fellow emigrants fell victim to drink and other vices. She wrote that any girl who could do washing, ironing and baking could earn twelve to fifteen dollars a month, but those who went further west would earn only five or six dollars a month. Her own story took a dramatic turn, which she left until the end of her letter: a man hired her off the ship and when his wife died a week later, he asked her to marry him. Having obtained the permission of her aunt, she married the wealthy man, who was much older than she was:

> I thought it more prudent to marry a man whom I considered more capable of supporting me and rendering me capable of sending you and the rest of the family some aid, than to marry a man who may leave me after, if he

was different to my views. Johanna lives with me. My husband has clad her respectably and would not let her go to hire out as he can keep her without expense, but pays her what he would give to strangers in order to help me with the housework.[38]

Johanna was her sister, apparently. The letter writer ended by wishing long life in health, wealth and prosperity to Henry Herbert.

William Talbot Crosbie presented another proposal to the Tralee board for the removal of a hundred inmates over sixteen from the workhouse. They would be 'distributed' for employment by himself and the farmers of the areas of Abbeydorney and Ardfert. Those selected were regarded as 'the very class whom it is most desirable should be snatched from the demoralising influence of the workhouse' and Crosbie's initiative was lauded and recommended to others.[39] Some of the selected inmates were 'paraded before the board, previous to leaving the house. They were all women, and looked most respectable and comfortable, all decently clothed at Mr Crosbie's expense. Mr Crosbie's conduct met with the greatest applause from the board.'[40]

The Jeanie Johnston

The best-known emigrant ship that sailed from Blennerville was the *Jeanie Johnston*, which made a total of sixteen transatlantic voyages between 1848 and 1855. The ship was built by Scotsman John Munn in Quebec and its maiden voyage was from Quebec to Liverpool, where it was bought by the firm of John Donovan and his son, Nicholas.[41] The ship had a capacity of 700 tons and was fitted out and adapted to suit passengers, particularly by raising the height between decks, and it proved a very comfortable and sea-worthy vessel. It sailed from Liverpool to Tralee in March 1848 with a varied cargo, which shows the range of goods imported to Tralee and sold by the Donovan firm: 160 tons of rock salt, 120 tons of coal and coke, 100 boxes of soap, 510 barrels of Indian meal, 10 sheets of lead, 50 barrels of tar, pitch and rosin, 120 crates of crown window glass, 30 bags of metal nails, 3 packs and 6 bundles of sundries, 6 logs of mahogany, 100 tons of Baltic timber, 8 pieces of oak and ash, 3,400 oak pipe staves, 60 casks and kegs of paint and painters' colours, 2 casks of spirit of turpentine, 3 pipes of oil, 40 boxes of tin, 900 bars of iron, 120 bundles of nail road iron, 30 barrels of Roman cement, 5 casks of sulphur, 3 fathoms of lathwood and 30 barrels of plaster of Paris.[42] Later cargoes on the voyage from Quebec consisted almost entirely of timber, as described in 1850: prime red and yellow pine timber, oak, ash, elm, birch, pine and spruce deals, oak pipe and barrel staves, spars and oars.[43]

The *Jeanie Johnston* featured regularly in the pages of the press, with Captain James Attridge, a native of Castletownshend, Co. Cork, being singled out for praise for his sailing skills and care for his passengers. The first voyage of the *Jeanie Johnston* from Tralee was in April 1848, as reported in the *Post*:

> The emigrants who were mostly comfortable farmers and tradesmen with their families, were greatly pleased with the comfort, room and regulation on board the barque, and all their friends who went to see them in the barque speak highly in praise of the care and attention paid by the owners, Messrs. Donovan, to the comfort of the passengers.[44]

The voyage from Tralee to Quebec could be completed in four weeks in very good conditions, but usually took six weeks. In 1852 one voyage took seventy-four days to reach Quebec.[45] Remarkably, no passenger ever died on the voyages of the *Jeanie Johnston*, and credit for this is attributed to Captain Attridge and the ship's doctor, Richard Blennerhassett, son of Dr Henry Blennerhassett of Tralee.

Grosse Isle in Quebec was the quarantine centre for arrivals by ship and Dr George Douglas, the medical superintendent there, had witnessed some appalling scenes, especially in 1847 and 1848. For example, one ship, the *Virginius*, was truly a 'coffin ship'. It had set out from Liverpool in May 1847 with 596 passengers, but had lost 158 at sea and, when it landed, it had 186 passengers who were 'more dead than alive'; stores had run out and all but two of the crew had died on the voyage.[46] Another ship, the *Jessie*, sailed from

Limerick to Quebec in 1847 and lost thirty of its 479 passengers.[47] In 1850 the same ship lost twenty-five passengers and sixty were hospitalised as soon as they arrived in Grosse Isle.[48] By contrast, when the *Jeanie Johnston* arrived in the autumn of 1849, Dr Douglas examined the passengers and declared that they were in such good health that they were not required to land at Grosse Isle.[49]

On 20 April 1850 the *Post* noted that the *Jeanie Johnston* was the only emigrant ship to sail from Tralee that year, whereas twelve ships had sailed at the same period in 1849, but it acknowledged that Kerry emigrants had left from other ports.[50] On its arrival in Quebec, a tribute by the passengers to Captain Attridge was published in a journal there and re-published in the *Post*. They noted that the voyage was marked by 'tempestuous weather', but Attridge's skills as a mariner were equal to the task and they expressed their appreciation for his 'affability and characteristic benevolence'. They also paid tribute to 'our much esteemed medical attendant, Dr Blennerhassett, of whom it is but justice to say that he spared no exertions on his part'. The newspaper notice was signed by twenty-four male passengers on behalf of all and it ended with a wish for Captain Attridge: 'May you live long and glide along the vale of life crowned with the best gifts of Heaven.'[51]

Dr Blennerhassett did not sail on all voyages, it seems, as noted in a newspaper tribute of late 1850. The *Jeanie Johnston* sailed from Tralee on 23 August but did not arrive in Quebec until 15 October, after experiencing 'many severe and dangerous storms'. The tribute in a Quebec newspaper was again addressed to Captain James Attridge, and clearly stated that there was no doctor on this particular voyage: 'The absence of a doctor on board your ship should never prevent persons from emigrating in her, so long as you, Sir, are commander, for your experience in that profession and the interest you have always taken (and we believe will long continue to take) render you a very good substitute.'[52]

All of the many tributes appear to have been unforced and genuinely felt and, when reprinted in the Kerry newspapers, were undoubtedly very beneficial to the business of the Donovans of Tralee. On this occasion the passengers added some practical considerations which further boosted the Donovans' business interests:

> We will also impress it on the minds of all our fellow countrymen (particularly all our friends in Kerry who may yet emigrate to America) the very great comfort, the regularity, and the clean manner in which the *Jeanie Johnston* is always kept; which is a large, firm and well ventilated ship, and one well adapted for the accommodation of passengers. Those advantages, together with your experience and the attention and kindness which have hitherto so characterised you, ought to be borne in mind by every person in our native county (Kerry) who may subsequently come out.
>
> Persons in Kerry are not at all aware of the many advantages acquired by coming direct from the port of Tralee, above going to Liverpool where they may perhaps be for a week (or even longer) under expense for diet, lodging etc. before they could match themselves with a ship, and even when they do so, they must provide sea store, as the food which they get cannot be used in too many cases, which often proves fatal to the poor emigrants.[53]

In July 1852 the *Quebec Morning Chronicle* carried another fine tribute addressed to Captain Attridge from the passengers of the *Jeanie Johnston*:

> Sir – We feel that we should appear ungrateful did we leave your ship without returning our sincere and grateful thanks for your unremitting kindness and attention to us during the voyage.
>
> The character you have long since won for yourself has been well preserved since our meeting with you and we trust that any of our friends who wish to follow us may be fortunate to meet with one possessed of so much skill and humanity. This, we have no doubt, is also the wish of our medical officer, Dr. Blennerhassett, whose unceasing attention to us shall not soon be forgotten.
>
> It must be a source of much gratification to you, as indeed it is to us that neither death nor sickness have made their appearance among us, owing, we consider under God, to the wise regulations that have been observed on board.

> Long may you continue to enjoy the high reputation you possess and long may you live to receive the thanks and blessings of your truly grateful and obliged passengers.[54]

In October 1853 the *Jeanie Johnston* was blown off course in a storm and put in to St Andrew's, New Brunswick. An emigration officer named Thomas Jones befriended and helped a man named John Gaynor and his two sons, Laurence and Stephen. The two children were suffering from frostbite and one was in danger of losing a foot. Thomas Jones himself cared for the two boys from December to April 1854.[55] In a letter of May 1854, which is archived in New Brunswick, Thomas Jones wrote as follows from St Andrew's, referring to passengers of the *Jeanie Johnston*:

> In my different communications to you respecting these emigrants, I told you of the probability of some of them becoming chargeable to the Province. Two children, Stephen and Laurence Gaynor have been so, from December to the end of April, when I found persons willing to take them off my hands. They were frost-bitten and otherwise sick for most of the winter. Their father, an old man, could obtain no kind of employment from 19 February to 28 March, after that period he was occasionally employed, when I reduced his rate of boarding from 11s 3d to 6s a week. Goggin with the two Doyles and Sullivan are similarly situated, with the difference that Doyle was injured on the railroad and Sullivan was badly frozen. All these people would have proceeded to Quebec, had they not been induced to remain with the expectation of finding permanent work on the railway.[56]

Jones submitted a request to his employers for £52 11s 3d to cover the expense of caring for these emigrants, supplying receipts. Passenger records for that particular voyage of the *Jeannie Johnston* have not survived, so it is not known where exactly the Gaynor family was from, but it very likely that they were from the Kerry Head area, where the surname is found.[57]

In 1855 the Donovans decided to sell the *Jeanie Johnston*. It ended its sailing days in 1858 when its cargo of timber began to absorb water, weighing down the ship. The crew abandoned it and it sank.[58] A replica of the *Jeanie Johnston* was built in Tralee in the 1990s and is now berthed at Custom House Quay in Dublin, where it is a major tourist attraction.

Tralee Workhouse

In March 1851 the guardians of Tralee Union were still smarting from the forced annexation of 'the nine northern divisions' with which they 'were swamped by the perverseness of the Commissioners'.[59] To add to their grievances, Captain Spark was transferred to the newly formed Dingle Union, and the Poor Law inspector of Killarney Union, Mr Horsely, was obliged to take on Tralee as well. The fact that they did not have the undivided attention of a designated inspector infuriated the Tralee guardians, especially as Dingle Union had its own inspector.

Horsely reassured the Tralee guardians that he could manage the two locations and he curried favour by praising their management: 'I went through all your establishments and found them in admirable order. I could discover no evidence of inattention on the part of the officers. Your average cost too is as low as in any other union.'[60] He found that in the main workhouse there was 'a very creditable attempt at industrial employment'. He explained patiently that 'the use of an inspector is to see the law carried out by the guardians, to co-operate with them in every way possible and to detect whatever may be wrong'. There was a mild rebuke in his reminder that 'the guardians are not merely expected to come and sit in their boardroom; if they do not look after the progress of discipline and economy, they are not guardians'.[61]

One practical decision made by Horsely was to have extra Masses on Sunday in the Rock Street and Ballymullen workhouses, because walking the inmates through the town to attend Mass was causing disciplinary problems, with some absconding and some plundering shops on the way.[62] Another was the proposed amalgamation of the hospitals attached to the workhouses of the Rock, Ballymullen, Waterloo, James Street, Blennerville, Riordan's and

Clahane.⁶³ Horsely also opposed a board decision to appoint an unqualified inmate as a workhouse teacher over another man who was qualified; the guardians believed that the saving involved was worthwhile, but Horsely saw it as an undesirable precedent to set.⁶⁴

There were great expectations of the newly installed capstan mill in Tralee workhouse in early 1851: 'As spring advances,' wrote the *Chronicle*, 'it will prove a most valuable test of destitution for able-bodied paupers lazily inclined.'⁶⁵ Capstan mills, designed by Richard Perrott, were installed in several workhouses around this time. A mill could employ up to a hundred inmates who pushed it round in a circle for hours. The Tralee capstan mill became the source of ructions several times during the year, beginning in March when about seventy young men refused to co-operate in working it and attacked the miller and the overseer. This '*émeute* of the grown lads' came before the board; sixteen of the boys faced expulsion. In the end, only the two leaders were expelled, and some alterations to the capstan routine were made so as to make the labour 'less continuous' for the boys.⁶⁶ However, there was another incident in July when the capstan boys were reported as ready to kill the master.⁶⁷ At the October Petty Sessions, eighteen paupers were sentenced to a month's hard labour for refusing to work the capstan mill and for breaking the wheel.⁶⁸

Numbers in the workhouses of Tralee were still a concern, with a total of 6,600 in March 1851, a figure that was over 500 higher than the number for which there was accommodation.⁶⁹ Even Captain Spark (prior to his move to the Dingle Union) agreed that there was not a single suitable building available in Tralee; he preferred to use a store rather than a private house because it would be cheaper and easier to ventilate. Spark proposed this solution: that all infirm persons and widows with two legitimate children should be discharged from the workhouse and placed on outdoor relief. This harsh proposal was opposed by Justin Supple, who said that their numbers amounted to 400 and that, if discharged, they 'would not have a place to put their head in'.⁷⁰ There was no recorded response from Spark.

When the matron of the workhouse was challenged about an order for

3,000 yards of linen, she told the board that that quantity would make only 1,000 shirts and she had to provide for 7,000.[71] From mid-May to mid-June 1851 there were over 7,000 inmates in the workhouses of Tralee, with a peak of 7,197 on 24 May. There was a proposal to build additional accommodation in the grounds of the main workhouse.[72] Beggars were also numerous in Tralee, with a large number of vagrants 'who prowl about our streets', about 1,600 altogether according to the *Post*.[73]

The *Post* was outraged at the numbers in Tralee workhouses in late April, claiming that '3,000 are grown, healthy, able-bodied persons living in idleness on the public'.[74] Newspapers in other parts of Ireland took up the story, with one referring to 'the monster evil of overcrowding in Tralee workhouse',[75] and another to 'the foul and unwelcome atmosphere in which 7,000 human beings are doomed to exist in idleness'.[76] However, in the second half of the year the numbers fell steadily, with 5,801 inmates recorded on 2 August and 3,900 on 6 December 1851.[77]

Auxiliary Workhouses

The board of guardian minutes for Tralee in 1851 show that the following abbreviations were used for their auxiliary workhouses: BV: Blennerville; BM: Ballymullen; R: the Rock; Rior: Riordan's (on High Street); Jas: James Street; Cla: Clahane; and C.I.: Castleisland. The abbreviation 'K' is used for one which cannot be identified.[78] Another auxiliary workhouse mentioned in the minutes was Busteed's.

The number of auxiliary workhouses varied according to need and the *Post* stated that there were ten in the union in March 1851.[79] However, in August 1851 one guardian, John Hurly, was not challenged or corrected when he referred to seventeen auxiliary workhouses in the union; perhaps some smaller buildings were used temporarily.[80] Justin Supple later spoke about the responsibilities of the board of guardians when they 'had to rent, fit-up and furnish at immense expense sixteen auxiliary workhouses' at a time when there were nearly 8,000 paupers in the union.[81]

Workhouse Incidents

One issue was bread. An inmate told a board member that if a pauper complained about the quantity of bread, the master would take it away and replace it with the same quantity of wood.[82] In Castleisland, the medical officer complained that the bread provided was of inferior quality and endangered the lives of patients: it was agreed to purchase shop bread in future.[83] But again in October, the bread was described as unfit for the sick, and the flour merchant and master baker were at odds about the cause. It was alleged that the baker's assistants were in the habit of drinking thirty or forty pints of the barm or yeast, which was a superior type of bitter ale.[84]

Other matters of concern in 1851 were accusations that the guardians were open to bribery and that Ballymullen workhouse with 987 inmates consumed 3,700 quarts of milk while Castleisland workhouse with 868 inmates used 4,300 quarts.[85]

Farmers were known to be employing young labourers wearing workhouse clothes, and in these cases the labourers were charged with stealing workhouse property. The farmers were criticised by magistrates for encouraging the abuse of public property, i.e. the uniforms.[86] Maurice Fitzgerald Sandes of Oakpark offered to take inmates out to work on his Brosna estates if the board would provide them with a suit of clothes. His request was denied by twelve votes to six.[87]

A Protestant inmate of Tralee workhouse, John Bonnett, wrote a letter complaining that he had been prevented from working at various jobs because of his religion, but his case was dismissed as without foundation.[88]

Rev. Samuel B. Leonard complained to the board about a man named Garret Neil of Ballyheigue. He had a wife and child living on a quarter of an acre in Ballyheigue while he and two other children received outdoor relief. The wife and children were causing a nuisance to farmers there, according to Leonard, by stealing sheep, and he wanted the family taken into the workhouse according to the letter of the Gregory Clause. Leonard was given an opportunity to make his case, but his request was summarily rejected. 'We cannot turn them out, or make this court a court of ejectment,' said guardian James O'Connell, adding that 'unfortunately there are too many people turned out of house and home in this country'. Justin Supple said, 'We are not here for the purpose of maintaining the "rights" of landlords by starving the people.' The chairman concluded, 'We will not interfere.'[89]

There were signs of growing resentment about the cost of the workhouses to the ratepayers and the perceived comforts of the paupers. Comparisons were made between Killarney, where the numbers in the workhouse had fallen by a third between November 1850 and November 1851, and Tralee, where they had fallen by only one-tenth. Noting that Tralee contained mainly women and children, the *Post* asked where the fathers were – 'shaking a free leg in Tipperary, England or America', it asserted, leaving the ratepayers 'to support their families in idle contented beggary, which is every day becoming more habitual'.[90] One woman whose husband had deserted her was refused entry to the workhouse unless he was with her; she called to a stranger in Church Street and asked him to look after her two children for a brief period, but she never returned and the children were then taken to the workhouse.[91]

Comparisons between the management of Killarney and Tralee workhouses arose frequently and questions were raised about the 'desperately profligate expenditure' in Tralee. There was grumbling that, although ratepayers – and even guardians – could not afford tea for themselves, workhouse officers in Tralee were provided with tea and sugar; it was pointed out that the same officers in Killarney workhouse did not have that privilege. Justin Supple stated that while Killarney Union might provide fewer creature comforts, they paid their officers higher salaries than Tralee Union.[92]

The *Post* also berated the Tralee guardians for their irregular and late attendance, for 'spending the day in babble', leaving no time to investigate applicants and then hurriedly admitting masses of paupers, 'and the end is you have 4,000 paupers snug and comfortable in your houses and the question is when or how will you get them out again'.[93] The *Post* was ever conscious of the institutionalisation of workhouse inmates and the possibility of them becoming dependent on welfare for a protracted period. 1851 ended with the revelation that there were 140 more paupers on the books of Tralee workhouse than were actually resident, and a discussion followed on the waste of public money involved.[94]

Listowel Workhouse

1851 was a truly appalling year for deaths in Listowel workhouses. In the first six months, 1,057 people died. During March 1851, 271 deaths were recorded, with a peak of sixty-six in the week ending 22 March. There were 4,983 people in the workhouses at that time.[95] Numbers in Listowel's workhouses peaked at 5,627 in May 1851 and there was a proposal to build additional accommodation for up to 1,000 near the main workhouse, but by the end of the year numbers had fallen to 2,444. There was a corresponding decline in the death rate.[96]

When deaths were at their peak in March 1851, Dr Thorpe reported as follows to the board, with his final recommendation sounding singularly hollow and suggesting a sense of fatalism about the death rate:

> Dr Thorpe regrets to point out to the guardians the still increasing amount of sickness and great mortality. The different additional places of accommodation for the sick which have been granted by the board are occupied and still many wards of the infirmary are over-crowded. Besides the dysenteric wards where there are eighty, which ought to be limited to fifty-six, the infirm wards also have too many occupants and Dr Thorpe is seriously embarrassed as to what provision he is to make for the several sick infirm sent from Clieveragh … Dysentery, chest affections [sic] and whooping cough have been vastly on the increase during the past week and have caused nearly the entire mortality. Dr Thorpe would impress upon the guardians the importance of substituting milk for coffee (when practible [sic]) in the general dietary of the paupers.[97]

Of the sixty-six deaths in the workhouse in the week of his report, Thorpe said that thirty-seven took place in the main workhouse and they comprised twenty-six females and eleven males. Twenty-three died of dysentery, six of chest infections and eight of other causes.

THE GREAT FAMINE

Table 1: Listowel workhouses: deaths recorded in 1850, 1851 and 1852

	1850	1851	1852
January	131	62	24
February	96	129	15
March	184	271	26
April	149	184	33
May	154	241	26
June	136	170	22
July	86	105	36
August	79	58*	21
September	63*	12**	7
October	82	26	12
November	90	35	10
December	63	15	12

* Deaths for one week not recorded
** Deaths for two weeks not recorded

Table 2: Listowel workhouses: deaths recorded in March 1851

Ages	Week ending 1 March	Week ending 8 March	Week ending 15 March	Week ending 22 March	Week ending 29 March
Under 2 years	4	6	3	5	7
2–5 years	10	7	9	7	8
5–9 years	7	8	12	20	20
9–15 years	6	8	9	17	5
Over 15 years	14	16	23	17	23

(Source: Board of guardian minute books, KCA)

It is strange that there appears to have been no great outrage in the press at the situation in the Listowel workhouses in 1851 and no reports of protests on the part of the clergy or other public figures. It may be that the press and public had become inured to the scale of deaths. However, a discussion did take place at a meeting of Killarney board of guardians where the members expressed concern at the number of workhouse deaths there – 112 in the month of March 1851. 'Is there nothing appalling in this – I will not hesitate to call it so – sacrifice of human life?' asked Mr Maybury, a Killarney guardian.[98] There were fifty-nine workhouse deaths in Tralee in the same month. It was pointed out that Tralee Union had three physicians while Killarney had only one; but a guardian noted that Listowel had very high death rates although it had four physicians. The conclusion was that it was not the number of medical officers in a union which made the difference, or their conscientiousness or their expertise, but the reluctance of the poor to enter the workhouse until they were at death's door.[99]

This concern was addressed by the Listowel guardians, who strongly refuted the view of Mr Duncan, inspecting officer, that overcrowding was the main cause of the high workhouse mortality, although they accepted that there was some temporary and limited overcrowding. The board members adopted Thorpe's position and cited factors such as the extremely harsh weather, the lack of outdoor relief and the failure of the potato crop of 1850 that resulted in people having only turnips for sustenance. The board believed that many people were brought to the workhouse only when they were at death's door in order that they would be buried in a coffin supplied by the union. Many of the guardians were said to be surprised that workhouse mortality was not even higher, because almost all deaths among the poorer classes took place within the workhouse. In discussing the strong aversion among the poor to entering the workhouse until near death, the board members argued that the extreme cold of the house, caused by excessive ventilation, was the chief deterrent. Regardless of how poor they were, people in north Kerry always had turf for fuel and therefore a warm cabin, they said, and 'those fires and that heated atmosphere are considered to be indispensable comforts and the loss of them among the greatest of their privations'.[100]

In December 1851 two boys died in Listowel workhouse after eating a poisonous root. They had been working on the training farm of the workhouse when they came across this root, named as *cicuta merculata*.[101] Another strange and tragic death was that of a boy who fell into the soup pot 'and was so scalded as to die four hours afterwards'.[102] Dr Thorpe informed the board that this was the third such fatality during his time as medical officer and the board agreed to install a protective barrier as recommended by him.[103]

Auxiliary Workhouses

Some limited information on conditions in the auxiliary workhouses of Listowel Union is recorded in the press. Banemore was visited by Dr Thorpe and Mr Duncan and they found that discipline was very lax there. The nurses were said to be starving the children and eating the bread themselves; the master was incompetent; and a number of disorderly female inmates were charged before a magistrate.[104]

The medical officer of the auxiliary workhouses in 1851 was Dr Enright and his reports were forcefully expressed. He was concerned that 300 patients were suffering from ophthalmia and he advised that in the overcrowded state of the schoolroom, spreading powdered lime on the floor could be a contributory factor. The practice was discontinued on his advice.[105] Dr Enright told the board that unless a fire was provided at Clieveragh auxiliary workhouse for the old and infirm, 'to whom warmth is nearly as necessary as food', it should be closed down as it was not fit to receive the infirm. He said that the diet at Bedford Infirmary was 'more calculated to sicken than to nourish' and that diarrhoea and dysentery were on the increase there. There were sixty patients in the hospital, which was intended to have a maximum of twenty. Of twenty-one deaths in his area of responsibility, eighteen were of children between two and nine years of age and were caused by dysentery and chest infections. His inability to separate the well from the ill meant that 'all are breathing a tainted atmosphere' and diseases spread rapidly.[106]

'TAKE FORTUNE'S TIDE – THE WORLD IS WIDE'

Dr Enright also complained that he could not travel to Gunsborough auxiliary workhouse because it was too far away and he would have to acquire a horse, which was too expensive for him. He requested that the master of Gunsborough should send the sick to Bedford Infirmary where he would be willing to attend them. The reply of the board showed that the members had lost patience with Enright; he was told that his salary had been raised to £80 in recognition of his additional duties and that the board would be glad to accept his resignation if he did not attend patients in Gunsborough workhouse.[107]

There was further conflict over religious matters in 1851 when Fr Denis O'Donoghue, curate in Listowel, claimed that Protestant clergymen were giving instruction to Catholic inmates, conducting their religious services while Catholics were present and distributing money to soupers or converts.[108] This led to an inquiry by the board. The two accused Protestant clergymen were Rev. Stamer of Ballybunion and Rev. Gibson of Kilflynn, who were acting as chaplains to the workhouse while Rev. Edward Denny was ill. They were accused of 'proselytising by bribery'. The two men did not deny that they had given money in charity to some workhouse inmates, but according to the *Post*, the affair was greatly exaggerated and it believed that the parish priest, Fr Mahony, was not supportive of his curate's accusations because he appeared 'heartily sick of the whole thing'.[109]

10

'TIMES ARE MENDING'

1852

It is a gratifying fact that we can say at last that times are mending.

Kerry Evening Post, 21 February 1852

The Great Exhibition in London had been the highlight of 1851 in England and the *Post* contrasted the mood in the two islands as follows: 'In England – all holiday, in Ireland – all hunger'.[1] England had 'a crystal palace by a crystal fountain' while Ireland had 'half-starved mendicants robbing turnip fields, or lurking ribbonmen murdering wayfarers, or half-clad emigrants, shoaling from the land of famine and ill-luck'.[2]

Nevertheless, the *Post* looked forward to improvements and was soon pleased to report 'signs of better times' in Kerry.[3] It cited more marriages at Shrovetide, especially among substantial farmers, fewer tenants flitting with their stock and crops, large quantities of sound potatoes in Tralee market and tenants paying their rents on time. Numbers receiving workhouse relief in Killarney had dropped from 4,400 in February 1851 to 2,400 in February 1852. In Kenmare and Cahersiveen, the number of paupers had fallen by 40 per cent. People receiving indoor relief in Tralee had peaked at over 7,000 in mid-1851, but numbers were now expected to fall to under 2,000, requiring the use of only the main workhouse. 'It is a gratifying fact that we can say at last that times are mending,' the *Post* declared with confidence.[4]

Not everybody in Tralee was as optimistic, however, and one person complained that the town was 'infested with beggars', some of them stout men who were begging from ladies 'more in a tone of menace than of entreaty'.[5] Emigration was high, and the *Post* wrote that 'the tide of emigration has set in both strong and early this year' with three ships owned by local businessmen in the harbour.[6] These were the *Jeanie Johnston* of Messrs Donovan, the *Lismahagow* of Messrs Kennelly and the *Maime* of Messrs Hickson. They all carried a full complement of passengers, with the *Lismahagow* taking thirty-seven young people from the townland of Curraheen, west of Blennerville, resulting in several houses being abandoned there. According to the *Post* these emigrants were not driven away by excessive rents or by extreme poverty, but rather made a choice to emigrate.[7]

By May five vessels had sailed from Tralee with about 1,400 emigrants; another 1,100 were expected to travel by July and a further 1,000 were estimated to have travelled via Cork, Limerick and Liverpool. This amounted to about 1.5 per cent of the population of Kerry, according to the *Post*. The emigrants came mainly from two classes: small farmers whose rent was between £12 and £20, who left with their families and with some money, and labourers who had been sent for and were supported by friends and relatives already in America. Those who had larger farms were not disposed to emigrate and were working with great energy on their lands.[8] Remittances from America supported the costs of emigration and the successful harvest season led to many people being able to afford the passage money.[9]

This 'Celtic exodus' was not viewed as a disaster, and for one category in particular, the *Post* was a strong advocate of emigration: those who had become institutionalised by spending many years in the workhouse. Noting that Tralee board of guardians was assisting inmates of the workhouse to emigrate if half the cost was funded by relatives, the paper argued that it should:

> … go farther and at one sweep, send across the Atlantic all those whom we have on a former occasion described as 'the children of the workhouse' – parties so long in the establishment as to have no sense of self-dependence,

so acclimatised, if we may use the word, to the atmosphere of the workhouse, as to have no wish to leave it.[10]

This, according to the *Post*, would prove a benefit to the individuals themselves, but also to ratepayers, by relieving them of the burden of long-term support. The attitude of the *Post* towards those who had become institutionalised in the workhouse is revealed in its conclusion that 'emigration is then the only way of getting permanently rid of that most useless class of the community'.[11]

Tralee

Mining Mania

The main commercial event of 1852 in Tralee was the mining mania that swept the town and brought an expectation of wealth in abundance which would provide employment, dispel poverty and empty the workhouses. The directors of the Royal Hibernian Mining Company arrived in Kerry amid great fanfare. A great public celebration (termed a *fête champêtre*) was planned for the opening of the company's mine shaft on the Headley estate near Castlemaine; 500 gold invitation cards were printed for the gentry, clergy, military officers and traders of Kerry and 1,000 green invitation cards for everyone else.[12] The *Post* declared that 'England expects that every man must do his duty' at the event to preserve decorum and to impress the directors of the company 'who had shown a spirit of generous and manly fraternisation' towards the county.[13] The fête came off 'with the most distinguished *éclat*'.[14]

There was more kow-towing to the mining company officials who visited Tralee, and a public holiday was declared in their honour, with the *Post* giving two pages of coverage to their visit.[15] The principal representative of the mining company was Henry Gibson, who confidently declared that Kerry was the Cornwall of Ireland. At the fête, there was a discharge of cannon for the directors and when Gibson appeared, the band played 'The Conquering Hero'. A great evening of celebration ended with a fireworks display.

As a cavalcade left Tralee for the fête and banquet at Castlemaine, the reporter of the *Post* observed hundreds of pauper children near the workhouse adjoining the old castle of Ballymullen and he confidently hoped that 'those young creatures, now an incumbrance to society and to themselves, would too find an industrial field for the exercise and development of those energies and powers of which the workhouse is at once the prison and the grave'.[16]

At the banquet, William Denny captured the spirit of the times as he painted a Utopian picture of Kerry's future after the development of mines:

> You would have your poorhouses cleared (cheers) – your surplus population employed – your artisans, your small tenant and your large tenant farmers, instead of seeking subsistence in a foreign soil, would be found here exercising their energies upon the mines that Nature seems to have scattered throughout his native land (loud cheers). Your landed proprietors too would be enabled to give that extensive employment that the pressure of public taxation now prevents them from doing.[17]

'It is the beginning of a great movement,' wrote the editor of the *Examiner*, 'by which the sphere of employment among the labouring population will be enlarged and this we look upon as a foundation … of a superstructure of national prosperity.'[18]

Henry Gibson visited schools in Castlemaine and Tralee, with gifts of money and bread for the children. He carried a bag full of three-penny coins to the value of five pounds and these he distributed to the children. The schoolmistress received half a guinea. He also made contributions of five pounds to Dr John McEnnery for distribution among the poor and of five guineas to Rev. Samuel B. Leonard for the Protestant Orphan Society. Gibson also distributed coins to the children of Presentation Convent school in Tralee. Fr Charles O'Callaghan, PP of Ballymacelligott, was another who received money and he too was charmed by the great Gibson, predicting that he would be 'a brilliant star yet in [the] Irish story'.[19] On hearing a rumour that 'a silver mine had been discovered in Ardfert' the *Examiner* speculated excitedly: 'Perhaps the Kerry diggings will yet astonish and attract the world.'[20]

The *Examiner* lauded Gibson, as 'the head, the chief, the great designer and the bold venturer', and stated that 'his liberality, his generosity, his straightforwardness, his indomitable spirit of enterprise and exertion have powerfully recommended him to the warm regards and to the esteem of Kerrymen'.[21] One Thomas D. Stack was inspired to write a poem in praise of Gibson, which began as follows:

> *Illustrious chief! To whom do now belong*
> *To guide my pen and raise this epic song,*
> *To welcome thee to Kerry's ancient shore,*
> *Her mines and treasures nobly to explore,*
> *To give employment to the woeful train,*
> *The sons of sadness, hunger, grief and pain.*[22]

Traders in Tralee benefitted from the visit of the mining magnates; in grossly exaggerated reports it was estimated that £5,000 was spent by them in the town and all articles of haberdashery in the shops were (wrongly) said to have sold out.[23] There was further jubilation when six hundredweight of lead ore was extracted from Clogher mine on the Blennerhassett estate.[24] The mining frenzy seemed to herald boom times for the traders of Tralee and the prospect of the railway being extended from Killarney added to the sense that good times were indeed coming.[25]

However, no fortunes were ever made from Kerry mines. Gibson and his partners were said to have become disillusioned with the level of co-operation they received from some Kerry landlords and the mining operations petered out.[26] There was litigation in England between the directors of the company and it was revealed that Gibson was not the man he appeared to be; he had not always gone by the surname Gibson and in his early life he had stolen a horse and gig and served a sentence of seven years' transportation to Australia. He had then lived in Canada and in Africa before settling in London.[27] If the people who had fawned over the visiting mining officials felt any embarrassment over their misplaced adulation, it was not apparent in the Kerry press; chief among the cheerleaders for Gibson were the newspaper editors themselves.[28]

Tralee Workhouse

In 1852 the master of Tralee workhouse, John P. O'Sullivan, suspected that the nurse tenders were in the habit of stealing items from the workhouse. In order to entrap them he instructed some of the boys to spy on them; as part of the plan, he arranged for the boys to carry out robberies in the house. When this became known, the *Examiner* was outraged that boys were being trained in spying and robbery at the ratepayers' expense – 'young spies in training, amateurs in the art of plunder, to practice hereafter in a wider field as finished masters'.[29] The *Examiner* lamented that the young paupers were not only exposed to suffering in the workhouse but also to vices: 'Excluded from the care of the public eye, from the protection and vigilance of parents, the children imprisoned in workhouses seem to be particularly fitted to receive the worst impressions that human nature is capable of receiving.'[30]

In January 1852 there were 3,928 people in the workhouses, compared with 5,245 twelve months earlier.[31] Several of the branch workhouses were closed down as the number of workhouse inmates fell after mid-1852. Castleisland auxiliary workhouse and fever hospital were closed in August, as it was decided that there was no further need for them; attempts to keep the fever hospital open were opposed by Mr Horsely who said that it could not continue once the workhouse was closed.[32]

Statistics published in September 1852 showed the changes in numbers of paupers in the workhouses from the previous year. In Listowel Union, numbers had fallen from 2,952 to 1,619, a decrease of 45 per cent.[33] In Tralee Union, the numbers had fallen from 3,694 to 2,550, a decrease of 31 per cent.[34] The *Chronicle* attributed the improvement to better management of the workhouses, improved conditions generally and emigration. Assisted emigration from the workhouses directly affected the figures, and the general emigration of labourers meant that more work was made available for able-bodied workhouse inmates.[35]

Numbers in Tralee workhouses fluctuated somewhat and by July 1853 there were 2,828 workhouse inmates in the union.[36] By August, however, it was clear that the numbers would soon fall 'considerably below 2,000', which meant that more branch workhouses could close.[37]

Listowel

For those who believed that the Famine was a visitation of God, or those who were superstitious, a disastrous event on Easter Sunday 1852 in Listowel might have been seen as yet another *dies irae* (day of wrath), after many such days in the town's recent history. A fire broke out in Michael Bourke's spirit store, opposite McElligott's Hotel, and spread rapidly to nearby houses. *Slater's Commercial Directory* of 1846 listed a public house and hardware store owned by Michael Bourke, and the Royal Hotel owned by Ellen McElligott, both in Church Lane. Most people were at Mass when the fire broke out at midday, and no lives were lost.

The blaze quickly spread, destroying the nearby premises of Nagle and O'Connor. Other houses or businesses destroyed were owned by families named Stack, Clifford and Stokes. One report stated that twenty-seven houses were ultimately destroyed by the fire and many people were made homeless; six of the houses were slated but the rest were thatched.[38] Another account stated that forty houses were destroyed.[39]

The first people to arrive at the scene quickly realised that houses should be pulled down to prevent the fire from spreading. The police, under Sub-Inspector Henry Smith, began to do this, at great risk to themselves. An eyewitness wrote that he was astonished to see fire breaking out in another street, separated from the original fire by several substantial three-storey houses. Once again, the role of leadership fell to two men who had displayed great commitment and civic spirit during the darkest days of the town: Fr Darby Mahony and James Murray Home. They took charge and showed their mettle in a crisis. An eyewitness described the scene:

> My attention was immediately after called to the lane leading from the town

to the convent and the workhouse, where the greater portion of the poorer inhabitants reside, whose houses are all thatched and the thatch being very dry, having had no rain for several weeks, the sparks were easily conveyed to those houses from Scanlons, the wind being in that direction at the time. It was generally supposed that nothing could save this part of the town from total ruin and only for the exertions of Rev. J. Mahony, P.P. and James M. Home Esq. who after receiving a great deal of opposition, at length succeeded in getting some of the owners to pull down their houses and thus save the rest, not a single house would now remain.[40]

The witness deplored the fact that the 'country people' did not come to the assistance of the townspeople and were more interested in looting. Dozens of wine and brandy bottles were found on the street with their necks broken, and when the widow Clifford moved her property out to the street, it was stolen. The witness, however, praised the police and those who helped to contain the fire, and reported that Lord Listowel was expected to come to the aid of those who had lost property.[41]

Landlords and Tenants
Sir John Benn-Walsh was a landlord who took a keen interest in the management of his estates around Listowel and regularly visited in person. In October 1852 he remarked on the general improvement in evidence around the countryside:

> It seems universally admitted that the country has greatly improved; prices are really good for stock, butter, pigs and sheep and while in the old days of outdoor relief there were 30,000 souls on the lists out of a population of 70,000, there are now not more than 1,500 and these principally children.[42]

The annual exhibition of the North Kerry Farming Society was held again in Ballinruddery. The quality of the stock was praised – bulls 'that would have done credit to any exhibition', Leicester sheep, superior pigs and handsome

Kerry cows. The *Chronicle* looked forward to a wider participation by farmers, now that 'they have to a great extent been scourged by the potato epidemic out of many of their ancient habits of husbandry'.[43] Among the notables at the dinner that evening were Lord Listowel, William Talbot Crosbie, St John Blacker, Sir John Benn-Walsh and Lieutenant Colonel Kitchener. Also present were seven farmers who were tenants of John Leahy from Clanmaurice, a sign that the society was becoming more inclusive. The main award went to Crosbie and in his speech he specifically encouraged the wider participation of tenant farmers. A representative of Clanmaurice farmers, Timothy Sheahan, was optimistic that their numbers would increase. Crosbie made these conciliatory remarks about the prospects for better relations between landlords and tenants:

> The predominant feeling in my mind at the present moment is that this assembling together of the several classes connected with the land and interested in the development of its resources affords such an opportunity for cultivating that great social and moral principle – a mutual cooperation in all things, in our relative positions, to advance each other's material interests and to sink all differences of opinion upon vexed questions in a sodality of cordial feeling. If by any mechanical or metaphysical process the minds and opinions of the present company could be analysed, you would find them on most subjects as far as north from south or east from west. But notwithstanding, we can all here assemble on a middle ground and bear testimony to the advantages that the principle of cooperation creates in giving an impulse to the social conditions of the country, as regards its agricultural and other interests. In the words of a statesman of the present day – we have a ground on which, instead of contending those subjects on which we are most likely to differ, we can prize those great truths in which we all agree.[44]

Listowel Workhouse

Instead of horror stories, newspapers now regularly carried normal advertisements for employment in the workhouse, including, for example, for a master weaver; the salary was £12 a year with rations of two pounds of bread and one pint of new milk daily. The person appointed was 'to instruct the boys in weaving linen, cotton and other woollen stuffs with hand or fly shuttles and he must be able to make and keep in repair all reeds, gears and other loom fittings of every kind'.[45] Other vacancies arose for an apothecary, a master baker and a rate collector.[46] The union also invited tenders for the supply of the best unground yellow and white Indian corn, barley and Egyptian wheat, which was to be properly kiln-dried and perfectly clean and fit for grinding, as well as the best coarse yellow Indian corn meal, Egyptian wheat meal and Patna rice.[47] This all demonstrates that the workhouse was returning to pre-Famine conditions.

Races at Ballyeagh

In a sign that normal life really was returning, the annual races on the strand at Ballyeagh near Ballybunion were reported on as having 'a large attendance of the elite of north Kerry, including Tralee'.[48] A grand ball was held in Ballybunion in the evening; it was 'numerously and respectably attended' and lasted until 5.30 a.m. when 'all separated, highly delighted with the evening they had spent and only regretting all was for this year over'.[49] In what was essentially a sports report, the reason for the low attendance of the ordinary people at the races was explained in passing remarks which today appear very casual and insensitive:

> Two capacious stands were erected, one for the *beau monde* and the other for the *bourgeoisie*. The peasantry were, as compared with olden days, 'nowhere', to use a sporting phrase. Indeed there could be no stronger evidence of the inroads which emigration, the workhouse and death have made amongst the once stalwart tillers of the soil than the strand of Ballyeagh on last Tuesday and Wednesday, for there is no amusement in which our people have always taken a warmer interest than in horse-racing. Among 'the last of the Mohicans' however, there was no lack of enthusiasm and that essentially Celtic element called 'fun'.[50]

AFTERMATH

Decline in Population, 1841–51

The census of 1851 showed that the population of Ireland was 6,552,385 people, compared with 8,175,124 in the census of 1841. Allowing for an increase in population between 1841 and 1846, the total loss of population during the Famine years is estimated at 2.5 million. Ó Murchadha states that the number of people 'who died of starvation, disease, and exposure during the famine was 1.1 million or 1.5 million if account is taken of averted births'.[1] Approximately one million people emigrated.

A comparison between census statistics for 1841 and 1851 shows that Ballinclogher in Listowel Union, between Abbeydorney and Lixnaw, was the most severely affected district electoral division (DED) in the county of Kerry, losing 57.38 per cent of its population between 1841 and 1851.[2] Killury DED lost 50.58 per cent of its population. Four district electoral divisions in Tralee Union lost over half of their population between 1841 and 1851. They were: Kilgobbin (54.95 per cent), Cordal (52.54 per cent), Scartaglin (52.43 per cent) and Carker (50.35 per cent).[3] There could be several reasons for this extreme loss, but death and emigration were undoubtedly among the main causes.

In a brief analysis of the 1851 census, the *Post* recorded the decline in the population of Tralee Union since 1841; it fell by 19 per cent, from 71,626 to 58,184. The population of Tralee town, however, increased by 28 per cent, from 13,120 to 16,828. The *Post* attributed this increase to the number of paupers admitted to the auxiliary workhouses, at least half of whom, it claimed, came from outside Tralee. In summary, the *Post* claimed that the actual number lost by death and emigration in Tralee Union amounted to about 15,000 people, or 21 per cent of its 1841 population.[4]

Using the filter of townlands rather than DEDs, close examination of census records shows even more acute declines in population in places.[5]

What follows is a list of some townlands that lost over 80 per cent of their population between 1841 and 1851.

In Iraghticonnor barony, the population of the townland of Kingsland in Duagh fell from 41 to one, a decrease of 97.5 per cent; Rathroe in Lisselton fell from 74 to 9, a decrease of 87.8 per cent. Listowel townland (as distinct from the town of Listowel) fell from 332 to 14, a decline of 95.8 per cent.

In Clanmaurice barony, the population in Ballinclogher East in Kiltomy parish fell from 165 in 1841 to 20 in 1851, a decrease of 87.9 per cent. Another area which stands out is Monument townland in Kilcaragh parish in Lixnaw. In 1841 there were 152 people in twenty-five houses, whereas in 1851 there were only twenty-five people in three houses. This decline of 83.5 per cent over ten years reflected the large-scale evictions on the Lansdowne estate in September 1850, as discussed in Chapter 8. Sackville in Ardfert parish fell from 319 to 57, a decrease of 82.1 per cent; Dromlegagh Demesne in Duagh fell from 99 to 17, a decrease of 82.8 per cent; and Aulanebane in Ardrahan fell from 143 to 22, a decrease of 84.6 per cent.

In Trughnanacmy barony, the population in Cordal West in Ballincuslane parish fell from 512 to 97, a decrease of 81 per cent; the population in Moanmore, Castleisland, fell from 176 to 11, a decrease of 93.8 per cent. In Lisheenbaun, Dysart, the population fell from 131 to 18, a decline of 86.3 per cent. Kilderry South in Kilcolman parish saw a decrease from 214 to 31, a decline of 85.5 per cent. Near Tralee, Listellick South fell from 42 people to 7, a decline of 83.3 per cent.

Pauper Burial Places in Tralee

In the autumn of 1853 Thomas B. Hurly, chairman of Tralee Borough Commissioners, read a letter signed 'An Irishman', which had been published in the (London) *Evening Standard*. The letter criticised the state of the graveyard at Rathass, Tralee. Hurly's reply was published in the *Post*.[6] He disputed the claim that skulls and bones were scattered around the burial ground and that bodies were left 'in all stages of decay, visible to spectators and prey to rats and vermin'. He was particularly outraged at the suggestion by the 'Irishman' that 'the sanctity of the tomb is scarcely known here'. Hurly responded:

> Was ever such monstrous falsehood uttered? It is, Sir, a foul lie on the people of Tralee and of Kerry. Where is the land beneath the sun where the dead are more deeply mourned and respected or their memory more dearly and fondly cherished than in Ireland? Was this wandering Irishman at the pyramids of Egypt when the grave opened wide its jaws to swallow down the famishing and famished people of Ireland? … Is it then monuments and pyramids this writer wants over the graves of the poor famished people of our workhouses?[7]

Hurly stated that between September 1850 and March 1853, '1,876 poor creatures have been interred from the workhouse alone'. He continued:

> I was the guardian who, when the dogs, also famished, came to make their ravages among the dead and, when other food could not be found for them sought to eat up the bodies of the poor, had appointed a person to watch over their graves. Oh! it is heartrending to recall the remembrance. The poor sufferers died in hundreds. They were brought to, I hope in God, though a promiscuous, yet not a dishonoured grave. They died in poverty but I trust it was a death for all and each to obtain a heavenly eternity. Yet they were cared for.[8]

He wrote that a man was still being provided with a gun, powder and ball to watch every night over the graves at Rathass. 'He has shot some of those famishing dogs as they attempted to crimson their mouths with the gore of human beings.' The burial grounds of Rathass had no more room, Hurly wrote, and the board of guardians had rented an acre of ground as a burial ground for paupers alone.[9] This probably refers to the graveyard known today as God's Acre.

God's Acre
Advertisements began to appear from mid-1851 for tenders for a new burial

ground near the town; an acre of coarse land was required, two miles from the workhouse.[10] A site at Ballybeggan was acquired in due course, and tenders were invited for enclosing it with a five-and-a-half-foot wall.[11] An iron gate was required and invitations to tender for it appeared in the press in 1854.[12] This appears to mark the beginning of the use of this plot for burials. This graveyard, called God's Acre, at Ballybeggan is preserved today as a memorial to Tralee's Famine victims. As it does not appear to have been opened until 1853 at the earliest, it might more accurately be described as the workhouse graveyard or the paupers' graveyard. It was still in use in 1900 and, in this poignant account, a writer describes the usual form of burial in this 'indescribably lonely spot':

> The body in a pauper's coffin is brought to the pauper's grave on a donkey cart or some such humble vehicle. A couple of paupers with grave-digging implements are in attendance. The melancholy task is soon finished and – if they think of it – a hastily muttered prayer is offered by the amateur grave-diggers who then slouch away from the forbidding place where they have laid their wretched fellow mortal. No mark is left on the rude mound to show that the newly interred person ever bore a name, or whether he or she belonged to the great community of Christians. There is at the present time only one grave distinguished by a rough wooden cross, emblem of the mercy which shall not fail even those who have been outcasts from their fellow creatures. But for this cross a stranger would pass this 'God's Acre' many times and never suspect the purpose for which it is used.[13]

The writer believed that more respect was due to 'the friendless dead' and recommended that the guardians should arrange for a clergyman to be present at the burial. 'It is absolutely revolting to see creatures made to God's likeness put into the earth as if they were inferior animals, born without souls or without hope of immortality.'[14] Eleven years earlier the burial of paupers without religious rites was deplored by the chairman of the board of guardians, Mr Murphy, who said that the two chaplains, Protestant and

Catholic, received good salaries and should attend at burials as part of their duties.[15] Clearly their practice had not changed by 1900.

Today in Tralee, people honour the Famine dead by visiting God's Acre to remember and to pray. A plaque reads: 'In memory of the many hundreds of unknown dead who were buried here in God's Acre during the Famine years and after. Erected by Tralee Urban District Council. 19 April 1997.' There is currently no public access to the small graveyard at the rear of County Buildings, but it is hoped that access will be provided in the future.

Ballymullen Auxiliary Workhouse

Ballymullen workhouse was finally closed in the autumn of 1855 and its inmates transferred to the main workhouse; at that time there were 988 inmates altogether in Tralee.[16] At the same time the board decided that the capstan mill could be disposed of, as the board believed that 'there will never again be a sufficient number of able-bodied men and boys receiving relief in this workhouse for the working of said mill'.[17]

Soon after Ballymullen workhouse closed, a newspaper advertisement stated that Ballymullen Distillery was available for rent from John Frederick Eagar.[18] The complex of buildings included three large stores; one had five floors and was 120 feet long and 25 feet wide; another had four floors and was 98 feet long and 20 feet wide; the third was 134 feet long and 25 feet wide. Other buildings included a corn kiln, a spirit store, a distillery house, a dwelling house 'with every accommodation requisite for a gentleman's family', two other 'commodious residences', a stable and coach-house and two large 'well-enclosed' yards, one 84 feet by 73 feet and the other 140 feet by 70 feet.[19] There was no reference to the complex's use as a workhouse for approximately seven years. There is, however, an indication as to why the distillery had closed down and had become available to rent as a workhouse: the advertisement stated that 'previous to the Temperance Movement, there was manufactured here 70,000 gallons of whiskey annually'.[20]

At least one of the former workhouse buildings still stands today in Ballymullen as a ruin; nearby are some other large buildings which may also have been part of the workhouse compound. In March 1852 the *Examiner* reported that a Mr James O'Connell offered a plot of ground as a pauper burial ground near the Ballymullen workhouse at a rent of £2 a year and this was 'at once approved of by the board'.[21] Close to the ruined building in Ballymullen today is an enclosed area where at least one yew tree is growing. As yew trees are usually associated with graveyards, it is possible that the enclosed area is another pauper graveyard.

Signs of Hope

The social and psychological impact on communities of a dramatic decline of population and the effects of the trauma of having endured and witnessed appalling events can only be imagined. Yet in the early 1850s there were signs of hope for the future.

Sir John Benn-Walsh visited his lands in north Kerry in the autumn of 1853 and was pleased to observe signs of improvement all round. 'The tenants are all in good spirits,' he wrote in his journal, 'and considerable improvement is perceptible.' Butter, oats, pigs and cattle were fetching high prices and the potato crop was free of blight. 'It is to be hoped the period of distress has passed away,' he wrote. He noted that there were 905 inmates in Listowel workhouse, about 700 of them children; a year earlier there had been 1,500 inmates. In Tralee workhouse, 'the matron … lamented over the emptiness of the house', with only 1,600 inmates; a year earlier there had been 2,700.[22]

The Cork Examiner of December 1856 cited some of the most obvious improvements in the country, which included a decrease in the number of paupers, more adequate wages and the introduction of machinery on farms:

> To those who can carry their recollections back a space of ten years, and think of the various forms of calamity and of misery through which at the commencement of that period she passed, it must appear that no country has ever, within the same period, made the same progress … It must be evident that the time would not be far distant when Ireland might take a place among the happiest and most prosperous nations of Europe.[23]

THE GREAT FAMINE

The sale of the large Locke estate in Kerry under the auspices of the Encumbered Estates Act showed how much had changed, according to *The Cork Examiner*, because it was expected to sell for about £40,000 but actually realised nearly £70,000. Not only that, but every penny of the purchase price was paid by residents of Kerry, some of them working farmers.[24] There appears to have been plenty of money in circulation, and James Murray Home of Listowel bemoaned the fact that farmers in Kerry had amassed £250,000, held in bank accounts, which he believed would have been better spent on more productive purposes, such as the extension of the railway from Tralee to Tarbert.[25]

The *Chronicle* believed that farming techniques had developed dramatically in the years since 1833, when proprietors had little interest in improving systems of tillage, green cropping, drainage, or breeds of cattle and sheep. In 1853 it surveyed the north of the county and saw:

> Sandes, Blacker, Hickie, Hewson, Elliott, all landed proprietors, tillers of the soil, and all showing a good example to their tenantry and neighbours. From thence we come along to Ardfert, Churchill, Fenit, back to Oakpark, Ballybeggan and Chutehall, the proprietors of which places have put their hand to the plough and we are sure they will not turn back.[26]

In 1856 *The Cork Examiner* noted that the social changes could be clearly seen on Sundays:

> If you wish to judge of the condition of the peasantry, go to the parish chapel on Sunday and see the congregation issuing from the devotions. Poor Paddy and his inalienable rags have given place to a sturdy well-fed, well-clad peasant; and though poverty is not yet banished, and misery, aye, abject misery still exists, yet as a whole it is in far smaller proportions than even in the years which preceded the famine. Contrast the appearance of the girls, smart, tidy, and smiling brightly in their Irish beauty, with the miserable creatures who seven or eight years ago might have been seen creeping out of the same place

of worship; and if you be an Irishman your heart will swell with pride and thankfulness looking on those future mothers of your race.[27]

In his Lenten pastoral of 1858 Bishop David Moriarty reminded people of how their lives had changed in the decade since the Famine: 'It cannot have passed from your memory how a few years ago, thousands amongst you had not what to eat [*sic*]. You remember how the old and the young melted away with hunger from off the face of the earth. God has sheathed his sword of vengeance and He no longer afflicts His people as before.'[28]

The twentieth anniversary of the Famine was obliquely adverted to by one local poet named Thomas de Cantillon Church. He regularly contributed poems and articles to the *Chronicle* and in 1867 he was particularly incensed by the actions of William Talbot Crosbie, who planned 'improvements' to his estate in Ardfert, which involved moving tenants from their holdings. In a long poem denouncing the landlord's evictions of families in the Commons area of Ardfert, de Cantillon gave this idealised picture of the lively village of his youth, and contrasted it with the depopulated village of 1867:

Where are all thy cottage homesteads that I've seen some years ago,
Sending forth their curling smoke wreaths in the early morning's glow?
Where the troops of sun-browned children whom I always loved to meet,
Where their peals of pleasant laughter soft resounded through the street?

Where are all thy bright-eyed daughters, modest-faced and pure and fair
Who lang syne were wont to wander up thy streets and down thy square?
All those beauteous splendid maidens that lived here in days of old,
Pleasant tongued and gay and blithesome, with blue orbs and locks of gold?

Where are all thy scions of manhood, strong of hand and bright of brain,
Whom I've seen in glowing autumn, mowing down the golden grain?
All those stalwart glorious fellows, light of foot at ball and goal,
Wielders of the stave and hurley, true of speech and brave of soul?

> *Ask the plague ship's floating prison, ask the broad Atlantic's wave,*
> *Ask the city and the prairie, ask the foreign nameless grave;*
> *Ask the pest house and the vile slum, ask them all, oh poet, and see*
> *The fate of all my gallant sons, and my daughters' purity.*[29]

I conclude by identifying with the editors of the *Atlas of the Great Irish Famine*, who wrote as follows on the completion of their research on the Famine: 'The dominant feeling is one of sadness – sadness for all that horror and all that suffering and sadness about the failures at all levels to stop that suffering.'[30] Ciarán Ó Murchadha also eloquently expressed my own sentiments about the events of the years 1845–52 when he wrote: 'Almost impossible to comprehend in its totality, even at the remove of more than a century and a half, the evidence left by this calamitous period, in its vastness and in its minute detail alike, remains deeply, powerfully shocking.'[31]

I am also conscious that for all the detailed accounts recorded in the pages of the press, many untold tragedies were played out on the lonely hillsides and boreens of Kerry. These were never recorded and will never be fully known. When writing a general history of Ballyheigue parish in 1994 I found a folklore memory recorded as follows: 'An old woman died in the bad times and the pigs ate her, God bless us and save us.'[32] I chose to omit this from the published book because it was so abhorrent, because it seemed to reflect badly on the community and because I reasoned that it was most likely an exaggeration. I now realise that such abominations did occur and that my decision was part of a characteristic blocking-out of the most shocking and disturbing Famine atrocities. This found expression in the 'dispassionate, sanitised approach' which Cormac Ó Gráda described as 'dominant in Irish historical scholarship' when he wrote in the 1980s, an approach which recoiled from detailing the full horrors which occurred in the Famine years.[33]

Human beings are not able to cope with too much reality. The question inevitably arises: why or how did communities forget or choose to obliterate the memory of these horrors? Why were the unspeakable incidents, the traumatic experiences, not remembered and passed down to future generations? Perhaps it was because the memory had to be suppressed in order for communities to survive and recover. 'Whereof one cannot speak, thereof one must be silent', in the words of the philosopher Ludwig Wittgenstein.

Another folk memory from Ballyheigue was related to me recently, concerning a man who transported bodies of Famine victims by horse-drawn cart for burial. After disposal of the bodies, he would take the cart to the shore and immerse it in the sea to let the waves cleanse it.[34] This happened on the same timeless shore where several women gathering seaweed had been drowned in 1847 and from which the Famine ships sailing out of Blennerville could be seen against the backdrop of majestic mountains across Tralee Bay, beginning their long voyage to Grosse Isle and other places.

A cleansing, purifying and renewing process has taken place in north Kerry over the decades since the Famine, and the memory of those who died has faded. The memory of those who worked strenuously on behalf of the ravaged people has also faded, although there are some half-hidden reminders. For example, in St Mary's Church in Listowel there is a stained-glass window in memory of Fr Darby Mahony, which few people ever see, as it is in the sanctuary area to the right of the altar. The window was installed in 1866 by Canon Michael McDonnell as a tribute to his predecessor and can be called an early Famine memorial, dating from its twentieth anniversary.[35] One of the two panels of the window shows Fr Mahony bringing Communion to a sick man, depicted as a biblical figure with beard and long hair and covered only in a loincloth. The youthful-looking priest wears liturgical vestments and has a halo. In contrast with his closeness to the sick man, three figures behind him are shrinking away, holding their garments to their mouths as if to protect themselves from infection. In the background are church buildings. At the base of the panel, and so in the forefront, is an emaciated child with an exposed ribcage lying on a bed of grass bordered with shamrock, or perhaps in a roadside grave. The image of the lonely, dead child is a haunting symbol of all who perished in the Famine, particularly the children, such as Michael and James Mitchell in December 1846, Daniel Griffin in March 1847 and the nameless waifs of the workhouses throughout those Famine years. The dead are also remembered in Listowel in the tranquil *Teampaillín Bán* where a plaque reads: '*Teampaillín Bán* (The Little White Churchyard) where very many nameless victims of the Irish Famine 1845–47 lie buried. Also buried here are others who died in the nearby workhouse built 1840. *Saibhreas na bhflaitheas dóibh.*'

Most of the research for this book was done during 2015–16 when there were daily reminders of the parallels between the horrors of the Famine years in Ireland and the desperate plight of migrants seeking refuge in Europe. One of the most heart-breaking images of 2015 was of the body of the Syrian boy Aylan Kurdi on a Turkish beach: a stark, shocking photograph which stirred the conscience and compassion of the world. The similarity with the image of the nameless child in the Listowel church window is chilling and disturbing.

Another haunting image is evoked in seven words in Irish on the Famine memorial beside the mass grave in Galey cemetery, which is between Listowel and Lisselton: *A mbás siúd a thug beatha dúinn*: It was their death which gave us life. These words carry a profound message for those of us who live in the same towns, villages and townlands, who travel the same roads, who farm the same land, who sport on the same strands, who shop and dine and conduct business on the same streets and even in the same buildings, who worship in the same locations if not the same churches, whose children attend national schools of the same names as in 1847, who bury our dead in the same cemeteries, whose county affairs are administered from the building which was the Tralee workhouse, who share the fruits of the steady progress and prosperity which have characterised the north Kerry area since the 1850s.

Notwithstanding the long silence that surrounded the Great Famine, its echoes are all around us. All those traumatic events and distant lives must never be forgotten. The Famine dead are worthy of more than the old epitaph, *pulvis, cinis et nihil*: dust, ashes and nothing. The final words on the Galey memorial are more fitting: *Ná déanaimís dearmad orthu*: Let us not forget them.

NOTE ON MANUSCRIPT SOURCES

Tralee Board of Guardian Minute Books, 1847

The minute books of the Tralee board of guardians covering the years from 1840 to 1845 and from 1853 onwards are available in Kerry County Archives in Tralee. The archives also hold the rough minute books of Tralee board of guardians for the period 1 April 1845 to 27 October 1846. The next book of rough minutes is from May 1851 to December 1851.[1]

There are no Tralee board of guardian records in Kerry County Archives for the crucial year of 1847. However, there are some records for 1847 in two other repositories: the National Library of Ireland and Trinity College Library. The National Library holds a bound volume of five separate 'Kopirite' duplicate books of a hundred pages each: Ms 7860. This manuscript is a carbon copy of a transcription of the minute book made in the 1950s. Ms 7860 begins with minutes of the board of guardians' meeting of 26 October 1846 and ends on page 51 of the fifth book with the minutes of 4 January 1848. The remaining pages contain extraneous material relating to 'Percy's Trust', 'Leigh's Trust' and financial details relating to the accounts of William M. Hickson. This material dates from a later period and there is no explanation of its significance or of the reason for its inclusion with the minutes.[2]

The provenance of the document in the National Library is unusual. The typed letter below, dated 28 November 1955, was received by the library from Mr Michael Glazier of the Kerry Bookshop in Tralee:

Dear Sirs

Some months ago the Minute Book of the board of guardians of Tralee Workhouse was discovered. It covers in detail the famine period in Tralee, giving full details of admissions, rejections and expulsions from the

Workhouse. It also gave details of the nursing conditions, punishments, diets, purchases etc. of the institution.

The original manuscript was in a very bad condition, and it is unlikely that the present owner will preserve it for long. Consequently we got his permission to make a copy and a duplicate copy of it. Part of the Ms. was illegible so we decided to have it carefully copied by hand. It took six weeks to complete and correct (making almost 500 quarto pages, with good margins).

The document is, perhaps, the most authorative [sic] source of conditions in Kerry in that period. The duplicate copy is for sale. If interested kindly let us know.

Yours faithfully
Mr M. Glazier

The offer was accepted by the National Library and Michael Glazier received £10 for the item. He wrote again on 9 January 1956: 'We enclose duplicate copy of minute book of Tralee Workhouse. We trust that you will be satisfied with same. We guarantee that the work is an exact copy. It had to be copied by hand for reasons already explained.'[3] The identity of the owner of the original of the minute book was not given. Michael Glazier was the editor of a journal entitled *The Kerry Annual*, of which at least one issue was published, in 1953. He emigrated to the United States and became a successful publisher of religious and historical books; he now lives in Florida. It is thanks to Michael Glazier's foresight that a copy of the minutes of Tralee board of guardians has survived in the archives.

Subsequent to that discovery, I learned from Shane Lehane's book *The Great Famine in Kerry* that the National Library of Ireland also holds a microfilm copy of the minute book of Tralee board of guardians (NLI POS 5648) covering the same period as Ms 7860. This is a microfilm of the original of the Glazier transcript. It is inaccurately catalogued as the 'Minute Book of Dingle Board of Guardians' and the original has been defaced on many pages by children's writing. A short note at the beginning of the microfilm states: 'Original in the possession of Dr Thomas Murphy, Dean of Medicine, University College Dublin (UCD). June 1964.' Dr Murphy was the head of the faculty of medicine of UCD at the time when the microfilm was made, and later president of UCD. He died in June 1997. Inquiries to the UCD Archives have established that the original manuscript is not among his papers there, so its present location is not known.

The Manuscripts Library of Trinity College, Dublin (TCD) holds the rough minute book of Tralee board of guardians for approximately the same period, TCD Ms 10499.[4] This was acquired at an auction held in Dublin by Mealys of Castlecomer in 1990. The first entry in this manuscript is dated 3 November 1846 and the final entry is a brief report of an aborted meeting of the board on 7 January 1848. The Trinity manuscript is an original document and so has the actual signatures of some of the board members. The differences in content between the National Library transcript and the Trinity College manuscript arise at the beginning and end of the documents, with other minor differences elsewhere. It is clear that the National Library manuscript was not transcribed from the Trinity College manuscript. Both of these manuscripts and the microfilm have been consulted for this book. Much of the information in the minutes concerns routine issues of correspondence, accounts and supplies to the workhouse, too detailed for inclusion here.

Famine Journal of Henry Nicholas Greenwell (1826–91)

Having come across the name of Lieutenant Henry Nicholas Greenwell in newspaper records and government reports of the period 1846–7 in Kerry, I searched online for further information on him. I discovered that his later life was spent in Hawaii, where he set up an extremely successful business, and where his name is remembered today as the founder of an extensive ranching empire which later developed into large-scale production of Kona coffee, exporting to Europe and the Americas. Kona coffee is one of the most expensive in the world and the name is exclusive to the Kona region in the western part of the island of Hawaii. The coffee won an award at the World's Fair in Vienna in 1873 and soon became an internationally famous brand. Greenwell Farms today comprises 150 acres of land. One of the visitor attractions of Kona is the Greenwell Store Museum at Kalukalu, a re-creation of the store established by H. N. Greenwell. Some of the ceiling boards are original and still have the initials HNG painted in black on them. After his death in 1891, his widow, Elizabeth, and their descendants continued to run the business.[5]

In late 2014 I made contact by email with Kona Historical Society to share the information I had found and to ask if the society might have any information on Greenwell's time in Kerry. I received a reply from Maile Melrose, great-granddaughter of H. N. Greenwell. Maile lives in Hawaii and she informed me that her ancestor's journal, written in Kerry in the winter of 1846–7, was extant and was held in the archives of Kona Historical Society. Maile and her sister, Amanda Barnes, who lives in England, had been collaborating on a transcription of the diary for some years. The journal covers the first six months of Greenwell's time in Kerry, from 18 September 1846 to mid-March 1847. His journal for the remaining six months has not been found.

On learning of my interest in the journal, Maile generously shared some extracts by email. Then, in February 2015, she and Amanda decided to travel to Ireland to walk in the footsteps of their great-grandfather and visit some of the places mentioned in his journal. They presented a digital copy of the journal of H. N. Greenwell to the archives of Kerry County Library in Tralee, where it is now available for consultation.

I am grateful to Kona Historical Society for permission to reproduce parts of the journal of H. N. Greenwell here, and especially grateful to Maile and Amanda for allowing me to avail of their transcription. Greenwell's handwriting is difficult to decipher, especially without prior knowledge of the family names and placenames of Co. Kerry. It is a credit to their commitment that they produced a full transcription of the journal and I was pleased to help identify some of the names in it. The bound journal is now in the archives of Kona Historical Society, located in the Jean Greenwell Archives and Library in the basement of Greenwell Store, where it can be consulted by appointment. The title page has this inscription: 'Presented to the Kona Historical Society on the occasion of the Greenwell Family Re-union, 1993, in honor of Marguerite (Bryant) and James Vanderbilt. Brysson Greenwell.' Brysson is a great-grandson of H. N. Greenwell.

ENDNOTES

ACKNOWLEDGEMENTS

1   Ó Murchadha, Ciarán, *The Great Famine: Ireland's Agony 1845–1852* (Continuum, London, 2011), p. 78.

INTRODUCTION

1   *The Times*, 4 October 1848.
2   'All Things Bright and Beautiful' by Cecil Frances Alexander, first published in 1848.
3   Ó Murchadha (2011), p. 10.
4   *Slater's Commercial Directory of Ireland 1846* can be viewed at www.failteromhat.com/slaterm.htm.
5   Baronies were another administrative division within counties. Tralee and its hinterland formed the barony of Trughnanacmy. Listowel Poor Law Union comprised the baronies of Clanmaurice and Iraghticonnor.
6   Legg, Marie-Louise, *Newspapers and Nationalism: The Irish Provincial Press, 1850–1892* (Four Courts Press, Dublin, 1999), appendix. Newspapers submitted self-descriptions to the National Press Directory and the quotation is from that source.
7   *Ibid*.
8   *Kerry Examiner* (hereafter *KEx*), 7 June 1850.
9   Michael Foley, *Death in Every Paragraph: Journalism and the Great Irish Famine* (Quinnipiac University Press, Quinnipiac, 2015), p. 7.
10 *Ibid*., p. 22.
11 *Ibid*., p. 39.
12 Cited in Mac Suibhne, Breandán and Dickson, David (eds), *The Outer Edge of Ulster: A Memoir of Social Life in Nineteenth-Century Donegal* (Lilliput Press, Dublin, 2000), p. 223.
13 Kinealy, Christine, *This Great Calamity: The Irish Famine 1845–52* (Gill and Macmillan, Dublin, 1994), p. 359.
14 Cited in Edwards, Robert Dudley and Williams, T. Desmond (eds), *The Great Famine* (Lilliput Press, Dublin, 1994), p. 315.
15 *The Kerry Evening Post* (hereafter *KEP*), 23 December 1846.
16 Ó Gráda, Cormac, *The Great Irish Famine* (Gill and Macmillan, Dublin, 1989), p. 41.

1   'A DARK AND WITHERED APPEARANCE': 1845

1   *KEP*, 23 August 1845.
2   Quoted in *KEx*, 26 August 1845.
3   *KEP*, 18 October 1845.

ENDNOTES

4 *KEx*, 24 October 1845.
5 National Archives of Ireland (hereafter NAI), Relief Commission Papers, RLFC/2/Z14284.
6 *Ibid.*
7 *KEx*, 28 October 1845.
8 *KEx*, 4 November 1845.
9 *Ibid.*
10 *KEx*, 14 November 1845.
11 Kinealy (1994), pp. 41–3. The early government responses are outlined here, when it was dealing with the 'chequered' nature of the crop failure.
12 NAI, Relief Commission Papers, RLFC/3/1/32.
13 *KEx*, 21 November 1845.
14 *KEP*, 5 November 1845.
15 *KEP*, 22 November 1845.
16 *KEx*, 9 December 1845. See Kieran Foley's essay, 'Killarney's Famine Story', in Larner, J. (ed.), *Killarney History and Heritage* (Collins Press, Cork, 2005), pp. 156–66, for a detailed study of the actions taken in Killarney.
17 NAI, Relief Commission Papers, 215700. Cited in full in Kissane, N., *The Irish Famine: A Documentary History* (Syracuse University Press and National Library of Ireland, Dublin, 1995), p. 30.
18 *Ibid.*

2 'SOFT WORDS NO MORE': JANUARY–JUNE 1846

1 *The Tralee Chronicle* (hereafter *TC*), 10 January 1846.
2 *Ibid.* The Corn Laws imposed tariffs on imported corn and kept prices high for the benefit of producers. Prime Minister Robert Peel opposed the Corn Laws and succeeded in having them repealed in June 1846, just before his resignation as prime minister.
3 *TC*, 24 January 1846.
4 *Ibid.*
5 Score ground was a small plot of land rented by a labourer to grow potatoes.
6 *TC*, 24 January 1846, quoting *KEP*.
7 *TC*, 24 January 1846.
8 *Ibid.*
9 *TC*, 28 February 1846.
10 *TC*, 7 February 1846.
11 *Ibid.*
12 *Ibid.*
13 *Ibid.*
14 *Ibid.* In the 1840s Ireland exported huge quantities of grain to Britain, where it was food for two million people. Ireland was the largest supplier of corn to Britain and it was a lucrative trade for Irish farmers and merchants. See Kinealy (1994), p. 4.
15 *TC*, 7 February 1846.
16 *Ibid.*

17 *Ibid.*
18 *Ibid.*
19 *Ibid.*
20 *KEP*, 7 February 1846.
21 Parliamentary Papers, National Library of Ireland (hereafter NLI): *Correspondence Explanatory of the Measures Adopted by Her Majesty's Government for the Relief of Distress Arising from the Failure of the Potato Crop in Ireland* (HMSO, London, 1846), p. 273.
22 See Kinealy (1994), pp. 54–60, for more information on the administration of public works.
23 *KEx*, 20 March 1846.
24 *TC*, 7 March 1846.
25 *TC*, 28 March 1846.
26 *KEP*, 18 April 1846.
27 *TC*, 30 May 1846.
28 *Ibid.*
29 *TC*, 6 June 1846.
30 *The Cork Examiner* (hereafter *CEx*), 11 May 1846.
31 *CEx*, 27 July 1846.
32 *Ibid.*
33 NAI, RLFC/3/1/1718, 22 April 1846.
34 *CEx*, 27 April 1846.
35 *TC*, 25 April 1846.
36 *CEx*, 11 May 1846.
37 O'Connor, J., *Workhouses of Ireland* (Anvil Books, Dublin, 1995), p. 238. The building became a hospital in the twentieth century and is now the Head Office of Kerry County Council.
38 *TC*, 28 February 1846, quoting *KEP*.
39 *KEP*, 1 April 1846.
40 Tralee board of guardians rough minute book, Kerry County Archives (hereafter KCA), BG/154/AA/1, 25 August 1846.
41 *TC*, 2 May 1846.
42 KCA, BG/154/AA/1, 16 June 1846. Also in *TC*, 20 June 1846.
43 KCA, BG/154/AA/1, 19 May 1846.
44 *TC*, 23 May 1846.
45 *TC*, 20 June 1846.
46 *TC*, 1 March 1845.
47 *KEx*, 24 April 1846.
48 *KEx*, 29 May 1846.
49 *TC*, 21 February 1846.
50 *Ibid.*
51 *TC*, 4 April 1846.
52 *Ibid.*
53 *KEP*, 29 April 1846.
54 *Ibid.*

55 *TC*, 2 May 1846, quoting *KEx*.
56 *Ibid*.
57 *TC*, 16 May 1846.
58 *Ibid*.
59 NAI, RLFC/3/1/3914.
60 *Ibid*.
61 Pierse, John, *Teampall Bán: Aspects of the Famine in North Kerry 1845–1852* (Listowel Tidy Towns Committee, Listowel, 2014), pp. 164–9 has more detail on this. See also O'Mahony, Maurice, 'Peirce Mahony, Landlord' in *Ballydonoghue Magazine* (1990), pp. 20–1.
62 Somerville, Alexander, *Letters from Ireland during the Famine of 1847*, edited by K. D. M. Snell (Irish Academic Press, Dublin, 1994), pp. 159–60.
63 *Ibid*.
64 *TC*, 7 March 1846.
65 NAI, RLFC/3/1823.
66 NAI, RLFC/3/1/3422.
67 *KEx*, 24 April 1846.
68 NAI, RLFC/3/1/4686, 24 July 1846. Brosna, Co. Kerry, is very close to Abbeyfeale, Co. Limerick, and had close links with Abbeyfeale Church of Ireland parish. Rev. Edward Norman was very active in establishing a Protestant community in Brosna.
69 *KEP*, 11 July 1846.
70 *KEP*, 8 April 1846.
71 *Ibid*.
72 NAI, RLFC/3/1/1088. See also Ó Conchubhair, Pádraig, *Thá Sinn Ocrach: Ballylongford and the Great Famine* (Ballylongford, 1997), p. 10.
73 *TC*, 11 April 1846.
74 *Ibid*.
75 *TC*, 25 April 1846.
76 *KEP*, 22 April 1846.
77 Ó Conchubhair (1997), pp. 8–9.
78 *KEP*, 19 September 1846.
79 NAI, RLFC/3/1/1709.
80 NAI, RLFC/3/1/368.
81 *Ibid*.
82 *TC*, 2 May 1846.
83 *Ibid*. The chair remains in Tarbert House to this day, with a silver plaque that reads: 'Presented to Robert Leslie Esq. of Tarbert House on attaining his majority, by his tenantry as a token of their esteem. April 30th 1846.'
84 *Ibid*.
85 *Ibid*.
86 *KEx*, 6 January 1846.
87 *Ibid*.
88 *Ibid*.
89 *KEP*, 7 January 1846.
90 NAI, RLFC/3/1/437.

91 NAI, RLFC/3/1/357.
92 NAI, RLFC/2/Z2808.
93 *Ibid.*
94 *KEx*, 31 March 1846. 'Slouke' here refers to sliuchán, or sleabhac, an edible seaweed. It is known as sloke or laver in English.
95 *TC*, 28 March 1846.
96 *KEx*, 31 March 1846.
97 *TC*, 11 April 1846.
98 *KEx*, 17 April 1846.
99 His twenty-six-page manuscript of 17 April, addressed to Mr E. B. Twistleton, Poor Law Commissioner, is held in the National Archives: NAI, RLFC/3/1694. The report of John Ball is published in full in Pierse (2014), pp. 173–83. All quotes in this section, unless otherwise indicated, are taken from Ball's report.
100 *KEP*, 2 May 1846.
101 *KEx*, 10 April 1846.
102 *KEP*, 14 April 1846.
103 *KEP*, 23 May 1846.
104 *CEx*, 15 May 1846, quoting *KEP*.
105 Kinealy (1994), p. 51.
106 *KEx*, 24 April 1846.
107 *KEx*, 9 June 1846.
108 *KEx*, 12 June 1846.
109 Ó Murchadha (2011), p. 46.
110 Kinealy (1994), p. 51.

3 'ON THE VERY VERGE OF FAMINE': JULY–DECEMBER 1846

1 *KEx*, 21 July 1846.
2 *KEx*, 24 August 1846.
3 *TC*, 29 August 1846.
4 *KEP*, 11 July 1846.
5 *Ibid.*
6 *Ibid. KEx*, 10 July 1846, described the incident as a strike.
7 *TC*, 31 July 1846.
8 *Ibid.*
9 *KEP*, 25 July 1846. This road is today's Basin Road.
10 *KEx*, 4 August 1846.
11 Events in Killarney and Listowel were reported in *TC*, 8 August 1846, and The Spa regatta was reported in *TC*, 29 August 1846.
12 *KEP*, 19 August 1846.
13 *TC*, 19 September 1846.
14 *Ibid.*
15 Woodham-Smith, Cecil, *The Great Hunger: Ireland 1845–49* (Penguin Books, London, 1991), p. 137.
16 *KEx*, 15 September 1846.

17 *Ibid.*
18 *Ibid.*
19 Kinealy (1994), p. 82.
20 See *Ibid.*, pp. 82–9, for a full treatment of these administrative arrangements.
21 *KEP*, 10 October 1846.
22 *KEx*, 20 October 1846.
23 *TC*, 3 October 1846.
24 *TC*, 10 October 1846.
25 *TC*, 31 October 1846.
26 *KEx*, 25 December 1846.
27 *TC*, 28 November 1846.
28 Non-payment was reported in *KEx*, 3 November, and the dismissals in *TC*, 5 December 1846.
29 *KEP*, 5 December 1846.
30 *KEP*, 28 October 1846.
31 *KEP*, 31 October 1846.
32 *CEx*, 23 November 1846, quoting *KEP*.
33 *Ibid.*
34 *KEP*, 31 October 1846.
35 *TC*, 31 October 1846.
36 *KEP*, 14 October 1846.
37 *TC*, 28 November 1846.
38 *The Tablet*, 9 January 1847.
39 *Ibid.*
40 *KEx*, 1 January 1847.
41 *KEP*, 23 December 1846.
42 *TC*, 5 December 1846.
43 *KEP*, 2 January 1847.
44 *TC*, 5 December 1846.
45 *CEx*, 2 December 1846. In general, horses were not to be used in public works, so as not to reduce the number of positions available for labourers.
46 *KEx*, 25 September 1846.
47 *Ibid.*
48 *TC*, 10 October 1846.
49 *KEx*, 25 December 1846.
50 *KEP*, 7 October 1846.
51 NLI, Ms 7860, 26 October 1846. See Note on Manuscript Sources, pp. 335–7.
52 *TC*, 7 November 1846.
53 *Ibid.*
54 NLI, Ms 7860, 10 November 1846.
55 *TC*, 28 November 1846.
56 *Ibid.*
57 *TC*, 8 December 1846.
58 NLI, Ms 7860, 8 December 1846.

59 *Ibid.*, 5 January 1847.
60 *CEx*, 13 November 1846.
61 *KEx*, 25 December 1846.
62 NAI, RLFC/3/2/12/26.
63 *KEx*, 1 September 1846.
64 *Ibid.*
65 *KEP*, 9 September 1846.
66 *TC*, 28 November 1846, quoting *KEx*.
67 *TC*, 1 December 1846.
68 O'Donnell, P. D., *The Irish Faction Fighters of the 19th Century* (Anvil Books, Dublin, 1975), p. 150, citing the *Limerick Herald*, 9 July 1834.
69 Gaughan, J. A., *Listowel and Its Vicinity* (Mercier Press, Cork, 1973), p. 148.
70 *TC*, 26 September 1846.
71 *Ibid.*
72 *KEP*, 15 August 1846.
73 Woodham-Smith (1991), p. 127.
74 NLI, PD, EPH, B18.
75 *KEP*, 30 December 1846.
76 *Ibid.*
77 *Ibid.*
78 *The Times*, 3 August 1846.
79 *KEP*, 23 December 1846. The O'Brien mentioned was William Smith O'Brien, nationalist leader.
80 *KEP*, 7 October 1846. Further information on the *Madagascar* can be found in Lynch, P. J., *Tarbert: An Unfinished Biography* (self-published, Shanagolden, 2008). It includes selections from letters written by the ship's surgeon, Dr Thomas Graham, describing some of his experiences while in Tarbert. He ministered to the local people when asked to and vividly described the hardships they endured.
81 *TC*, 10 October 1846.
82 NAI, RLFC/3/2/12/28.
83 *Ibid.*
84 Ó Murchadha (2011), pp. 62–4.
85 *KEx*, 1 December 1846.
86 *Ibid.*
87 *TC*, 28 November 1846.
88 *Ibid.*
89 *KEP*, 2 December 1846.
90 *TC*, 5 December 1846.
91 Journal of Lieutenant H. N. Greenwell, 14 December 1846, pp. 100–1. The original of this manuscript is held in Kona Historical Society Archives, Hawaii. A digital copy of the journal is now in Kerry County Archives, Tralee. For substantial extracts from Greenwell's journal, see MacMahon, B., 'The Famine Journal of Lt H. N. Greenwell, 1846–7', in *Journal of the Kerry Archaeological and Historical Society* (hereafter *JKAHS*), Series 2, Vol. 13 (2015), pp. 5–50. See also *History Ireland*, Vol. 24, No. 4 (July-August 2016) for a shorter version.

92 See O'Neill, Thomas P., 'The organisation and administration of relief, 1845–52', in Edwards and Williams (1994), p. 226.
93 Journal of Lieutenant H. N. Greenwell, p. 55.
94 *TC*, 28 November 1846.
95 *KEP*, 28 November 1846.
96 *TC*, 28 November 1846.
97 Quoted in *KEP*, 28 November 1846.
98 *TC*, 28 November 1846.
99 *Ibid.*
100 *KEP*, 28 November 1846.
101 *TC*, 28 November 1846.
102 *KEP*, 28 November 1846.
103 *TC*, 30 May 1846.
104 *KEx*, 15 September 1846.
105 *CEx*, 9 November 1846.
106 *TC*, 5 December 1846.
107 *TC*, 17 October 1846.
108 NAI, RLFC/3/2/12/1–7.
109 *TC*, 21 November 1846.
110 *Ibid.*
111 *Ibid.*
112 *KEx*, 20 November 1846.
113 *Ibid.*
114 *KEP*, 7 November 1846.
115 *KEP*, 2 December 1846.
116 *KEP*, 16 December 1846. The claim that Indian meal was rotting on board the *Madagascar* was refuted by Captain Burney when he invited local officials to inspect storage arrangements. See Lynch (2008), p. 37. The term 'Whig' referred to the Liberal Party, which was in government and which the *Post* opposed, favouring instead the Tory or Conservative Party.
117 *KEP*, 16 December 1846.
118 *KEP*, 19 December 1846.
119 *Ibid.*
120 *KEP*, 23 December 1846.
121 *KEx*, 25 December 1846. Also reported in *The Freeman's Journal*, 30 December 1846.
122 *The Tablet*, 9 January 1847, quoting *KEx*.
123 *Ibid.*
124 *Ibid.*

4   'A CHILL FEELING OF DESPAIR': JANUARY–JUNE 1847

1 *KEP*, 2 January 1847.
2 *Ibid.*
3 Ó Murchadha (2011), p. 78.

4   *The Tablet*, 9 January 1847.
5   *KEP*, 6 January 1847.
6   *KEx*, 5 January 1847.
7   *KEx*, 8 January 1847.
8   *Ibid.*
9   *Ibid.*
10 *CEx*, 15 January 1847.
11 *TC*, 9 January 1857, quoting *KEx*.
12 *KEx*, 8 January 1847.
13 *KEP*, 6 January 1847.
14 *TC*, 16 January 1847.
15 *Ibid.*
16 *The Nation*, 27 February 1847.
17 *KEP*, 6 February 1847.
18 *KEP*, 17 February 1847, citing *KEx*.
19 *KEP*, 3 March 1847.
20 *The Nation*, 20 February 1847, citing *KEx*.
21 *KEP*, 27 January 1847.
22 *CEx*, 7 April 1847.
23 *Ibid.*
24 *KEP*, 17 January 1847.
25 *KEx*, 26 January 1847.
26 *KEP*, 17 March 1847.
27 *KEP*, 6 March 1847.
28 *KEP*, 20 February 1847.
29 *KEP*, 2 January 1847.
30 *TC*, 16 January 1847.
31 *Ibid.*
32 *KEP*, 31 October 1846. Henry Stokes was not related to the Tralee family of Day Stokes; he was from a distinguished Dublin medical family.
33 *TC*, 16 January 1847.
34 *KEx*, 5 January 1847.
35 *Correspondence from January to March 1847 Relating to the Measures Adopted for the Relief of Distress in Ireland*, Board of Works Series, Second Part (London, 1847) p. 100.
36 *Ibid.*
37 *KEP*, 24 March 1847.
38 *KEP*, 27 March 1847.
39 *KEP*, 13 February 1847.
40 NLI, Ms 7860, 26 January 1847.
41 *Ibid.*
42 *TC*, 17 April 1847.
43 *Ibid.*
44 *KEP*, 24 March 1847.
45 *KEP*, 10 March 1847.

46 *KEP*, 17 March 1847.
47 'Report upon the Recent Epidemic Fever in Ireland', *Dublin Quarterly Journal of Medical Sciences*, Vol. 7 (1849), pp. 86–7.
48 *KEP*, 24 March 1847. For more on the innovative medical practices of Dr Crumpe see Fitzsimons, Bob, 'Medicine and Society in 19th-Century Kerry: A Life of Francis Crumpe, M.D.', *JKAHS*, No. 27 (1994), pp. 5–88.
49 *KEx*, 23 March 1847.
50 *KEP*, 7 April 1847.
51 *KEx*, 23 March 1847.
52 *KEP*, 27 March 1847.
53 *KEP*, 3 April 1847.
54 *KEx*, 16 April 1847.
55 *KEP*, 17 April 1847.
56 *Ibid.*
57 *KEP*, 14 April 1847.
58 NLI, Ms 7860, 13 April 1847.
59 *KEP*, 6 March 1847.
60 *Ibid.*
61 *KEP*, 12 June 1847.
62 *KEP*, 3 April 1847.
63 *Report of the British Association for the Relief of the Extreme Distress in Ireland and Scotland* (Richard Clay, London, 1849), p. 79. Macadamising was the process of breaking stones for use in road making and binding them with tar or bitumen in a process named after its inventor, John McAdam.
64 *Northern Whig*, 11 May 1847. Cited in Kinealy (1994), p. 173.
65 *KEP*, 14 April 1847.
66 *TC*, 17 April 1847.
67 *KEP*, 28 April 1847.
68 *Ibid.*
69 *KEP*, 10 April 1847.
70 *KEP*, 13 January 1847.
71 *KEP*, 20 March 1847.
72 *KEx*, 19 March 1847.
73 *Ibid.*
74 *Ibid.*
75 *KEP*, 24 March 1847.
76 *KEP*, 1 May 1847.
77 *Ibid.*
78 *KEP*, 8 May 1847.
79 *KEP*, 3 March 1847. The quarterly assize courts were occasions of pomp and ceremony in Tralee; they were presided over by a visiting judge who was welcomed with deference and elaborate courtesy.
80 *KEP*, 23 June 1847.
81 *Ibid.*
82 *TC*, 31 July 1847.

83 *Ibid.*
84 *KEP*, 7 November 1849. The Encumbered Estates Act enabled landlords who were unable to meet their financial obligations because of reduced incomes during the Famine years to sell their estates.
85 Woodham-Smith (1991), p. 299.
86 *KEx*, 26 February 1847.
87 *Ibid.*
88 *KEP*, 2 January 1847.
89 NLI, Ms 7860, 29 December 1846.
90 *KEx*, 8 January 1847.
91 *KEP*, 6 January 1847.
92 *KEP*, 16 January 1847.
93 NLI, Ms 7860, 9 February 1847.
94 *Ibid.*, 13 January 1847.
95 Kelly, John, *The Graves Are Walking: The History of the Great Irish Famine* (Faber and Faber, London, 2012), p. 210.
96 NLI, Ms 7860, 29 June 1847.
97 KCA, BG/154/A/1, 18 February 1845.
98 *Ibid.*, 16 June 1846.
99 *Ibid.*, 30 June 1846.
100 *Ibid.*, 1 September 1846.
101 NLI, Ms 7860, 8 June 1847.
102 KCA, BG/154/A/1, 18 February 1845.
103 NLI, Ms 7860, 8 June 1847.
104 *Ibid.*, 12 January 1847.
105 *Ibid.*, 6 April 1847.
106 *Ibid.*, 16 March 1847.
107 Numbers from NLI, Ms 7860.
108 This list of names is found in Trinity College, Dublin (hereafter TCD), Ms 10499, 12 January 1847; and in the microfilm at NLI, POS 5648, 12 January 1847 (for more on these, see 'Note on Manuscript Sources', pp. 336–7). A similar list is in the transcript NLI, Ms 7860, 12 January 1847, but in this the names of Patrick Bailey and Mary Sullivan are omitted. Rubeola was measles and variola was the virus which caused smallpox.
109 TCD, Ms 10499, 19 January 1847.
110 KCA, BG/154/AA/1, 29 September 1846.
111 *Ibid.*, 6 October 1846.
112 NLI, Ms 7860, 23 March 1847.
113 *Ibid.*, 8 June 1847.
114 *Ibid.*, 1 December 1847.
115 *Ibid.*, 4 January 1848.
116 *Ibid.*, 9 March 1847.
117 *CEx*, 5 April 1847.
118 NLI, Ms 7860, 15 June 1847.
119 *Ibid.*, 7 September 1847.

120 *Ibid.*, 30 March 1847.
121 *Ibid.*, 6 April 1847.
122 *Ibid.*, 15 June 1847.
123 *Ibid.*, 28 September 1847.
124 *Ibid.*, 18 May 1847. This letter was recorded in the Trinity College manuscript and was transcribed in full in the NLI manuscript.
125 Cited in Kinealy (1994), p. 195.
126 *Ibid.*, p. 125.
127 Woodham-Smith (1991), pp. 317–18, quoting Lt Hotham's report to the Treasury.
128 *Ibid.*, p. 318.
129 Ó Murchada (2011), pp. 103–4.
130 KCA, BG/154/AA/1, 11 August 1846.
131 *Ibid.*, 21 July 1846.
132 *Ibid.*, 18 August 1846.
133 NLI, Ms 7860, 24 June 1847.
134 *Ibid.*, 25 May 1847.
135 *Ibid.*
136 *Ibid.*, 1 June 1847.
137 *Ibid.*, 15 June 1847.
138 *KEP*, 20 January 1847. The writer was laying the blame for Famine deaths at the door of the government in London.
139 *Correspondence from January to March 1847 Relating to Measures Adopted for the Relief of Distress in Ireland*, Commissariat Series, Second Part (HMSO, London, 1847), p. 210.
140 *KEP*, 14 April 1847, quoting *KEx*.
141 *Ibid.*
142 *KEP*, 8 May 1847.
143 *KEP*, 16 June 1847.
144 *KEP*, 1 May 1847.
145 *KEP*, 17 March 1847.
146 *Correspondence from January to March 1847 …*, Board of Works Series, Second Part, p. 101.
147 *Ibid.*
148 *Ibid.*
149 *Ibid.*, p. 242.
150 KCA, Greenwell Journal, 6 March 1847.
151 *Ibid.*, 13 February 1847. See also *Correspondence from January to March 1847…*, Board of Works Series, Second Part, p. 242. The phrase 'near the causeway' almost certainly refers to Causeway, as Greenwell goes on to refer to 'the parish priest, Mr Eugene McCarthy'.
152 KCA, Greenwell Journal, 6 March 1847.
153 *Correspondence from January to March 1847…*, Commissariat Series, Second Part, p. 210.
154 NAI, RLFC/3/2/12/29.
155 *Ibid.*

156 *KEP*, 1 May 1847.
157 *Report of the British Association …* (1849), p. 78.
158 *KEx*, 30 April 1847.
159 *Ibid.*
160 *Ibid.*
161 *Ibid.*
162 *KEx*, 23 March 1847.
163 *KEP*, 22 May 1847.
164 *KEP*, 30 January 1847.
165 *Ibid.*
166 *Correspondence from January to March 1847…*, Commissariat Series, Second Part, pp. 130–1.
167 Mitchel, John, *Jail Journal* (M. H. Gill, Dublin, 1913), p. xxxix.
168 *TC*, 20 February 1847.
169 *TC*, 30 January 1847.
170 *Ibid.*
171 *Correspondence from January to March 1847* …, Commissariat Series, Second Part, pp. 130–1.
172 *Ibid.* 'Raiment' is an archaic word for clothing.
173 *KEx*, 23 February 1847.
174 *Ibid.*
175 *KEx*, 16 March 1847.
176 *The Nation*, 15 May 1847.
177 *KEx*, 16 March 1847. There are more extracts on Ardfert from the newspapers of 1846 and 1847 in O'Connor, T., *Ardfert in Times Past* (Foilseacháin Bréanainn, Ardfert, 1999), pp. 158–62.
178 *The Freeman's Journal*, 11 May 1847.
179 *KEx*, 21 May 1847.
180 *The Tablet*, 29 May 1847.
181 *TC*, 19 June 1847.
182 *The Tablet*, 19 June 1847.
183 Condon, Kevin, *The Missionary College of All Hallows, 1842–1891* (All Hallows College, Dublin, 1986), pp. 81, 191. See also: O'Shea, Rev. Kieran, 'David Moriarty (1814–1877) I: The Making of a Bishop', *JKAHS*, No. 3 (1970), p. 92.
184 The Moriarty letters are in the archives of All Hallows College, Dublin, now part of Dublin City University. I am grateful to Fr John Joe Spring and to Greg Harkin for their assistance in accessing the letters.
185 *KEP*, 13 February 1847.
186 *Correspondence from January to March 1847* …, Commissariat Series, Second Part, pp. 130–1.
187 *KEx*, 23 November 1847.
188 *KEx*, 21 May 1847.
189 *KEx*, 4 June 1847.
190 The word 'myrmidon' refers to a hired ruffian.
191 *KEx*, 4 June 1847.

192 *KEP*, 16 June 1847.
193 *KEP*, 12 June 1847.
194 *Ibid.*
195 *TC*, 19 June 1847.
196 *KEP*, 21 August 1847. For more on the Labouchere scheme, named for Chief Secretary Henry Labouchere, see Kinealy (1994), p. 99.
197 *TC*, 19 June 1847.
198 *KEx*, 15 June 1847.
199 *KEx*, 18 June 1847.
200 *KEP,* 19 June 1847.
201 *KEx*, 19 January 1847.
202 *KEP*, 27 January 1847.
203 *Ibid.*
204 *KEx*, 16 February 1847.
205 *Ibid.*
206 *KEP*, 27 February 1847.
207 *KEx*, 2 March 1847.
208 NAI, RLFC/3/2/12/1-7.
209 *Ibid.*
210 *KEx*, 16 February 1847. It is not clear whether the estimate of sixty to seventy weekly deaths refers to Ballyheigue alone or to the wider district of the united parishes. The three incidents cited happened in Ballyheigue but the words 'this extensive parish' might indicate the wider area.
211 Crawford, E. Margaret, 'Food and Famine', in Póirtéir, Cathal (ed.), *The Great Irish Famine* (Mercier Press, Cork, 1995), p. 65.
212 *KEx*, 16 February 1847.
213 NAI, RLFC/3/2/12/2.
214 *TC*, 27 March 1847.
215 NAI, RLFC/3/2/12/2.
216 Reports in *KEP,* 21 July and 29 December 1847.
217 *TC,* 22 May 1847.
218 *Ibid.*
219 *KEP,* 26 May 1847.
220 Ó Murchadha (2011), p. 67.
221 *TC,* 16 January 1847.
222 *TC,* 9 January 1847.
223 *KEP*, 17 February 1847.
224 *KEP*, 13 February 1847.
225 *KEx*, 16 February 1847.
226 *The Nation*, 27 February 1847.
227 *KEx*, 23 February 1847.
228 *KEP*, 7 April 1847.
229 *KEP*, 31 March 1847.

5 'WHAT UNDER HEAVEN ARE THE PEOPLE TO DO?': JULY–DECEMBER 1847

1. Kelly (2012), p. 333.
2. Kinealy, Christine, *Charity and the Great Hunger in Ireland: The Kindness of Strangers* (Bloomsbury, London, 2013), p. 35.
3. Broderick, Eugene, 'The Famine in Waterford as Reported in the Local Newspapers', in Cowman, Des and Brady, Donald (eds), *The Famine in Waterford, 1845–1850: teacht na bprátaí dubha* (Geography Publications, Dublin, 1995), p. 167.
4. Kinealy (2013), p. 6. Trevelyan's role is discussed in detail in general histories of the Famine.
5. The 'Gregory Clause' was introduced by Sir William Gregory, MP, of Coole Park, Co. Galway, as part of the 1847 Poor Law Extension Act.
6. *KEP*, 21 August 1847.
7. *KEx*, 27 August 1847.
8. The Dingle rowing contest was reported in *KEx*, 17 September; The Spa regatta 'for the benefit of poor fishermen and their families' in *KEx*, 21 September 1847; and Killarney regatta in *TC*, 18 September 1847.
9. *KEx*, 17 August 1847.
10. *KEP*, 18 September 1847.
11. *KEP*, 29 September 1847.
12. *KEP*, 2 October 1847.
13. *Ibid*.
14. Wikipedia entry on Douglas Labalmondière: https://en.wikipedia.org/wiki/Douglas_Labalmondière (accessed January 2017).
15. *KEP*, 22 September 1847.
16. *KEP*, 9 September 1847.
17. See MacMahon (2015).
18. *KEx*, 1 October 1847.
19. Kinealy (2013), pp. 112–13.
20. *Ibid*., p. 113.
21. *The Times*, 9 October 1847.
22. Ó Murchadha (2011), p. 159, quoting *The Times*.
23. *Ibid*., p. 194.
24. Kinealy (1994), p. 351.
25. NLI, Ms 7860, 31 August 1847.
26. A. J. Hotham to Poor Law Commissioners, 5 November 1847. National Archives, Kew, London, Treasury Papers, T64 367A. Also in *Papers Relating to Proceedings for the Relief of the Distress and State of the Unions and Workhouses in Ireland*, Fourth Series (HMSO, London, 1847), pp. 187–8.
27. *Ibid*.
28. *Ibid*.
29. *KEP*, 15 September 1847.
30. *Ibid*.
31. *KEP*, 18 September 1847.

ENDNOTES

32 *Southern Reporter*, 12 October 1847.
33 *KEP*, 20 November 1847.
34 *Ibid.*
35 *KEP*, 1 December 1847.
36 *TC*, 25 September 1847.
37 *KEP*, 15 September 1847.
38 *KEP*, 6 November 1847.
39 *Ibid.*
40 *KEP*, 17 November 1847.
41 *Ibid.*
42 *Ibid.*
43 *KEP*, 20 November 1847.
44 *Ibid.*
45 *KEP*, 22 September 1847.
46 *KEP*, 13 October 1847.
47 *Ibid.*
48 *Ibid.*
49 *Ibid.*
50 NLI, Ms 7860, 9 November 1847.
51 *KEP*, 30 November 1847.
52 *KEP*, 20 November 1847.
53 NLI, Ms 7860, 1 December 1847.
54 *KEP*, 1 December 1847.
55 *Ibid.*
56 *KEP*, 8 December 1847.
57 *KEP*, 20 June 1849.
58 *KEP*, 16 May 1849.
59 *Papers Relating to Proceedings for the Relief of the Distress and State of the Unions and Workhouses in Ireland*, Fifth Series (London, 1848), p. 298.
60 *Ibid.*
61 *Ibid.*
62 Dingle Poor Law Union was established in 1848. A workhouse was built near Dingle town in 1849.
63 *KEP*, 4 December 1847.
64 *TC*, 2 October 1847.
65 *KEP*, 29 September 1847.
66 *Ibid.*
67 *KEP*, 25 August 1847.
68 *KEP*, 16 May 1849.
69 See 'Aftermath', p. 326.
70 *KEP*, 13 July 1847.
71 *KEP*, 26 November 1847.
72 *Papers Relating to Proceedings for the Relief of the Distress …*, Fifth Series, pp. 341–2.
73 *TC*, 27 November 1847.
74 *Ibid.*

75 *Ibid.*
76 *Ibid.*
77 *TC*, 25 September 1847.
78 *Ibid.*
79 *Ibid.*
80 *Ibid.*
81 *Ibid.*
82 Donovan, T. M, *A Popular History of East Kerry* (Talbot Press, Dublin, 1931), p. 76.
83 *KEP*, 19 December 1847.
84 *KEP*, 8 and 11 December 1847.
85 *KEP*, 19 December 1847.
86 *Ibid.*
87 *TC*, 14 August 1847. This comprehensive list is headed 'Statement of Relief Works' and it gives locations, costs and other details of a large number of road projects supervised by R. Bevan, engineer, in Clanmaurice, Iraghticonnor and part of Trughnanacmy. A sketch-map of some Famine roads in north Kerry by Tomás Kelly, based on details in this source, is published in Crowley, John, Smyth, William J. and Murphy, Mike (eds), *Atlas of the Great Irish Famine, 1845–52* (Cork University Press, Cork, 2012), Fig. 5b, p. 467.
88 *TC*, 27 November 1847.
89 *Ibid.*
90 *Ibid.*
91 *Ibid.*
92 *KEP*, 1 December 1847. 'Trow' is an archaic term for 'to think' or 'believe'.
93 *Papers Relating to Proceedings for the Relief of the Distress* …, Fifth Series, p. 349. Killury is rendered as Killeery in this document, most likely because of a transcription error.
94 *Ibid.*, p. 350. Ballyden seems to be another transcription error, possibly for Ballyduff.
95 Donnelly, James S. Jr, 'Mass Eviction and the Great Famine', in Póirtéir (1995), p. 160.
96 Delaney, E., *The Curse of Reason: The Great Irish Famine* (Gill and Macmillan, Dublin, 2012), p. 173.
97 *Papers Relating to Proceedings for the Relief of the Distress* …, Fifth Series, p. 350.
98 O'Donnell, Ruán, *A Short History of Ireland's Famine* (O'Brien Press, Dublin, 2008), p. 103.
99 *Papers Relating to Proceedings for the Relief of the Distress* …, Fifth Series, p. 350.
100 *Ibid.*, p. 351.
101 *Ibid.*
102 *Ibid.*
103 *Ibid.*, pp. 351–2.
104 Quoted in O'Reilly, Hugh, 'The Presbyterian Mission in Kerry, 1840–1860: Background to Home Mission', *Bulletin of Presbyterian Historical Society of Ireland*, No. 39 (2015), pp. 20–34. I am grateful to Linde Lunney for drawing my attention to this article.

105 Ó Cathaoir, Breandán, 'Famine Diary', *The Irish Times*, 20 December 1997.
106 *KEP*, 20 June 1847.
107 *Irish Ecclesiastical Gazette*, 9 January 1891.
108 *TC*, 2 June 1849.
109 *CEx*, 8 February 1847.
110 *TC*, 11 July 1846.
111 *KEP*, 31 March 1847. Abraham Beale was a Quaker and a member of a Cork business family. He died in August 1847 of typhus fever contracted during his humanitarian work. See Kinealy (2013), p. 82.
112 *TC*, 5 February 1848. There is a memorial plaque to Jeremiah O'Leary in the Church of St Stephen and St John in Castleisland.
113 *KEP*, 2 December 1848.
114 *KEP*, 3 April 1847.
115 *KEx*, 14 May 1847.
116 O'Shea, Fr Kieran, 'In the Line of Duty: Priests Who Ministered to the Famine Victims', in Michael Costello (ed.), *The Famine in Kerry* (Kerry Archaeological and Historical Society, Tralee, 1997), pp. 28–31.
117 *KEx*, 25 January 1847.
118 *KEx*, 2 July 1847.
119 O'Shea, Kieran, 'The Nuns in Kerry: Unsung Heroes of the Famine', in Costello (1997), p. 55.
120 *Ibid.*, pp. 55–7. See also Pierse (2014), pp. 70–9.
121 O'Shea, 'The Nuns in Kerry', in Costello (1997), p. 56.
122 *Ibid.*
123 Moriarty, David, *Sermons* (Gill, Dublin, 1907), pp. 37–8.
124 *KEx*, 7 September 1847.
125 *The Tablet*, 9 January 1847.
126 *KEP*, 28 June 1847.
127 *KEP*, 8 September 1847.
128 *KEx*, 9 July 1847.
129 *Ibid.*
130 *Berrow's Worcester Journal*, 19 August 1852, cited in Murphy, J. A. and Chamberlain, E., *The Church of Ireland in Kerry: A Record of Church and Clergy in the Nineteenth Century* (ebook available at www.lulu.com), p. 180.
131 *The Freeman's Journal*, 6 June 1849, cited in Murphy and Chamberlain, p. 180.
132 *KEx*, 8 October 1847. See also O'Reilly (2015), p. 21.
133 *KEP*, 29 September 1847.
134 Edwards and Williams (1994), p. 226.
135 *Ibid.*
136 *TC*, 4 December 1847.
137 *KEP*, 8 December 1847.
138 *TC*, 23 November 1850.
139 *Fourth Report from the Select Committee of the House of Lords Appointed to Inquire into the Operation of the Irish Poor Law* … (London, 1849), pp. 850–1.
140 *KEx*, 28 January 1850.

141 Daly, Mary E., 'The Operations of Famine Relief, 1845–47', in Póirtéir (1995), pp. 133–4.

6 'GRAVES CALL TO YOU FOR VENGEANCE': 1848

1 *Dublin Evening Packet*, 1 January 1848.
2 Dublin Diocesan Archive, Murray Papers, 33/6/14, 5 February 1848.
3 *Ibid.*, 33/6/20/1, 6 March 1849.
4 Kinealy (2013), p. 114.
5 Kinealy, Christine, *A Death-Dealing Famine: The Great Hunger in Ireland* (Pluto, London, 1998), p. 233.
6 *Papers Relating to Proceedings for the Relief of the Distress ...*, Fifth Series, pp. 300–1.
7 *Ibid.*
8 *Ibid.*, p. 296.
9 *Ibid.*, pp. 300–1. See also *Papers Relating to Proceedings for the Relief of the Distress and State of the Unions and Workhouses in Ireland*, Sixth Series (London, 1848), pp. 772–86.
10 *KEP,* 12 July 1848.
11 *Ibid.*
12 *KEP*, 23 August 1848.
13 *KEP*, 13 September 1848.
14 *KEP*, 20 September 1848.
15 *TC*, 5 February 1848.
16 *TC*, 26 February 1848.
17 *TC*, 22 April 1848.
18 *KEx*, 20 June 1848.
19 NLI, Ms 7860, 30 March 1847.
20 *KEP*, 8 April 1848.
21 *Report of the British Association ...* (1849), p. 141. The association spent £2,892 in relief work in Dingle Union, £3,991 in Caherciveen Union and £7,680 in Kenmare Union.
22 *Ibid.*, Appendix B III, No. 4, p. 166.
23 *Ibid.*, p. 165.
24 *Papers Relating to Proceedings for the Relief of the Distress ...*, Sixth Series, p. 251.
25 NAI, ED2/19/No. 21.
26 *Papers Relating to Proceedings for the Relief of the Distress ...*, Fifth Series, p. 292.
27 Ó Conchubhair, Pádraig, 'The Church Education Society, Ballylongford and the Famine', *The Kerry Magazine*, No. 7 (1996), pp. 20–3, especially p. 21.
28 *Report of the British Association ...* (1849), p. 165.
29 *Ibid.*, p. 42.
30 Lord Robert Clinton, report from Tralee, 30 March 1847, in *Report of the British Relief Association ...* (1849), pp. 79–80.
31 Kinealy (2013), p. 192.
32 Quoted in Crowley *et al.* (2012), p. xii.
33 *Papers Relating to Proceedings for the Relief of the Distress ...*, Sixth Series, p. 256.

34 *Ibid.*
35 *Ibid.*, p. 260.
36 *Ibid.*, p. 261.
37 *Papers Relating to Proceedings for the Relief of the Distress ...*, Fifth Series, p. 271.
38 *Ibid.*
39 *Papers Relating to Proceedings for the Relief of the Distress ...*, Sixth Series, p. 257.
40 *Ibid.*, p. 259.
41 *Ibid.*, p. 268.
42 *Papers Relating to Proceedings for the Relief of the Distress ...*, Fifth Series, p. 360.
43 *Ibid.*
44 *Papers Relating to Proceedings for the Relief of the Distress ...*, Sixth Series, p. 262.
45 O'Connor (1995), p. 237. The workhouse was destroyed by fire in 1922, during the Civil War. There are few traces of it today, but the site is now the location of Listowel Community Hospital.
46 *Papers Relating to Proceedings for the Relief of the Distress ...*, Fifth Series, pp. 356–8.
47 *Ibid.*
48 Pierse (2014) includes extracts from Captain Spark's reports, pp. 138ff.
49 *KEx*, 25 February 1848.
50 *Ibid.*
51 O'Connor (1995), p. 101.
52 *TC*, 19 February 1848.
53 *Ibid.*
54 *Ibid.*
55 *KEx*, 28 November 1848.
56 *TC*, 30 September 1848.
57 *Ibid.*
58 *Ibid.*
59 The *Chronicle* records one of the curates as being called Martin McMahon, but this is probably a misprint for Mathias McMahon.
60 *TC*, 30 September 1848.
61 *TC*, 21 October 1848.
62 *KEP*, 4 November 1848.
63 Quoted in *TC*, 21 April 1849.
64 *KEP*, 23 December 1848.
65 *KEP*, 29 November 1848.
66 *KEx*, 28 November 1848.
67 The letter was reprinted in the *Kerry Sentinel* at a later period of land agitation and the information here is based on that source. The *Sentinel* introduced the letter as 'the first public letter from a pen which has often since lent powerful and timely aid to the cause of our country'. It stated that the letter was published in *The Nation* more than thirty-six years earlier, but I have not found it in that paper in 1848. All quotes from the letter are taken from the *Kerry Sentinel*, 2 May 1884.
68 *The Nation*, 20 August 1859.
69 Journal of Dr Thomas Graham cited in Lynch (2008), p. 66.

70   *TC*, 19 February 1848.
71   *Ibid.*
72   *TC*, 24 June 1848.
73   *Ibid.*
74   *Ibid.*
75   Ó Cathaoir, Breandán, 'The Rising of 1848', *History Ireland*, Issue 3, Vol. 6 (Autumn 1998). More information available online at: www.historyireland.com/18th-19th-century-history/the-rising-of-1848/.
76   *KEP*, 5 August 1848.
77   *CEx*, 9 August 1848.
78   *KEP*, 9 August 1848.
79   *KEP*, 18 October 1856.
80   *KEP*, 12 August 1848.
81   *KEP*, 9 August 1848.
82   *KEP*, 12 August 1848.
83   *KEP*, 27 September 1848.
84   *CEx*, 29 September 1848.
85   *KEP*, 27 August 1848.
86   *TC*, 26 August 1848.
87   *TC*, 9 September 1848.
88   *KEx*, 24 October 1848.
89   *KEP*, 8 December 1849.
90   *KEP*, 3 January 1849.

7   'THE POOR ARE SINKING': 1849

1   Statistics from Kinealy (1994), p. 251.
2   Alphonse de Lamartine led the Second Republic in France for a large part of 1848.
3   *KEP*, 3 January 1849.
4   Listowel board of guardians' minutes, KCA, BG/112/A/2.
5   KCA, BG/112/A/2, 30 January 1849.
6   *KEP*, 3 January 1849.
7   *Ibid.*
8   Noted in KCA, BG/112/A/2, on 10 April, 25 July and 23 August 1849.
9   *Ibid.*, 6 December 1849.
10 *Papers Relating to the Relief of the Distress and State of the Unions and Workhouses in Ireland,* Eighth Series (London, 1849), pp. 141–3.
11 *KEP*, 28 April 1849.
12 *KEP*, 16 May 1849.
13 *KEP*, 2 June 1849.
14 *KEP*, 13 July 1850.
15 *KEP*, 2 June 1849.
16 *KEP*, 18 July 1849.
17 Kinealy (2013), p. 5.
18 *TC*, 15 September 1849.

19 *Ibid.*
20 *TC*, 2 June 1849.
21 *KEP*, 7 February 1849.
22 *KEP*, 10 March 1849.
23 *KEP*, 9 May 1849.
24 *CEx*, 16 May 1849.
25 *KEP*, 21 March 1849.
26 *KEP*, 22 June 1850.
27 *Ibid.*
28 Kennedy, Liam, Ell, Paul S., Crawford, E. M. and Clarkson, L. E., *Mapping the Great Irish Famine* (Four Courts Press, Dublin, 1999), p. 123.
29 Ó Murchadha (2011), p. 168.
30 *KEP*, 14 April 1849.
31 *KEP*, 25 April 1849.
32 *Ibid.*
33 *CEx*, 27 April 1849.
34 KCA, BG/112/A/2, 2 May 1849.
35 *KEx*, 11 May 1849.
36 *KEP*, 26 May 1849.
37 *Ibid.*
38 *KEP*, 19 May 1849.
39 *KEP*, 5 May 1849.
40 *KEP*, 26 May 1849.
41 *KEP*, 30 May 1849.
42 *KEP*, 20 June 1849.
43 Kennedy *et al.* (1999), p. 123.
44 Ó Murchadha (2011), p. 168.
45 *KEP*, 1 August 1849.
46 *KEP*, 23 June 1849.
47 *KEP*, 20 June 1849.
48 *Ibid.* I did not find any evidence that this plan was completed.
49 *KEx*, 31 August 1849.
50 Ó Murchadha (2011), p. 164.
51 Kinealy, Christine, *Apparitions of Death and Disease* (Quinnipiac University Press, Connecticut, 2014), p. 27.
52 *CEx*, 30 May 1849.
53 *TC*, 17 February 1849.
54 *KEP*, 17 November 1849.
55 *CEx*, 7 February 1849.
56 *KEx*, 13 April 1849.
57 *KEP*, 14 April 1849.
58 *KEx*, 20 April 1849.
59 *Ibid.*
60 *Ibid.*
61 *CEx*, 25 April 1849.

62 *KEP*, 28 April 1849.
63 *CEx*, 4 May 1849.
64 Toal, Caroline, *North Kerry Archaeological Survey* (Brandon Books, Dingle, 1995), pp. 28–34. I have not found the location of Cloarbougher or Beendhuve.
65 *CEx*, 4 May 1849.
66 Letter of 28 April 1849. Cited in Kinealy (2014), p. 28.
67 See Gray, Peter, *Famine, Land and Politics: British Government and Irish Society 1843–50* (Irish Academic Press, Dublin, 1999), pp. 314–15.
68 Cited in Gray (1999), p. 333.
69 Osborne, S. G., *Gleanings from Ireland* (T. and W. Boone, London, 1850), pp. 254–6.
70 Cited in *CEx*, 19 July 1850.
71 *Ibid.*
72 Kinealy (1994), p. 357. There are parallel situations today: for example, during an acute accommodation crisis in Ireland, *The Sunday Times* of 18 December 2016 carried a report that a tenant received notice of a rent increase of almost 40 per cent on the day when the government introduced legislation to impose a cap of 4 per cent on rent increases.
73 *KEP*, 16 May 1849.
74 *TC*, 8 December 1849.
75 *KEP*, 22 December 1849.
76 *Ibid.*
77 *KEP*, 6 October 1849.
78 *KEP*, 20 October 1849.
79 *KEP*, 22 December 1849.
80 *KEP*, 24 March 1849.
81 *KEP*, 8 December 1849.
82 KCA, BG/112//3, 6 December 1849.
83 *KEP*, 8 December 1849.
84 KCA, BG/112/A/2, 28 March 1849.
85 Information drawn from KCA, BG/112/A/2.
86 KCA/BG/112/A/2, 14 December 1848.
87 *Ibid.*, 2 May 1849.
88 *Ibid.*, 5 September 1849.
89 *KEP*, 18 July 1849.
90 *Ibid.*
91 *KEP*, 20 October 1849.
92 *CEx*, 17 August 1849.
93 *Ibid.*
94 *TC*, 29 September 1849.
95 *CEx*, 14 January 1850. Only Crowley's responses are recorded and not the actual queries, and the time period to which these figures refer is not specified.
96 *Ibid.*
97 *CEx*, 29 August 1849.
98 Cited in *KEx*, 2 February 1849.
99 Cited in *TC*, 7 April 1849.

100 *KEP*, 28 March 1849.
101 *KEP*, 21 February 1849.
102 *KEP*, 18 August 1849.
103 *KEP*, 4 January 1843; see also *KEP*, 4 January 1845.
104 *CEx*, 28 December 1847.
105 *CEx*, 28 January 1850.
106 *KEP*, 22 December 1852.
107 Gray (1999), p. 66.
108 *TC*, 1 March 1851.
109 *KEP*, 24 July 1852.
110 *KEP*, 26 September 1849.
111 *Tralee Mercury*, 3 November 1832. 'Jobber' was a derogatory term to describe someone who made private profit out of public office.
112 *KEP*, 26 September 1849.

8 'AN UNPRECEDENTED AND UNEXPECTED INFLUX OF PAUPERISM': 1850

1 Kennedy *et al.* (1999), p. 127.
2 *KEP*, 30 March 1850.
3 *KEP*, 18 July 1849.
4 *KEx*, 5 April 1850.
5 *KEP*, 13 April 1850.
6 *KEP*, 3 April 1850.
7 *KEP*, 6 April 1850
8 *Ibid*. 'Ukase' was the Russian term for an edict of the Tsar of Russia.
9 *Ibid*.
10 *TC*, 20 April 1850.
11 *TC*, 11 May 1850.
12 *KEP*, 3 April 1850.
13 *TC*, 20 April 1850.
14 *Ibid*.
15 *Ibid*.
16 *Ibid*. Another consequence of the boundary changes was that 180 children were removed from Tarbert to a new workhouse in Glin, taking them farther away from their families – see *TC*, 25 May 1850.
17 *TC*, 20 April 1850.
18 *Ibid*.
19 *Ibid*.
20 *Ibid*.
21 *KEP*, 20 April 1850.
22 *KEP*, 17 April 1850.
23 *TC*, 25 May 1850.
24 *Ibid*.
25 *Ibid*.

26 *Ibid.*
27 *CEx*, 14 June 1850.
28 *Ibid.*
29 *TC*, 2 March 1850.
30 *TC*, 25 May 1850.
31 *TC*, 4 May 1850.
32 *KEx*, 5 July 1850. Waterloo Lane was in the Island of Geese area of Tralee.
33 *TC*, 25 May 1850.
34 *Ibid.*
35 *CEx*, 24 May 1850.
36 *KEx*, 17 May 1850.
37 *KEP*, 13 November 1850.
38 *CEx*, 10 May 1850.
39 *KEx*, 17 May 1850.
40 *The Tablet*, quoted in *TC*, 25 May 1850.
41 *TC*, 9 November 1850.
42 *TC*, 30 November 1850.
43 *TC*, 9 November 1850. Ophthalmia, or xerophthalmia, is a deficiency of vitamin A which causes blindness. It was particularly prevalent among children. In 1851 Dr William Wilde recommended regular doses of cod liver oil as a cure, but this effective treatment was not widely adopted until sixty years later. (Crawford, 'Food and Famine', in Póirtéir (1995), pp. 71–3.) Whiskey was cheaper and more readily available than imported wine.
44 KCA, BG/154/AA/2, 31 May 1851.
45 *CEx*, 13 July 1850.
46 *KEP,* 4 January 1851.
47 *Ibid.*
48 *TC*, 20 April 1850.
49 *KEP,* 4 May 1850.
50 *TC,* 15 June 1850.
51 KCA, BG/112/A/3, 9 February 1850.
52 *Ibid.*
53 *Ibid.*, 23 February 1850.
54 *Ibid.*
55 *CEx*, 1 February 1850.
56 *Ibid.*
57 *TC,* 15 June 1850.
58 *Ibid.*
59 Pierse (2014), p. 23.
60 KCA, BG/112/A/3, 28 March 1850.
61 *KEP*, 12 January 1850.
62 *Ibid.*
63 *Ibid.*
64 *Ibid.*
65 *Ibid.* Mr Phillips was indeed a very conscientious official and he played an important

administrative role in Listowel Union for five years; his signature is found in the minute books every week. He was obliged to resign, along with the matron Miss Fitzelle, when it was discovered that she had tried to conceal the birth of their child and had placed the baby in the workhouse; KCA, BG/112/A/8, 29 November 1852.
66 *CEx*, 16 January 1850.
67 KCA, BG/112/A/3, 21 March 1850.
68 *Ibid.*, 14 March 1850.
69 *Ibid.*, 4 April 1850.
70 *Ibid.*, 14 March 1850.
71 *Ibid.*, 21 March 1850.
72 *Ibid.*, 23 March 1850.
73 *Limerick and Clare Examiner*, 24 April 1850.
74 KCA, BG/112/A/3, 25 April 1850.
75 *TC*, 5 January 1850.
76 Pierse (2014), pp. 35ff.
77 KCA, BG/112/AA/1, 2 May 1850.
78 KCA, BG/112/A/3, 21 March 1850.
79 *Ibid.*
80 *Ibid.*, 4 April 1850. The Visiting Committee of a Poor Law Union comprised a number of guardians who were meant to visit the workhouse each week to inspect its administration, to ensure that inmates were properly treated and to listen to any complaints. They recorded their findings in the visitors' book. For further information see www.workhouses.org.uk/admin/index.shtml.
81 KCA, BG/112/A/3, 4 April 1850.
82 *TC*, 23 November 1850.
83 *TC*, 15 October 1852.
84 *Kerry Sentinel*, 30 October 1895. See MacMahon, Bryan, 'George Sandes of Listowel: Land Agent, Magistrate and Terror of North Kerry', *JKAHS*, Series 2, Vol. 3 (2013), pp. 5–56.
85 *KEP*, 20 April 1850.
86 *Ibid.*
87 *KEP*, 15 May 1850.
88 *KEP*, 31 July 1850.
89 *KEx*, 12 April 1850.
90 The letter is quoted in full in Ó Ciosáin, Micheál, *Cnoc an Fhómhair* (An Sagart, Maynooth, 1988), pp. 181–6.
91 *Ibid.*
92 *KEx*, 18 October 1850.
93 *Ibid.*
94 Lyne, Gerard, *The Lansdowne Estates in Kerry under the Agency of William Steuart Trench, 1849–72* (Geography Publications, Dublin, 2001), p. 201.
95 *CEx*, 18 September 1850.
96 *TC*, 5 October 1850.
97 *KEx*, 4 October 1850.
98 *CEx*, 7 October 1850.

99   Lyne (2001), p. 199.
100 *Ibid.*, p. 195.
101 *TC*, 5 October 1850.
102 *TC*, 12 October 1850.
103 *TC*, 1 June 1850.
104 *TC*, 21 September 1850.
105 *Ibid.*
106 *KEx*, 5 July 1850.
107 *Ibid.*
108 *Ibid.*
109 *KEx*, 11 October 1850.
110 *KEx*, 18 October 1850.
111 *KEx*, 4 October 1850.
112 *KEP,* 30 October 1850.
113 *TC*, 2 November 1850.
114 *KEP,* 2 November 1850.
115 *TC*, 2 November 1850.
116 *Ibid.*
117 *Ibid.* This man's death may have been the last starvation death in Kerry. Ó Murchadha (2011), pp. 177–8, concluded that the last traceable death from starvation in Ireland in the Famine years was that of an unnamed man in Ennis in April 1851, but there were inquest verdicts of death by starvation in Dungarvan, Co. Waterford as late as July 1851. Jeremiah Crowley died on the roadside and Thomas Whelan was brought to the workhouse where he died. Two other men were in an advanced state of exhaustion from hunger – see *The Freeman's Journal,* 14 July 1851.
118 *TC,* 2 November 1850.
119 *Ibid.*
120 *Ibid.*
121 *TC,* 9 November 1850.
122 *The Nation*, 31 January 1885.
123 *KEx*, 17 May 1850.
124 *Ibid.*
125 *TC,* 18 May 1850.
126 *KEx*, 7 June 1850.
127 *TC*, 1 June 1850.
128 *Ibid.*
129 *TC,* 15 June 1850.
130 *KEP*, 18 January 1851.
131 *Ibid.*
132 *Ibid.*
133 *Ibid.*
134 Diary of Archdeacon John O'Sullivan, Kerry Diocesan Archives. Extracts from the diary were provided in a private communication from the late Fr Kieran O'Shea.
135 *TC,* 21 September 1851. Bere is a type of barley.
136 *KEP*, 4 January 1851.

137 *KEP*, 11 January 1851.
138 Caird, James, *The Plantation Scheme, or The West of Ireland as a Field for Investment* (William Blackwood and Sons, Edinburgh and London, 1850), pp. 96–7.

9 'TAKE FORTUNE'S TIDE – THE WORLD IS WIDE': 1851

1 *TC*, 2 November 1850.
2 *TC*, 16 November 1850. Kitchener had purchased land in north Kerry under the Encumbered Estates Act and his son Horatio Herbert, who became Field Marshal Kitchener, was born at Gunsborough in June 1850.
3 *KEP*, 8 February 1851.
4 *KEx*, 8 November 1850.
5 *KEP*, 8 February 1851.
6 *KEP*, 27 August 1851.
7 *KEP*, 12 July 1851.
8 *KEP*, 26 April 1851.
9 *KEP*, 22 November 1851.
10 *KEP*, 27 August 1851.
11 *CEx*, 24 October 1851.
12 Fr Mathias McMahon's long letter was published in *The Nation*, 15 November 1851, under the heading 'The Great Crow-bar Exhibition in Kerry'.
13 *Ibid.*
14 *Ibid.*
15 Lucid, Geraldine, 'Nineteenth Century Emigration from Kerry', in Kelly, Liam, Lucid, Geraldine and O'Sullivan, Maria (eds), *Blennerville: Gateway to Tralee's Past* (Foras Áiseanna Saothair, Tralee, 1989), p. 134.
16 *Ibid.*, p. 134.
17 *Ibid.*
18 *KEP*, 30 April 1851.
19 The poem 'A Call for Emigrants' was in *KEP*, 2 June 1849. The warning to emigrants was in *KEP*, 16 June 1849.
20 *KEx*, 3 June 1851.
21 *KEP*, 30 May 1849.
22 *KEP*, 4 January 1851.
23 *KEP*, 4 April 1849.
24 *The Freeman's Journal*, 10 January 1851.
25 *KEP*, 4 January 1851.
26 *Ibid.*
27 *Ibid.*
28 *KEP*, 28 May 1851.
29 *KEP*, 12 April 1851.
30 *KEP*, 1 February 1851.
31 *KEP*, 4 June 1851.
32 *TC*, 12 April 1851.
33 *Ibid.*

34. *Ibid.*
35. *Ibid.*
36. English, Michael, *Sailing the Jeanie Johnston* (Collins Press, Cork, 2012), p. 35.
37. *KEP*, 7 June 1851.
38. *Ibid.*
39. *KEP,* 12 July 1851.
40. *KEP*, 16 July 1851.
41. Detailed information on the history of the Donovan family and their business interests can be found in O'Mahoney, Vincent, *Merchant Princes: The Remarkable Story of Tralee's Milling Families* (self-published, Tralee, 2016).
42. *KEP*, 25 March 1848.
43. *KEP*, 31 July 1850.
44. *KEP*, 26 April 1848.
45. English (2012), p. 47.
46. *KEP*, 1 September 1847. See also Quigley, Michael, 'Grosse Isle: Canada's Island Famine Memorial', *History Ireland*, Issue 2, Vol. 5 (1997). In this essay the number of passengers given is 476. The passengers were the unfortunate tenants of the notorious Major Denis Mahon of Strokestown, Co. Roscommon, who was assassinated on 2 November 1847.
47. *KEP*, 21 July 1847.
48. *KEP*, 30 October 1850.
49. *KEP*, 24 October 1849.
50. *KEP*, 20 April 1850.
51. *KEP*, 15 June 1850.
52. *KEx*, 8 November 1850.
53. *Ibid.*
54. *KEP*, 21 July 1852.
55. Information from Helen O'Carroll, curator of Kerry County Museum. Further details on Famine emigration from Kerry can be found in Kelly *et al.* (1989) and in Moloney Caball, K., *The Kerry Girls: Emigration and the Earl Grey Scheme* (The History Press Ireland, Dublin, 2014).
56. Thomas Jones, Correspondence (1854), RS555, Provincial Archives of New Brunswick, Canada. I am grateful to Rob Gemmell for this document.
57. A well-known TV scriptwriter named Larry Gaynor, who worked with the Canadian Broadcasting Corporation and who died in 2010, was descended from Laurence. (Information from Helen O'Carroll.)
58. English (2012), p. 59.
59. *TC*, 29 March 1851.
60. *KEP*, 12 April 1851.
61. *Ibid.*
62. *KEP*, 30 April 1851.
63. *KEP*, 12 April 1851.
64. *TC*, 5 April 1851.
65. *TC*, 25 January 1851.
66. *KEP*, 2 April 1851.

67 *KEP*, 5 July 1851.
68 *KEP*, 29 October 1851. See Pierse (2014), pp. 155–6, for information on the Listowel capstan mill.
69 *KEP*, 24 May 1851.
70 *Ibid.*
71 *TC*, 12 April 1851.
72 KCA, BG/154/AA/2, 17 May 1851.
73 *KEP*, 24 May 1851.
74 *KEP*, 30 April 1851.
75 *Limerick and Clare Examiner*, 24 May 1851.
76 *Armagh Guardian*, 7 June 1851.
77 KCA, BG/154/AA/2.
78 *Ibid.*, 24 May 1851.
79 *KEP*, 29 March 1851.
80 *KEP*, 16 August 1851.
81 *KEP*, 18 February 1852.
82 *TC*, 23 August 1851.
83 *KEP*, 5 July 1851.
84 *KEP*, 29 October 1851.
85 *TC*, 26 July 1851.
86 *KEP*, 29 October 1851.
87 *KEP*, 30 March 1852.
88 *TC*, 5 July 1851.
89 *KEP*, 19 April 1851.
90 *KEP*, 10 December 1851.
91 *KEP*, 9 April 1851.
92 *KEP*, 5 February 1851.
93 *KEP*, 10 December 1851.
94 *KEP*, 25 December 1851.
95 Statistics from KCA, BG/112/A/5.
96 *Ibid.*
97 KCA, BG/112/AA/1, 27 March 1851.
98 *KEP*, 3 May 1851.
99 *Ibid.*
100 KCA, BG/112/A/5, 3 April 1851.
101 *KEP*, 6 December 1851.
102 *TC*, 9 August 1851.
103 KCA, BG/112/A/5, 29 July 1851.
104 *TC*, 13 April 1850.
105 KCA, BG/112/A/4, 19 December 1850.
106 KCA, BG/112/A/5, 27 March 1851.
107 KCA, BG/112/A/4, 6 February 1851.
108 *KEP*, 21 June 1851.
109 *KEP*, 25 June 1851.

10 'TIMES ARE MENDING': 1852

1. *KEP*, 3 January 1852. The Great Exhibition of the Works of Industry of All Nations was an exhibition held in the specially built Crystal Palace in Hyde Park, London, from May to October 1851. It was visited by approximately six million people.
2. *Ibid.*
3. *KEP,* 21 February 1852.
4. *Ibid.*
5. *TC,* 23 July 1852.
6. *KEP*, 20 March 1852.
7. *KEP,* 27 March 1852.
8. *KEP,* 19 May 1852.
9. *KEP,* 15 September 1852.
10. *KEP*, 2 September 1852.
11. *Ibid.*
12. *KEP,* 22 May 1852.
13. *Ibid.*
14. *KEP*, 2 June 1852
15. *Ibid.*
16. *Ibid.*
17. *Ibid.*
18. *KEx,* 8 June 1852.
19. *KEx,* 15 June 1852.
20. *Ibid.*
21. *KEx,* 8 June 1852.
22. *Ibid.*
23. *Ibid.*
24. *KEP*, 3 July 1852.
25. *KEP*, 20 November 1852.
26. *KEP*, 29 September 1852.
27. *CEx*, 20 August 1852.
28. It is noteworthy that as recently as 2009, Connemara Mining PLC found high levels of zinc near Castlemaine. It was reported that 'rock samples containing over 51 per cent zinc have fuelled speculation that hundreds of jobs may be created' – see *The Kerryman*, 25 September 2009.
29. *KEx,* 27 April 1852.
30. *Ibid.*
31. *KEP,* 21 January 1852.
32. *KEx,* 10 August 1852.
33. *KEP*, 25 September 1852.
34. *TC,* 17 September 1852.
35. *TC,* 24 September 1852.
36. *TC,* 8 July 1853.
37. *CEx,* 1 August 1853, citing *KEP*.
38. *TC,* 17 April 1852.

39 *The Freeman's Journal*, 16 April 1852.
40 *TC*, 24 April 1852. Fr Gaughan refers to the incident and records the local memory that Fr Darby Mahony had 'read the book' over the fire. In folk memory, this had the effect of limiting the effects of the fire. (Gaughan (1973), p. 195.) See also www.listowelparish.com/history.
41 *TC*, 24 April 1852.
42 Donnelly, James S. Jr, 'The Journals of Sir John Benn-Walsh Relating to the Management of His Irish Estates 1823–1864', *Journal of the Cork Historical and Archaeological Society*, Vol. lxxx, No. 230 (July–Dec. 1974), pp. 86–123, at p. 119.
43 *TC*, 15 October 1852.
44 *Ibid.*
45 *TC*, 10 January 1852.
46 *TC*, 23 October, 27 October and 21 August 1852 respectively.
47 *TC*, 16 June 1852.
48 *TC*, 10 September 1852.
49 *KEP*, 11 September 1852.
50 *TC*, 10 September 1852. *The Last of the Mohicans: A Narrative of 1757* was a popular novel by James Fenimore Cooper, first published in 1826.

AFTERMATH

1   Ó Murchdha (2011), pp. 179–80.
2   The National Centre for Geocomputation based in the National University of Ireland, Maynooth, makes it possible to compare census statistics over time. See http://airo.maynoothuniversity.ie/mapping-resources/airo-research-themes/historical-mapping/population-change-1841-2002-kerry.
3   *Ibid.*
4   *KEP*, 24 December 1851.
5   See Census of Ireland 1851: www.dippam.ac.uk/eppi/documents/13125/page/160677.
6   *KEP*, 12 October 1853. The letter of 'An Irishman' was also published in *The Times* of 23 September 1853.
7   *Ibid.*
8   *Ibid.*
9   *Ibid.*
10 *KEP*, 13 August 1851.
11 *TC*, 30 September 1853.
12 *KEP*, 7 January 1854.
13 *Kerry Sentinel*, 17 November 1900. Cited in Costello (1997), pp. 10–11.
14 *Ibid.*
15 *Kerry Sentinel*, 27 April 1889.
16 *KEP*, 22 August 1855.
17 *Ibid.*
18 *KEP*, 3 November 1855.
19 *Ibid.*

20 *Ibid.*
21 *KEx*, 30 March 1852.
22 Donnelly (1974), pp. 121–3.
23 *CEx*, 22 December 1856.
24 *CEx*, 19 December 1856.
25 *TC*, 19 December 1856.
26 *TC*, 15 July 1853.
27 *CEx*, 22 December 1856.
28 Moriarty, David, *Allocutions to the Clergy and Pastorals of the Right Rev. David Moriarty, Bishop of Kerry* (Browne and Nolan, Dublin, 1884), p. 302.
29 *TC*, 5 July 1867.
30 Crowley *et al.* (2012), p. xvi.
31 Ó Murchadha (2011), p. 78. Ó Murchadha was referring specifically to the first six months of 1847.
32 National Folklore Collection, University College Dublin, Ms 658, p. 291.
33 Ó Gráda (1989), p. 41n.
34 Information from Johnny Leen of Ballyheigue and Switzerland.
35 See www.listowelparish.com/history.

NOTE ON MANUSCRIPT SOURCES

1 KCA, Tralee board of guardians' rough minutes, BG/154/AA/1 and BG/154/AA/2.
2 I first learned of this source from O'Connor (1995), in a note on p. 284.
3 NLI, Ms 7860.
4 I am grateful to John Pierse for drawing my attention to this manuscript in Trinity College.
5 Further information is found on the website www.konahistorical.org.

BIBLIOGRAPHY

Books and Articles

Bary, V., *Houses of Kerry* (Ballinakella Press, Whitegate, County Clare, 1994)
Caird, J., *The Plantation Scheme, or The West of Ireland as a Field for Investment* (William Blackwood and Sons, Edinburgh and London, 1850)
Condon, K., *The Missionary College of All Hallows, 1842–1891* (All Hallows College, Dublin, 1986)
Costello, M. (ed.), *The Famine in Kerry* (Kerry Archaeological and Historical Society, Tralee, 1997)
Cowman, D. and Brady, D. (eds), *The Famine in Waterford, 1845–1850: teacht na bprátaí dubha* (Geography Publications, Dublin, 1995)
Crowley, J., Smyth, W. J. and Murphy, M. (eds), *Atlas of the Great Irish Famine, 1845–52* (Cork University Press, Cork, 2012)
Delaney, E., *The Curse of Reason: The Great Irish Famine* (Gill and Macmillan, Dublin, 2012)
Donnelly, J. S. Jr, 'The Journals of Sir John Benn-Walsh Relating to the Management of His Irish Estates 1823–1864', *Journal of the Cork Historical and Archaeological Society*, Vol. lxxx, No. 230 (July–Dec. 1974), pp. 86–123
Donnelly, J. S. Jr, *The Great Irish Potato Famine* (Sutton, Stroud, 2001)
Donovan, T. M., *A Popular History of East Kerry* (Talbot Press, Dublin, 1931)
Dorian, H., *The Outer Edge of Ulster: A Memoir of Social Life in Nineteenth-Century Donegal*, edited by Breandán Mac Suibhne and David Dickson (Lilliput Press, Dublin in association with Donegal County Council, 2000)
Doyle, J. F., 'The Tralee Workhouse and the Poor Laws 1832–50', *Journal of the Kerry Archaeological and Historical Society*, Series 2, Vol. 9 (2009), pp. 55–76
Edwards, R. D. and Williams, T. D. (eds), *The Great Famine* (Lilliput Press, Dublin, 1994)
English, M., *Sailing the Jeanie Johnston* (Collins Press, Cork, 2012)
Fitzsimons, B., 'Medicine and Society in 19th-Century Kerry: A Life of Francis Crumpe, M.D.', *Journal of the Kerry Archaeological and Historical Society*, No. 27 (1994), pp. 5–88
Foley, M., *Death in Every Paragraph: Journalism and the Great Irish Famine* (Quinnipiac University Press, Quinnipiac, 2015)
Gaughan, J. A., *Listowel and Its Vicinity* (Mercier Press, Cork, 1973)
Gray, P., *Famine, Land and Politics: British Government and Irish Society 1843–50* (Irish Academic Press, Dublin, 1999)
Guerin, M., *Listowel Workhouse* (self-published, 1996) (copy in Kerry County Library, Tralee, Local Studies Department)
Kelly, J., *The Graves Are Walking: The History of the Great Irish Famine* (Faber and Faber, London, 2012)
Kelly, L., Lucid, G. and O'Sullivan, M. (eds), *Blennerville: Gateway to Tralee's Past* (Foras Áiseanna Saothair, Tralee, 1989)
Kennedy, L., Ell, P. S., Crawford, E. M. and Clarkson, L. E., *Mapping the Great Irish Famine* (Four Courts Press, Dublin, 1999)
Kinealy, C., *This Great Calamity: The Irish Famine 1845–52* (Gill and Macmillan, Dublin, 1994)
Kinealy, C., *A Death-Dealing Famine: The Great Hunger in Ireland* (Pluto, London, 1998)
Kinealy, C., *Charity and the Great Hunger in Ireland: The Kindness of Strangers* (Bloomsbury, London, 2013)

Kinealy, C., *Apparitions of Death and Disease* (Quinnipiac University Press, Connecticut, 2014)
Kissane, N., *The Irish Famine: A Documentary History* (Syracuse University Press and National Library of Ireland, Dublin, 1995)
Larner, J. (ed.), *Killarney History and Heritage* (Collins Press, Cork, 2005)
Legg, M., *Newspapers and Nationalism: The Irish Provincial Press, 1850–1892* (Four Courts Press, Dublin, 1999)
Lehane, S., *The Great Famine in Kerry: A Study of Its Impact in the Poor Law Unions of Dingle and Killarney, 1845–52* (Cló Inis na Bró, Tralee, 2015)
Lynch, P. J., *Tarbert: An Unfinished Biography* (self-published, Shanagolden, 2008)
Lyne, G., *The Lansdowne Estates in Kerry under the Agency of William Steuart Trench, 1849–72* (Geography Publications, Dublin, 2001)
MacMahon, B., 'George Sandes of Listowel: Land Agent, Magistrate and Terror of North Kerry', *Journal of the Kerry Archaeological and Historical Society*, Series 2, Vol. 3 (2013), pp. 5–56
MacMahon, B., 'The Famine Journal of Lt H. N. Greenwell, 1846-7', *Journal of the Kerry Archaeological and Historical Society*, Series 2, Vol. 13 (2015), pp. 5–50
Mac Suibhne, Breandán and Dickson, David (eds), *The Outer Edge of Ulster: A Memoir of Social Life in Nineteenth-Century Donegal* (Lilliput Press, Dublin, 2000)
McMorran, R., 'Archdeacon Rowan, founder of *The Kerry Magazine*', *The Kerry Magazine*, No. 1, (1989), pp. 3–6
McMorran, R. and O'Keeffe, M., *A Pictorial History of Tralee* (R. McMorran and M. O'Keeffe, Tralee, 1995)
Miles, K., *All Standing: The Remarkable Story of the Jeanie Johnston, the Legendary Irish Famine Ship* (Simon and Schuster, New York, 2013)
Mitchel, J., *The Last Conquest of Ireland (Perhaps)* (R. and T. Washbourne, Glasgow, 1861)
Mitchel, J., *Jail Journal* (M. H. Gill, Dublin, 1913)
Moloney Caball, K., *The Kerry Girls: Emigration and the Earl Grey Scheme* (The History Press Ireland, Dublin, 2014)
Moriarty, D., *Allocutions to the Clergy and Pastorals of the Right Rev. David Moriarty, Bishop of Kerry* (Browne and Nolan, Dublin, 1884)
Moriarty, D., *Sermons* (Gill, Dublin, 1907)
Murphy, J. A. and Chamberlain, E., *The Church of Ireland in Kerry: A Record of Church and Clergy in the Nineteenth Century* (ebook available at www.lulu.com)
Ó Cathaoir, B., 'The Rising of 1848', *History Ireland*, Issue 3, Vol. 6 (Autumn 1998)
Ó Ciosáin, M., *Cnoc an Fhómhair* (An Sagart, Maynooth, 1988)
Ó Conchubhair, P., 'The Church Education Society, Ballylongford and the Famine', *The Kerry Magazine*, No. 7 (1996), pp. 20–22
Ó Conchubhair, P., *Thá Sinn Ocrach: Ballylongford and the Great Famine* (self-published, Ballylongford, 1997)
Ó Gráda, C., *The Great Irish Famine* (Gill and Macmillan, Dublin, 1989)
Ó Murchadha, C., *The Great Famine: Ireland's Agony 1845–1852* (Continuum, London, 2011)
O'Connor, J., *Workhouses of Ireland* (Anvil Books, Dublin, 1995)
O'Connor, T., *Ardfert in Times Past* (Foilseacháin Bréanainn, Ardfert, 1999)
O'Donnell, P. D., *The Irish Faction Fighters of the 19th Century* (Anvil Books, Dublin, 1975)
O'Donnell, R., *A Short History of Ireland's Famine* (O'Brien Press, Dublin, 2008)
O'Mahoney, V., *Merchant Princes: The Remarkable Story of Tralee's Milling Families* (self-published, Tralee, 2016)
O'Mahony, M., 'Peirce Mahony, Landlord', *Ballydonoghue Magazine* (1990)

O'Reilly, H., 'The Presbyterian Mission in Kerry, 1840–1860: Background to Home Mission', *Bulletin of Presbyterian Historical Society of Ireland*, No. 39 (2015), pp. 20–34

O'Shea, K., 'David Moriarty (1814–1877) I: The Making of a Bishop', *Journal of the Kerry Archaeological and Historical Society*, No. 3 (1970), pp. 84–98

O'Shea, K., *The Diocese of Kerry, Formerly Ardfert: Working in the Fields of God* (Éditions du Signe, Strasbourg, 2005)

Osborne, S. G., *Gleanings from Ireland* (T. and W. Boone, London, 1850)

Pierse, J. D., *Teampall Bán: Aspects of the Famine in North Kerry 1845–1852* (Listowel Tidy Towns Committee, Listowel, 2014)

Póirtéir, C. (ed.), *The Great Irish Famine* (Mercier Press, Cork, 1995)

Quigley, M., 'Grosse Isle: Canada's Island Famine Memorial', *History Ireland*, Issue 2, Vol. 5 (1997)

Report of the British Association for the Relief of the Extreme Distress in Ireland and Scotland (Richard Clay, London, 1849)

'Report upon the Recent Epidemic Fever in Ireland', *Dublin Quarterly Journal of Medical Sciences*, Vol. 7 (1849), pp. 86–88

Somerville, A., *Letters from Ireland during the Famine of 1847*, edited by K. D. M. Snell (Irish Academic Press, Dublin, 1994)

Swords, L., *In Their Own Words: The Famine in North Connacht 1845–49* (Columba Press, Dublin, 1999)

Toal, C., *North Kerry Archaeological Survey* (Brandon Books, Dingle, 1995)

Woodham-Smith, C., *The Great Hunger: Ireland 1845–49* (Penguin Books, London, 1991)

Newspapers

Armagh Guardian
Cork Examiner, The
Dublin Evening Packet
Freeman's Journal, The
Irish Ecclesiastical Gazette
Irish Times, The
Kerry Evening Post, The
Kerry Examiner
Kerry Sentinel
Kerryman, The
Limerick and Clare Examiner
Nation, The
Southern Reporter
Sunday Times, The
Tablet, The
Times, The
Tralee Chronicle, The
Tralee Mercury

Parliamentary Papers

Correspondence Explanatory of the Measures Adopted by Her Majesty's Government for the Relief of Distress Arising from the Failure of the Potato Crop in Ireland (HMSO, London, 1846)

Correspondence from January to March 1847 Relating to Measures Adopted for the Relief of Distress in Ireland, Commissariat Series, Second Part (HMSO, London, 1847)

Correspondence from January to March 1847 Relating to the Measures Adopted for the Relief of Distress in Ireland, Board of Works Series, Second Part (HMSO, London, 1847)

Fourth Report from the Select Committee of the House of Lords Appointed to Inquire into the Operation of the Irish Poor Law ... (HMSO, London, 1849)

Papers Relating to Proceedings for the Relief of the Distress and State of the Unions and Workhouses in Ireland, Fourth Series (HMSO, London, 1847)

Papers Relating to Proceedings for the Relief of the Distress and State of the Unions and Workhouses in Ireland, Fifth Series (HMSO, London, 1848)

THE GREAT FAMINE

Papers Relating to Proceedings for the Relief of the Distress and State of the Unions and Workhouses in Ireland, Sixth Series (HMSO, London, 1848)
Papers Relating to the Relief of the Distress and State of the Unions and Workhouses in Ireland, Eighth Series (HMSO, London, 1849)

Manuscripts

David Moriarty Letters, Archives of All Hallows College, Dublin
Diary of Archdeacon John O'Sullivan, Kerry Diocesan Archives, Killarney
Duplicate copy of minutes of Tralee board of guardians, October 1846 to January 1848, Ms 7860, National Library of Ireland
Journal of Lieutenant H. N. Greenwell, September 1846–1847. Original held in Kona Historical Society Archives, Hawaii. Digital copy in Kerry County Archives, Tralee
Listowel board of guardians' minutes, Kerry County Archives, BG/112/A
Microfilm of minutes of Tralee board of guardians October 1846 to January 1848, OS 5648, National Library of Ireland
Murray Papers, 33/6/14, Dublin Diocesan Archive, Clonliffe, Dublin
Relief Commission Papers (RLFC), National Archives of Ireland, Dublin
Rough minutes of Tralee board of guardians, Ms 10499, November 1846 to January 1848, Trinity College Manuscript Library, Dublin
Thomas Jones, *Correspondence* (1854), RS555, Provincial Archives of New Brunswick, Canada
Tralee board of guardians' minutes, Kerry County Archives, BG/154/A and rough minutes, BG/154/AA
Treasury Papers, T64 367A, National Archives, Kew, London

Theses

Foley, Kieran, 'The Killarney Poor Law Guardians and the Famine, 1845–52', MA thesis, University College Dublin, 1987. (Copy in Kerry County Library, Tralee, Local Studies Department)
Foley, Kieran, 'Kerry during the Great Famine, 1845–52', PhD thesis, University College Dublin, 1997. (Copy in Kerry County Library, Tralee, Local Studies Department)

Websites

http://airo.maynoothuniversity.ie/mapping-resources/airo-research-themes/historical-mapping/
www.dippam.ac.uk/eppi/documents/
www.failteromhat.com/slaterm.htm.
www.historyireland.com
www.irishnewsarchive.com
www.konahistorical.org
www.listowelparish.com
www.odonohoearchive.com
www.workhouses.org.uk/Ireland/

INDEX

A

Abbeydorney 85, 88, 108, 131, 138, 141–144, 202, 203, 252, 299, 324
Abbeyfeale 37, 38, 45, 215–217, 253
Aghadoe 249
Aghamore 226
Aghavallin 182
Ahanagran 282, 283
Ahern, John 162
Alexander, James 137, 148
Alton, Dr 40, 69, 72, 96, 103, 107, 108, 116, 117, 120, 165, 262
Annagh Island 65, 107
Ardfert 28, 42, 57, 58, 69, 85, 114, 137–144, 188, 196, 203, 252, 253, 258, 261, 299, 317, 325, 330, 331
Ardoughter 149, 247
Asdee 20, 81, 84
Attridge, James 300–302
Aulanebane 325
Austin, Mr 209

B

Bailey, Julia 118
Bailey, Patrick 121
Balfour, Captain 160
Ball, John 56, 57, 173
Ballinahaglish 295
Ballinascrena 239
Ballinbranhig/Ballinvranig 239
Ballinclogher 279, 324, 325
Ballincus(h)lane 78, 155, 171, 183, 287, 325
Ballineanig 89
Ballingarry 10, 215, 216
Ballinoe 174, 279
Ballinorig 252
Ballinruddery 292, 321
Ballybeggan 34, 38, 64, 167, 260, 327, 330
Ballybunion 47, 53, 64, 85, 87, 130, 132, 133, 186–188, 199, 210, 212, 226, 265, 275, 282, 284, 285, 287, 290, 313, 323

Ballydonoghue 47
Ballydonoghue House 248
Ballyduff 24, 57, 148, 173, 174, 210, 214, 247, 275, 283
Ballyeagh 64, 76, 86, 154, 323
Ballyheigue 24, 27, 28, 42, 51–58, 62, 88, 144–148, 150, 173–176, 180, 182, 198, 202, 210, 211, 221, 223, 224, 233, 234, 239, 252, 253, 272, 280, 307, 332, 333
Ballyhorgan 248
Ballylongford 28, 47, 48, 62, 81, 84, 133, 134, 135, 182, 202, 203, 214, 243, 248, 265, 282, 283
Ballymacelligott 126, 148, 171, 317
Ballymullen 34, 109, 164, 165, 194, 195, 225, 231, 259, 262, 263, 304, 306, 307, 317, 328, 329
Ballymullen Barracks 32, 72, 162, 232
Ballyrobert 137
Ballyseedy 14, 70, 114, 231
Banemore 265, 274, 312
Banna 139, 140, 161, 252
Barden, William 121
Barton, Thomas 124
Bartregaum 295
Bateman, John 171
Bateman, Rowland 69, 115, 170
Beaufort 229
Beecher, Anne 231
Beendhuve 239
Behane, Thomas 119
Benmore 247, 275
Benner, Mr 114
Benn-Walsh, John 44, 235, 246, 247, 276, 290, 321, 322, 329
Bessborough, Earl of 10, 89
Bevan, Mr 99, 111, 112
Blacker, St John 243, 244, 248, 275, 284, 322, 330
Blennerhassett, Arthur 229
Blennerhassett, Dr Henry 37, 41, 74, 300
Blennerhassett, Henry 14, 114

Blennerhassett, Mr 70
Blennerhassett, Richard 300–302
Blennerhassett, William 171
Blennerville 68, 70, 88, 97, 113, 161, 162, 165, 230, 260, 299, 304, 306, 315, 333
Boherbee 107, 115, 232
Boherbue 210, 284
Bolger, James 63, 66, 86
Bonnett, John 307
Botend, John 89
Bourke, Michael 320
Boyle, Richard 247
Breen, Bess 118
Brereton, Mr 40
Brereton, Mrs 231
Brick river 44, 57, 149, 169
Bridge Street, Tralee 197, 224, 231
Brien, John 118
British Relief Association 9, 108, 135, 165, 166, 192, 198, 199, 207, 224
Bromore 282
Brosna 17, 32, 45, 46, 59, 77, 126, 199, 215, 216, 229, 249, 250, 279, 307
Brosnan, Joan 119
Browne, Dan 214
Browne, John 89
Busteed, Barbara 231
Busteed, William 231
Byrne, John 231
Byrne, Patrick O'Loughlin 20, 26
Byrne, P. R. L. 124

C

Caherina 63
Cahersiveen 35, 314
Caird, James 288, 289
Carberry, John 223
Carker 324
Carmody, Maurice 137
Carrahoonaremela 283
Carrigafoyle House 47
Carroll, Biddy 121
Cashen 44, 64, 85, 154, 226, 287
Cashman, Mr 88
Castlegregory 24, 26, 91, 116, 230
Castleisland 17, 28, 35, 43, 45, 46, 59, 68, 77, 78, 126, 154, 155, 160, 165, 170, 172, 182, 183, 189, 217, 223, 229, 249, 258, 259, 260, 285–287, 306, 307, 319, 325
Castlemaine 184, 316, 317
Castletownshend 300
Causeway 24, 25, 27, 28, 51, 56, 57, 88, 99, 149, 150, 173, 174, 210, 234, 235, 247, 266, 279–281, 287
Chambers, Betty 69
Cheevers, P. 135
Chestnut, William 66
Churchill 330
Chute, Captain 103
Chute, Dr 262, 263
Chute, James P. 53–57, 146, 148, 182
Chute, Pierce 258
Chute, Richard 256, 257
Chute, Rowland 258
Chute, William 103, 122, 160, 165
Chutehall 330
Clahane 149, 305, 306
Clandouglas 267
Clanmaurice 28, 36, 42, 68, 100, 131, 133, 173, 281, 291, 322, 325
Clarendon, Lord 10, 171, 240, 244
Clinton, Robert 108, 109, 135, 165, 200
Cloarbougher 239
Clogher 318
Clogherbrien 107, 109, 295
Collinson, Daniel 171
Collis, Stephen E. 47, 169, 290
Condran, Michael 128, 129
Connell, Edward 279
Connell, John 226
Connell, Michael 91, 92
Connor, Cornelius 119
Connor, Cornelius (relieving officer) 266, 267
Connor, John 221
Connor, Timothy 149
Cooke, James 201, 221, 223
Coolaclarig 283
Cor(a)bally 239
Cordal 324, 325
Cork 26, 35, 46, 59, 68, 148, 248, 295–297, 315
Corkaguiny 35, 68, 89, 100, 117, 126, 166, 214
Corridon, Patrick 285

INDEX

Costello, David 132
Cournane, Kitty 225
Cournane, Tom 139
Creagh, John 56
Crompane 44
Crosbie, Francis 96, 148, 231
Crosbie, James 224
Crosbie, Michael 231
Crosbie, Pierce 55, 56, 88, 148, 174, 223, 224
Crosbie, William Talbot 42, 57, 58, 67, 114, 137, 141–144, 169, 170, 203, 244, 253, 258, 290, 299, 322, 331
Crotto 239
Crowley, Catherine 118
Crowley, James 247, 248, 275, 276
Crumpe, Francis 104, 105, 161
Currane, James 121
Cushion, Maurice 27

D

Davis, Captain 230
Davitt, Michael 284
Day, Agnes 231
Day, Edward Fitzgerald 247, 248
Day, John Fitzgerald 148
de Cantillon Church, Thomas 331
de Courcy McGillycuddy, Daniel 256, 258
de Rothschild, Baron Lionel 108
Delahunt, Thomas 231
Dennis, Meade C. 244, 265, 273–275, 284, 290
Denny, Anthony 95, 182, 184
Denny, Arthur 66
Denny, Barry 96, 184
Denny, D. 96
Denny, Edward 18, 38, 59, 96, 101, 110
Denny, Henry 66
Denny, Mr 40, 43, 225, 262, 264, 275
Denny, Rev. Edward 313
Denny, William 18, 38, 63, 66, 103, 288, 295–297, 317
Denny Street, Tralee 63, 107, 110, 184, 197, 231
Derrymore 67, 97, 98
Derrymore Point 65
Derryreagh/Derryra 239

Devane, Timothy 124
Devine, Michael 184, 230
Dexter, Joseph 53, 85
Dicksgrove 45
Dillon, T. A. 160
Dingle 19, 28, 48, 66, 72–74, 90, 92, 100, 110, 126, 154, 165, 166, 184, 195, 198, 209, 230, 264, 304, 305, 336
Donnelly, James S. 176
Donohue, Thomas 124
Donovan, Bridget 223
Donovan, John 299
Donovan, Messrs 96, 101, 299, 300–303, 315
Donovan, Nicholas 295–299
Donovan, T. M. 172
Dooling, Thomas 226
Doon 67, 295
Doonard 282
Dorian, Hugh 23
Douglas, George 300, 301
Driscoll, Michael 221, 222
Driscoll, Norry 285
Driscoll, Timothy 279
Dromkeen 55, 202, 234, 243
Dromlegagh 325
Drummond, Colonel 171
Drummond, Mr 63, 66, 96, 160
Duagh 156, 173, 181, 215–217, 279, 325
Dublin Castle 27, 38
Duncan, Mr 265, 268, 311, 312
Dunne, Maurice 258
Dysart 78, 325

E

Eagar, James Raymond 20
Eagar, Jeffrey 20
Eagar, John F. 20, 109, 164, 165, 328
Enright, Dr 312, 313
Enright, Fr 226
Enright, Patrick 121
Enright, Thomas 66, 107, 184

F

Fairfield, Charles G. 77, 103, 162, 163, 170, 171, 231, 244
Fairfield, William 231

Falvey, D. 124
Falvey, Hugh 196
Falvey, Jeremiah 184
Farmer's Bridge 99
Feale Bridge 253
Feale river 44, 149, 169, 226
Fenit 17, 31, 160, 275, 288, 330
Fitzgerald Day, Robert 247
Fitzgerald, Fr 144
Fitzgerald, Richard 50, 51
Fitzgerald, Thomas 208
Fitzmaurice, Oliver 156, 279
Fletcher, R. B. 26, 47, 75, 148
Flynn, Denis 137
Flynn, Jeremiah 98
Flynn, Patrick 121
Foley, Fr 282, 283
Foley, Patrick 66
Foley, P. T. 96
Frawley, Ellen 81, 82
Frawley, John 81, 82

G

Gale river 44, 149, 169
Gaynor, John 303
Geary, Stephen 92
Gibson, Henry 316–319
Gibson, John 156
Gibson, Rev. 313
Glazier, Michael 335, 336
Glenderry 243
Glenflesk 184
Godfrey, William 200
Goggin, John 137
Gorham, Elizabeth 231
Gorham, Mr 74
Gray, Peter 249
Greenwell, Henry Nicholas 13, 84, 85, 100, 130–134, 142–144, 155–157, 209, 337–339
Gregory Clause 154, 176–178, 212, 307
Griffin, Daniel 98, 333
Griffin, Mary 119
Griffin, Patrick 121
Grogan, Michael 118, 119
Grosse Isle 300, 301, 333
Gun, William 235

Gun, Wilson 42
Gun, George 132
Gunsborough 133, 313
Guranaclouna 283

H

Hanafin, Biddy 121
Hancock, Mr 39
Hanrahan, John 123, 124
Harenc, Mrs 275, 284
Harnett, Cornelius 24, 91
Harnett, Danny Dan 215, 217
Harnett, E. 171
Harold, James 230
Hart, Captain 207, 209, 210, 221
Hartnett, Timothy 208
Harty, Maurice 279
Hawkshaw, H. 26, 160
Headley, Lady 45, 249, 250
Herbert, Captain 100
Herbert, Henry Arthur 154, 171, 249, 250, 263, 279, 292, 294, 295, 298, 299
Herbert, Thomas 287
Hewson, George 169, 330
Hickie, William 47, 330
Hickson, Robert C. 32, 34, 68
Hickson, William 68, 244, 290, 335
Higgins, Deborah 118
Hilliard, George 256, 258
Hogg, Matthew 274
Home, James Murray 18, 41, 42, 143, 169, 170, 244, 245, 266, 267, 291, 320, 321, 330
Horsely, Mr 304, 305, 319
Hotham, A. J. 157, 159, 160, 162, 164–166, 192, 194, 195, 199
Houlihan, Daniel 208
Howard, Daniel 121
Huggard, William 124
Huolahan, Daniel 247
Hurly, Francis Newton 189, 282
Hurly, John 29, 31, 33, 35, 40, 67, 103, 127, 196, 225, 254–258, 263, 264, 295, 306
Hurly, Robert Conway 230
Hurly, Thomas B. 297, 325, 326
Hutchins, Captain 85, 87
Hynes, James 121

INDEX

I

Iraghticonnor 42, 100, 173, 281, 292, 325
Irremore 17, 235
Isten, Michael 124
Iveragh 26

J

James Street, Tralee 260, 304, 306
Jeanie Johnston 298–304, 315
Jeffcott, Mr 96
Jeffcott, Richard 258
Jerningham, F. W. 69
Jones, Thomas 303
Julian, Christopher 86

K

Kavanagh, Pat 162
Kenefick, Mr 215
Kenmare 28, 90, 100, 294, 296, 314
Kennedy, Mary 97, 98
Kerry Head 147, 150, 243, 248, 252, 253, 303
Kilcolman 325
Kilconly 77, 239
Kilcredan 85
Kilcummin 89
Kilfahadoge 282
Kilflynn 20, 138, 173, 239, 252, 313
Kilgarvan 184
Kilgobbin 37, 108, 231, 324
Killahan 138, 141, 142, 226, 252
Killarney 29, 52, 59, 64, 85, 90, 95, 100, 154, 210, 249–252, 267, 294, 295, 298, 304, 308, 311, 314, 318
Killeentierna 78, 287
Killehinny 243, 282
Killelton House 47
Killorglin 59
Killury 24, 27, 28, 57, 88, 144, 147, 149, 150, 175, 176, 180, 211, 233–235, 239, 248, 280, 324
Kilmore 52, 149, 214
Kilmoyley 24, 88, 138, 139, 144–147, 174, 175, 200, 201, 223, 261
Kilmurry 183
Kilquane 89
Kilrush 48
Kiltomy 169, 170, 203, 325
Kitchener, Henry Horatio 290, 322
Knockavuhig/Knockavaghig 239
Knocknagoshel 20

L

Labalmondière, Douglas 85, 100, 101, 125, 155, 156
Lassinagh 70
Latchford, John 122, 124
Lawlor, Dr 231
Lawlor, Patrick 139
Lawrence, Henry 28, 52, 53, 57
Leahy, Elizabeth 231
Leahy, John 239
Leahy, Mr 256, 257
Leahy, P. 296
Leahy, Richard 68
Leahy, Thomas 121
Leamington 139
Lee, John 124
Leensbawn 282
Lenamore 283
Leonard, Maurice 264–266, 270, 296
Leonard, Samuel B. 307, 317
Leslie, Robert 49, 50, 169, 173
Leyne, Cornelius 127
Limerick 42, 46, 48, 85, 135, 137, 148, 172, 215, 229, 301, 315
Linehan, Jane 118, 119
Lisheenbaun 325
Lislaughtin 283
Lislaughtin Abbey 81
Lisselton 136, 187, 238, 282, 325, 334
Listowel 11, 13, 14, 17, 19, 21, 24–26, 41–43, 47, 51, 55, 59, 64, 75–77, 82, 84, 85, 100, 129–131, 133, 134, 140, 143, 148, 153, 157, 167–169, 173–175, 180, 181, 185, 188, 189, 198–200, 204–207, 209, 221, 223, 234, 235, 241, 243–246, 252–254, 256, 257, 260, 261, 264–268, 270–272, 274, 280–282, 287, 290, 291, 296, 309–313, 319–322, 324, 325, 329, 330, 333, 334
Listowel, Lord 18, 41, 42, 44, 143, 235, 284, 290, 292, 321, 322

381

Liverpool 35, 68, 248, 299, 300, 302, 315
Lixnaw 17, 56, 140, 156, 170, 203, 235, 267, 276, 278, 279, 284, 324, 325
Long, John 208
Lucas, Edward 27
Lumsden, Mr 96
Lynch, John 30–35, 37, 38, 40, 43, 66, 67, 70, 74, 96, 103, 116, 167, 196–198, 217
Lynch, Mary 119
Lynch, Mr 268, 269
Lyne, Patrick 138

M

Macintosh, Archibald 170, 171, 183, 287
Magee, John 56
Maharees 26
Mahony, Constable 230
Mahony, James 223
Mahony, Jeremiah (Darby) 21, 41, 76, 129, 188, 208, 269, 273–275, 313, 320, 321, 333
Mahony, John 121
Mahony, Kean 161
Mahony, Peirce 43, 44, 243, 244, 246, 250, 251, 253, 272
Mahony, Thomas 137
Mann, Robert 48, 49, 137, 138
Mason, Frederick 214
Mason, Oliver 52
Mason, Oliver William 226, 227
Maulin 239
Maunsell, F. R. 45, 78–80, 154, 182
Mawe, John 208, 227
McCarthy, Charles 118
McCarthy, Daniel 47, 50, 62, 81–84, 135, 173, 208, 214
McCarthy, Eugene (Owen) 25, 27, 28, 55, 57, 88, 133, 144–146, 149, 174–178, 180, 182, 191, 198, 202, 208, 210, 221, 233, 280, 281
McCarthy, Florence 208
McCarthy, Isabella 231
McCarthy, John 162, 196, 258
McCarthy, Mary 119, 121
McCowen, T. 124
McCrystal, Dr 270
McDonnell, Michael 333

McElligott, Ellen 320
McElligott, Patrick 47
McEnnery, David 69
McEnnery, John 21, 41, 66, 71, 72, 94–96, 140, 184, 186, 196, 217, 225, 317
McGuire, William 121
McKennedy, Denis 68, 82
McMahon, Martin 208
McMahon, Mathias 50, 210–212, 275, 282–285, 290–293
McMahon, T. 124
McQuinn, Michael 138
Meredith, William 45, 78
Milltown 59, 88, 109, 200
Mitchel, John 137, 200, 213–215
Mitchell, James 24, 91, 333
Mitchell, Michael 24, 91, 333
Moanmore 325
Mollineux, Mortimer 285
Moore, Francis 137–139, 141, 142, 144, 261
Moore, Thomas 208
Moran, Jeremiah 121
Moriarty, Catherine 97, 98
Moriarty, David 139, 140, 186, 331
Moriarty, John 119
Moriarty, Mr 273
Moriarty, Oliver 146, 147
Morris, Richard 119
Moyvane 136, 199
Mulchinock, J. 96
Mulchinock, Mary 118
Mulgrave Bridge 68
Murphy, Cornelius 123
Murphy, Mr 327
Murphy, Thomas 337

N

Nash, Mr 296
Nash, Robert 231
Naughten, Richard 45, 77
Neligan, Michael 223
Newcastlewest 217
Norman, Edward 45, 46, 216

O

Oakpark, Tralee 115, 170, 307, 330

INDEX

O'Brien, Thomas 137
O'Brien, William Smith 80, 213, 215, 217, 218
O'Callaghan, Charles 317
O'Connell, Daniel 10, 20, 135, 190, 213, 250, 281
O'Connell, Fr 260
O'Connell, James 96, 258, 262, 308
O'Connell, Jeremiah 208
O'Connell, John 154
O'Connell, M. 96
O'Connell, Morgan John 217
O'Connell, Rickard 253
O'Connell, Thomas 56, 164
O'Connor, Gerard 258
O'Connor, John 129, 189, 208, 267, 268, 282
O'Connor, Thomas 56, 134, 169, 214, 263
O'Donnell, John 98, 231
O'Donoghue, Denis 313
O'Donoghue, John 184
O'Flaherty, Edward 154
O'Gorman, Richard 215, 217
O'Halloran, Michael 147
O'Leary, Arthur 119
O'Leary, Jeremiah 154, 170, 171, 183, 249, 285–287
O'Leary, John 95
O'Leary, Philip 287
Osborne, Sidney Godolphin 240, 241
O'Shea, Kieran 184
O'Sullivan, George 97
O'Sullivan, Jeremiah 138, 139, 208
O'Sullivan, John 287
O'Sullivan, John P. 319
O'Sullivan, Margaret 196

P

Payne, Thomas 124
Perrott, Richard 305
Petty-Fitzmaurice, Henry (Marquis of Lansdowne) 276–279, 284, 294, 325
Phelan, Denis 204, 205
Pierce, John 56, 235, 279
Plummer, Richard 27, 28, 149
Pope, William 56, 88, 234
Purtill, Mary 266

Q

Quakers (Society of Friends) 110, 137, 141, 148, 183, 185
Quebec 293, 298–301, 303
Quill, Patrick 230

R

Rae, Curry 258
Rathass 39, 97, 107, 232, 325, 326
Rattoo 24, 27, 28, 55, 57, 88, 144, 146, 150, 175, 176, 180, 202, 211, 233–235, 239, 243, 275, 280
Raymond, Hugh 231
Raymond, Mr 284
Rice, Dominic 56
Rice, George 142
Rice, Justin 56, 235
Rice, Mr 268
Roche, D. 171
Rock 97, 115, 260, 264, 304, 306
Rock Street, Tralee 113, 165, 304
Roonagra 283
Routh, Captain 209
Routh, Richard 81, 82
Rowan, A. B. 37, 66, 96, 101, 108, 112, 155, 182, 197
Rusheen 283
Rushy Park 283
Russell, John 9, 89, 105, 106, 158, 178, 218
Russell, John Norris 59, 85–87, 96, 172
Ruttle, Christopher 223
Ruttle, John 223

S

Sallowglen 135, 199
Samuels, Mr 146, 148, 149
Sandes, Charles L. 135
Sandes, Fitzmaurice 182
Sandes, George 212, 267, 272–274, 282, 330
Sandes, John 137
Sandes, Maurice Fitzgerald 307
Sandes, Stephen C. 47, 48, 134, 169, 248
Sandes, Thomas 48, 135
Sandes, W. S. 214
Sandes, William Gough 174, 235

Sandes Jr, William 209
Sayers, John 119
Scariff 207
Scartaglin 324
Scollard, J. 132, 133, 136
Sealy, John 162, 169, 254, 285, 286
Sears, Denis 98
Shea, Denis 121, 122
Sheahan, Cornelius 272, 273
Sheahan, Timothy 322
Sheehy, John 27, 28
Skibbereen 68, 82, 109, 214
Smith, Henry 320
Smith O'Brien, William 216
Smyth, James 209
Somerville, Alexander 44
Spark, Thomas 157, 168, 178–181, 198–209, 254–259, 264, 297, 304, 305
Spa, The 64, 65, 70, 154
Spratt, Rev. Dr 182
Stack, Edmond 124, 125
Stack, James 285, 297
Stack, Mr 43
Stack, Thomas 318
Stamer, John 187, 188, 226, 285, 313
Stewart, P. 124
Stokes, Bridget 140
Stokes, Edward 130
Stokes, George Day 63, 66, 95, 96, 101, 155, 157, 161, 171
Stokes, Henry 35, 66, 89, 99
Stokes, John Day 14, 32, 37, 41, 67, 74, 96, 99, 101, 103, 112, 117, 160–162, 166
Stokes, Oliver Day 169
Stokes, Patrick 43
Stokes, William 23
Stoughton, Thomas A. 211, 212, 248
Stoughton, William 96, 211, 279, 280
Strokestown 227
Strzelecki, Paul 108, 189, 199, 224, 225
Stuart, Commander 100, 129, 134
Sullivan, Mary 121
Sullivan, Myles 119
Supple, Justin 38, 40, 92, 213, 214, 217, 249, 258, 282, 305, 306, 308
Supple, Kerry 206, 235
Supple, Mr 262, 264, 296

T

Tangney, James 162, 163
Tangney, John 119
Tarbert 42, 47–51, 62, 81, 85, 90, 109, 134, 135, 137, 172, 173, 199, 213, 229, 248, 256, 282, 288, 292, 330
Taulaght 31
Taylor, William 55
Teeraclea 282
Thomas, John 121
Thompson, Peter 35
Thompson, W. 162
Thorpe, Gabriel 268–271, 309, 311, 312
Touhy, Patrick 184
Touhy, Peggy 119
Trant, Thomas P. 35
Trench, William Steuart 277–279
Trevelyan, Charles Edward 93, 153, 157, 258
Trinity College, Dublin 18, 23, 150, 226, 235, 239, 335, 337
Trughnanacmy 68, 100, 325
Tubrid 252, 295, 296
Tullomore 86
Twiss, Francis 91, 221
Twiss, George 183
Twistleton, Edward 10, 240

W

Walker, Mr 85
Walsh, James 136, 208, 238, 282, 284, 285
Walsh, Mr 132
Walsh, Thomas 127
Waterloo 260, 304
Whedall, Henry 139
Williams, John 172
Woodlock, Fr 140
Wren, George 214
Wyse, Sub-Inspector 160, 215

Y

Yescombe, Mrs Massy 135

www.ingramcontent.com/pod-product-compliance
Lightning Source LLC
Chambersburg PA
CBHW061252230426
43665CB00026B/2909